Uncle John's
ACTION-PACKED
BATHROOM READER

No. 37

PORTABLE
PRESS

Portable Press

San Diego, California

Portable Press / The Bathroom Readers' Institute
An imprint of Printers Row Publishing Group
9717 Pacific Heights Blvd, San Diego, CA 92121
www.portablepress.com • mail@portablepress.com

Correspondence regarding the content of this book should be sent to Portable Press / The Bathroom Readers' Institute, Editorial Department, at the above address.

Publisher: Peter Norton • Associate Publisher: Ana Parker
Editorial Director: April Graham
Art Director: Charles McStravick
Production Team: Beno Chan, Julie Greene

Creator: Javna Brothers LLC

Interior and Infographics Designer: Linda Lee Mauri
Cover Design: Linda Lee Mauri

Image credits: Darumo/iStock via Getty Images, Designer_things/iStock via Getty Images, M-A-U/iStock via Getty Images, Hiznysyahril - stock.adobe.com (cover); Icons-Studio - stock.adobe.com (6, 340, 385–386); top dog - stock.adobe.com (26–27); stocksnapper/iStock via Getty Images, wynnter/iStock via Getty Images (31); Igor Zakowski/iStock via Getty Images (104); Happy Dragon - stock.adobe.com, Paul Kovaloff - stock .adobe.com (135); filo/DigitalVision Vectors via Getty Images, Quarta_/iStock via Getty Images (199); Julia Henze/iStock via Getty Images, -VICTOR-/DigitalVision Vectors via Getty Images (251); iKonStudio/ iStock via Getty Images, wetcake/DigitalVision Vectors via Getty Images (270); LIORIKI - stock.adobe.com (281–283); Amguy/iStock via Getty Images (332); Mgogo - stock.adobe.com (354–355); mutsMaks/iStock via Getty Images (384)

"A book read by a thousand different people is a thousand different books." —Andrei Tarkovsky

Library of Congress Control Number: 2024933882

ISBN: 978-1-6672-0603-5

Printed in India

28 27 26 25 24   1 2 3 4 5

OUR "REGULAR READERS" RAVE!

I buy one every year to give myself for Christmas! That way I know I am going to get at least one present I really, really want!

—Dee M.

These books are awesome on history and knowledge!

—Heather W.

Love all the Uncle John's books. Nice easy read and interesting stories.

—Sandra K.

I have been buying these books for years for my husband. He's an avid bathroom reader and this is perfect reading material for those times. Lots of interesting facts. I read it too!!

—Nora H.

Another fun, interesting, and educational read by Uncle John.

—Scott V.

Buy these books for my husband and he has every one of them. Please don't stop publishing them.

—Arlene S.

Always interesting and fun.

—Rosie

A must buy.

—Reg F.

Great read for the bathroom.

—Sandra T.

With ANY of Uncle John's odd-ball stories & trivial bits of truthful information, you'll never spend idle time sitting on the throne! Tons of info. that you can share & amaze your friends!

—Glenn A.

CONTENTS

Because the BRI understands your reading needs, we've divided the contents by length as well as subject.

Short—a quick read

Medium—2 to 3 pages

Long—for those extended visits, when something a little more involved is required

GOOD NEWS!
Medium

IT'S A WEIRD, WEIRD WORLD
Short

Medium

LANGUAGE ARTS
Short

Medium

LAW AND ORDER
Medium

Long

LET'S EAT
Short

Medium

*   *   *

WHALE, EVERYBODY ELSE IS DOING IT

Also known as killer whales, young orcas have been observed engaging in behaviors that don't seem to serve a purpose beyond being fun, or because they've seen other orcas doing it. In other words, according to animal behaviorists, they're following the crowd and participating in fads. In the summer of 2022, multiple news reports were filed about orcas ramming into ships off the coasts of western European countries, seemingly unprovoked. The animal behavior scientists think the orcas were just having a good time, akin to light teenage rebellion or mild vandalism, or that the water that whooshes off the rudder during the hit feels good. In 1987, orcas from three different pods in the waters outside Seattle were seen wearing dead salmon on their nose—an activity that lasted for only about six weeks, because, like a fad, the novelty wore off. In 2023, juvenile orcas in coastal British Columbia engaged in messing with prawn and crab traps.

INTRODUCTION

Like so many American kids, I loved comic books growing up. Superman, Spider-Man, Batman, Captain America, Silver Surfer...I was a fan of all the heroes, and was in awe of the unique abilities that helped each one triumph over the bad guys time after time. For years, I made a monthly trek to the comic-book shop to buy the latest issue of each of my favorites, devoured them as quickly as I could, then spent an agonizing few weeks waiting to find out what happened in the next installment.

Of course, gone are the days when we had to wait a whole month between issues to get our superhero fix. Whether you like Marvel or DC, live action or cartoons, these days—with movies, streaming shows, and social media posts all in abundance—there's a seemingly endless supply of superhero stories to keep us engaged. But there's still one limited, collectible publication that folks can't wait to snatch up as soon as it's released, and that's the book you have in your hands: the annual Uncle John's Bathroom Reader. And, as always, this year's edition is

ACTION-PACKED

Comic books make for excellent bathroom reading, if you hadn't already figured that out; in fact, it may have been one of the many times I brought those comics with me on a toilet trip that I began to realize my own destiny as a superhero of sorts. I may not have heat vision or the ability to fly, but I do have a super-sized plunger and one noteworthy capability: a superhuman memory for fun facts and terrific trivia. I decided to use my powers for good and, 37 years ago, set off on my mission to defeat that most evil of villains that terrorizes all of us at some point: bathroom boredom.

Join me in my quest! Here are just some of the weapons we have at our disposal in this year's Bathroom Reader.

ACTION: Real-life survival stories straight out of Hollywood, wacky races for anyone who wants to do more than just run, death by flying cow (and other strange ways people went out), and people who got themselves stuck—literally—in some difficult situations.

POP CULTURE: The wildest stats of Tom Brady's career, amusement parks that flopped, conspiracy theories you won't believe people believe, the rise and fall of Lollapalooza, game show facts, and famous folks serving jury duty (celebrities—they *are* just like us!).

LAUGHS: The strangest things found in library books, the wide array of items you can buy from Japanese vending machines, baby names gone wrong, and the most awkward AI-generated inspirational posters.

LANGUAGE: Commonplace terms invented by U.S. presidents, all the slang you need to know to help you finish that jigsaw puzzle, our favorite pun-derful craft beer names, and the origins of English phrases involving the word *cake*.

HISTORY: The larger-than-life wrestler who helped Jewish GIs beat the Nazis, fad diets through the ages, a few of the (hundreds of) attempts to assassinate Fidel Castro, the coffee crisis in East Germany, and the man who created the Dewey Decimal System.

FOOD: The origins of our favorite salad dressings, funeral food traditions, and the weirdest cheeses from around the world (you've been warned).

HEROES: Everyday folks (and everyday kids!) who ended up saving the day, thrift store finds worth plenty of dough, animals that turned out not to be extinct after all, and good old-fashioned nice stories.

And much, much more!

Big thanks to all my heroic sidekicks at the Bathroom Readers' Institute who have contributed to this year's collection—I couldn't keep saving the day without these talented folks.

Gordon Javna	Angela Garcia	Bruce Langley
Jay Newman	Traci Douglas	Paul Rubenfeld
Brian Boone	Linda Lee Mauri	Thomas Crapper

And of course we must thank our loyal readers, who continue to support this annual endeavor. Whether or not you read this book in your own secret (bathroom) lair, your support of our work makes you *our* heroes!

Happy reading, and, as ever,
Go with the flow!

—Uncle John and the BRI Staff

YOU'RE MY INSPIRATION

It's fascinating to see where the architects of pop culture get their ideas.

PEE-WEE HERMAN

When Paul Reubens was a member of the improv comedy troupe the Groundlings in 1977, he came up with a goofy character who would bomb at a comedy club because he couldn't remember punchlines—an actual problem that Reubens had—so he'd laugh nervously. That laugh provided the basis for the character; Reubens got the name "Pee-wee" from a brand of harmonica, and Herman was the last name of an energetic kid he'd known in his youth.

SPIDER-MAN

The Spider was a popular 1930s pulp magazine about an antihero millionaire who wore a black hat and cloak, along with fake vampire fangs, to fight the bad guys with his pair of Browning .45 automatics. Marvel guru Stan Lee grew up reading those comic-book precursors. "[To] my impressionable, preteen way of thinking, the Spider was the most dramatic character I had ever encountered." But he was inspired only by the name; "Everything else about our new character would be completely different." (Lee based Spider-man's boss, *Daily Bugle* publisher J. Jonah Jameson, on "a grumpy, irritable" version of himself.)

THE ANKLE MONITOR

In 1983, a New Mexico judge named Jack Love was reading a 1977 *Spider-man* comic strip in which the hero gets tagged with a "radar device" bracelet—now the bad guys can keep tabs on him. Love thought that a tracking device could keep low-level offenders out of overcrowded jails. It turned out that two Harvard University grad students had invented such a device in the 1960s, but had run out of funding. Love hired an engineer to complete the work: they came up with the ankle bracelet and launched the National Incarceration Monitoring and Control Services (NIMCOS).

THE OSCAR STATUETTE

Officially called the Academy Award of Merit, the world's most recognizable trophy was designed by MGM art director Cedric Gibbons in 1928. Although the Motion Picture Academy's official history says that it came from his imagination, legendary Mexican director, screenwriter, and actor Emilio "El Indio" Fernández claimed that he was asked to pose nude for Gibbons to sketch him. Fernández had the same V-shaped, muscular physique as the statue. (Its nickname might have come from Academy librarian Margaret Herrick, who said the statue looked like her Uncle Oscar.)

Readers Oren Jopko and Sam Rotelick call these running feet "blurbies"
(which Uncle John agrees is a lot more fun than "running feet"!).

TOILET TECH

Better living through bathroom technology.

THE HEAT IS ON

Product: LumaWarm

How It Works: Whether it's due to a draft from a window or because of a poorly placed air conditioner vent, or just because all those ceramic fixtures always seem to be naturally chilly, the toilet seat can be one of the coldest places in a home. And it's certainly an unpleasant and uncomfortable surprise when you're not expecting your bare bottom to make contact with something seemingly ice-cold. Enter the LumaWarm, a sophisticated electronic heated toilet seat with several luxurious features. At the push of a button, the LumaWarm heats to one of three preprogrammed temperature settings in about five minutes' time. It also comes equipped with a stay-on blue night-light to help navigate a middle-of-the-night bathroom trip—when the toilet seat would otherwise be at its absolute coldest.

Cost: $119–$159

A BRIGHT IDEA

Product: LumiLux Toilet Light

How It Works: Speaking of bathroom lights, it's nice to leave one on throughout the night to illuminate any 2:00 a.m. potty emergencies. But a night-light casts light across the whole bathroom, which could pull you out of your sleepy state and make it hard to fall back asleep after you've done your business. And it's a waste of electricity. That's why the LumiLux is such an innovation. Smaller than a smartphone, it clips onto any standard toilet and is programmed to light up only when it senses movement, providing just enough light to guide a user to the commode, and staying on long enough for a bathroom session before clicking off after the user has flushed and gone back to bed. Bonus: the LumiLux can be programmed to light up in one of 16 different colors.

Cost: $17

IF YOU CAN'T SEE IT, IT'S NOT DIRTY

Product: Grout Pen

How It Works: One of the toughest, trickiest, and grossest parts of cleaning a bathroom is keeping the grout—the caulked areas between individual shower or floor tiles—tidy and white. The Grout Pen from the Rainbow Liquid Chalk Specialists doesn't actually remove dirt and grime from grout, but it makes it a nonissue. Presented like a felt-tip marker, it's a tube of liquified white chalk. Users simply draw over the brown or black-

stained lines, and the Grout Pen's nontoxic white paint covers everything up. And it's available in two sizes, for narrow dirty grout or wide dirty grout.
Cost: $8.99–$11.99

SIT DOWN AND BE COUNTED

Product: Heart Seat
How It Works: In 2023, a medical technology company called Casana received FDA approval for the world's first "smart" toilet seat. Like other "smart" home gadgets, the Heart Seat measures, collects, and tracks data that it intuitively gathers: in this case, it can measure a user's heart rate, oxygen saturation levels, and blood pressure. Those can all be used to keep tabs on cardiovascular and respiratory health and for identifying warning signs of serious health issues. And it does it all by sensing what's going on in the blood, heart, lungs, and veins just by the weight of a rear end.
Cost: Unknown as of press time, but it will likely be a prescription-only item and carry a high price tag; Casana used $44 million to develop the Heart Seat.

UNAFFORDABLE LUXURY

Product: Numi 2.0
How It Works: Bathroom fixture company Kohler made the Numi 2.0 Smart Toilet available to the public in 2022. It's loaded with features that turn using the facilities into a luxurious experience. The Numi has sensors that can tell when a user is approaching (and leaving), so the lid opens and closes automatically. A touch-screen display allows multiple users to set their profiles—such as what temperature and pressure they want the bidet to use to clean them up when they're done, what temperature they want the heated seat, and if they'd like the built-in speaker system (powered by Amazon's Alexa technology) to play music when they sit down to cover up any sounds their body might make. It's also got an illuminated display (for when nature calls in the middle of the night) and a charcoal-powered deodorizing system.
Cost: $11,500

SHOW SOME BACKBONE

Product: Vertebrae
How It Works: This all-encompassing bathroom fixture from Design Odyssey is so named because it looks like a human spine with all of those bones sticking out. It's also much more than a toilet—the Vertebrae is an entire bathroom's worth of necessities in one tall, space-saving silver tower. A sink, toilet, and shower are housed in modules within the column, and each swings out when needed. A user could even use all three at the same time, if they're so inclined.
Cost: $15,000

When a one-month-old baby looks up at your face, all he sees is a blur.

YOU MUST BE "THIS" OLD

Ironically, this page about the little-known things you can and cannot do when you reach a certain age is open to readers of all ages.

Nationally, sports betting is restricted to those aged 21 and over. But not horse racing. In most areas where playing the ponies is legal, you must be 18 to place a bet—you just can't do it in a bar or in a casino.

About two-thirds of world nations enforce a minimum legal drinking age of 18. So although consumers of alcohol must be 21 in the U.S., they can travel outside the country and legally imbibe. And in the U.S., 18-year-olds can sell alcohol as employees of stores, bars, and restaurants—but they can't drink any.

In the U.S., you have to be 21 to buy nonalcoholic beer, but you can legally consume it if you're at least 18.

It's illegal to purchase a gun if you're under 18 (and some states restrict the sale of certain firearms to people 21 and older), but it's also against the law to buy certain other weapons and weapon-like objects unless you're a legal adult, including pocketknives, hunting knives, paintball cartridges, pepper spray, BB guns and ammunition, and slingshots.

In most jurisdictions, you can become a licensed driver at age 16. Across the U.S., you must be 21 to apply for a large vehicle license, giving you the legal documentation to drive a semitruck or bus. It's also impossible to get a pilot's license or sign up to drive for a rideshare service such as Uber or Lyft if you're under 21.

Many legal and financial privileges and benefits instantly become available to you upon your 18th birthday. You can open a checking account (without a parent as a cosigner), file a lawsuit, enlist in the military, buy a car, purchase real estate, buy stocks and other commodities, sign up for a credit card, legally change your name, and register your last will and testament.

In most states, 21 is the age of majority for both adopting a child and donating one's eggs so that other couples may conceive a child.

Some random things anyone under the age of 18 may not purchase: disposable lighters (to discourage minors from smoking), propane tanks, fireworks, cough syrup (because it can be used like a drug), keyboard cleaning spray (because it can be used like a drug), spray paint (to limit its use for graffiti), and dry ice.

Stay in the plane, kid: you have to be 18 years old to skydive.

Due to habitat loss and light pollution, nearly one-third of the world's firefly species are in danger of extinction.

HOW TO BE A HARBINGER HOUSEHOLD

*Did you ever love a new electronic gadget, snack food, or soda flavor,
and then a few months later notice it had completely disappeared from
stores? Bad news: you may be part of a harbinger household.*

EPIC FAIL

In the worlds of marketing, advertising, and general merchandise and food
distribution, there's a term that gets thrown around a lot: harbinger. Outside of
that context, harbinger is generally followed by the words "of doom" or "of failure"—
within the business world, the rest of those phrases is simply left unsaid. "Harbinger
households" describes certain individuals or families whose early and enthusiastic
adoption of a product indicates that it's going to spectacularly flop among the general,
wider population.

It's like an accidental negative test market for a new food, beverage, or consumer
good, discovered after the fact. According to a few studies conducted by researchers at
major American universities, harbinger households share some eerie similarities, and
they tend to buy the same types of flop products over and over.

IDENTIFYING THE HARBINGER

According to the research, harbinger households are slightly more likely to be found
on the West Coast than in the rest of the country, and in nonurban areas (suburbs
or rural communities). They earn slightly more money than average, they tend to be
led by less-educated single parents, tend to be larger families, shop at warehouse stores
such as Costco, and use a lot of coupons. Other than those things, harbingers are
spread evenly (or randomly) across all other demographic indicators.

Harbingers even tend to congregate—certain zip codes are rife with these
loser-pickers who consistently and continually bet on the wrong foods, drinks,
political candidates, clothing choices, and real estate choices. And if they move,
they overwhelmingly, and somehow, move into another harbinger-identified zip
code. In other words, harbinger households aren't losers...but they inadvertently
and subconsciously know how to spot them.

BUYING IN

Perhaps because of the coupons—one big way major distributors and manufacturers
advertise a product at its launch—harbinger households are early adopters of new

What are houndstooth, buffalo check, gingham, black watch, madras, and tartan?
Types of plaid.

flavors and concepts. That may be why the same buying habits appear among harbingers spread across the country. For example, studies show that people who purchased a lot of Diet Crystal Pepsi—transparent sugar-free cola—in the 1990s were the same consumers who bought Colgate Kitchen Entrees—frozen meals produced by a toothpaste company—a decade prior. And those who bought oral care products such as newfangled toothbrushes or toothpastes that didn't stick around similarly choose hair-care items that don't last long on store shelves.

BACKING THE WRONG HORSE

Researchers investigated the broader spending habits of identified harbinger households and found that their ability to pick flops extended into real estate and political donations. Homes that buy quick-disappearing, widely maligned stuff such as Crystal Pepsi and Watermelon Oreos are more likely to direct their political donations to congressional and senatorial candidates that wind up losing their races. And those harbinger households and the harbinger-heavy districts in which they live just might be cursed. Research indicates that harbinger zip codes enjoy smaller home value increases over time, lower than national and even regional trends.

Adding insult to injury: harbingers aren't very fashionable individuals, it would seem. One harbinger study focused on clothing choices. Just like when it comes to selecting snack foods, sodas, neighborhoods, and political candidates, those identified by academics as harbingers predominantly purchased clothing from large chain stores that was discontinued within a few months. Basically, they're buying clothes that are more unappealing to the rest of the world.

THE HARBINGER HOUSEHOLD CHECKLIST

Here are some products that harbinger households seemingly loved...but nobody else did, leading to their quick discontinuation. Did you ever buy any of these?

Microsoft Zune (an iPod competitor)

Cheetos Lip Balm

Frito-Lay Lemonade

Tropicana Twister Orange Soda

Lifesavers Soda

Cosmopolitan Yogurt

McDonald's Arch Deluxe

Doritos 3D

WebTV

Frito-Lay WOW Chips (made with Olestra, a fat-free oil substitute that led to anal leakage)

Watermelon Oreos

Josta (an exotic energy drink made by Pepsi)

Coca-Cola with Lemon (or Lime)

Pepsi Blue

New Coke

Movie Pass

Sega Dreamcast

Amazon Fire Phone

Coors Rocky Mountain Sparkling Water

Sony Betamax

In 2010, some city councilmembers in Elmhurst, Illinois, tried to make "eye-rolling" illegal. The motion failed. (Eye-roll.)

THE WAY BACK TIMES

These weird, old-timey newspaper stories are more than just great bathroom reading—
they offer a glimpse into what life and language were like in centuries past. We're glad
to know that Bathroom Reader–worthy news stories have always taken place.

"O, DAMMIT" WANTS NAME CHANGED.

Because he can't tell whether people are calling him or merely venting injured feelings when they say "O, Dammit." Orlando Dammit seeks to have his name changed, says an Elmsford, N.C. dispatch.

—Richmond (KY) Climax, 1913

PUTS AUTO FIRE OUT WITH SLICES OF BREAD

PARIS, Ky. (AP)— Henry Short has a new fire fighting technique. When wiring in his auto caught fire, he called the fire department, then grabbed a loaf of bread and wrapped the slices around the burning wires.

When the fire fighters arrived, the blaze was out.

—Newark (OH) Advocate, 1958

KISS TIME LIMIT ALL A MISTAKE

TULSA, OK., Oct. 13 (UP)—Mayor Olney Flynn, who had been pictured as a man opposed to lengthy kissing in public places, said tonight it wasn't necessarily so.

Not so long ago the mayor was plugging for a city ordinance to limit the public kiss to one minute because wives and sweethearts lingered too long in the embrace of their returning servicemen at bus and train depots, but he said he'd decided it was all a mistake.

—Pittsburgh Press, 1945

Antone Fratus of Provincetown selected his pillow as a safe place for keeping money and there deposited $300 [$8,500 today] in an envelope. His two-year-old child found the envelope and shoved it through an open grate into the fire. There was $290 in bills, which were destroyed and a $10 gold piece was found in the ashes.

—Boston Evening Transcript, 1890

WAS HORSE INTOXICATED?: Judge "Passes It Up" In a Suit for Damages.

Milwaukee, Wis.— Whether or not a horse was intoxicated was made a part of an argument of a case in Judge Otto H. Bredenbach's branch of the civil court recently.

Michael Iglinski sued William Koontz for $1,000, charging that the defendant drove an automobile into his buggy, throwing his wife out. Some testimony tended to show that the buggy was zigzagging along the road.

The attorney for the plaintiff in his argument declared that there was no evidence to show that the horse was drunk. The court found for the defendant without deciding the horse's condition.

—Stevens Point (WI) Journal, 1916

Actual headline: "Man Who Spent £12,480 to Become a Dog Terrifies Real Dogs in the Street."

Weather's Not To Blame For Youth's Frost-Bitten Hand

Philadelphia – (AP) – Thomas Folweiler, 17, has a frost-bitten hand—but the weather's not to blame.

An ice cream vending machine into which he plunked a nickel jammed and his hand got stuck trying to pry loose a package.

Firemen worked half an hour and finally demolished the machine before freeing him.

—*Intelligencer Journal* (Lancaster, PA), 1943

He Found a Way to Run Guests Off

LOS ANGELES, Aug. 29 (AP)—Mrs. Eloise Garry Stern testified in a divorce hearing that her husband, Frederick Henry Stern, a writer, kept their guests waiting three hours for dessert while he read his poetry to them.

"Every time we had company the evening would end with the guests going home in disgust," she said.

Mrs. Stern was granted a divorce.

—*Greenwood (MS) Commonwealth*, 1941

SCHOOL REVEILLE STIRS POLICE CALL

It was the first day of school and it stirred up quite a commotion in outer Monroe Avenue.

In fact there was such a commotion in one household at about 7:15 a.m. that neighbors called police. Police of the University Avenue Station reported the disturbance was merely a father trying to get his children up to go to school. They didn't record the ultimate outcome.

—*Democrat and Chronicle* (Rochester, NY), 1942

ROBBER ROBS TAXI ROBBERS: THEN HE IS TWICE FLEECED, ONCE BY WOMAN— PRISONER TELLS HOW HE BLUFFED BANDITS.

New York.—A robber who robbed the robbers who stole $25,000 from two bank messengers in the financial district a few weeks ago was afterward robbed twice himself. Such was the chapter added to the "taxicab holdup story" by the confession of Marreo Arbano.

Arbano is anything but a robber in appearance. He is only five feet tall, weighs 100 pounds and wears spectacles. He gave himself up, and told police how he walked into a saloon where the five taxicab bandits were dividing the $25,000 loot, and by "pure bluff" was given $10,000.

As he left the saloon he was in turn held up by two companions and had to divide with them.

With $3,000 he fled to Havana, Cuba. In Havana he became acquainted with a woman, and after a night of drinking said he found himself short $2,500, which he says the woman had stolen.

The police so far have recovered only $2,000 of the original loot, and on this account heavy bond was required.

—*Sausalito (CA) News*, 1912

CORPSE SPOILS WAKE; REFUSES TO STAY DEAD

New York, June 16.— An hour after she had been prepared for burial today, Mrs. Rebecca Senpz sat up in her coffin.

Physicians were summoned by the woman's children and relatives this afternoon and at five o'clock, after she had suffered a paralytic stroke, she was

Your body is 60 percent water, and your brain is 60 percent fat.

pronounced dead. Ice was packed about her body and candles were lighted. Neighbors who came in to console the woman's children, were standing about the coffin when the body stirred. Mrs. Senpz sat up and asked for a drink.

Physicians said that she would recover.
—*Modesto (CA) Morning Herald*, 1922

SUGGESTIONS FOR CHRISTMAS PRESENTS

A nice book of postage stamps.
A bottle of ketchup.
A new fangled toothbrush.
A cook book.
Some selected pen points.
Some cigar coupons.
A box of matches.
—*Mount Vernon Argus* (White Plains, NY), 1923

"Grand Whiskerino"

In Chicago assembled the annual convention of the International Association of Specialty Salesmen. Said their President: "This year we decided to find the man with the longest beard in the country, to appear at our convention!" He then introduced Hans W. Langseth, 77, of Barney, N.D. Mr. Langseth carries his 17-foot beard inside his waistcoat—in a bag. The specialty salesmen conferred upon him the title of Supreme Grand Whiskerino of the Universe.
—*TIME* **Magazine**, 1923

Vengeful Man Barks Like Dog

MONTGOMERY, Ala., March 21. (UP) — Marion D. Perry today appealed a $10 fine imposed after neighbors hailed him into court on charges of sitting on his porch at night and barking like a dog.

Perry told the judge that the barking of the neighbors' dogs kept him awake and he was only retaliating.
—*Asheville (NC) Citizen*, 1950

HE WANTS IT BACK

SYLACAUGA, Ala., Dec. 1 — Hewlett Hodges of Sylacauga today retained the Talladega law firm of Love and Hines to recover the meteorite that struck his wife and home yesterday.

Atty. Huel Love said that if the meteorite is not returned within a reasonable time suit will be filed against "whatever party has it," adding that the Air Force was expected to return it later today.

Love said Hodges had received telephone calls from institutions and individuals throughout the country offering fantastic prices for the fragment.
—*The Birmingham (AL) News*, 1954

Jockey Wins Race, Then Falls From Saddle, Dead

New York, June 4.— After piloting Sweet Kiss to an easy victory in the steeplechase at Belmont Park today, Rider Frank Hayes rode to the judge's stand and fell from the saddle, dead. It was the first time he had jockeyed a winning jumper.

When Sweet Kiss gracefully leaped the last barrier and straightened out for the run to the wire, Hayes was seen swaying in the saddle. Attendants hurried toward him when the race ended, but he toppled to the track before they reached him.

Hayes was 35 years old. His death was said to have been due to heart failure, induced by weight reduction.
—*The Owensboro (KY) Messenger*, 1923

"The Scully Effect" is the increased number of women in STEM fields as a direct result of the role of FBI Special Agent Dr. Dana Scully (Gillian Anderson) on *The X-Files*.

UNCLE JOHN'S STALL OF SHAME

Not everyone deserves to make it into the Stall of Fame—and for a good reason. That's why Uncle John created the "Stall of Shame."

Honoree: Wilson High School in Florence, Alabama
Dubious Achievement: Prohibiting privacy in a public privy
True Story: Vaping in school bathrooms is an ongoing issue, and it reached a boiling point at Wilson High in September 2019 after a student was found passed out in a stall. Principal Gary Horton blamed the incident on vaping, and then took the drastic step of removing stall doors from the boys' restrooms.

The outcry from students and parents was immediate. "I don't like it," said one parent. "They take their only private place in the school that they can do their business." Principal Horton explained that he didn't remove all of the stall doors, and that the measure "was only temporary." Then he quickly had the doors put back.

Honoree: Purple, a Wi-Fi company based in Manchester, England
Dubious Achievement: Playing a dirty trick on their customers
True Story: For two weeks in 2017, Purple quietly slipped a "community service clause" into its terms and conditions for new customers. In that span, 22,000 people signed up without realizing that by clicking "I agree," they consented to performing 1,000 hours of community service. Doing what? Disgusting tasks, including cleaning portable toilets at a music festival and manually removing sewer blockages. Purple's point was to press people to read the fine print. The laws are iffy as to whether users are legally bound to show up for their crappy community service, but in 2014, cybersecurity firm F-Secure ran a similar gag allowing people to use the company's Wi-Fi hotspots in exchange for the users' firstborn children—that so-called "Herod clause" was not legally binding. (Good thing, since six people agreed to it.)

Honoree: Patrick Beeman of Sheboygan, Wisconsin
Dubious Achievement: Stuffing stuff where no stuff should be stuffed
True Story: In at least 12 incidents from 2017 to 2019, Beeman would sneak into empty women's restrooms with a random object—usually a bottle that he'd found in the trash—drop it into a toilet, flush, and hurry out...leaving a flood of damage behind. After the serial toilet clogger was caught (because he even did it at his place of employment) and put on trial, his only defense was that he sometimes has "urges" to

In 2023, one out of every four songs that reached the U.K. Top 40 featured samples from older songs.

clog toilets. A judge gave Beeman 150 days in jail and three years' probation. "I need to make things right and pray for forgiveness every day," he said at his sentencing.

Honoree: A Chinese man identified only as Wang
Dubious Achievement: Turning bathroom breaks into a bathroom broke
True Story: Often, the only respite from workplace drudgery is the hallowed bathroom break. It's a time to sit back and recharge. That's why coworkers get so irked when one of their kind abuses this right. But there are few who've abused the bathroom break like Wang. To be fair, he did have an excuse to be in there more than most people, as he'd recently undergone anorectal surgery and therefore had to go a lot. But when upper management started tracking his bathroom usage in 2015, they fired him. Why? Of the 22 bathroom breaks that Wang took—in only 10 workdays— the shortest one was 47 minutes; the longest was six hours. Wang sued to get his job back but was denied on the grounds that a six-hour bathroom break surpasses "reasonable and normal physiological needs."

Honorees: Two unidentified juveniles from House Springs, Missouri
Dubious Achievement: Blowing an innocent restroom (and then some) to smithereens
True Story: Northwest Jefferson County Sports Complex has ball fields, pickleball courts, a skate park, a walking trail, and, in the middle of it all, a nice little building with a concession stand and public restrooms. At least it had that building until the Fourth of July in 2023. At around 10:30 p.m., someone called police to report that about 20 people were gathered around the restrooms lighting off fireworks. By the time a squad car arrived, the people were gone and so was the restroom. Two teenagers (who were captured a few weeks later) apparently had enough firework power to bring down the men's room roof and half of the building with it, including an entire wall. "It's really uncivilized behavior," said Parks and Recreation director Tim Pigg. "It's not funny, it's not cute, and it's going to cost a lot of money." About $150,000. And thanks to the "not funny" teens, Pigg had to close the entire complex for two weeks in the middle of summer. Local news station KSDK spoke for everyone: "This is why we can't have nice things."

*　*　*

LEARN A NEW WORD

Mizzle (v.): to rain in very small drops; lighter than a drizzle, which has more moisture. It's also a Briticism that means "to abscond with something and quickly flee." (In a sentence: *I put my wipers on constant when it drizzles and on intermittent when it mizzles.*)

Now you know: Twix (the candy bar) is a portmanteau of "Twin Sticks."

DIDION'S BIBLE

As a journalist, memoirist, novelist, and critic, Joan Didion was one of the most profound writers the U.S. and the 20th century produced. In works such as The Year of Magical Thinking, Slouching Towards Bethlehem, *and* Play It as It Lays, *she offered crucial, enlightening, and unsettling insights into life and the world.*

"We tell ourselves stories in order to live."

"To free us from the expectations of others, to give us back to ourselves—there lies the great, singular power of self-respect."

"You have to pick the places you don't walk away from."

"There's a point when you go with what you've got. Or you don't go."

"I am what I am. To look for reasons is beside the point."

"We forget all too soon the things we thought we could never forget."

"Time is the school in which we learn."

"I don't think anybody feels like they're a good parent. Or if people think they're good parents, they ought to think again."

"I think we are well advised to keep on nodding terms with the people we used to be, whether we find them attractive company or not. Otherwise they turn up unannounced and surprise us, hammering on the mind's door at 4 a.m. of a bad night."

"The fear is not for what is lost. What is lost is already in the wall. What is lost is already behind the locked door. The fear is for what is still to be lost."

"In time of trouble, I had been trained since childhood, read, learn, work it up, go to the literature. Information was control."

"As time goes by I think that men who were unable to make choices were more right than those who made them. Because there are no clean choices."

"I'm not telling you to make the world better, because I don't think that progress is necessarily part of the package. I'm just telling you to live in it. Not just to endure it, not just to suffer it, not just to pass through it, but to live in it. To look at it. To try to get the picture."

"Do not whine...Do not complain. Work harder. Spend more time alone."

"Memory fades, memory adjusts, memory conforms to what we think we remember."

"Was there ever in anyone's lifespan a point free in time, devoid of memory, a night when choice was any more than the sum of all the choices gone before?"

"I'm not interested in the middle road—maybe because everyone's on it."

"Life changes in the instant. The ordinary instant."

"I don't know what I think until I write it down."

A 2016 paper found judges in Louisiana were more likely to give harsher sentences after their favorite college football team lost a close game.

BEHIND THE LINES

Every screenwriter dreams of writing a line of dialogue that achieves movie immortality. But it also takes good direction, great acting, and more than a little good luck. (Of course, in some cases, the line just needs to be included in the trailer.) Here are the origins and impacts of some of the silver screen's most enduring quotes.

Famous Line: "Release the Kraken!"

Said by: Greek god Zeus (Liam Neeson) in *Clash of the Titans* (2010)

Story: This corny catchphrase came from the pen of revered English playwright Alan Beverley Cross, who wrote the screenplay for 1981's *Clash of the Titans*. Despite the fact that silver screen legend Sir Laurence Olivier delivered the line in it, the original *Titans* is known more for Ray Harryhausen's stop-motion creature animation than for Cross's dialogue. Olivier's version of Zeus is more subdued, and his delivery of the line is more reluctant, than Liam Neeson's take in the remake: The camera zooms in to Neeson's bearded Zeus, his head cocked at an angle. He pauses dramatically before growling, "Release the Kraken!"

Thanks to the movie trailer—which was plastered all over TV and amassed millions of views on YouTube—the line became a catchphrase before the movie was even released. It was later named one of *TIME* magazine's top 10 "Buzzwords of the Year" for 2010. Then the definitions started piling up on Urban Dictionary. (Our favorite: "Release the Kraken: to take an epic s***.") In the era of social media, the Kraken has achieved immortality in the form of countless memes.

It's ironic, then, that a line—and a movie—that become indelibly linked to Greek mythology gets so much of it wrong. When writing the 1981 screenplay, Cross took more than a few creative liberties. For one, in the original myth, the sea monster was the whale-like Cetus, and it was sent by Poseidon, not Zeus. Oh, and there was no Kraken in Greek mythology at all—the Kraken is a mythological Scandinavian sea monster first described in modern times only in the 1700s. (Details, details.)

The Kraken made a foray into politics in November 2020, following the contested U.S. presidential election. Lawyer Sidney Powell appeared on Fox Business and threatened that Donald Trump's legal team would soon present evidence of massive voter fraud. Trump, she said, won the election "in a landslide...We are talking about hundreds of thousands of votes." Then she added, "I'm going to release the Kraken." With that, the line trended on Twitter...and Powell received a titanic amount of mocking. Why? Because in both versions of *Clash of the Titans*—spoiler alert—the Kraken loses.

Houseflies can see behind themselves.

Famous Line: "I'm going to make him an offer he can't refuse."

Said by: Don Vito Corleone (Marlon Brando) in *The Godfather* (1972)

Story: "In that case, I will make you an offer that no one would decline." That line comes from French author Honoré de Balzac's 1835 novel, *Le Père Goriot*. American author Mario Puzo was so inspired by that book that he quoted a passage from it to open his best-selling 1969 novel, *The Godfather.*

While writing his book (working title: *Mafia*) about the Corleones, a fictional Italian American crime family, Puzo reportedly labored over the "offer" line. Then he labored over it even more while working on the screenplay with director and cowriter Francis Ford Coppola. In fact, this movie quote is so iconic that it generated headlines in 2016 after Puzo's literary archives were unsealed. Handwritten notes over the typed screenplay reveal that the filmmakers tried a few different wordings.

In the novel, Vito says, "I'll make him an offer he can't refuse." During script revisions, the line was almost shortened to a command: "Make him an offer he can't refuse." At another point the line was crossed out and replaced with a handwritten "I'll reason with him." By the time it shows up in the film, the original beginning "I'll make him" was lengthened to "I'm going to make him an offer he can't refuse."

Variations of the line are later said by two other characters (and then in the two Godfather sequels), but it's Brando's cold, calm delivery that became iconic. Said softly into the ear of his worried godson Johnny Fontane (Al Martino), it turns out to be a really gruesome "offer" that culminates with a Hollywood producer waking up in bed next to the severed head of his thoroughbred horse. Now maybe that producer will change his mind and cast Johnny in his next movie.

The line came in second in the American Film Institute's venerated "100 Years...100 Movie Quotes" list (after *Gone with the Wind*'s "Frankly, my dear, I don't give a damn") and has been parodied countless times, proving all that laboring was worth it.

Bonus: Puzo made other indelible marks on culture—not only did he come up with "godfather" as a term for a Mafia boss, he also coined the phrase "sleep with the fishes."

Famous Line: "Hey, Malkovich, think fast!"

Said by: An extra in *Being John Malkovich* (1999)

Story: It's a weird scene in a weird movie. John Malkovich (John Malkovich) has just traveled through a portal that leads into his own mind and been dumped out on the side of the New Jersey Turnpike at night. Disoriented and angry, he's walking alongside traffic when a passenger in a passing truck yells, "Hey, Malkovich, think fast!" and then chucks a beer can at the back of his head. Malkovich shrieks and yells an expletive. This clever bit of writing from Charlie Kaufman's Oscar-nominated screenplay (his first) shows the character's life spinning out of control, thus creating empathy for him.

According to (most) "famous ad-libs" lists, none of it was planned—not the line, the throw, or Malkovich's *real* reaction. The source for this claim is a 59-second YouTube video (with around a million and a half views) purported to be director Spike Jonze telling the story in the DVD commentary: "That was not in our script at all. We had some extras that had snuck some beer on set and they got pretty lit." He said that they had to up that extra's pay from $100 (for a nonspeaking role) to $700.

It's a funny story, except it isn't true. For one, there is no commentary for *Being John Malkovich*. For some reason, a prankster did a so-so impression of the director's voice and recorded one minute of fake commentary. Strangely, every comment on the YouTube video pointing this out gets deleted, and if you try to click on a video of the cast and crew actually setting up the shot, it says, "Video unavailable."

In an "Ask Me Anything" on Reddit, the *real* John Malkovich told it this way: "Spike Jonze wanted to cut it because we were late that night and he felt no one would be able to hit me on the head with a half-full can of beer from a passing car, and about 70 or 80 sets of hands shot up on the crew saying they would like to try. Eventually the task fell to Johnny Cusack's writing partner and he nailed it on the first try."

Famous Line: "That'll do, pig."

Said by: Farmer Arthur Hoggett (James Cromwell) in *Babe* (1995)

Story: Australian producer George Miller is best known for the Mad Max franchise, so it came as a bit of a shock that he'd make a family friendly, talking-animal comedy-drama about a pig that competes against sheepdogs in a herding competition (which makes the underdog a pig). Miller and director Chris Noonan collaborated on the screenplay, and by all accounts they did *not* get along during filming. But one thing they did agree on: keeping the last line of the 1983 novel *The Sheep-Pig* (renamed *Babe, The Gallant Pig* in the U.S.) by English writer Dick King-Smith. But they did make one change. The book ends with:

> "That'll do," said Farmer Hogget [sic] to his sheep-pig. "That'll do."

One word was added for the movie: "That'll do, pig. That'll do."

For James Cromwell, the Oscar-nominated role revived his career—lucky considering that he'd originally balked because his character has only 17 lines. But it was his heartfelt delivery of that final line, staring straight into the eyes of his beloved pig, that struck a chord with the public. Like any skilled actor, Cromwell channeled that emotion from deep within—in this case, his troubled relationship with his father, who never supported his dreams to become an actor. When Cromwell, whom the makeup department had aged for the role, looked down at the camera, he didn't see a reflection of himself in the lens, he instead saw his father. And he nailed the delivery in one take. "Although I said, 'That'll do, pig. That'll do,' what I heard was, 'That'll do, Jamie. That'll do.'"

What's the difference between *lasagna* and *lasagne*?
The former is singular; the latter is plural.

JUST PLANE WEIRD

*If you happen to be reading this book on an airplane, you might want
to save this article for when you're back on the ground.*

✈ CHICKEN AND STUFFING

The Transportation Security Administration, the federal agency in charge of airport
security checks, allows passengers to bring fresh meat in their carry-on luggage
(with some caveats). TSA agents deal with a lot of food transit during the busy
Thanksgiving travel season but were still left baffled in November 2022 when a man
attempting to board a flight at Florida's Fort Lauderdale–Hollywood International
Airport placed on the conveyer belt X-Ray a portable cooler containing a whole, raw
chicken wrapped in a thin plastic bag. TSA agents examined the chicken and found
that it was a stuffed chicken—the man had shoved a handgun into the body cavity.
Unlike poultry, guns are not allowed in carry-on luggage.

✈ THE AIR UP THERE

In January 2023, Daniel David Becon took a long transatlantic flight, leaving Miami for
London. Two hours into the eight-hour trip, he left his seat at the back of the plane in
economy class and moved to an empty seat in the more expensive business-class area.
A flight attendant noticed and ordered him to return to his seat; Becon refused, and
he offered to pay for the upgrade. When told that wouldn't be possible, Becon came
unglued, swearing, shouting, and spitting at the flight attendant while standing on the
seat. When the worker attempted to leave the situation, Becon punched him in the
face. Headed back to his economy seat, Becon shouted more swears, shoving another
flight attendant along the way. The pilot turned around and landed back in Miami
where Becon was arrested. The reason he'd tried to get out of his original seat: another
passenger seated near him couldn't stop letting out noxious farts.

✈ A ONE-PLANE DOGFIGHT

Because of events that transpired on a routine hour-long flight from Geneva,
Switzerland, to Paris in June 2022, two Air France pilots were suspended and
reprimanded by their employer. One pilot said an "inadvertent blow" delivered
from one to the other shortly after takeoff triggered a full-scale physical fight. That
led to the seemingly attacked pilot grabbing the other by the collar, and mutual
collar-grabbing and slapping ensued. Flight attendants noticed the ruckus and broke
it up, but not until after one pilot threw a "wooden object" at the other. The flight

On *Star Trek*, Dr. McCoy's medical instruments were Swedish salt shakers.

completed its journey, with one flight attendant staying in the flight deck to ensure the pilots didn't fight anymore.

✈ MID-FLIGHT CAT-ASTROPHE

A March 2021 Tarco Aviation flight from the Sudanese capital of Khartoum to Qatar was forced to return to its point of departure less than half an hour after takeoff. The reason: the pilot was attacked by an irate cat. According to witnesses, the cat, not belonging to anyone on board, had apparently been in the cockpit prior to takeoff, and when it woke up mid-flight, it was so upset that it lashed out at the pilot, then resisted the flight attendants that attempted to wrangle it. Investigators believe that the cat wandered into the airport the night before the flight, entered the plane (grounded for cleaning) looking for a place to sleep, and dozed off until the flight was in progress.

✈ BEE CLEVER

A May 2023 Delta Airlines flight from Houston to Atlanta scheduled to leave at 12:25 p.m. didn't depart until 4:30 because of a bee infestation. For reasons never made clear, a massive swarm of bees amassed on one of the plane's wings and wouldn't leave of their own volition. Beekeepers wouldn't be allowed to touch the plane, and pest-control agents wouldn't be allowed to spray the plane; in desperation, airline crew tried to blow exhaust at the bees. It briefly upset some of the swarm, but the bees stayed put. What finally worked: the pilot just moved the plane. As soon as the engine turned on and the aircraft started to back up, the bees flew away.

✈ COBRA IN THE COCKPIT

Life imitated art on a small plane flying out of South Africa in April 2023 (if you consider the silly 2006 B movie *Snakes on a Plane* to be art). While flying four passengers in a small private plane, pilot Rudolf Erasmus said he felt "something cold" on his back. He looked down and saw the head of a snake slither down under his seat. Particularly worrisome—it was a Cape Cobra, a reptile native to South Africa and known and feared for its especially toxic venom. After taking a few minutes to gain his composure, Erasmus let his passengers know that there was a snake on the plane and was met with a "stunned silence." The pilot called air traffic control and received permission to make an emergency landing in Welkom, South Africa—meaning he had to spend another 15 minutes flying a plane while a cobra sat at his feet. "I kept looking down to see where it was. It was happy under the seat," he said. An emergency team and a snake handler met the plane on the runway. No one was injured, although crews searched the plane for two days...and never found the snake.

Elephants lack sweat glands; they stay cool in part thanks to "hot spots" across their bodies that allow heat to escape.

QUIRKS OF LANGUAGE

If you're new to our language, sorry. English really is confusing, but it's also fascinating...once you get past the confusion. Here's some stuff about it.

PRESENT THE PRESENTS

Did you ever notice that a lot of words that can be both a noun and a verb have something in common? Their pronunciation changes depending on their part of speech: nouns stress the first syllable in a word, and verbs stress the second. This is called *initial stress derivation*, and you can see it in action in these sentences:

- I want to con*vert* the *con*verts.
- I sus*pect* that I'm a *sus*pect.
- I must pro*test* at the *pro*test!
- I shall in*sult* you with an *in*sult.
- Let's ad*dress* the change of *ad*dress.
- We must com*bat* the desire for *com*bat.

Not all noun-verb pairs do this—about 170 in total. How many others can you think of?

HELLO MUDDER, HELLO FODDER

Native English speakers should have no trouble saying "this and that" and "although the father lathers," but that soft *th* sound appears in only English and a few other languages. It's called a *dental fricative*, and is made by lightly pressing the tip of the tongue against the upper teeth. In most of the world, there is no soft *th* sound, which is why you might hear a non-English speaker say what sounds more like, "Dere is a deer over dere."

OF THEE I SAY

There's actually a certain way we're supposed to be pronouncing the word *the* according to what follows it, but depending on where you're from, you might not follow this rule. To find out, say this sentence out loud: "The egg is on the stove." The proper pronunciation is, "*Thee* egg is on *thuh* stove." That's because a long *e* goes before a word that starts with a vowel or a vowel sound, as in "*thee* orangutan" and "*thuh* gorilla." There is an exception—if you want to emphasize the word after *the*, whether it begins with a vowel or a consonant, you can elongate your *the*, as in "Uncle John's is *thee* book to read in the bathroom." But remember, this pertains only to how you say it; it's always spelled T-H-E, regardless.

The Pentagon isn't in Washington, D.C.; it's in Arlington, Virginia, on the spot where a large hemp farm once stood.

OLD FISH

Lox is a very special word. Most people use it in the context of "lox and bagels," as it means "smoked salmon." But that word, say linguists, could be the oldest word in existence that hasn't changed pronunciations. How old? About 8,000 years, give or take. The word came from what is now called Indo-European—the common language that, according to the going theory, existed millennia ago before branching off into Greek, Latin, English, and 400 others. The only change *lox* has undergone? It used to mean "salmon," not specifically smoked salmon.

YOUR ABCs AND THEN SOME

English didn't always have 26 letters. Six more were lost as Old English transitioned to Middle and then Modern English. Trade and warfare brought previously isolated bands of Europeans together, where they swapped words and pronunciations. Then, after the printing press was invented around 1436, placing individual letters by hand was time-consuming. To save printers space and money, some letters got chopped and were replaced by letter combinations:

- **Eth (ð):** pronounced like the *th* in *they* or *those*
- **Wynn (ρ):** the *w* sound, which had been represented by *uu*—but *w* won out over *ρ*
- **Thorn (þ):** the *th* sound in *thick* and *thin*
- **Ash (æ):** a short *a,* as in *hat.*
- **Ethel (œ):** the *oi* in *oil*—eventually replaced those two letters (and *oy*)
- **Yogh (ʒ):** Like the silent *gh* in *thought* or *though*—but it wasn't totally silent: it was voiced at the back of the throat, as in the Scottish word "loch"

WHY NO MEESE?

The Old English word for *goose* was *gōs.* The plural form was *gōsiz.* That's why the plural of *goose* is *geese.* The word *moose* came to English in the 1600s from the Native American family of languages called Algonquian, which called it a *moòs.* That's why the plural of *moose* is not *meese.* So, what is the plural of *moose? Moose.*

WHO AND *WHOM* MADE EASY

Who is the subject of a sentence: *who* causes the action. The object of the sentence is *whom:* something happens to *whom.* It's just like *he* and *him: he* (or *who*) causes something to happen to *him* (or to *whom*). Still confused? Remember the phrase "for whom the bell tolls." And if you're still confused after that? Just avoid it altogether.

Hall of Fame pitcher Nolan Ryan holds 51 Major League records, including most strikeouts (5,714) and most no-hitters (7).

THE FELINE TIMELINE, PART I

Whether you're a cat person or not, you might be curious to know how this secretive predator kneaded its furry little paws into the fabric of society. Here's the first of our articles that investigate the history and mystery of Felis catus.

Hello, Kitty!

Abraham Lincoln once observed, "No matter how much the cats fight, there always seem to be plenty of kittens." And then some! These days, there are so many cats... that we don't even know how many cats there are. Worldwide estimates range from 300 million to 1 billion; the U.S. has the most, with an estimated 60 to 86 million kept as pets, and up to 40 million more that are stray or feral.

That places the domestic house cat among the most successful predator species on Earth. And it's all thanks to its peculiar relationship with *our* species. "The house cat has gained ground from the Arctic Circle to the Hawaiian archipelago, taken over Tokyo and New York, and stormed the entire continent of Australia," writes cat-behavior expert Abigail Tucker in her book *The Lion in the Living Room*. "And somewhere along the way, it seized the most precious and closely guarded piece of territory on the planet: the stronghold of the human heart." (Except for Uncle John's.)

Our story technically starts back when the first opportunistic wildcats slunk their way into early human settlements. But we'll begin just a bit earlier than that...

10.8 million years ago	The first mammals that will later be assigned to the family *Felidae* appear. Over time, the feline family tree will break up into eight major phylogenetic lineages that will later evolve into the "big cats" that make up the genus *Panthera* (lions, tigers, leopards, jaguars, and panthers), and the smaller *Felinae* genus (lynxes, bobcats, ocelots, leopard cats, and wildcats).
10,000 years ago	The African wildcat (*Felis silvestris lybica*), which looks uncannily like a modern house cat (*Felis catus*), encounters early modern humans living in the Fertile Crescent (the Middle East and North Africa), who are just beginning to grow and store grains. That attracts mice and rats, which attract the wildcats, thus beginning an uneasy truce between felines and humans.
9,500 years ago	In the village of Shillourokambos on the island of Cyprus in the Mediterranean Sea, a Neolithic human is buried in an elaborate grave, right next to a cat. Archaeologists will later deem this the earliest

One difference between planets and stars in the night sky: planets don't twinkle. (They're too close to Earth.)

evidence of cats having a special place among people (many millennia earlier than previously thought), as the animals could have arrived on Cyprus only by boat. However, this particular cat is more likely a tamed wildcat than a domesticated house cat.

4400 BC

Wildcats begin showing up in greater numbers in the Middle East. They live much like today's feral cats do—on the edges of population pockets, taking advantage of the rodents while keeping clear of the people—until they don't. It's around this time that the domestic house cat starts to become its own species. Called the Egyptian Mau, this first cat breed has some slight but significant differences from the wildcat—not the least of which is a more kitten-like appearance. However, when compared to other domesticated animals like dogs, hooved mammals, and poultry—which differ drastically from their wild counterparts—domestic cats mostly retain their wild traits, physical *and* behavioral. Whatever factors have led to this change in their DNA is still unknown, but the going theory is that cats, like dogs before them, "self-domesticated" among humans by figuring out ways to get fed.

3500 BC

Cats become domesticated in China, much in the same way they were in Egypt. However, the Chinese tame the leopard cat, a more robust relative of the African wildcat (with spots like a leopard). When they later come in contact with the Egyptian Mau, cats will begin to branch out into breeds.

1950 BC

It's the first "cat pic"! An Egyptian fresco depicts a cat in a field about to pounce on a rat. Cats don't just kill rodents, they also provide protection from deadly cobras, which pose a serious threat to people living near the Nile River. The cat's ferocity—combined with its soft fur and soothing purr—earns it a hallowed place in Egyptian society. Contrary to popular belief, cats aren't worshipped as gods. Rather, the Egyptians view them as vessels that the gods inhabit.

1425 BC

The first known cat to have a name is called Nedjem. (It means "sweet.") This is significant because it not only shows that cats are moving from alleys into homes, but that friendlier cats are being favored. By using selective breeding to get the most desired features and personalities, Egyptians basically "invent" the modern house cat.

1353 BC

Egyptian Prince Thutmose loves his favorite cat, Ta-Miu ("She-Cat"), so much that, after her death, she is mummified and laid to rest in a

Emil Jannings's claim to fame: in 1929, he won the first Academy Award ("Best Actor" for the movies *The Last Command* and *The Way of All Flesh*).

fancy limestone sarcophagus befitting a human nobleman. Carvings on the sarcophagus depict the cat before a table laden with sacrifices; the inscription reads, "I myself am placed among the imperishable ones that are in the Sky / For I am Ta-Miu, the Triumphant."

1070 BC After 2,000 years being depicted with the head of a lioness, the Egyptian goddess Bastet is now depicted with the head of a house cat—another sign that the wildcat truly has become domesticated.

500 BC The Egyptians' love of the house cat becomes the main driver for the species' spread across the known world. First, cats are taken to the Phoenicians, situated near both Cyprus and Egypt; the Phoenicians introduce them into Greece and Rome, where they make themselves right at home. (Libertas, the Roman goddess of freedom and independence, is often depicted with a cat lying at her feet.) As the Roman Empire takes over Europe, so to do cats. It's also around this time that Egyptian cats arrive in China in greater numbers.

AD 75 The word that will become *cat* first appears in the Late Latin word *cattus*, which means "domestic cat" (replacing *feles*). The word will enter West Germanic circa 400 as *katte*, and into Old English circa 700 as *catt*. By the 15th century, the Modern English spelling will be finalized, as seen here in William Shakespeare's *The Tempest*: "They'll take suggestion as a cat laps milk."

985 Like the Romans before them, the Vikings employ cats for pest control on their ships. They land in Newfoundland, becoming the first known Europeans to sail to the Americas. Although there isn't any archaeological evidence, it's speculated that the Vikings brought cats with them. This is a possible origin of the Maine Coon breed.

1233 The Middle Ages are bad for cats. Once considered "vessels of the gods" by the Egyptians, they're labeled agents of Satan by the Catholic Church when Pope Gregory IX issues *Vox in Rama*. This decree goes into lurid details about a coven ceremony where witches kiss a black cat's behind before engaging in an orgy that conjures Lucifer (who has cat legs). Thus begins the popular association of witches with cats, especially black cats.

1347–52 Life gets even worse for cats during the Black Death, a series of bubonic plague outbreaks that kill an estimated 25 million Europeans. The spreaders are infected fleas that jump from mice, rats, dogs, and cats (and humans) onto humans. But thanks to the anti-cat stigma already in place, cats take the brunt of the blame and are killed en masse—often brutally. Ownership of a cat becomes illegal in many places. Result: European cats are nearly wiped out. In their absence, mice and rat populations flourish, as do illness outbreaks. Only when the connection is made that cats may bring plague deaths down by keeping rodents in check are they allowed back into homes. Now revered as saviors, cats spread even faster throughout the Old World.

1352– 1767

Tamra Maew ("The Cat Book Poems") is a collection of manuscripts from Siam (modern-day Thailand). The book has the first known descriptions of Siamese cats, described as "rare as gold."

1380s

An hole he foond, ful lowe upon a bord
Ther as the cat was wont in for to crepe

These lines from Geoffrey Chaucer's "The Miller's Tale" are the first written mention of a cat hole, the precursor to today's cat door. (This lays to rest a common myth that Isaac Newton invented the cat door in the late 1600s.)

1400– 1782

During the European witch trials, between 40,000 and 60,000 women are executed by the Catholic Church. In many cases, simply owning a cat—especially a black cat—can lead to an accusation of witchcraft. The cats often suffer the same fate as their owners.

1492

Columbus sails the ocean blue...and cats do, too. The Age of Sail sees cats landing on Plymouth Rock with the Pilgrims, and patrolling the first permanent Colonial settlement at Jamestown. But it is at sea where these feline friends eventually make their mark. Ships' cats, as they're known, are crucial for killing rats—which eat food stores and chew through ropes. Cats also boost crew morale, as they are said to bring good luck.

1758

Carl Linnaeus, the Swedish botanist famous for formalizing binomial nomenclature (the system of giving names to organisms), proposes the scientific name for the domestic cat: *Felis catus*.

OK, time for a catnap. When you wake up, give your arms and legs a good licking and then run as fast as you can over to page 368!

The word *opera* is the plural of *opus*.

CAT PEOPLE

People who like cats explain why.

"IN ANCIENT TIMES CATS WERE WORSHIPPED AS GODS; THEY HAVE NOT FORGOTTEN THIS." —Terry Pratchett

"There are two means of refuge from the miseries of life: music and cats." —Albert Schweitzer

"Even the smallest feline is a masterpiece of nature." —Leonardo da Vinci

"I have lived with several Zen masters—all of them cats." —Eckhart Tolle

"Time spent with a cat is never wasted." —Colette

"The phrase 'domestic cat' is an oxymoron." —George F. Will

"One cat just leads to another." —Ernest Hemingway

"If you really want to learn about life, get a cat." —James Cromwell

"The trouble with a kitten is that eventually it becomes a cat." —Ogden Nash

"The problem with cats is that they get the exact same look on their face whether they see a moth or an axe murderer." —Paula Poundstone

The working title of 1984's *Indiana Jones and the Temple of Doom* was *Indiana Jones and the Temple of Death*.

"You know my philosophy when it comes to cats, babies, and apologies. You gotta let them come to you."
—Ted Lasso

"Cat people are different, to the extent that they generally are not conformists. How could they be, with a cat running their lives?"
—Louis J. Camuti

"I have felt cats rubbing their faces against mine and touching my cheek with claws carefully sheathed. These things, to me, are expressions of love."
—James Herriot

"Way down deep, we're all motivated by the same urges. Cats have the courage to live by them."
—Jim Davis

"If animals could speak, the dog would be a blundering outspoken fellow; but the cat would have the rare grace of never saying a word too much."
—Mark Twain

"Throw a stick, and the servile dog wheezes and pants and stumbles to bring it to you. Do the same before a cat, and he will eye you with coolly polite and somewhat bored amusement."
—H. P. Lovecraft

"Cats can work out mathematically the exact place to sit that will cause most inconvenience."
—Pam Brown

"I like cats a lot. I've always liked cats. They're great company. When they eat, they always leave a little bit at the bottom of the bowl. A dog will polish the bowl, but a cat always leaves a little bit. It's like an offering."
—Christopher Walken

Gorillas fart almost constantly.

ANOTHER AUDREY HOPBURN?

Thanks to the craft beer movement, there are thousands of small-batch beers made by small breweries throughout the U.S. and Europe. And to differentiate themselves, they all seem to have a goofy, funny, or eyebrow-raising name. Here are some of the silliest ones we've found.

Parking Violation

Juicebox Hero

Cinna-Mom on French Toast

Men in Bock

Hazed and Confused

Peter Piper Peppered Pale

4 Hop Men of the Apocalypse

Elvis Crack

Mother Fuggle Brown Ale

Geriatric Hipster Club

Pickleodeon

The Great Big Kentucky Sausage Fest

Moose Drool

Barbarian Streisand

Respect Your Elderberries

668: The Neighbor of the Beast

Tactical Nuclear Penguin

Tart Side of the Moon

Sky Hag

Ill Tempered Gnome

Dan's Pink Skirt

Haulin' Oats

I'll Be Bock

Ratsalad

Village Idiot

Complicated Passwords

Turn Your Head and Coffee

Human Blockhead

Yellow Snow

Java the Nut

Buzz Lightbeer

Grand Pappy's Sugar Shack

Audrey Hopburn

Whitney Brewston

Mrs. Stoutfire

Tamarind Diaz

Punk in Drublic

99 Red Baboons

Pathological Lager

Questionable Advice

Back Sack & Quack

Drink of Me Fondly

Wheat the Parents

Spruce Willis

Pancakes 'n' Hotpants

Stop, Hop, & Roll

Boom Shaka Lager

Smooth Hoperator

This Is Why We Can't Have Nice Things

Don't Wait in Line For This

Czech Your Head

Random Name Generator

I'll Have What the Gentleman on the Floor Is Having

Named in honor of 9-year-old Amber Hagerman, AMBER in AMBER Alert System is an acronym for "America's Missing: Broadcast Emergency Response."

LOCAL HEROES

You're going about your day, minding your own business,
when all of a sudden—BOOM!—you're face-to-face with a life-and-death situation!
What do you do? Do you freeze up and hope someone else helps?
Or do you step up and be a hero?

THE BLIZZARD OF '22

Joey White sure needed a hero. A "gentle soul" is how his boss, Ray Barker, described him. By December 2022, White, 64, had spent 42 years working as a janitor at the North Park Theatre in Buffalo, New York. Being cognitively challenged, "Joe is used to his pattern," Barker told the *Washington Post*. "For someone who's used to being in a pattern, I think it's hard not to engage that pattern." That's why, the day before a fierce winter storm was about to hit, Barker called White and insisted that he not come to work the next day. White's sister, Yvonne, also warned him to stay home. But White was beholden to his pattern. Some time on December 23 (it's unsure exactly when), he left the group home where he lives and walked nine miles to the movie theater, just as the worst blizzard to hit Buffalo in 50 years was getting going. No one was at the theater, so White went inside to warm up for the night and left sometime before dawn. He trudged several miles through subzero temps, high winds, and rising snow until he became stuck in a snowbank.

Sha'Kyra Aughtry was awoken at 6:30 a.m. on Christmas Eve by what she later described as cries of agony. The mother of three boys looked out her window and saw an older balding man—Joey White—struggling in the deep snow. Aughtry woke up her boyfriend; they went outside in the blizzard, freed the stranger, and carried him inside.

White was incoherent, and his hands were severely frostbitten. Aughtry had to use a hair drier to unfreeze his clothes from his skin. After deducing that their guest was cognitively challenged, Aughtry asked White if there was anyone she could contact. Thankfully, he knew his sister's phone number, so Aughtry called Yvonne and told her that her brother was safe for now, but he needed serious medical attention...which was all but impossible in the blizzard. Aughtry estimates she called 911 around 100 times, but the roads were impassable.

So Aughtry, her sons, and her boyfriend put their holiday plans aside to tend to White. They fed and bathed him and washed his clothes. When Christmas arrived and emergency vehicles still couldn't get to her house, Aughtry took to social media for help: "I've been very private and sensitive about this situation," she stated in a livestream video, but, "This man is not about to die over here." Within half an hour, several good Samaritans arrived with snow plows and a four-wheel drive, and they got White to the hospital.

The doctors said it was going to be a long recovery, but thanks to Aughtry and her family, Joey White survived the Blizzard of '22 that killed 35 people in the Buffalo area. White's boss, Barker, called what Aughtry did "an act of goodness...Joe won't be able to express his gratitude fully, but he will feel it emotionally." Yvonne added, "I cannot wait to hug her."

SEE SOMETHING, SAY SOMETHING

In October 2021, Nadia Popovici, a 22-year-old University of Washington graduate about to enter medical school, was attending the home opener of her favorite NHL hockey team, the Seattle Kraken. She was sitting in the front row, right behind the visiting Vancouver Canucks' bench. At the end of the game (the Kraken lost), Popovici was about to leave when she noticed that one of the visiting team's equipment managers, Brian "Red" Hamilton, had an irregular mole on the back of his neck.

Thanks to her time spent volunteering in hospitals, Popovici knew right away that he should have that looked at ASAP. But because of the plexiglass, she couldn't simply yell over to him. She needed to be more discreet. So she typed a message on her phone, in a large font so he could see it, and then waited until he was almost done gathering up the equipment—and everyone else had left the bench. Then Popovici tapped on the plexiglass. Hamilton swiveled around and saw this message: "The mole on the back of your neck is possibly cancerous. Please go see a doctor!"

A bit unnerved, Hamilton gave Popovici a quick glance and left (he admits that at first he "didn't give her the time of day"). She could only hope he'd take the message seriously.

A month and a half later, Popovici woke up on New Year's Day (after spending New Year's Eve answering calls at a suicide hotline) to find out that the Canucks were looking for her! It turned out that Hamilton did heed her advice, and the mole turned out to be a type-2 malignant melanoma.

Hamilton posted a message looking for the "very special woman" who "changed my life." Popovici went to the Kraken game that day, where she was introduced and received huge applause from the crowd. After the game, on a Zoom press conference, Hamilton said that not all heroes wear capes: "She didn't take me out of a burning car like the big stories but she took me out of a slow fire, and then words out of the doctor's mouth where if I ignored that...I wouldn't be here." For her good deed, the Kraken and the Canucks awarded Popovici with a scholarship to medical school.

The incisors of rodents never stop growing.

WORKING ON THE CHAIN GANG

June of 2017 had Georgia's law enforcement officers on edge after two inmates riding in a prisoner transfer bus killed two guards and escaped (they were later captured). A few days later, on a scorching summer day, a Polk County deputy (name not released in press reports) was overseeing six inmates who were working in a cemetery when he collapsed and lost consciousness. No one else was around—all the inmates had to do was take his gun and run. They could be long gone before anyone figured out what happened.

According to one of the inmates, Greg Williams, they didn't even think about running. "It wasn't about who is in jail and who wasn't. It was about a man going down, and we had to help him." They used the deputy's cell phone to call 911 and removed his bulletproof vest to cool him down, then they waited beside their patient until paramedics arrived. The deputy (who was suffering from complications from an earlier brain surgery) made a full recovery. The department threw the inmates a pizza party, and they all had their sentences reduced.

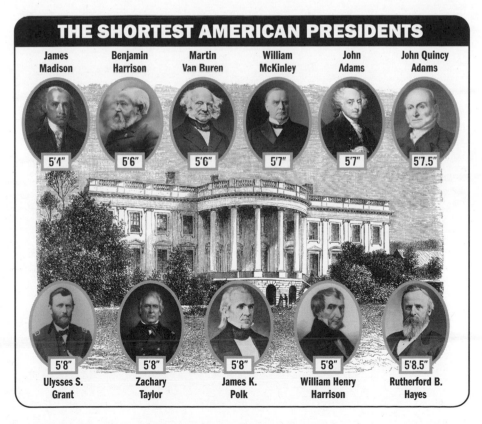

THE SHORTEST AMERICAN PRESIDENTS

James Madison	Benjamin Harrison	Martin Van Buren	William McKinley	John Adams	John Quincy Adams
5'4"	5'6"	5'6"	5'7"	5'7"	5'7.5"

Ulysses S. Grant	Zachary Taylor	James K. Polk	William Henry Harrison	Rutherford B. Hayes
5'8"	5'8"	5'8"	5'8"	5'8.5"

ONE-TRICK KITCHEN PONIES

Kitchen gear manufacturers routinely trot out new, supposedly must-have items that purport to fix a problem that home cooks didn't even know they had. Result: bizarre gadgets, sold in catalogs and via infomercials, that do just one thing—and sometimes ridiculously at that.

The Bacon Master

The user drapes slices of raw bacon over both sides of a shelf in the middle of the gadget. Then they put a metal door (that looks like a mailbox) over the top, sealing the bacon inside. With an adjustment of the crispiness dial, the bacon cooks while draining grease into a trap. It's essentially a toaster. **Cost:** $30.

Asparagus Peeler

Uncle John hasn't heard of anybody peeling off the outer layer of an asparagus. But if you ever need to, for whatever reason, a simple and cheap potato or vegetable peeler does the trick. But this gadget purports to provide the perfect thickness for asparagus peeling—and asparagus peeling only—while resembling any other vegetable peeler. **Cost:** $9.

Tuna Press

The Tuna Press is a piece of blue plastic with two small handles (which are shaped like fish). It fits over a standard can of tuna. Open the can as usual, place the Tuna Press on top, flip it over, and drain the water out through the Tuna Press's little holes. In case using the can lid to help drain the tuna isn't good enough for you, you can replace that lid with a plastic doodad. **Cost:** $8.

Ham Dogger

At backyard cookouts, the choice is usually "hamburger or hot dog?" With this gadget, the answer is "both!" It's a plastic mold in the shape of a frankfurter. Users are directed to stuff it with ground beef, creating a hamburger that's shaped like a hot dog. **Cost:** $9.

Double Waffle Bowl Maker

The ice cream cone was invented at the 1904 World's Fair when an ice cream seller ran out of dishes and spoons and asked a waffle vendor to make cones—edible containers. But then here comes the Waffle Bowl Maker: basically a waffle iron. Users pour in batter and receive two waffle cones shaped like bowls, suitable for filling with ice cream...and requiring the use of a spoon. **Cost:** $40.

Some states require only two years of practicing law before a lawyer can become a judge.

Motorized Ice Cream Cone

This labor-saving device makes all the effort that comes with licking or with turning your wrist while eating an ice cream cone a thing of the past. It looks just like an ice cream cone, except that it's made of plastic and requires batteries. Scoop some ice cream inside and at the push of a button, the device rotates the ice cream as you hold it up against your tongue. **Cost:** $10.

Egg Cuber

This doesn't cook eggs, nor does it cut them. Instead, by way of massage and force, it turns a normal, oblong egg—which the user has already hardboiled—into the shape of a cube. And then you've got a cube-shaped hardboiled egg to do with as you please. **Cost:** $12.

RoboStir

Place this battery-powered tripod device into a pot of food that needs to be constantly stirred as it heats. A rubber-tipped anchor keeps the gadget in place while three other rubber tips at the end of thin wires flail around through the sauce or stew, keeping up a constant stirring motion. **Cost:** $30.

Nana Saver

For when you just can't finish an entire banana, you can place what's left into this yellow banana-shaped piece of plastic. It forms a seal on the clean-cut edge of the fruit to prevent it from browning so quickly. Nana Saver is also available in green and not-curved, marketed as the "Cucumber Saver." **Cost:** $11.

Sunnyside Egg Shaper

Eggs are commonly associated with breakfast, and this gadget really lets a diner know that they're eating food in the morning. Place the Sunnyside Egg Shaper, a piece of plastic shaped into a mold, into a skillet. Carefully separate the egg as you pour it into the stencil—white into the larger section, and the yolk into the little round area. As the egg cooks, it'll take the shape of the stencil: the yolk will look like the sun, and the whites, a fluffy cloud. Because it's morning. **Cost:** $12.

Table Tap

The struggles of slightly tipping a pitcher of water to pour the contents into a glass are over. This water container looks like a massive chemistry beaker. Fill with liquid, and then hold a glass under the protruding tube while squeezing the handle of a separate rubber tube. That forces the water out of the pitcher and into the glass—no lifting or moving required. **Cost:** $250.

Bed bugs appeared on earth 100 million years before beds did.
They may have originally fed on dinosaur blood.

MOSTLY DEAD

You're in a room with a coffin, when you hear a knock...from inside the coffin!
Does this really happen? Yep. How? Because pronouncing someone dead isn't as
straightforward as just feeling for a pulse. Sometimes, even medical professionals botch
this seemingly simple diagnosis. And the results are as terrifying as you'd imagine.

AWAKE AT THE WAKE

In June 2023, a 76-year-old retired nurse named Bella Montoya was rushed to the
state hospital in Ecuador, suffering cardiopulmonary arrest and showing signs of a
stroke. Efforts to revive her were unsuccessful, and the doctor on duty pronounced
her dead. She was issued a death certificate and transferred to a funeral home in
nearby Babahoyo. Later that day, her family and friends gathered to pay their respects.
"After about five hours of the wake," Montoya's son told the Associated Press, "the
coffin started to make sounds. My mom was wrapped in sheets and hitting the coffin,
and when we approached we could see that she was breathing heavily." Paramedics
soon arrived and took Montoya back to the same hospital that had declared her dead.
She was placed in intensive care, where she was kept under "permanent surveillance"
and lasted another seven days before dying for real. Then she was taken to the same
funeral home where she'd woken up. At last report, the government had opened an
investigation into the hospital's practices.

GASPING FOR AIR

An unidentified 66-year-old Iowa woman with Alzheimer's disease was moved into her
nursing home's hospice care unit a few days after Christmas in 2022 due to "senile
degeneration of the brain." A few days later, on January 3, a staffer couldn't detect a
pulse, and the woman wasn't breathing, so she was pronounced dead at around 6:00 a.m.
At 7:30 a.m., a funeral director and a nurse placed the woman in a body bag and
zipped it up. About an hour later, when staffers at the funeral home unzipped the
bag, they "observed [the resident's] chest moving and she gasped for air." That was
according to the Iowa Department of Inspections and Appeals report. The woman
died two days later, and the care facility was hit with $10,000 in fines.

IT'S A CATALEPSY

Rosa Isabel Céspedes Callaca was in a horrific car accident in April 2022. Her three
children were hospitalized, and Callaca—who suffered severe internal injuries and

showed no signs of life—was pronounced dead. And it really seemed like she was dead until her funeral, when she started knocking from the inside of her coffin. When the funeral director opened the lid, "She opened her eyes and was sweating. At that moment I went to my office and proceeded to call the police." They got Callaca back to the hospital as fast as they could, but her "resurrection" was short-lived. She died a few hours later. This particular misdiagnosis was blamed on a condition called *catalepsy*, "characterized by a trance or seizure with a loss of sensation and consciousness accompanied by rigidity of the body." In other words, she only appeared dead.

LOOK WHO'S LOOKING

Named for the biblical story of Jesus resurrecting Lazarus, "Lazarus syndrome" is a rare occurrence in which a patient who was administered CPR is pronounced dead and then later regains blood flow. Technically called *autoresuscitation*, of the 65 documented cases between 1982 and 2018, 18 patients made a complete recovery. An unfortunate incident that occurred in the Detroit, Michigan, suburb of Southfield in August 2020 has been blamed on the Lazarus effect. Paramedics rushed to the home of 20-year-old Timesha Beauchamp, who had cerebral palsy and was unresponsive. After 30 minutes of CPR, they called it. Later, an emergency room doctor "pronounced the patient deceased based upon medical information provided." Several hours later, funeral home staffers unzipped the body bag, and Beauchamp's eyes were "wide open." They put her on the table and detected faint breathing. "They were about to embalm her, which is most frightening, had she not had her eyes open," said her family's lawyer. A spokesman from the Southfield Police and Fire Departments said they "feel terrible about this" but insisted that they followed all the proper protocols. Beauchamp died two months later. (Her family blames the death on brain damage caused by the paramedics not giving her oxygen after pronouncing her dead; city officials believe the young woman experienced a case of Lazarus syndrome.)

SLICE OF LIFE

In November 2020, a 32-year-old Kenyan man named Peter Kigen was taken to a hospital for a "stomach ailment." For some reason—the details are fuzzy on this one— he was pronounced dead. Then he was taken directly to the mortuary for embalming; when they cut into his leg to begin the blood draining, Kigen screamed and the workers ran away, thinking a dead body had returned to life. He made a full recovery, and his family announced they are accusing the hospital of negligence. "I cannot believe what just happened," said Kigen. "How did they establish that I was dead? I did not even know where I was when I regained consciousness, but I thank God for sparing my life. I will serve him for the rest of my life."

English singer Gary Numan is 13 days older than English actor Gary Oldman.

I SPY...AT THE MOVIES

You probably remember the kids' game "I Spy, with My Little Eye..."
Filmmakers have been playing it for years. Here are some in-jokes and
gags you can look for the next time you see these movies.

DIRTY HARRY (1971)

I Spy: A movie marquee for Clint Eastwood's directorial debut, *Play Misty for Me*

Where to Find It: In the most famous scene in *Dirty Harry*, when Detective Callahan (Eastwood) foils a bank robbery on his lunch break and delivers his famous "'Do I feel lucky?' Well, do you, punk?" speech, he walks across the street. The marquee can be seen on a theater in the background. (*Play Misty for Me* was released in October 1971, two months before *Dirty Harry* hit theaters.)

VICE (2018)

I Spy: A photograph of director Adam McKay's heart attack

Where to Find It: "There is a scene when [Vice President Dick] Cheney is getting all the unfiltered intelligence," said McKay. "There's a shot, it almost looks like an octopus, people don't quite know what it is." What is it? "That's my heart attack!" As in, the actual black-and-white photo of McKay's blocked artery (that he asked his doctor if he could keep) from a heart attack he suffered while making the movie.

ONCE UPON A TIME IN HOLLYWOOD (2019)

I Spy: Cars from other Quentin Tarantino movies

Where to Find Them: More than 2,000 vintage cars were needed for Tarantino's dark tale about the 1969 Charles Manson murders. The cream-colored 1966 Cadillac Coupe DeVille owned by Rick (Leonardo DiCaprio) in the movie belonged to Michael Madsen, who drove the same Caddy while portraying Mr. Blonde in *Reservoir Dogs* (1992). The sky blue 1968 Volkswagen Karmann Ghia convertible that Cliff (Brad Pitt) drives was also driven by Uma Thurman in *Kill Bill: Vol. 2* (2004).

GODZILLA (1998)

I Spy: A not-so-subtle dig at the two most famous movie critics

Where to Find It: In Roland Emmerich's poorly received reboot of the Japanese monster movie, the monster Godzilla is in New York with a new look. The city's bumbling Mayor Ebert (Michael Lerner) and his equally ineffective aid Gene (Lorry Goldman) are named after—and even look like—Roger Ebert and Gene Siskel. In case you don't immediately get that they're based on Siskel and Ebert, at one point they stick their thumbs up. Why? Because the critics had trashed Emmerich's two previous hits, *Independence Day* and *Stargate*. Not surprisingly, they didn't like *Godzilla*, either. On their movie-review TV show *Siskel & Ebert*, both critics agreed that Emmerich's revenge was "petty." And even worse, complained Siskel, if the producers were going to go through the trouble of putting the pair in a monster movie, they should have at least taken advantage of the opportunity to have the monster eat them or squash them.

BACK TO THE FUTURE (1985)

I Spy: Edward Van Halen

Where to Find It: After traveling back to 1955, Marty (Michael J. Fox) has to scare his future father George (Crispin Glover) into going to a school dance. While George is sleeping, Marty, wearing a hazmat suit, puts headphones around George's ears and inserts into a Sony Walkman a cassette tape labeled "Edward Van Halen." Then some serious shredding is heard as Marty says in a robotic voice, "My name is Darth Vader. I am an extraterrestrial from the planet Vulcan!"

In 1985, Van Halen was one of the biggest bands on the planet, and the original plan was to feature one of their songs in the scene. However, lead singer David Lee Roth wasn't interested—none of the band members were, except for lead guitarist Eddie. Nearly three decades later, he copped to his uncredited cameo: "It was just me playing a bunch of noise." (It was actually part of the film score he did for 1984's *The Wild Life*.) Because the band hadn't given their permission, the movie couldn't legally use the name "Van Halen." So the tape that Marty puts in the Walkman says "Edward" above "Van Halen"—Eddie's legal name, not the band's name. Problem solved.

THE SUPER MARIO BROS. MOVIE (2023)

I Spy: The original voice of Mario

Where to Find It: In a movie packed with references to other Nintendo games, the one that raised the most eyebrows was the character of Giuseppe, who appears at the pizzeria in the beginning. He's voiced by Charles Martinet, who'd been voicing Mario in video games since 1991. (Some fans were bothered that Chris Pratt was cast in the movie role instead of Martinet.) Giuseppe is working on an arcade game called *Jump Man* that looks just like 1981's *Donkey Kong*, which launched the Mario Bros. franchise.

Bonus Fact: Jumpman was the original name of the mustachioed character in development in the 1980s. Then one day Mario Segale, landlord of Nintendo's American headquarters, stormed in and demanded his rent. They changed the character's name to Mario in Segale's "honor."

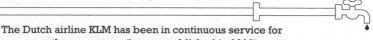

The Dutch airline KLM has been in continuous service for more than a century (it was established in 1919).

DUMB CROOKS

Here's proof that crime doesn't pay.

TO CATCH A THIEF

In December 2018, a 26-year-old Oregon man named Adam Valle strolled up to a bicycle rack right next to the front door of the Gladstone Police Department. Valle's face was masked and he wore a dark hoodie. He approached the bike rack with a large pair of bolt cutters, then got down on one knee and started trying to cut a bike chain, but he was having difficulty.

Meanwhile, only a few feet away—*inside* the station—several befuddled cops were watching the attempted thieving unfold live on the security monitor. Within 30 seconds, an officer stepped out and startled Valle, who was still struggling to cut the chain. He held up the bolt cutters in a threatening manner, and the cop held up his Taser. Valle sat down next to the bike and gave himself up. At least his "perp walk" was shorter than most.

ON GRAND THEFT AUTOPILOT

Nymea Cropper, a bail bondswoman from Charlotte, North Carolina, was walking into the jailhouse to post bond for a client in late December 2022. Anthony Goddard, whose bond had just been posted by another bondsman, was walking out of the jailhouse. They walked right past each other. Then Goddard, who was initially incarcerated for stealing a car, walked up to Cropper's car...and stole it...in broad daylight...in full view of a security camera. Cropper described Goddard as "the boldest and the dumbest criminal in the city," but as of this writing, he has yet to be caught.

In 2022, Dublin, California, police reported that an alleged car thief named Brandy Jones—who'd twice been convicted of stealing cars in the past—showed up for her court appearance...in another stolen car. She left in a police car.

HIT THE ROAD, JACK

In December 2021, a 23-year-old brazen thief (unnamed in press reports) stole all four tires from a Dodge Challenger that was for sale in the lot of a Washington state car dealer. The man then rolled the tires over to his own Dodge Challenger, parked in a lot across the street, and started to put them on. Then a police car pulled up and the thief jumped in to his car and tried to make a quick getaway! Two problems: His car was propped up on the jacks, and the tires were still on the ground.

Future *Star Wars* creator George Lucas is credited as a cameraman on the Rolling Stones' 1970 concert film, *Gimme Shelter*...

THE UNMASKED MAN

All that Paul Green had to do was wear his mask. Everyone else at England's Liverpool railway station—where Green, 38, boarded a train—was wearing theirs. After all, this incident occurred in January 2021 amidst strict COVID-19 protocols. But because Green was maskless, he drew the attention of British Transport Police officers. When Green departed the train at Wigan station, still without a mask on, they questioned him. Green was uncooperative, so officers searched him and found 544 grams of heroin and 101 grams of crack cocaine. Total street value: more than £60,000 ($75,000 U.S.). Green was sentenced to 40 months in prison.

IF YOU CAN'T BEAT 'EM

In August 2022, Thomas Ngcobo, 40, applied for a job at the Mpumalanga, South Africa, police department. But after he didn't hear back, he went to the station to find out why his application was held up. Instead of getting an update, he was arrested. Turns out, Ngcobo was a wanted man for committing fraud seven years earlier. He'd stolen more than £1,000 worth of hardware products that he was supposed to deliver to customers, and had been on the run ever since. The theft was registered at the same police station he later applied to—and the cops knew he did it. According to U.K.'s *The Mirror*, "The Provincial Commissioner...welcomed the criminal's capture and alerted fugitive suspects that there is no running away from the law." (Especially when they run straight *toward* the law.)

DUMB, DUMBER, AND DEMO

A couple (unnamed in press reports) entered a phone store in Belfast, Maine, in May 2022. While the woman distracted sales associate Ned Lally by disputing their bill, the man tried to clandestinely steal one of the demo phones. He tampered with one, damaging it, and then yanked another off its cord—setting the alarm off. The couple hurried out of the store with their stolen phone, leaving Lally dumbfounded.

He went on Facebook and wrote, "Good evening, Waldo County! Did you and/or your significant other just steal one of our demo phones...moments after having me look up your account, which provides your address, phone number, [Social Security number] and any and all other possible demographic information that might be helpful to law enforcement?" He also pointed out that a demo can't be configured like a real phone, so it's basically worthless. "Well, Maine's Dumbest Criminals, have I got some news for you both: you should be expecting a visit from some men and/or women in blue."

...though none of his footage, shot at the 1969 Altamont Free Concert, made it into the final cut.

MOUTHING OFF

SILLY QUOTES

...from silly movies.

"At first I did not know it was your diary, I thought it was a very sad handwritten book."

—Brynn, *Bridesmaids*

"Supper time was the best! Nothing could beat Mom's homemade, vitamin-rich, soy-based, germ-free, fat-free fiber cookies."

—Jimmy, *Bubble Boy*

Ghostface: Do you know where I am? I could be anywhere. I'm like the wind, baby. Yeah, where am I?
Cindy: Um...you're behind the couch.

—*Scary Movie*

"I'm just like any modern woman trying to have it all. Loving husband, a family. It's just, I wish I had more time to seek out the dark forces and join their hellish crusade."

—Morticia, *Addams Family Values*

"Santa's gonna eat through these guys like a plate of cookies!"

—Santa Claus, *Violent Night*

"WHAT'S THE MATTER, COLONEL SANDERS, CHICKEN?"

—Dark Helmet, *Spaceballs*

Dr. Rumack: Elaine, you're a member of this crew. Can you face some unpleasant facts?
Elaine: No.

—*Airplane!*

"They've done studies, you know. Sixty percent of the time, it works every time."

—Brian Fantana, *Anchorman*

"If there is anything that this horrible tragedy can teach us, it's that a male model's life is a precious, precious commodity. Just because we have chiseled abs and stunning features, it doesn't mean that we too can't not die in a freak gasoline fight accident."

—Derek, *Zoolander*

"Don't make me put the cat down and punch you!"

—Det. Mullins, *The Heat*

WE, THE JURY

Jury duty is a huge inconvenience. With work, child care, and other obligations,
who has the time? Can I get out of this? It's possible. But perhaps after having
more information about how important the jury system is to maintaining a
free society, you'll be (slightly) more inclined to do your civic duty.

Peer Pressure

Here's a scary scenario: You're on trial, and your life as you know it hangs in the balance. In the end, your fate won't be decided by the lawyers (who spent several years in law school), or by the judge (law school plus years in the courtroom). Nope—your fate will be decided by a jury of your peers. A dozen or so regular folks with zero formal law training...who couldn't even get out of jury duty. Good luck!

Framed like that, the whole jury system seems like it shouldn't work—until you take a closer look at it. For starters, the jury trial is one of the earliest forms of government still in use, and it's the only form—other than voting—that allows regular citizens to not just participate in government, but to help make bonding decisions. Once a jury has rendered its verdict, it cannot be overturned by the lawyers or the judge. Juries also help to keep people in power—be they from the government or the private sector—in check. "The framers of the constitutions strove to create an independent judiciary but insisted upon further protection against arbitrary action," wrote 18th-century British statesman William Blackstone. "Providing an accused with the right to be tried by a jury of his peers gave him an inestimable safeguard against the corrupt overzealous prosecutor and against the compliant, biased, or eccentric judge."

Before we get into the history of the jury, here's a quick primer.

Juries 101

There are two main classifications of juries in the United States: the *petit jury* and the *grand jury*. The petit jury is the one you're most familiar with—6 to 12 adults from all walks of life, sitting in a box on one side of the courtroom, usually close to the judge and the witness stand. As temporary "officers of the court," jurors observe the entire case before deliberating behind closed doors; then, if they come to a unanimous vote (or a majority vote, in some cases), they render a verdict. If they can't come to a decision, it's called a "hung jury" and the case is retried with a new jury.

Petit jurors preside over two types of cases: criminal and civil. In criminal cases, they must listen carefully to the instructions from the judge, to the arguments from the lawyers, and to the witness testimony, to be the "finders of facts" and then determine—beyond a reasonable doubt—whether the criminal defendant (the accused)

Hannah Stilley's claim to fame:
she's possibly the earliest-born person (1746) ever to be photographed (1840).

is guilty or not guilty. In civil cases (disputes between people or entities wherein the infraction wasn't charged as a crime), the jury decides which party is most at fault—or liable. In some states, juries also decide on penalties or prison sentences, or both.

A grand jury, as its name implies, is larger. Randomly selected from the same registry as petit jurors, anywhere from 16 to 23 grand jurors are presented with evidence and must decide if there's enough probable cause for formal charges to be brought. Most criminal trials begin this way in the U.S. and Liberia; all other countries that previously used the grand jury practice ended it long ago in favor of preliminary hearings—sans a jury—to determine charges.

The only requirement to serve on a jury is that you be a registered voter over the age of 21. (There are disqualifications, such as permanent medical excuses or being a convicted felon.) Your name goes into a pool, and then, when you least expect it, you receive a notice in the mail summoning you for service. Still, few who get called actually end up serving on a jury. If you do, you'll be told not to discuss the case with anyone while it's in progress. If the case is newsworthy, the jury will likely be *sequestered*, meaning you stay in a hotel with no access to news or loved ones until the end of the trial, so your opinions can remain free from outside influence.

Living History

Sitting among a jury of your peers goes back more than a millennium in Europe, and even further back to ancient times. More than 4,000 years ago, the Egyptians utilized the *Kenbet*, a council of eight elders (four from each side of the Nile) who adjudicated local disputes and other small claims. They acted more as judge *and* jury.

One of the first modern-style juries showed up circa 600 BC in the first democracy in the Western world: Athens, Greece. The jury that presided over the trial of Socrates in 399 BC consisted of 500 men over the age of 30, chosen by lot. The charge: impiety, or a lack of reverence for the gods. Things didn't look good for the famous philosopher, considering that every juror had to swear an oath to those same gods.

Why so many jurors? Because, the thinking went, it's a lot harder to bribe hundreds of men than a dozen. Socrates didn't help himself by openly mocking the jurors during the sentencing phase of his trial. He was found guilty and sentenced to death. He accepted the verdict, as he "owed it to the city under whose laws [he had] been raised to honor those laws to the letter."

Later, when Rome became Europe's cultural hub, it appropriated Greek culture, including its justice system. During the Roman conquests of Europe, the seeds for juries were planted all over the continent. Later, when Western democracy started taking a foothold around the first millennium AD, the jury began its comeback. Good thing, too, considering what it replaced.

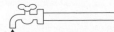

There's a lighthouse in La Coruña, Spain, that's been in operation since the first century AD.

Trial by Torture

"If she weighs more than a duck, she's a witch!" That's how the villagers in *Monty Python and the Holy Grail* conduct a trial, and it's not much of a stretch from the truth. Called "trial by ordeal," guilt was determined, for example, by holding a woman accused of witchcraft underwater: if she drowned, she was innocent; if she floated, she was guilty...and then executed. Trials by fire were even more gruesome. The accused would be forced to walk barefoot over hot coals while holding a red-hot iron. Three days later, a priest would inspect the wounds: if God had healed them, the accused was innocent; if the wounds were festering, guilty. Those kind of trials took place all the way into the Middle Ages.

But the seeds of the modern jury were planted in the ninth century in response to the Holy Roman Emperor Charlemagne's "trial by cross" system, in which both the accused and the accuser stood on either side of a cross with their arms outstretched; whoever kept their arms up the longest won the case. In 819, Charlemagne's son and coruler, Louis the Pious, deemed this method "a mockery of Christ" and instead proposed that court cases be decided by a "jury of administrative inquiry" consisting of 12 of the "most credible men."

The Magna Carta

Despite Louis's efforts, juries didn't really start to take hold until 1215. That's when the *Magna Carta Libertatum* (Latin for "Charter of Freedoms") laid the groundwork for representative democracy in England by stripping the crown of its absolute power. Written by barons who were growing tired of tyranny, the Magna Carta gave us this: "No mal [defendant] shall be taken, outlawed, banished, or in any way destroyed, nor will we proceed against or prosecute him, except by the lawful judgment of his peers and by the law of the land."

Over the next few centuries, the rights of British subjects to receive a fair trial depended on who possessed the crown. For example, in the 1500s, Henry VIII corrupted a system known as the Star Chamber, a closed-door session of common-law judges and "privy counselors" (king's advisors) originally established to ensure that when those in power stood trial, they wouldn't receive special treatment. Henry VIII's Star Chamber consisted of his own loyal advisors, and he used it to punish anyone who threatened his rule.

It wasn't until the British Bill of Rights was signed in 1689 that a trial by jury truly was the law of the land.

The American Revolution

The British Empire spread the jury system to India, Australia, and North America. In the 1620s, shortly after arriving in Plymouth, the Pilgrims decreed that "all criminal

The eagle on the back of the $1 bill was based on "Peter the Mint Eagle," a frequent avian visitor at Philadelphia's U.S. Mint building in the 1830s.

facts...betweene man and man should be tried by the verdict of twelve honest men." The Colonies' first jury trial took place in 1630 after John Billington was charged with the murder of John Newcomin. (The verdict: guilty.)

In a twist of fate, it was an English-style jury trial in 1735 that helped spark the American Revolution. The defendant was *New-York Weekly Journal* publisher John Peter Zenger, who'd run a story about the removal of Justice Lewis Morris from the bench. The article criticized the man who ordered the removal: England's Royal Governor William Crosby, who was so incensed by the criticism that he charged Zenger with seditious libel. But thanks to the rules enacted by Crosby's own government, the jurors did as they were instructed and based their ruling on the facts: that everything Zenger's newspaper printed was true. He was found not guilty.

That could have happened only with a jury of common men, and it set a precedent: as long as newspapers told the truth about England's injustices—most notably the unfair taxation wrought by the Stamp Act of 1765—then they couldn't be punished for libel. "The trial of Zenger in 1735 was the germ of American Freedom," noted Founding Father Gouverneur Morris.

The right to a jury trial is so important that it was included in the United States Bill of Rights. John Adams painted a grim picture of the alternative: "Representative government and trial by jury are the heart and lungs of liberty. Without them we have no other fortification against being ridden like horses, fleeced like sheep, worked like cattle, and fed and clothed like swine and hounds."

Twelve Angry Women

Women winning the right to serve on juries took longer than their winning the right to vote in elections (that happened in 1920). The arguments against women jurors originated in English common laws that classified wives as the property of their husbands. Women were deemed "too sentimental" for juries, and they were too necessary to running the household.

Massachusetts, for instance, assembled the first jury with a Black man in 1860, but wouldn't allow women jurors until 1950. The first American female jurors served in 1870 in the Wyoming Territory, which the previous year had granted women the right to vote. But that was a rare exception; by 1900, juries did not include women.

Women's rights groups fought throughout the first half of the century without much success, until a string of heartbreaking court cases started to shift the conversation. In Florida in 1957, an abused housewife fought back against her husband with a baseball bat, and he died two days later. It took the jury composed entirely of men only 25 minutes to convict the wife, who was sentenced to 30 years in prison. (That happened to be the same year as the classic Hollywood film *12 Angry Men*, which dramatized the intricacies of the jury-deliberation process.)

Where to begin? Worldwide, there are more than 300 music genres.

As more cases like the Florida one made headlines, states variously began to loosen the rules. In some states, women had to "opt in" to be placed on the juror list, whereas men were automatically registered. In others, a woman could "opt out" of jury duty on the basis of being a woman. In 1968, Mississippi became the last state to allow women jurors.

The Jury in Peril

The main reason juries have lasted for so long is because they really do work. Multiple studies have shown that—thanks to the vigorous selection process—the people who end up serving on juries (usually) take their duties seriously. That makes it more difficult for the corrupt and the powerful to stack the jury or bribe jurors.

Despite their success (or, perhaps, because of it), Steve Sussman, a famous trial lawyer who founded the Civil Jury project at New York University School of Law, notes that there are now fewer cases being tried by jury. "In 2018, for example, 0.5 percent of federal civil cases were tried before juries—down from 5.5 percent in 1962."

As we regular folks find fewer outlets to address our grievances, and the powerful few find new ways to game the system, it's more important than ever to answer the call of jury duty. You might just save the republic. And it can even be fun!

For some strange-but-true jury duty stories, report to page 193.

*   *   *

FEELING WOOLGETHERED?

Tangier Island is set 12 miles off the coast of Virginia. It's home to only 450 people, most from families who have been on the island for centuries. Tangier residents have their own accent (a mix of Southern and British) and their own slang terms.

Hucky: dirty

Yorn: yours

Punched tar: a flat tire

Ain't hard favored: an ugly person

Iggy: headed to

Fuzz cod: a storm is coming

Woolgethered: confused

Dry as Peckard's cow: thirsty

Nippity cut: too good to be true

He's got Fredericks: broke

Came night as peas.: "I almost fell off the boat."

If you're an average American dog owner, you'll spend $730 this year on your pooch.

BRADY BY THE NUMBERS

It's not just that the legendary NFL quarterback was that good, or that he played for so long. What's amazing is how he was so good for so long—more than 20 years. Here's a look back at the facts and figures of the career of Tom Brady, one of the all-time greats.

- Tom Brady is the first and only QB in NFL history to throw at least three touchdowns in one game on 100 or more occasions.

- Tom Brady played—and beat—all 32 NFL squads.

- In the 2007 season, Tom Brady guided the New England Patriots to a perfect 16-0 regular season record, only the second undefeated season in NFL history.

- Tom Brady's average win-loss regular season record as a starting quarterback: 12-4.

- Of all the Super Bowls ever mounted, Tom Brady played in nearly one-fifth of them.

- Tom Brady's New England Patriots won 17 division titles in 19 seasons. They also went to 13 AFC Championship games, including 8 in a row.

- With 35 career wins, no quarterback has more postseason victories than Tom Brady. It's not even close— second on the list is Joe Montana, with 16.

- More than 90 different NFL players caught a Tom Brady pass in a regular season game. More than 30 caught one in the playoffs.

- Tom Brady is the only quarterback to win a Super Bowl in three different decades, and the only QB selected to two different all-decade teams.

- Tom Brady leads the NFL's all-time list in passing touchdowns (649), passing yards (89,214), completed passes (7,753), games started (333), and games won (251).

- With 102,614 total passing yards, Tom Brady is the only NFL player to ever amass more than 100,000 yards in that category.

- At age 40, Tom Brady became the oldest-ever NFL MVP. At 43, he became the oldest-ever Super Bowl MVP, and, at age 44, the oldest-ever quarterback to earn a Pro Bowl selection.

- Tom Brady leads the NFL in all-time most Pro Bowl selections (15) and Super Bowl MVP awards (5).

- Tom Brady is the first quarterback to start and win a Super Bowl for teams in both the AFC (New England Patriots) and the NFC (Tampa Bay Buccaneers). He's the only player to be named Super Bowl MVP for two different franchises.

- Tom Brady is the first player to win multiple Super Bowls after age 40.

- Tom Brady has personally played in more playoff games than 13 NFL franchises—put together—and has more Super Bowl championships (7) than any individual franchise.

A 20-oz. Dunkin' Donuts "Pumpkin Swirl Frozen Coffee" contains 46 teaspoons of sugar...and no pumpkin.

I'M STUCK!

Now you're stuck reading this article about people who got stuck!

Stuck in the Rocks

In 2016, a student identified only as Sevilay K. was visiting a scenic marina in Samsun province, Turkey, with some friends when she decided to get a sunset selfie with her phone. Looking for the best angle, she climbed up onto the breakwater, which consists of large boulders fitted together like puzzle pieces to block big waves. Sevilay got to the top, positioned herself for the shot, held out her phone, and dropped it. She tried to snag it but ended up slipping and falling between two boulders. Her phone was out of reach, but that was the least of her worries; she was stuck! The more Sevilay tried to free herself, the more stuck she got. Her friends scrambled up to help her, but there was nothing they could do—she was wedged in tight.

Firefighters were called out and used an array of tools in an attempt to widen the gap between the rocks enough to lift her out. Sevilay had cuts and bruises but was otherwise OK. She didn't get her selfie, but it wouldn't have mattered if she had, because she didn't get her phone back, either.

Stuck in a Mine Shaft

In 2018, John Waddell, 62, drove out to the remote Arizona desert to explore an abandoned gold mine. Miles away from cellular service, Waddell walked right past the signs cautioning people not to enter. He lowered himself in with a rope, but about halfway down, the carabiner broke and Waddell fell about 50 feet. Next thing he knew, he was stuck at the bottom of a mine shaft with broken bones and no way to call for help. Worse yet, he wasn't alone in there; there were rattlesnakes!

Good thing for Waddell that he'd made a pact with his friend, Terry Shrader: "He had called me Monday and told me he was coming to the mine. And we always had a deal, if he is not back by Tuesday..." Waddell wasn't back by Tuesday, so Shrader headed out to the mine himself. When he parked his truck and got out, "I could hear John hollering, 'Help! Help!'"

Shrader had to drive back to cell service to call 911. A professional mountain rescue team set up a pulley system with hundreds of feet of rope. More than six hours later, Waddell was out of the mine and on the way to the hospital. He'd made it one night, but who knows how much longer he would have been able to fend off the rattlesnakes. (According to Shrader, Waddell killed three of them.)

Stuck on a Plane

Tiffani Adams was one of the few passengers on a 90-minute evening flight from Quebec City to Toronto in 2019. At some point, she fell asleep while lying across a row of seats. When she woke up, everything was pitch black, and she was freezing! Adams later wrote on Facebook that she was "full on panicking." She called a friend, but the phone battery died before she could explain her predicament. "I think I'm having a bad dream bc like seriously how is this happening!!?!" Adams later wrote. She slowly felt her way in the dark and reached the cockpit, where she found a flashlight. Then she tried the "walky-talky thingys," but there was no power. She couldn't even charge her phone. Adams shined the flashlight out the windows, hoping to catch someone's attention, but nobody saw. Then she walked to the main cabin door, pulled the big lever, and opened it. It was too far to jump—at least 40 feet—but Adams managed to get the attention of a luggage cart driver.

The ordeal that she first mistook for a nightmare ended up giving her real nightmares: "I haven't got much sleep since the reoccurring night terrors and waking up anxious and afraid I'm alone locked up in someplace dark." Air Canada said it reached out to Adams, was "very concerned" about the incident, and would "take a look into it."

Stuck in a Grease Vent

On a Sunday night in December 2018, an unidentified 29-year-old man—we'll call him Slim—climbed to the roof of an out-of-business Chinese restaurant in San Lorenzo, California. Slim took off his coat and then slid his slender 5-foot-9 frame into the grease vent; authorities suspect he was attempting to enter the restaurant in order to rob copper and steel wires to recycle for cash. Boy, was the vent greasy. Slim shimmied down feet first only to discover that the vent didn't go straight down to the kitchen—it took a 90-degree turn. Slim wasn't quite slim enough to shimmy through the bend, nor could he shimmy back up. So, there he was, stuck in a squatting position with his arms raised above his head, covered head to toe in rancid grease wearing only a pair of pants and a thin T-shirt.

Two days passed.

Igor Campos, who owns a tax business next to the restaurant, showed up to work on Wednesday morning and...is that someone moaning? "I keep hearing this 'uh, uh,'" he told a local news station. So he walked around the rear of the building and heard it louder, "and I'm like, 'Who can it be?'" It was Slim!

Slim barely had enough strength left to call for help. Good thing Campos heard him. "Given another day," said Alameda County Police spokesman Sgt. Ray Kelly, "there's a good chance he may not have made it." Still, it wasn't a simple rescue;

Jonathan Goldsmith, who played "The Most Interesting Man in the World" for Dos Equis beer, played a "Red Shirt" on *Star Trek*...and didn't die.

firefighters were unable to pull him up or down—for fear of injury—so they dismantled the entire duct system. When they finally freed him, the would-be burglar was cold, dehydrated, disoriented, exhausted, very sore, and he smelled horrible. "But we decided to be a little compassionate," said Kelly. "We figured he's been through enough, and it is in the holiday spirit," so he wasn't charged.

Stuck in the Mud

After he was arrested for attempted murder, Christopher Lee Pray was deemed psychiatrically unfit and then sent to Oregon State Hospital. One night in September 2023, Pray had a fight with another inmate and was taken to the emergency room. He was fitted with handcuffs, ankle shackles, and a belly restraint. At around 10:45 p.m., after his van arrived back at OHS, the driver got out and walked around to the other side, while Pray made his way to the driver's seat and sped away. Alerts were sent throughout the region to be on the lookout for an "extremely dangerous" fugitive. At some point Pray ditched the van, along with his restraints (though it's unclear how), and continued on foot. But it was dark, and the small pond he tried to cross was actually just a big mud puddle surrounded by thick brush. Pray made it 75 feet from shore and could go no more.

The next morning, a passerby on a footbridge called 911 to report a body in the muddy pond, with only the head and shoulders above the surface. Firefighters who responded determined the body was alive and got to work. They extended the ladder over the pond, climbed out, and threw down a rope. According to Lt. Laurent Picard, "At that point, one of our firefighters was able to pull him out of this muck enough that we were able to drag him to shore." None of the rescuers had any idea their victim was a dangerous escaped mental patient. Not that it mattered; Pray was weak—he'd been stuck in the mud for 12 hours—but he was with it enough to give a fake name to firefighters and to the staff at the hospital where he was taken for treatment. One hospital staffer recognized him, and he was taken back into custody. "We had no idea who this person was," said Picard, who called it his strangest rescue in his 27 years as a firefighter. "And frankly, it doesn't matter to us when there's a life threat, we're there to save lives."

* * *

HAVE YOU EVER NOTICED...

That almost all aquatic animals have dark backs and light bellies? It's a camouflage device called *countershading*, and it can be seen in penguins, ducks, alligators, orcas, dolphins, and countless more predators and prey. From below, the light bellies make the animals harder to distinguish from the sky; from above, the dark backs make them harder to distinguish from the water.

What do horses and saltwater fish have in common?
The same number of Americans keep them as pets (2.2 million).

JUST JOKES

Readers are always sending us great (and not-so-great) jokes. It would be selfish to keep the laughs all to ourselves.

A clown held the door open for me. What a nice jester!

"Does this bus go to Duluth?"

"No, it goes 'beep, beep.'"

Did you hear that NASA is launching a new mission to say sorry to the aliens? They're calling it Apollo G.

I have an inferiority complex, but it's not a very good one.

Q: What's the one time "I'm sorry" and "I apologize" don't mean the same thing?

A: At a funeral.

The shy climatologist was at a party and started talking about global warming. It was a real icebreaker.

Whenever my girlfriend is sad I let her draw things on me. You know, a shoulder to crayon.

My husband and I laugh about how competitive we are. But I laugh more.

Q: How did the hipster burn his mouth?

A: He ate his pizza before it was cool.

I used to live on a houseboat and dated the girl next door. Eventually, we drifted apart.

I saw my math teacher with a piece of graph paper. I think she might be plotting something.

I'm trying to organize a hide-and-seek tournament, but it's really hard to find good players.

A cheese factory exploded in France. Da brie was everywhere.

"Doc, unnecessarily complicated buildings make me crazy!"

"Hmm. It would seem you have a complex complex complex."

Parallel lines have so much in common. It's a shame they'll never meet.

They told me to stop impersonating a flamingo. I had to put my foot down.

Q: Why aren't DJs allowed in the fish market?

A: They're always dropping the bass.

I told the weight lifter to stop making sudden loud noises. He was quite disgruntled.

Did you hear about the guy who can't hear low- or midrange frequencies? He's in a world of treble.

Five out of six people agree that Russian roulette is safe.

Q: Why did the ghost go to rehab?

A: He was addicted to boos.

My grief counselor died the other day. He was so good at his job I don't even care.

Life has three unwritten rules: 1. 2. 3.

When President Jimmy Carter traveled to Portland, Oregon, in 1978, he stayed with local residents Paul and Janet Olson in their regular ol' home.

PRESIDENTIAL COINAGES, PART I

We're not talking about their images on the change in your pocket—we're talking about terms, phrases, and downright flubs from our commanders in chief. We won't sugarcoat it, nor will we bloviate: a few of these origins are iffy, though none should be called fake news. Just don't misunderestimate us, OK?

BLAH BLAH BLAH!

U.S. presidents sure do talk a lot—it's in their job description. Because they're presidents, more of what they say gets recorded for posterity than most of what's said by anyone else, so it's not surprising that a slew of new words and phrases—and new meanings of existing ones—have been credited to these Oval Office inhabitants. It certainly doesn't surprise lexicographer Paul Dickson. "A number of them showed great cleverness," he told *Voice of America*. "They often have to think on their feet... and sometimes there isn't an existing word to say what they mean. And they just make one up." Arguably, some other presidents have shown less cleverness, but their words have lived on as well. And sometimes just being president is enough to get someone credited with a neologism. Here are some examples from Dickson's 2013 book, *Words from the White House: Words and Phrases Coined or Popularized by America's Presidents*, along with some from our files.

ADMINISTRATION

Coined by: George Washington (1789-97)

Meaning: In government, a collective term for all the people who serve directly under an executive officer

Origin: When the first president took office, there wasn't a name for the group of people who worked in the executive branch, so he co-opted the word *administration*. From the Latin word meaning "cooperation," it simply meant "the management of public affairs." Washington cemented its modern meaning in his farewell address: "In reviewing the incidents of my administration, I am unconscious of intentional error."

Bonus Word: Washington invented the presidential cabinet—a group of advisors who inform the president's decisions—though he didn't want to call it a *cabinet* (a British term). Instead, he referred to them as "the gentlemen of my family." When Thomas Jefferson (one of those gentlemen) took over in office, he started calling the group his cabinet.

Tool timeout: Tim Allen was offered $50 million to do one more season of *Home Improvement*. He turned it down.

BLOVIATE

Coined by: Warren G. Harding (1921–23)

Meaning: "The art of speaking for as long as the occasion warrants, and saying nothing"

Origin: That definition came from Harding himself, and while he didn't coin this word, he expanded its meaning. *Bloviate* had been around since the 1840s, and simply meant "to talk at length." It had no negative political connotation...until Harding became known for his long-winded speaking style, which he himself described as "bloviation." That, by the way, wasn't a word when Harding said it—which irked writers such as H. L. Mencken, who said Harding's grasp of English "reminds me of a string of wet sponges; it reminds me of tattered washing on the line; it reminds me of stale bean soup, of college yells, of dogs barking idiotically through endless nights." Mencken may not have liked it, but *bloviation* lives on to this day.

THE BUCK STOPS HERE

Popularized by: Harry S. Truman (1945–53)

Meaning: When someone in charge accepts responsibility rather than pinning it on someone else

Origin: Poker players in the 19th century would place a marker, or *buck* (a term possibly taken from a knife with a buckhorn handle), in front of the dealer; if that person didn't want to deal, they "passed the buck." The phrase came to be used for anyone who shirks responsibility, and President Truman often said his own variation, "the buck stops here." He was famously given a placard for his desk with that phrase on one side (and "I'm from Missouri" on the other). Truman and that placard exposed the phrase to a national audience, and we still use it today.

Bonus Words: Truman also popularized "If you can't stand the heat, get out of the kitchen," and the still-useful term *do-nothing Congress*.

FAKE NEWS

Popularized by: Donald J. Trump (2017–21)

Meaning: False or misleading information presented as news; or something you don't agree with

Origin: Neither *fake* nor *news* is a very old word; both date back to the early to mid-19th century. And the first time *fake news* appeared in print was 1894. That verifies that Trump did not coin *fake news*, despite his claims to the contrary.

It's likely he saw *fake news* in online articles from 2014 on—that's when Buzzfeed News media editor Craig Silverman started using the term to describe propaganda

According to the latest research:
"You are more likely to make immoral decisions while speaking a second language."

websites masquerading as news sites. Even though the phrase was out there, it didn't become part of the national conversation until 2017 when Trump, during a press conference, called CNN "fake news" (and Buzzfeed a "failing pile of garbage"). Now the phrase is uttered—either in seriousness or in jest—when someone wishes to discredit or dismiss a story or source they object to: "That's fake news!"

Bonus Words: According to Dictionary.com, Trump is credited with coining *bigly* (even though he says he was saying "big league"), *yuge* (for "huge"), and *bing bong*.

GAG RULE

Coined by: John Quincy Adams (1825–29)

Meaning: A directive prohibiting public discussion of a particular matter

Origin: To once again quote lexicographer Paul Dickson: "We're really creating our own institutions through language. So, when John Quincy Adams creates the word *gag rule*, or somebody creates another word that actually fits into what we do, once you have a word for it, then it becomes a reality." Adams was serving in the U.S. House of Representatives in 1836—yes, after his presidency—when pro-slavery Congressmen passed a rule "forbidding debate, reading, printing of, or even reference" to the growing number of antislavery petitions being sent to Congress. Adams vowed to defeat this "gag rule" (which he might have co-opted from the term *gag law* that showed up a few years earlier). And he did defeat the gag rule, though it took him until 1844. The phrase has since been assigned to any measure that aims to quell a discussion.

GAME PLAN

Popularized by: Richard M. Nixon (1969–74)

Meaning: A strategy worked out in advance

Origin: This phrase comes from American football coaching staffs in the late 1940s, and it remained a sports-specific term until the 1970s. Then came President Nixon, a former college football player, who used it in phrases such as "economic game plan" and "2nd term game plan."

Bonus Word: Nixon has also been credited with the term *solid majority*.

Join the lunatic fringe on page 184 for more presidential coinages.

*　　*　　*

FARTS IN THE NEWS

In 2019, Joann Rogers, widow of beloved children's show host Fred "Mr." Rogers, revealed that her late husband thought farts were hilarious. Even in public: "He would just raise one cheek and he would look at me and smile."

The most common months for birthdays:
July through September. The least common: January.

FAMILIAR PHRASES

We use these phrases all the time, but most of us have no idea where they come from. Well, don't worry—the BRI has the answers.

"HIT THE GROUND RUNNING"

Some word-origins books trace this idiom—which means to begin an endeavor with vigor and focus—back to World War II, when U.S. Army paratroopers landed in combat situations and literally had to "hit the ground running" to avoid getting shot. But it had already been in use for at least 50 years, as evidenced by this 1895 *Evening News* story called "The King of All Liars": "The bullet went under me. I knew he had five more cartridges, so I hit the ground running and squatted low down when his gun barked a second time." The phrase took on its figurative sense before the war as well, as evidenced by this excerpt from the October 1940 *Hayward Daily Review*: "It sometimes seems to me that the young idea nowadays wants to hit the ground running and to tell the old editors how to run things."

"PIPE DREAM"

If you have a pipe dream today, it means you long for something you want to have, attain, or make happen that has very little chance of occurring. If you were in the western U.S. in the 1870s and you had a pipe dream, it meant you were hallucinating after smoking an opium pipe. Opium dens were popular back then. By 1890, the phrase had taken on its figurative meaning, first showing up in print in the *Chicago Daily Tribune*, which noted that air travel "has been regarded as a pipe-dream for a good many years."

"SPOILER WARNING"

People have been ruining stories—books, plays, movies, shows—for other people by giving away the ending for eons, but the first person to call this a *spoiler* was humor writer Doug Kenney in a 1971 *National Lampoon* column called "Spoilers," where he gave away the endings to such popular films as *Citizen Kane* and *Psycho*, along with a few Agatha Christie murder mysteries. "Spoilers! What are they? Simply the trick ending to every mystery novel and movie you're ever liable to see. Saves time and money!" The phrase caught on in early 1980s proto-internet Usenet groups with science-fiction fans urging one another not to spoil the ending of *Star Trek II: The Wrath of Khan*. (Spoiler alert! Spock dies.) The phrase went mainstream thanks to sci-fi author Spider Robinson. In his book reviews, he'd add "spoiler warning" before giving away plot points.

Actual headline: "John Cena Surprises 8-Year-Old Boy with Cancer on His Birthday."

"GREEN THUMB"

Some linguists have speculated that the phrase was inspired by Geoffrey Chaucer's 1386 work, *The Canterbury Tales*, wherein the Miller "hadde a thombe of gold." The golden thumb (a.k.a. the Midas touch) comes from ancient Greek mythology. But there's scant evidence to connect it to "green thumb." A few possible origins: During the reign of King Edward I (1272–1307), a reward supposedly went to the serf who had the "greenest fingers" after shelling the king's beloved peas. It might also come from the pagan god of spring, Green Man. Or it may be literal: the algae that grows on pots turns gardeners' digits green. It might not refer to gardening, but to "green" as a metaphor for the environment, as in "green movement." Although some dictionaries trace it back to the U.S. only as far as the 1930s, the first time it showed up in print was in an English newspaper in 1907: "my friend has what old country women call 'a Green Thumb,' that is to say, the gift of making anything and everything grow." Interestingly, the term "green thumb" caught on only in the United States. In England, the power is referred to as "green fingers," which showed up about the same time as "green thumb" and was popularized by a radio show called *In Your Garden*. It's also "green fingers" in Australia thanks to a 1957 gardening TV show called *Green Fingers*.

"A NEW LEASE ON LIFE"

In England in the early 19th century, when medicine and surgical techniques still hadn't advanced much since the Middle Ages, getting sick or injured was a lot more deadly than it is today. When a patient did recover from an illness, they were said to have a "new lease of life." (The word *lease* meant the same thing it does today.) In England and most other countries, it's still "a new lease *of* life." American English speakers changed "of" to "on" in the 1930s, but it's still "of" everywhere else.

"THAT'S MY STORY, AND I'M STICKING TO IT"

The identity of whoever told the original story that they originally stuck to has been lost to history, but the phrase might have come from mid-20th-century mobsters during police interrogations: "That's my story, copper! And I'm stickin' to it!" But the first verifiable occurrence comes from a 1993 Collin Raye country song (written by Lee Roy Parnell and Tony Haselden), where the narrator gets caught in a lie by his wife and drawls, "That's my story, and I'm sticking to it." A few years later, when comedian Colin Quinn sat behind the "Weekend Update" desk at *Saturday Night Live*, he ended each segment with the catchphrase, cementing it in popular culture.

Jimmy the raven appeared in over 1,000 movies from the 1930s to the 1950s. He was said to have the intelligence of an eight-year-old child.

FARTS IN THE NEWS

This just in: phbblbbttt!

THE FARTINATOR

In September 2023, *Business Insider* dropped this bombshell report: "Miriam Margolyes says Arnold Schwarzenegger only farted in her face because she farted next to him first." Here's the scoop: Margolyes, best known as Professor Sprout from the Harry Potter movies, played an evil Satanist in the 1999 Schwarzenegger-starring horror movie, *End of Days*. In a 2022 interview, Margolyes complained that, during filming, Schwarzenegger "farted in my face…deliberately" because "he didn't like me." A year later, in her memoir, *Oh Miriam! Stories from an Extraordinary Life*, Margolyes added some background info: "In the anxiety of our rehearsals, I allowed a medium-strength fart to escape. The sound effect was inevitable but there was no odourama, I assure you. Arnie, however, leapt upon my transgression with frenzy. He couldn't stop talking about it, constantly referring to it, showing his shock and revulsion."

Later, when it came time to film her character's death scene, the action star got his revenge: "Arnie had me pinned under him, utterly at his mercy. It was then he delivered the coup de grâce (or should I say, coup de disgrâce?). He farted, loudly, purposefully, and malevolently, directly into my face—and then laughed uproariously." Four years later, Schwarzenegger was elected governor of California.

"WITH FULL INTENT"

City police in Vienna, Austria, want it to be known that no one will be arrested for *accidentally* "letting one go," but if you do what this guy did? The culprit (unnamed in press reports) was sitting on a park bench, and after an unspecified verbal altercation, he stood up and looked right at the cops. Then, according to police and as repeated in news outlets all over the world, he "let go a massive intestinal wind apparently with full intent." Police added, "our colleagues don't like to be farted at so much." The farter was fined €500 ($565).

POLICE INFORMANT

In July 2019, officers in Liberty, Missouri, were closing in on a suspect wanted for possession of a controlled substance, but the perp was hiding—that is, until he let one rip, giving away his location and swiftly leading to his capture. The cops later went on Facebook and issued this warning: "If you've got a felony warrant for your arrest, the cops are looking for you and you pass gas so loud it gives up your hiding spot, you're definitely having a 💩 day."

Mexican zoo officials were arrested in 1993 after purchasing a black-market gorilla… that turned out to be an FBI agent in a gorilla suit.

"ONE OF US HAS POLLUTED THE AIR"

During a session in the Kenyan regional assembly in August 2019, Assemblyman Juma Awuor was speaking about providing more shade to sunny markets when a group of assemblymen started arguing nearby. Speaker Edwin Kakach interrupted Awuor and asked the group what was going on. Julius Gaya replied, "Honorable Speaker, one of us has polluted the air and I know who it is." He pointed to another assembly member, but the accused responded, "I am not the one. I cannot do such a thing in front of my colleagues." Whoever did it, *really* did it, because soon Kakach ordered a recess and told everyone to come back with air fresheners. "Whatever flavor you will find in any office, whether it's vanilla or strawberry." The smell dissipated before any air fresheners were obtained and lawmakers were able to resume their session.

DEVILED EGGS

GAMINGbible.com reported in 2023 that an Xbox gamer took to Reddit to complain that he'd received a notice from Microsoft: he had to change his gamertag, even though he'd had that username for seven years. Without providing a reason, the tech giant said he could no longer be known as "Satan Farted." The chief question in the comments (and among Uncle John's staff): did Microsoft have a problem with "Satan" or with "Fart"? We may never know.

"SHOULD MY BOYFRIEND STOP FARTING IN FRONT OF ME?"

In March 2023, in its relationship column "You Be the Judge," the *Guardian* asked its readers to help settle a domestic dispute between Astrid and her boyfriend, Alex. Astrid's complaint: Alex's farting. "It's offensive, it stinks, it's disrespectful, and it kills the romance between us."

Alex's counterargument: "Farting is healthy, and it's funny, too. Besides, hers smell worse than mine." Astrid flatly denies that, saying that Alex's farts are so smelly that she has to "leave the room for at least five minutes to let it disperse." He says that the fact that they're both vegetarians does help with the smell, but, "I agree with her that it takes away from the sexiness of the relationship. It's not a good idea to just let rip in front of your partner all the time. But we've been together so long now, so it's kind of like whatever." He also said, "Upon reflection, though, I do find it funnier when one of my friends or I fart than when Astrid does. Is that sexist? Probably."

Astrid again: "Farting in front of anyone is not a symptom of societal collapse—but it is morally offensive and kills the romance when you do it in front of your partner. It also signifies a breakdown in respect. That may sound extreme but I stand by it. Farting is also really gross. You could be forcing fecal particles up people's noses. Ew."

Guardian readers were split nearly evenly in their opinions: 51 percent said that Alex should clench his cheeks more, and 49 percent said that Astrid should lighten up.

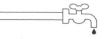

Odd New York City fashion fad from 1894:
wearing a chained chameleon as "living jewelry."

WHEN WORLDS COLLIDE

People and animals occupying the same space at the same time...with memorable results.

THE BUTTERFLY EFFECT

During a third-round match at the 2021 Australian Open, Japanese tennis sensation Naomi Osaka was about to serve when a spectator called out, "There's a butterfly on your leg!" Osaka looked down, and sure enough, there was an orange-and-black butterfly parked on her shin. She paused the game, gently removed the butterfly into her hand, walked over to the sideline, and placed it on the railing (to mild applause). Then the butterfly flew up and landed right on Osaka's face! "It just wants to hang out with you, Naomi," joked the announcer. "This is a singles match, not doubles!" With a smile, she removed the butterfly and once again placed it on the railing, where it stayed. The crowd cheered as Osaka returned to the court. Then she won the match, and then the tournament. (And she showed up at the next tournament wearing butterfly-print tennis shoes.)

OUT OF BODY EXPERIENCE

In May 2018, Jeremy and Jennifer Sutcliffe of Corpus Christi, Texas, were cleaning up their yard ahead of a cookout with their daughter and two grandkids. As Jennifer was weeding her garden, she didn't see the coiled-up western diamondback rattlesnake until it was almost too late. The three-foot-long reptile rattled its tail and raised its head in striking position. "Snake!" she screamed. Jeremy, who'd been mowing the lawn, ran over with a shovel. Seeing that the rattler had his wife cornered against the house, he saw no other choice but to chop its head off. Crisis averted.

But there was still the matter of disposal. "The smart thing would have been for Jeremy to scoop it up with a shovel of course," said Jennifer, "instead of trying to pick it up with his hand."

But that's what Jeremy did, a full ten minutes after the decapitation. As he reached down toward the rattlesnake's head, it struck and sank its teeth into his hand. He tried to get it off, but it kept biting...and emptied every last bit of deadly venom. (Yes, snakes can do this: being cold-blooded, they take longer to cool down after decapitation, and they can still bite up to an hour later.)

Jennifer helped Jeremy to the car and sped toward the nearest hospital, but he was in such bad shape that they had to stop so he could be airlifted the rest of the way. It took 26 doses of antivenin, and then three days on a ventilator in an induced coma, to keep

Watermelons are technically considered both a fruit *and* a vegetable.

Jeremy from dying. He lost two fingers and his kidneys nearly shut down. If all that wasn't bad enough, now he suffers from a condition called megacolon. And the Sutcliffes are both still afraid of their yard. "I'll see a crumpled up bunch of leaves that got stuck under a plant," said Jennifer, "and it gives me a heart attack because I think it's a snake."

OTTER 841

In July 2023, a 40-year-old software engineer named Joon Lee was surfing at a popular spot in Santa Cruz, California, when a sea otter swam up and started pestering him. "I tried to paddle away," he said, "but I wasn't able to get far before it bit off my leash." Then the animal hopped up onto Lee's surfboard and started biting it to pieces! Lee tried to push the otter off, but it remained "fixated" on his board. Lee wasn't injured (unlike his board), but the attack had wildlife officials concerned. This particular otter—a female known as Otter 841, who was born in captivity but released back to the wild—had been going after surfboards for a couple of years, and now it was acting more brazen than ever.

That's not a good sign for this threatened species. California sea otter numbers, once in the hundreds of thousands, are down to about 3,000. The animals usually avoid people, but as more and more swimmers, kayakers, and surfers try to get close to these cute animals for a selfie or a viral video, it can create dangerous situations. "What we're seeing with 841 is that loss of predator-avoidance behavior, and it can turn into something really quite intensive," said Gena Bentall, who founded the nonprofit research organization Sea Otter Savvy. "People want to view them as cuddly pets and don't give them the respect to view them as wild animals that need space and respect." There is an effort underway to capture 841 and return her to Monterey Bay Aquarium, but so far "she's been quite talented at evading us." At press time, the surfboard-chomping sea otter was still on the loose.

HUNGRY, HUNGRY HIPPO

A group of young children were playing at home near Lake Edward on the Uganda-Congo border when one of the lake's residents—a full-grown hippopotamus—started charging them. The kids scattered, but two-year-old Iga Paul wasn't fast enough, and the hippo scooped the boy up in its powerful jaws. The 3,000-pound animal had the child in its mouth, with only his legs sticking out, while neighbors were screaming that the child was dead. But one neighbor named Chrispas Bagonza yelled at and threw rocks at the hippo until, finally, it spat the boy out. They took Paul to the hospital, where he was treated for cuts and bruises and given a rabies shot. Otherwise, the toddler was OK...physically. His father said he's still afraid of animals—even on TV—and suffers from nightmares. But thanks to one brave neighbor, the boy survived. Around 500 other hippo-attack victims per year are not as fortunate.

A STINGING SENSATION

Swiss triathlete Daniela Ryf had already won the Ironman World Championship triathlon in Kona, Hawaii, three times. The event includes a 2.4-mile swim, followed by a 112-mile bike race, and then a 26-mile marathon. At the 2018 event, Ryf was all set for a four-peat until two minutes before the start. She was doing her warm-ups in Kailua Bay when a jellyfish stung her armpit, and then another jellyfish stung her *other* armpit! "I was like, oh no. I tried to convince myself it didn't happen." Armpits are one of the worst places for a swimmer to be stung. "I really didn't know if I was going to make it, actually, if I'm going to just drown," Ryf said later. But once the race started, so did she. First, her arms got so numb that she could barely lift them, then the burning kicked in. She nearly quit at one point but still managed to complete the swim, nine minutes behind the leader (and surprised to find she wasn't in last place).

Thankfully, Ryf was able to make up for lost time during the bike race. Then she had an extra spring in her step during the marathon. She finished first, beating her own record by 20 minutes. When asked how she treated the jellyfish stings before getting on the bike, Ryf answered, "There's two things you can do. You can put vinegar on it. They didn't have vinegar in that tent." So, "I improvised." (She wouldn't elaborate, but the other way most people try to treat a jellyfish sting is to pee on it.)

RIDE ALONG

This final encounter is a "hoot." Because it happened on Christmas Eve in 2015, we're giving this story of Officer Lance Benjamin's experience a holiday spin.

> 'Twas the night before Christmas, and all through the town,
>
> Drove a cop named Lance, who had his window rolled down.
>
> He turned on a side street at a leisurely pace.
>
> Oh no! "Something has hit the left side of my face!"
>
> A *football*, he thought, but felt "scratching and pecking."
>
> Then his car nearly did some serious wrecking!
>
> "Went into a ditch, avoided some trees," he scowled.
>
> And on the seat next to him: a surprised little owl!
>
> Lance had some cuts and got a heck of a fright.
>
> The owl flew off in the Louisiana night.
>
> If you drive in Covington on 12/24,
>
> Put those windows up—for this is where owls soar!

By the time you finish reading this, your body will have made more new cells than there are people in the United States: 25 million.

YOU NAMED YOUR BABY *WHAT?*

For a new parent, it's a very important duty—almost sacred—to choose the perfect name for a new perfect little baby. And sometimes parents select what they think is the best name, or what they want to be the right one, and the outside world doesn't agree it's such a good idea. Here are some stories about baby name controversies.

French Tries

Parents in France are free to name their children whatever they like—up to a point. Law enforcement agencies around the country are encouraged to use their best judgment and report to the federal government when parents register a newborn with a name considered offensive or inappropriate. This oversight is part of a law that went into effect in 1993, and the government has occasionally nixed a baby name.

- A lower court tried to stop a couple with the last name of Renaud from naming their daughter Megane, because "Megane Renaud" would sound too much like the name brand of a popular French car, the Renault Mégane. The couple was able to legally proceed with their choice.

- The government forced the parents of a baby girl they wanted to name Fraise (French for "strawberry") to choose Fraisine instead, on the basis that the kid might be teased someday.

- In 2015, a judge forced a couple to name their daughter Ella instead of their first choice: Nutella, the name of a chocolate hazelnut spread well-known in France.

The Choice of a New Generation

In 2019, a 46-year-old woman made headlines when she earned her doctorate degree in higher education leadership after defending her dissertation about how an unusual name, or one associated with a particular ethnicity, can adversely affect perceptions of the name's owner in the classroom. The newly graduated PhD herself had what could be considered an odd name, bestowed on her by her mother with the aim that it would earn her attention and take her to unique places in life. The woman has two sisters with "ordinary" names—Robin and Kimberly—so her moniker is certainly the outlier in the family. Nevertheless, and despite the findings of her dissertation, Marijuana Pepsi Vandyck is now a doctor.

Early Education

A man seeking advice on the Internet forum site Reddit complained about his sister, identified only as Katie, a graduate of the Yale School of Law engaged to a neurosurgeon who graduated from Stanford Medical School. The Reddit poster was uninvited from the wedding after he criticized the names Katie and her husband planned to give their unborn twins. "It wasn't right to give the boys names that would put them under immense pressure to succeed," the poster argued. The names the soon-to-be parents selected: Yale and Stanford.

Combination Mock

In 2023, another individual seeking life advice about a name-based situation surfaced on Reddit, this time asking for opinions on what strangers thought about the unique, invented name she devised for her yet-to-be-born daughter. The woman (unnamed in reports) wanted to name her baby after all four of her own grandparents—two grandpas named Christopher, and grandmas Quinn and Florence. "I love the name but have gotten mixed feedback," she said. "I am thinking of calling my daughter Quiftopher." "That name is hideous," one commentator said, while another suggested it's "borderline child abuse." At the end of the conversation, the mother-to-be said she "might have to rethink" her idea. No word on what name the baby girl ended up with.

Seems Fishy

In 2022, the parliament of Taiwan debated passing a new law that would prevent citizens from filing for official, legal name changes too many times. That was a response to hundreds of Taiwanese people changing their name to one particular word, and then changing it back, all to get some free food—a debacle that became known in the local media as "the salmon chaos." Back in March 2021, Taiwanese restaurant chain Sushiro ran a campaign offering all-you-can-eat sushi to the entire party of anyone who had the Chinese language characters *gui yu* in their name—which are also the characters for "salmon." Plenty of people (and their families) got free sushi in that way, and so did 331 people who legally changed their name to some variation of Salmon, including names that translate to "Dancing Salmon" and "Salmon Dream."

A Slice of the Absurd

At the end of 2013, parenting website BabyCenter analyzed data from across the United States to determine the most-used names for newborns that year. Rising quickly in popularity—growing by more than 450 percent from 2012—was Cheese. While BabyCenter's cross section analyzed 500,000 records and found nine kids—both boys and girls—born in 2013 named Cheese, the overall data was much higher. There were four million babies born in the U.S. that year, meaning as many as 72 of them were given the name Cheese. Analysts were stumped about the increase of Cheese babies; no news or pop culture events pointed to the trend, unlike the rise of Khaleesi as a girl's name in the 2010s, taken from the hit TV show *Game of Thrones*.

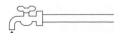

Cockroaches and termites are closely related to praying mantises.

JANE GOODALL

British naturalist Jane Goodall (born 1934) became famous for her groundbreaking studies of chimpanzees—which changed the very definition of humanity (because humans no longer thought we were the only animal that makes tools). As these quotations show, Goodall has learned quite a lot about her own species, as well. And she doesn't mince words.

On Human Nature

"What makes us human, I think, is an ability to ask questions, a consequence of our sophisticated spoken language."

"There seems to be a disconnect between our clever brain and our compassionate heart."

"Let us not forget that human love and compassion are equally deeply rooted in our primate heritage."

"We have so far to go to realize our human potential for compassion, altruism, and love."

"It actually doesn't take much to be considered a difficult woman. That's why there are so many of us."

On the Animal Kingdom

"I wanted to talk to the animals like Dr. Dolittle."

"I like some animals more than some people, some people more than some animals."

"Chimpanzees, more than any other living creature, have helped us to understand that there is no sharp line between humans and the rest of the animal kingdom."

"You cannot share your life with a dog...or a cat, and not know perfectly well that animals have personalities and minds and feelings."

"One million species are in danger of extinction. So what I say to the business community is: Just think logically. This planet has finite natural resources."

"Anyone who tries to improve the lives of animals invariably comes in for criticism from those who believe such efforts are misplaced in a world of suffering humanity."

"If we kill off the wild, then we are killing a part of our souls."

On the Current State of Affairs

"You cannot get through a single day without having an impact on the world around you."

"The greatest danger to our future is apathy."

"Hope does not deny the evil, but is a response to it."

"Like our intellect, social media in itself is neither good nor bad—it is the use to which we put it that counts."

"Lasting change is a series of compromises. And compromise is all right, as long as your values don't change."

"Change happens by listening and then starting a dialogue with the people who are doing something you don't believe is right."

Hope for the Future

"I truly believe that the number of good and decent people in the world form by far the greatest percentage of the world population."

"I do have reasons for hope: our clever brains, the resilience of nature, the indomitable human spirit, and above all, the commitment of young people when they're empowered to take action."

"Nature can win if we give her a chance."

SURVIVAL STORIES

If you ever find yourself lost, stranded, trapped, or in any life-and-death situation, there are countless tips for how to stay alive. But the most important tip is this: never give up.

WINE AND LOLLIPOPS

A 48-year-old woman whom police identified as Lillian has mobility issues that make it difficult for her to walk any sort of distance. That could be what kept her alive after her car got stuck in mud in the Australian outback in May 2023. Why? If she'd left the car to try finding help, she would have been exposed to near-freezing nighttime temperatures, and she was 37 miles from the nearest town. Lillian took a wrong turn on her way to Dartmouth Dam for a day trip; she hit a dead end in the Mitta Mitta bushland and got stuck while trying to turn around.

The dense eucalyptus forest made it difficult to see the ground from above, but the dirt road provided a bit of a clearing, so Lillian stayed there to be visible to search and rescue personnel...who had their work cut out for them. "The area is so vast," said a spokesperson on day four of the search. "We're talking about hundreds of kilometers that Lillian might be in. We don't have a starting point at the moment."

They needed to find Lillian fast: she was almost out of the few car snacks and lollipops she'd packed for her two-hour drive. She also had a bottle of wine that she'd planned to give to her mother. Lillian doesn't drink, but without any other fluids in the car, she had no other choice than to drink the wine herself to survive. Thankfully, on day five of the search, a helicopter pilot saw her waving from the road. When rescuers arrived on the ground, Lillian had just enough strength left to bow in appreciation, then they escorted her to their truck. Aside from dehydration, Lillian was fine.

SMOKE SIGNALS

In May 2022, a 51-year-old man was hiking along the top of a steep ridge called Munra Point in the Columbia River Gorge, about 40 miles east of Portland, Oregon. According to OregonHikers.org, "Munra is a non-maintained trail. Hikers have been seriously injured falling from the summit ridges. Use extreme caution near the summit of Munra and do not climb the chimney to the summit ridge unless you will be able to safely climb back down unassisted." This unidentified man didn't heed those warnings. And because the trail climbs 2,000 feet in two miles, few people hike it—especially on cold, overcast days with rain and patchy fog.

News reports were unclear about how long the man had been stranded up on the rocky summit, but at some point, he came up with the idea to light a "signal

A raindrop isn't just water. Each one forms around a *cloud condensation nucleus*, a tiny particle of dust, salt, smoke, or pollution.

fire"—not dissimilar from the smoke signals that Native Americans are known for. It's also uncertain how long the fire had been going before someone noticed the smoke from the river below at around 10:30 a.m. (which means the man had spent at lease one night on the exposed summit). After spotting the man with binoculars, the good Samaritan called police, who enlisted the help of an elite rescue team called the Hood River Crag Rats. It took the rescue team about three hours to get to the man's "precarious position." The hiker was suffering from the early stages of hypothermia; his choice of hiking trail was questionable, but had he not thought to light the fire, it's likely he would have perished on the mountaintop.

THREE DAYS IN GATOR LAND

One afternoon in July 2022, Eric Merda—who owns an irrigation installation company in Florida—finished work early, so he decided to explore the countryside near Sarasota. After driving down a random dirt road, he decided to take a short hike—so short that he didn't think to bring his phone. But Merda, 43, quickly discovered how easy it is to get turned around in the overgrown swampland. Unsure which way to go, he kept trudging through it until he reached the shore of Lake Manatee, an alligator habitat. By this point, it was getting dark, and Merda was so cut up from the brush he'd been trudging through that the thought of navigating all the way around the 1,200-acre man-made reservoir was too much. So he put aside thoughts of the gators and decided to swim. Merda wasn't even halfway across when he realized he needed to move faster, so he took off his heavy work clothes and boots. Now naked, he started swimming the backstroke as fast as he could.

Then he saw them—a pair of beady eyes—approaching fast just above the water. Next thing Merda knew, an alligator had clenched its jaws around his right arm and was pulling him under. Merda fought his way back to the surface, but then, "That's when the gator did the death roll and took off with my arm," he later told the *Washington Post*.

Merda somehow made it to shore. What was left of his arm ended just below the shoulder; the wound wasn't bleeding, but severed bone was sticking out through mangled flesh. "The pain was absolutely excruciating. I mean, I didn't stop screaming."

But he was disoriented and still miles from a populated area. Once again, Merda started trudging through thorny swampland along the lakeside—only now without any clothes or boots, or a right arm. Where the underbrush became too thick, he had to walk chest deep in the lake, and was nearly attacked by another alligator.

It took Merda three days—living on flowers and dirty water, and with his nub attracting flies—to finally find another person. Less than half an hour after that, Merda was being airlifted to a hospital. Facing a long recovery, he quit the sprinkler business and became a motivational speaker and comedian.

As of early 2022, there were 8,261 satellites orbiting Earth, with more than 3,000 of them belonging to the U.S.

ALTERNATE TV GUIDE

*Some actors are so closely associated with a specific role or TV series that it's
hard to imagine they weren't the first choice. But it happens all the time.*

GUNSMOKE, STARRING RAYMOND BURR

For the entirety of the ensemble Western *Gunsmoke*'s 635-episode, 1955–1975 run,
James Arness headlined the cast as U.S. Marshal Matt Dillon. Before and concurrent
to the TV version, William Conrad voiced the character in the original radio program,
but CBS executives didn't think he looked the part enough to reprise the role in a
visual medium. Raymond Burr was also considered, but Arness won the role over Burr
because producers and executives thought Burr was too heavyset to play the heroic
lawman—the same reason they rejected Conrad. Two years later, Burr was cast in the
title role on *Perry Mason*...and was ordered by CBS to lose weight or lose the job.

I LOVE LUCY, STARRING BEA BENADERET

Benaderet is famous for a couple of roles on classic TV shows: motel proprietor Kate
Bradley on *Petticoat Junction* and the voice of Betty Rubble on *The Flintstones*. She
nearly played a big role on what's arguably the most popular and enduring early TV
show of all. When Lucille Ball got the green light from CBS to start casting *I Love
Lucy*, she first turned to her frequent radio partner Bea Benaderet—who just weeks
earlier had already agreed to play Blanche Morton on *The George Burns and Gracie
Allen Show*. Benaderet had to turn down *I Love Lucy*; Vivian Vance would instead play
the role of Lucy's best friend, Ethel Mertz.

HAPPY DAYS, STARRING AN EX-MONKEE

In the 1970s, ABC would routinely air rejected pilots as episodes of its anthology
series *Love, American Style*. In 1972, an installment called "Love and the Television
Set," originally created as a pilot for a show titled *New Family in Town*, was broadcast;
the episode starred Ron Howard as 1950s teenager Richie Cunningham. After the
blockbuster success of the similarly nostalgic *American Graffiti* (also starring Howard)
in 1973, ABC wanted a TV show in the same vein, and asked *New Family in Town*
creator Garry Marshall for a reworking. An executive told Marshall that the show,
retitled *Happy Days*, needed a tough-guy character, a rebel or "greaser" in the mold
of James Dean or Marlon Brando. That character became the iconic Fonzie, and
producers reached out to two former members of the made-for-TV band the Monkees
to audition: Micky Dolenz and Michael Nesmith. Both gave good reads but lost the
part to Henry Winkler. When each screen-tested against the rest of the cast, Dolenz

Prince Fielder finished his MLB career with 319 home runs—just like
his dad, Cecil Fielder, who also finished with 319 home runs.

and Nesmith, both over 6 feet tall, towered over the others and made it difficult for the camera operators to frame all the actors in one shot. Winkler, all of 5'6", got the job—basically because he was short.

MORK AND MINDY, STARRING RICHARD LEWIS

Cashing in on a suggestion from his young *Star Wars*–loving son, *Happy Days* creator Garry Marshall added some science-fiction elements to his 1950s-set sitcom. The 1978 episode "My Favorite Orkan" introduced a wacky extraterrestrial named Mork from the planet Ork, meant to set up the spin-off series *Mork and Mindy*. The last two actors that producers auditioned were veterans of the Los Angeles stand-up comedy circuit: the self-deprecating and nervous Richard Lewis and the improv-oriented wild man Robin Williams. The comics were told to deliver their lines in an original "alien" voice; the best Lewis could do was a Scandinavian accent. He called off his own audition, telling the producers, "You know, Robin Williams is next. He is Mork, and if he doesn't get this, then you are all crazy." Williams indeed landed the part.

WONDER WOMAN, STARRING ANGIE BOWIE

Angie Bowie, a model and socialite most known in the mid-1970s for her connection to major rock stars of the era—she was married to David Bowie and claimed to be the inspiration for the Rolling Stones hit "Angie"—attempted to parlay her fame into an acting career. She landed rights to the Black Widow and Daredevil characters and took promotional photos for use in (unsuccessfully) shopping a television series based on the Marvel superheroes. She also auditioned for the TV movie that would become *Wonder Woman*. Tennis player turned actor Cathy Lee Crosby got the gig (but declined to reprise the role for the series, ceding it to Lynda Carter) over Bowie. Producers were pleased with Bowie's performance but were displeased with her insistence on not wearing a bra for the screen test.

ALL THAT, STARRING EMMA STONE

Nickelodeon scored a huge hit in the 1990s with *All That*, a sketch-comedy series modeled after *Saturday Night Live* but with a cast of teens and preteens performing age-appropriate material. Stars like Nick Cannon and SNL's Kenan Thompson got their start on *All That*, but not future Academy Award winner Emma Stone. At age 12, she attended an open audition, but was inadvertently unprepared. "Five minutes before I went in the room they said, 'You need to have three characters,'" she told *The Tonight Show with Jimmy Fallon*. In a panic, Stone created three characters off the top of her head. "I remember that one was a cheerleader that couldn't spell what she was cheering." Another was a babysitter possessed by a demon.

Treadmills were originally designed as a form a punishment in Victorian England.

FRASIER, STARRING JOHN LITHGOW

In 1984, *Cheers* added a new character in the form of Dr. Frasier Crane, a pompous intellectual and psychiatrist who dates Shelley Long's character, Diane Chambers. Kelsey Grammer got the part and it became his signature role—he'd play Frasier on *Cheers* through 1993, then for another 11 years on the spin-off *Frasier*, winning four Emmy Awards along the way. The part of Frasier was originally written by *Cheers* creators specifically for John Lithgow, best known in the mid-1980s for back-to-back Oscar-nominated performances in the acclaimed films *The World According to Garp* and *Terms of Endearment*. Lithgow said no, later revealing on *Watch What Happens Live with Andy Cohen* that at the time, he considered himself a serious, films-only actor, and that TV was "beneath his dignity." He later got over that attitude, and during *Frasier*'s run on NBC in the 1990s, Lithgow starred as an alien occupying a human body on his own NBC sitcom, *3rd Rock from the Sun*. In three of the years that Grammer didn't win an Emmy for *Frasier*, Lithgow took home the award for *3rd Rock*.

FRIENDS, STARRING TIFFANI THIESSEN

In 1994, Tiffani Thiessen had just finished a long run playing girl next door and teen idol Kelly Kapowski on the Saturday-morning high-school sitcom *Saved by the Bell* and its short-lived prime-time spin-off, *Saved by the Bell: The College Years*. She turned to more grown-up roles and landed an audition and a screen test for an NBC sitcom in the works called *Six of One*. An ensemble show about a group of pals in their twenties living in New York City, Thiessen impressed producers with her performance as Rachel Green, who runs away from her wedding to make a go of life on her own. That show became *Friends*, and as the rest of the cast filled out, Thiessen got left out. "I was just a little too young," Thiessen later said. She was 20 at the time, and lost the role to then-25-year-old Jennifer Aniston.

*   *   *

TWO OLD HOLLYWOOD DIVORCE STORIES

- Rod Cameron was a major star of Hollywood Westerns in the 1940s and 1950s. It was a minor scandal in 1960 when he announced that he was divorcing his wife of ten years, Angela. It caused another scandal when just a few months later, he married Dorothy Alves-Lico—his ex-wife's mother.

- Popular 1920s silent film and Broadway ingenue Madge Bellamy was married to her second husband, financial trader Logan Metcalf, for less than a week. Four days after their Tijuana wedding in 1928, Bellamy filed for divorce. The reason? Metcalf's daily breakfast of ham and eggs was too "plebeian" for her.

African wild dogs communicate by sneezing.

TALES FROM THE OZZYVERSE

By the 1980s, rock 'n' roll stars had reached peak debauchery. The godfather of that debauchery was the "Prince of Darkness" himself: Ozzy Osbourne (born in 1948 and amazingly still alive at the time of this writing). With his first band, Black Sabbath, Ozzy perfected the role of the heavy-metal front man. But it wasn't until he went solo that he really went off the rails on a crazy train. Kids, don't try this stuff at home. Or anywhere. (Especially at the Alamo.)

DOVE AT FIRST BITE

In 1981, two years after Osbourne was fired from Black Sabbath for "being loaded all the time" (though he claims he also left because the others "wanted to sound like Foreigner"), he was attending an event at CBS records for the U.S. release of his first solo album, *Blizzard of Ozz*. As with most Ozzy stories, the details are fuzzy. The original plan was for Osbourne to give a short speech and then release three doves as a sort of "peace offering." But he was drunk on brandy, and as he foggily recalled, "I just remember this PR woman going on and on at me. I pulled out one of these doves and bit its f***ing head off. Just to shut her up. Then I did it again... that's when they threw me out. They said I'd never work for CBS again." But the bird, Osbourne later explained, had died shortly before the ceremony. "So rather than waste it, I bit its head off. You should have seen their faces." He added that it tasted like "tomato sauce."

THIS IS NOT A TOY

After school one day in 1982, 17-year-old Mark Neal was hanging out with his friend Carmen Kelly when Mark's little brother came home with a dead bat. Carmen had an idea; she told Mark to put it in the freezer and then—when he would come to play Des Moines in two weeks—throw it at Ozzy Osbourne! Osbourne's *Diary of a Madman* tour was making news for bizarre theatrics including a catapult raining raw meat down on the crowd and a dwarf that was "hanged" from a small gallows.

On the night of the concert—after sneaking the thawed-out dead bat (in a baggie) past security—as Neal recalled, he "got right down in front, right in front of [the bass player]. I tossed [the bat] up onstage and it landed in front of him. He...motioned Ozzy over. Ozzy came over, picked it up, and the rest is history."

News spread fast that Ozzy Osbourne had bitten the head off a live bat on stage. Des Moines Mayor Pete Crivaro wanted answers, demanding to know "if the performer violated an agreement on the use of animals in his act." Animal rights groups called for the singer's arrest.

Osbourne's response: "I thought it was one of these toy bats, so I pick it up, bite the thing's head off, and suddenly everybody is freaking out." But that's what that tour had devolved into: "Eventually, people started to throw things on stage with nails and razor blades embedded in them," he said. "Joke shop stuff, mainly, like rubber snakes and plastic spiders." This was no joke, though. Osbourne was taken to the hospital, and had to spend every night for the next three weeks—while on tour—getting rabies shots: "One in each arse cheek, one in each thigh, one in each arm. Every one hurt like a bastard." Biting the bat wasn't that pleasant, either: "My mouth was instantly full of this warm, gloopy liquid, with the worst aftertaste you could ever imagine. I could feel it staining my teeth and running down my chin."

ANT MISBEHAVIN'

In 1984, while on tour with Mötley Crüe, Ozzy Osbourne and Crüe bassist Nikki Sixx had a "gross-out contest." As Sixx recalled, Osbourne asked for a straw and then "walked over to a crack in the sidewalk and bent over it. I saw a long column of ants... and as I thought, 'No, he wouldn't,' he did. He put the straw to his nose and...sent the entire line of ants tickling up his nose with a single, monstrous snort." Cool story, but did it happen? Ozzy's wife, Sharon, writes about it in her book, but his guitarist, Jake E. Lee (the only one there not on drugs), says that it wasn't ants: "He snorted a little spider." As for Ozzy, he has no recollection of the incident...or the tour.

FORGET THE ALAMO

Why was Ozzy wearing Sharon's dress? Because she'd hidden his clothes. They were in a San Antonio, Texas, hotel room in 1982—shortly before Osbourne divorced his first wife to marry Sharon, who was managing him at the time. He wasn't even sure what city he was in when he put on her dress and ventured outside to find more alcohol (Sharon had hidden his clothes in an attempt to keep him inside). First things first, though: Osbourne stumbled across the street and peed on the base of a 60-foot-tall statue. And not just any statue: the Cenotaph, dedicated to the Texans who lost their lives in the 1836 Battle of the Alamo...which happened to be located directly across the street from Osbourne's hotel. He was arrested and, in yet another public scandal, he was banned for life from not just the Alamo but San Antonio, too. (Ten years later, he made a public apology to the city and a large donation to the organization that runs the Alamo grounds, and all was forgiven.)

"They are not so beautiful as they were said to be, for their faces had some masculine traits," wrote Christopher Columbus about mermaids. They were actually manatees.

GET AHOLD OF YOURSELF, DAD!

Sharon married Ozzy despite his antics and started him down the road to recovery, but it was a bumpy ride. After an unsuccessful rehab stint in 1984, five years later, in a stupor, Ozzy attacked his wife and was arrested for attempted murder, and then sent to treatment for six months. Sharon stuck with him (and made their family reality TV stars). After a few hiccups here and there, Ozzy got sober for good in 2013. "It's a very selfish disease," he said of his drug and alcohol problem. "You don't think about it because you're loaded." It wasn't until Osbourne's son Jack told him he didn't care about all the riches and fame, he just wanted a father, that Ozzy made the commitment to quit. "I'd give whatever materialistic things [my kids] ever wanted," said Osbourne. "But the most important person wasn't there." He said it's a miracle he made it out alive: "I should have been dead 1,000 times."

* * *

DINO PEBBLES AND OTHER DISCONTINUED BREAKFAST CEREALS

Waffelos

Crazy Cow

Choco Donuts

Rainbow Brite

Sprinkle Spangles

Banana Frosted Flakes

Mr. Wonderfull's Surprize

Fruity Marshmallow Krispies

Baron Von Redberry

Smurf-Berry Crunch

Yummy Mummy

Sir Grapefellow

Dino Pebbles

Pac-Man

C-3PO's

Mr. T

In 1976, Barbara Cartland wrote a world record 23 novels.

HOW MANY SHEETS OF TOILET PAPER THICK IS IT?

Uncle John sees the world through a bathroom-shaped lens, so naturally he asked us to figure out the heights of various things in terms of toilet paper. Enjoy this truly useless page of trivia and learn how many sheets of two-ply toilet paper you'd need to get the job done.

Your thumbnail: 3

DVD: 4

A thick-cut potato chip: 8

A Popsicle stick: 9

A standard McDonald's hamburger patty: 38

An iPhone 14 Pro: 46

This book: 149

A Rubik's Cube: 329

The largest diamond ever discovered, the Cullinan, at its thickest spot: 347

A roll of toilet paper (lying on its flat side): 671

A Subway foot-long sandwich (stood up on its end): 1,644

An Academy Award statuette: 2,018

A toilet bowl (from the floor to the rim): 2,166

An adult male golden retriever: 3,529

An LG 65" flat-screen television: 3,930

NBA star Victor Wembanyama: 11,579

The World's Largest Roll of Toilet Paper in Branson, Missouri: 17,445

The faces on Mount Rushmore: 107,576

An average small-town water tower: 265,355

The Statue of Liberty: 546,847

The Washington Monument: 995,082

The highest point of the St. Louis Arch: 1,129,553

Chicago's Willis Tower: 2,599,765

Burj Khalifa, the tallest building on earth: 4,870,588

Four pilot/actor "Living Legends of Aviation" award recipients:
Tom Cruise, Morgan Freeman, John Travolta, and Harrison Ford.

LES PHRASES DE QUEBECOIS

Canada is officially a bilingual nation, but most of its French speakers live in Quebec, where more people speak French than they do English. Quebecois French is very different from the French used in France and elsewhere, with its own quirks, phrases, idioms, and expressions. Like these.

Attache ta tuque
Literally: attach your knitted cap
Meaning: hold on tight

Fais-le au plus sacrant
Literally: do it the most slammingly
Meaning: do it fast

C'est le fun
Literally: that is fun
Meaning: that's awesome

Franchement
Literally: frankly
Meaning: really

La blonde
Literally: the female with blond hair
Meaning: girlfriend

Chanter la pomme
Literally: sing the apple
Meaning: talk to someone flirtatiously

Partir sur une balloune
Literally: leave on a balloon
Meaning: party until you can no longer party

Être paqueté
Literally: to be packaged
Meaning: drunk

Virer une brosse
Literally: throw away a brush
Meaning: hit the town for a night out

Être sous raide
Literally: to be insufficiently rigid
Meaning: hungover

J'ai mon voyage
Literally: I have my trip
Meaning: I'm done with this conversation!

Tu me gosses
Literally: you're gobbling me
Meaning: you're bugging me

Avoir le feu au cul
Literally: have a fire in one's butt
Meaning: feeling angry

Cogner des clous
Literally: bang one's nails
Meaning: fighting the urge to sleep

J'ai la langue à terre
Literally: I have my tongue on the ground
Meaning: I'm hungry; I'm tired

Lache pas la patate
Literally: don't release the potato
Meaning: don't give up

Avoir des vers dans le cul
Literally: have worms in one's butt
Meaning: feeling anxious

Être vite sur ses patins
Literally: quick on one's skates
Meaning: smart or clever (often used sarcastically)

Caller l'orignal
Literally: imitate a moose
Meaning: vomit

Correct
Literally: correct
Meaning: OK, as in "everything's fine" or "you OK?"

Coupe Longueuil
Literally: Longueuil haircut
Meaning: named after a Montreal suburb where it was popularized in the 1970s, it's the French-Canadian term for the hairstyle known in the U.S. as a mullet

Australia has 65 wine regions.

SALAD DRESSING ORIGINS

*Here's how some enterprising cooks and business-minded folks came up with
the best-known varieties of the best part of any salad: the dressing.*

RANCH

The mildly peppery, mostly smooth, creamy style of dressing really did originate on
a ranch. Gayle and Steve Henson founded the Hidden Valley Ranch—a vacation or
"dude" ranch—outside Santa Barbara, California, in 1954. Predating the California-
based, vegetable-oriented health-food craze of the 1970s, the Hidden Valley Ranch
served its guests lots of raw veggies. To get folks to eat them in the 1950s and 1960s
(when the standard American diet consisted primarily of meat, potatoes, and well-
cooked vegetables), the Hensons needed a dip and dressing as crowd-pleasing as
possible. They struck on a recipe that combined mayonnaise, buttermilk, and various
fresh herbs and spices. Guests *loved* the dressing, so much so that many asked for the
recipe when they left the Hidden Valley Ranch. The Hensons weren't willing to give
that up, so instead they sold packets of the spice mixture that could be added to mayo
and buttermilk at home.

In 1972, the Hensons sold the recipe, along with the brand name of Hidden
Valley Ranch, to the food division of Clorox for $4 million. Initially sold in packets—a
reformulated blend of spices and dried buttermilk to be added to milk—the company
began bottling it fully ready in 1983. Within a decade, ranch (from all manufacturers)
was the best-selling dressing in the U.S.

FRENCH

Before the 1930s, "French dressing" was what is now referred to as a vinaigrette.
Cooks and chefs took their cues from French cuisine, regarded as the best in Western
culture, and a dressing bearing that distinction was as simple as a salad dressing could
get: a mixture of vinegar and olive oil, sometimes with Dijon mustard, garlic, and
salt. Modern French dressing, found in bottles or on salad bars, is based off that basic
vinaigrette, with the addition of sugar, paprika, and tomato puree (or even ketchup),
making for a creamy, sweet, and tangy orange sauce.

This newer French dressing is anything but French, created by a Chicago-based
food company founded by Italian American Louis Milani. In 1938, the company
debuted Milani's 1890 French Dressing, said to be "blended in the tradition of the
original world recipe." They called it "French" to sound European, and put "1890"
on the label to make it seem old-fashioned. It was really just a tomato vinaigrette with

They got their start on *Star Search*:
Justin Timberlake, Leann Rimes, and Beyoncé.

lots of sugar added to cut the bitterness. The dressing was a success nonetheless and supplanted the unaltered vinaigrette as *the* French dressing in North America.

NEWMAN'S OWN

Movie star Paul Newman found bottled salad dressing too sweet and bogged down by chemicals for his liking, so he made his own at home. After gifting bottles of a mustard vinaigrette he mixed up in a bathtub at his Westport, Connecticut, home in the early 1980s, Newman and a friend, writer A. E. Hotchner, decided to start a small company to sell the dressing in stores. In 1982, they put together a taste test with local caterer Martha Stewart (prior to her launch to stardom), and feedback was so positive that Newman declared himself "the salad king of New England"—and named his dressing Salad King. Local grocery store operator Stew Leonard liked the dressing and said he'd sell it, but only if Newman put his name and face on the bottle.

The actor found the idea of promoting himself as a grocery product crass, but got around his aversion by deciding he'd give all proceeds to charity. The renamed Newman's Own teamed with dressing manufacturer Ken's Foods to produce an initial batch of 10,000 bottles—which sold out in two weeks. That initial dressing became the first in the Newman's Own line, which now includes products such as salsa, popcorn, cookies, juice, pet food, and more, all with natural and organic ingredients, and with all profits (hundreds of millions of dollars so far) going to charity.

GREEN GODDESS

George Arliss was one of the most popular theatrical actors of the 1920s, and one of his biggest hits on Broadway was 1921's *The Green Goddess*, an adventure set in India in which the actor portrayed a rajah. Arliss reprised the role in the 1923 film version, and Philip Roemer—the executive chef at San Francisco's Palace Hotel, where Arliss was staying at the time—was inspired to make a superior salad dressing in the actor's honor.

Green goddess dressing started with a blend of vinegar and mayonnaise, into which Roemer whipped a great deal of ingredients, mostly herbs and vegetables including parsley, tarragon, chives, and scallions, as well as chopped anchovies. The classically trained Roemer was likely also inspired by *sauce au vert*, or "green sauce," a very old French condiment served with eel in the court of King Louis XIII in the 17th century. The dressing spread through the hotels and high-end kitchens of the United States, with many chefs tweaking the recipe, using sour cream instead of mayonnaise, or adding new herbs such as basil and chervil. Common in restaurants of all kinds by the 1960s, green goddess was bottled for the first time in 1970 by dressing company Seven Seas.

Want fries with that? Research known as the "Ketchup and Mustard Theory" says the combination of red and yellow might make you crave French fries.

Q&A: ASK THE EXPERTS

Here are more answers to life's important questions from the people who know—trivia experts.

NO POTTY BREAKS

Q: *How do bears go to the bathroom when they're hibernating?*

A: "Bears do not need to pee when they are hibernating. If they did they would have a problem with the balance of fluids in their body, since bears neither drink nor eat during hibernation. The only water that bears lose in hibernation is the air that they breathe out. But it is replaced with water that is produced when fat decomposes through the process of burning fat, and that keeps the bear from being thirsty." (From *How Long Can a Fly Fly?* by Lars-Åke Janzon)

HOT AND COLD

Q: *Why does glass shatter if it gets too hot or too cold too quickly?*

A: "The natural brittleness and poor conductivity of glass make it susceptible to cracking when it experiences a rapid change in temperature from hot to cold or vice versa. Contemplate what happens, for instance, when boiling water is poured into a cold glass jar. Because glass has a low heat-flow efficiency, the heat that is transferred from the water to the jar's bottom travels relatively slowly to the top of the jar. Since glass expands when heated, the jar's bottom will quickly swell, and—what is most critical—without a corresponding expansion in the upper part of the jar. This disparity creates a structural stress that cracks the doomed glass." (From *The New Kitchen Science*, by Howard Hillman)

SEEING GREEN

Q: *Why does cheap jewelry make your skin turn green?*

A: "Costume jewelry labeled as being made of nickel and even pieces that are silver- or gold-plated often contain copper or copper alloys (a blend of metals that has copper as a component). As we know from seeing corroded pennies on the sidewalk and the Statue of Liberty's complexion, copper is great at oxidizing to a green hue... The minerals and chemicals in your sweat can react with the copper content of your jewelry to cause the green tint to transfer to your skin." (From *USA Today*)

ALL FOR U

Q: *Why are the seats on public toilets U-shaped?*

A: "The original purpose for the U-shaped seat, according to...the International Association of Plumbing and Mechanical Officials[,] was to aid women...The open

The only number with the same value as its number of letters: four.

seat was designed to allow women 'to wipe'...without contacting a seat that might be unhygienic. The U-shaped seat in public restrooms is a requirement of IAPMO's Uniform Plumbing Code. On its own, the code doesn't have any legal force, but city, county, and state governments do frequently adopt it (or a variation) as law. It currently applies, in some form, to more than half the population of the U.S. and the world." (From *Slate*)

ORANGE YOU GLAD YOU ORDERED DECAF?

Q: *Why do pots of decaffeinated coffee in restaurants have orange lids and handles?*

A: "Decaffeinated coffee first arrived in America via the German company Sanka. Sanka (a portmanteau of the words sans and caffeine) sold its coffee in stores in glass jars with orange labels. The bright packaging was the company's calling card, and because it was the first decaffeinated coffee brand to hit the market, consumers started looking for the color when shopping for decaf. In 1932, General Foods...purchased Sanka and got to work promoting it. To spread the word about decaf coffee, the company sent orange Sanka coffee pots to coffee shops and restaurants around the country. Even if the waitstaff wasn't used to serving two types of coffee, the distinct color of the pot made it easy to distinguish decaf from regular. The plan was such a success that orange eventually became synonymous not just with Sanka, but all decaf coffee." (From *Mental Floss*)

SMELLS LIKE AN INJURY

Q: *What causes the bad smell when you take off a bandage?*

A: "Maceration often occurs during treatment of wounds because the skin under the bandage becomes wet due to perspiration, urine or other bodily fluids. The excess moisture is sometimes called hyperhydration...Although most maceration clears up quickly once the skin is exposed to fresh air and allowed to dry, sometimes skin that experiences long periods of maceration is vulnerable to fungal and bacterial infection. As opportunistic organisms affect the area, it may become itchy or develop a foul odor." (From *How Stuff Works*)

SCARED SHEET-LESS

Q: *Why are ghosts in old paintings, books, and movies depicted as floating white blobs?*

A: "The root of it lies in the fact that, up until the 19th century, the dead were almost always wrapped in burial shrouds, rather than placed in coffins. In poorer families, the recently deceased were simply wrapped up in the sheet from their death bed, and secured inside by a knot tied at either end...By the 1400s, people reporting supernatural phenomena almost always described apparitions as being clad in their death shrouds...These ideas were compounded by theatrical presentations of spirits and hauntings throughout the 19th and into the early 20th century." (From *KQED*)

Believe it or not, your pinky is your strongest finger.

BUTTING THE LAW

Q: *Why do airplanes still have ashtrays if they banned smoking on flights years ago?*
A: "Smoking has been universally banned on aircraft globally, and many airlines already began to phase out smoking since the 1980s...So why do aircraft still have ashtrays? The answer is because people will and do still ignore the rules. And so, just in case passengers are absent-minded and place an aircraft's safety in danger by smoking in the lavatories, it remains a Federal Aviation Administration (FAA) requirement to have an ashtray. Rather than a non-compliant passenger putting a cigarette butt in the trash and potentially causing a cabin fire, ashtrays remain as a safe place to put out a cigarette should a passenger decide to break the law." (From *Forbes*)

COCK-A-DOODLE-DECIBELS

Q: *Do roosters hurt their own ears with their extremely loud crowing?*
A: "Audio recordings at the level of the entrance of the outer ear canal of crowing roosters...show that a protective mechanism is needed as sound pressure levels can reach amplitudes of 142.3 dB...Micro-CT scans of a rooster and chicken head show that in roosters the auditory canal closes when the beak is opened. In hens the diameter of the auditory canal only narrows but does not close completely. A morphological difference between the sexes in shape of a bursa-like slit which occurs in the outer ear canal causes the outer ear canal to close in roosters but not in hens." (From *Zoology*)

A BLOODY DIFFICULT SIGHT

Q: *Why do some people faint at the sight of blood?*
A: "Syncope, from Greek sunkopē (sun-, 'together' and koptein, 'strike, cut off'), refers to a sudden loss of consciousness as a result of a temporary decrease in the blood flow supplying the brain. When syncope is caused by certain triggers, like the sight of blood or an intense emotion, it is called 'vasovagal syncope' or 'reflex syncope.' Most individuals with vasovagal syncope experience a prodrome, which is a period of symptoms lasting at least a few seconds just prior to losing consciousness." (From *Osmosis*)

BAD APPLES

Q: *Can one bad apple spoil the whole barrel?*
A: "Once an apple is rotten or has physical damage, (i.e., a bruise), it produces ethylene, which in turn leads to a slightly increased internal temperature causing a breakdown of chlorophyll and the synthesis of other pigments. The starch in the fruit is converted to simple sugars and at the same time, pectin, a component of fiber that cements the cell walls together, begins to disintegrate thereby softening the tissue. Once this happens, it starts a chain reaction, stimulating the process in other apples." (From McGill University Office for Science and Society)

World record for counting to one million:
Jeremy Harper of Alabama did it in 89 days (for 16 hours a day).

THE FIX IS IN

On at least a few occasions, major American sports were subject to predetermined outcomes engineered by professional, criminal gambling rings. How did they do it? They got the outcomes they wanted by purchasing the services of those who could affect the results: referees and players.

EVENT: MULTIPLE GAMES THROUGHOUT THE 2006–2007 NBA SEASON

Background: Jimmy "The Sheep" Battista worked with an illegal, underground, high-stakes gambling circuit. He was an intermediary broker, or a "mover," wagering on sports on behalf of his clients with bookmakers, both legal and illegal. He sought out Tim Donaghy, whom he'd known for 25 years since they both went to the same Philadelphia-area high school, and who now worked as a referee in the NBA. Donaghy would call Battista's assistant, Tommy Martino, and speak in code: Donaghy indicated he'd throw the game for the home team if he asked about Martino's brother who lived nearby; for the away team, he'd asked about his brother who lived in Florida. Battista would try to wager about $1 million on a single game. If Donaghy successfully fixed the game, the referee would collect a $2,000 fee (plus bonuses).

How They Did It: Donaghy would "announce" his winner the night before the game, giving Battista the chance to manipulate the bookmakers' odds by placing huge bets on both sides. This would get the point spread down to under six, which Donaghy said was the maximum amount of score differential he could have on a game. For example, in a Boston Celtics vs. Philadelphia 76ers game, Donaghy had to get the spread above 2.5; so he called two suspect fouls on Philadelphia's top scorer, Andre Iguodala, in the third quarter. Iguodala was sent to the bench, giving Boston a chance to recover, cover the spread, and win the game as planned. In a Seattle Sonics vs. Dallas Mavericks game, Donaghy called 11 straight fouls against Seattle, including one with 23 seconds left. Dallas made two free throws, increasing its final lead to eight points—and the spread was covered. Donaghy's picks won their games more than 70 percent of the time.

Outcome: Donaghy pleaded guilty to federal charges of conspiracy to transmit gambling information and conspiracy to commit wire fraud, and was sentenced to 15 months in prison.

EVENT: THE 1919 WORLD SERIES

Background: Approached by powerful organized crime gamblers from New York, eight members of the 1919 American League champion Chicago White Sox agreed to lose the World Series on purpose. The reason, according to some of the parties involved: team owner Charles Comiskey egregiously underpaid them relative to other, less-accomplished players in the league. Fed up with the owner's supposed stinginess, the players were willing to accept the offered payout of the gambling organization: $10,000 to each player if they lost four games.

How They Did It: The White Sox's starting pitcher in game 1: 29-game winner Eddie Cicotte. Arguably the best pitcher in the league at the time, Cicotte was also the ringleader of the White Sox conspiracy. In his second pitch of the game, he struck (and walked) Cincinnati Reds batter Morrie Rath. In the fourth inning, his pitching suddenly grew so wild and terrible that he gave up five runs in that inning alone. The Reds won the game, 9 to 1. In Game 2, White Sox star pitcher Lefty Williams experienced a sudden inability to strike out batters in the fourth inning, and the runs he gave up directly led to a 4 to 2 Reds win. In the middle of the series, according to some players' sworn testimony, they called off the fix—because they had yet to be paid the full amount due, being given just $10,000 total. It was too late, though—the early losses were too much to overcome, and the White Sox lost the championship, 5 to 3 in a best-of-9 series.

Outcome: The scandal was discovered in 1920, and the eight players involved all earned lifetime bans from professional baseball.

EVENT: THE 1918 WORLD SERIES

Background: According to a deposition given regarding the 1919 World Series fix, pitcher Eddie Cicotte claimed he and his teammates thought throwing the games would be no big deal—because across town, the year before, the Chicago Cubs had supposedly conspired to lose *their* World Series against the Boston Red Sox. And for the same reasons: team ownership had been so withholding of promised salaries that some players decided to accept an unnamed gangster's offer of $10,000 for each of them if they were to lose.

How They Did It: Cicotte didn't name names, but some peculiar plays from the Cubs' performance stick out. While baserunners rarely get picked off by pitchers, outfielder Max Flack got picked off twice in Game 4. On another occasion, he reportedly pretended not to listen to pitcher Lefty Tyler tell him to play right field deep to accommodate long-ball hitter Babe Ruth—who hit a pitch deep into right that Flack otherwise would've easily fielded, but instead resulted in a two-run triple. In Game 6, Flack so badly bobbled an otherwise easily fielded fly ball that it was ruled an error; he took so long to throw it into the infield that two runners scored. Those wound up the winning runs of the game—and the series—for the Red Sox.

Outcome: Aghast and embarrassed about the 1919 World Series, Major League Baseball declined to investigate the 1918 World Series.

Alice's Adventures in Wonderland author Lewis Carroll coined the words *portmanteau* and *chortle* (which is a portmanteau of *chuckle* and *snort*).

DUSTBIN OF HISTORY: MAN MOUNTAIN DEAN

Who do you get when you combine Andre the Giant, Hulk Hogan, the Rock, and Captain America? The greatest pro wrestler you've never heard of: Man Mountain Dean.

LITTLE-KNOWN BIG MAN

"He's a former cop who never made an arrest, a former Indian fighter who never saw an Indian, and a college graduate who never learned the English language." That's how sportswriter Edwin Pope described 1930s professional wrestler Frank "Man Mountain Dean" Leavitt, adding, "But into 25 years on the mat, Man Mountain Dean packed more of a lifetime than Methuselah, who in 969 years was never recorded as mastering the hammerlock." This was from Leavitt's 1953 obituary. Pope had no idea of another of Leavitt's accomplishments: playing a key role in helping to defeat the Nazis in World War II. Here's his larger-than-life story—declassified.

Born in the Hell's Kitchen neighborhood of Manhattan, New York, in 1891, Frank Leavitt had gotten so big by the age of 14 that he was able to lie his way into the U.S. Army. (It was more than his size that got him in; even then, Leavitt had the gift of gab. After all, he literally grew up on Broadway—the famous theater district—where his father was a stage manager, and tough-guy movie star George Raft lived down the street.) After enlisting, the nearly six-foot-tall, 300-and-some-pound baby-faced teenager served along the Texas-Mexico border until he was shipped off to France in World War I, where he saw combat duty and lived to tell about it.

After the war, Leavitt was recruited to play football for five colleges, though he attended classes at none of them (he maintained he dropped out of school in the fifth grade). Then he played for the fledgling New York Brickley Giants in the precursor to the NFL, where it's said he even faced off against the greatest athlete of the time, Jim Thorpe. But the game of football was too small for Leavitt's oversized personality.

THE HELL'S KITCHEN HILLBILLY

Though Greco-Roman wrestling goes back to ancient times, the modern sport of pro wrestling started in Europe in the early 19th century and took hold in the U.S. after the Civil War as a form of cheap entertainment. Because watching a "real" wrestling match can be a slog, some early wrestlers added costumed theatrics and invented rivalries. And they scripted the fights. While most sports fans—especially

The first battlefield tanks in World War I had to be cranked like a Model T to start.

boxing fans—dismissed pro wrestling as fake, the sport came into its own in the 1920s. And Leavitt, who was a star wrestler in the army, wanted a piece of the action. His first wrestling persona, "Soldier Leavitt," didn't really catch on, so he grew a beard and became "Hell's Kitchen Hillbilly," and then "Stone Mountain Leavitt," though promoters on a German tour complained that the name meant nothing. Leavitt's wrestling career sputtered along until a string of injuries knocked him out of the sport.

In 1925, Leavitt landed a new job as a traffic cop in Miami, where his gargantuan size and gregarious personality made him a local celebrity. Local leaders even sent him around the country to promote Miami in other cities. Alas, Leavitt's cop days were cut short after he was fired for visiting the mansion of infamous gangster and part-time Miami resident Al "Scarface" Capone, who, unbeknownst to Leavitt, was under police surveillance.

But before he got fired, fate had stepped in. While Leavitt was directing traffic one day, a young woman named Dorris Dean almost hit him with her car. "I gave her hell," he later said, "and then I married her." Dorris became Leavitt's manager and biggest fan (she was known to jump in the ring with a chair when he needed help). She also came up with the name "Man Mountain" and booked him a tour in Germany. The name "Leavitt" was "too Jewish" for that country in the 1930s, so he borrowed her maiden name and he became Man Mountain Dean.

FROM THE SQUARE RING TO THE SILVER SCREEN

Man Mountain Dean was such a big hit in Germany that Dorris booked him a U.K. tour. That's where he broke into movies—and filled out his trademark burly beard—as a stunt double for one of the most renowned (and largest) actors of the time, Charles Laughton. All told, Leavitt acted or did stunt work in 30 movies, five of them playing himself—most famously in *Gladiator* with comedian Joe E. Brown.

But it was in the wrestling ring where Leavitt was happiest. He fought in 504 bouts and—even though he usually played the villain—he became the sport's biggest champion and defender. At his peak, he was earning $1,500 per match. (The average *annual* income at the time was only twice that amount.) And like any good wrestler worth his persona, Man Mountain Dean had a signature move: the "blimp fall." Per the *Atlanta Constitution*: "he leaped high into the ozone, distended his limbs and plopped the south end of his massive carcass kerplunk on the victim's tummy."

Always up for a new challenge, in 1938, Leavitt ran for a seat in the Georgia state legislature, but dropped out, saying, "If I stay in politics, I'll slug somebody for sure...if I tried that on one of these politicians, I'd land in jail and be sued for all I own. Wrestling is on the level, but politics..."

Approaching 50, Leavitt retired to his farm in Georgia for some peace and quiet.

The GPS—or global positioning system—consists of only 24 satellites.

THE RITCHIE BOYS

Then World War II interrupted everything. Leavitt, ever the patriot, reenlisted in 1941. Too old for combat duty, Master Sergeant Leavitt was stationed at Camp Ritchie in Maryland. Until that point, the site had been a mountainside vacation resort; now, it was a secret military intelligence training center.

Leavitt was assigned to a unit of German-born Jewish immigrants who'd fled the Nazi regime. Now they were being trained to go back to Germany and gather information as translators, spies, and interrogators. Any one of these dangerous jobs might require hand-to-hand combat—which is where Man Mountain Dean came in. He taught the recruits—some as young as 19—how to fight, but that was just the beginning. The young men took to their gargantuan, now-clean-shaven commander right away. They got along because he wasn't a soldier, and neither were most of them: they were intellectuals who would go on to become doctors, teachers, lawyers, and writers (including future *Catcher in the Rye* author J. D. Salinger). Leavitt taught them about American culture and the proper use of slang; he told exciting stories of his adventures (some of them true). During war simulations, Leavitt drew on his acting skills to play notorious German Luftwaffe commander Hermann Göring.

The Ritchie Boys shipped out to Normandy in 1944. Thanks in no small part to Leavitt's training, "this extraordinary unit was responsible for more than half of all combat intelligence gathered on the Western Front, their work pivotal to the Allies' victory." That's according to the 2022 *Sports Illustrated* article that was the first to report the wrestler's wartime heroics.

After the war, even though he never finished school, Leavitt attended the University of Georgia–Atlanta (now Georgia State University) to study journalism. But a heart attack in 1953 cut his life short. He was 61.

INTO THE DUSTBIN

So why isn't Frank Leavitt better known today? In a way, he was the Babe Ruth of pro wrestling...but his sport wasn't nearly as prominent. Despite wrestling's small-but-loyal fan base, boxing was much more popular, and names like Jack Dempsey and Joe Louis have endured. Leavitt did all he could to champion the pastime he loved, but it would take until the 1980s—when big personalities including Andre the Giant and Hulk Hogan became famous outside of the sport—for wrestling to finally go mainstream.

Another reason Leavitt was swept into the Dustbin of History: Camp Ritchie was classified. Ever duty-bound, he never uttered a word in public about what went on there; even his family members were unaware of what he'd done. Now that the documents have been declassified and the remaining former Ritchie Boys are starting to speak out, this larger-than-life figure deserves a place in the history books.

Your stomach acid can dissolve some types of metal.

PEACE, LOVE, SEATBELTS

To reduce traffic accidents, U.S. transportation departments have been posting clever electric road signs—which multiple studies have shown actually work. Some of the funnier ones:

TEXTING & DRIVING IS CLEVER, SAID NO ONE EVER

GET YOUR HEAD OUT OF YOUR APPS

TEXTING WHILE DRIVING? OH CELL NO

DON'T DRIVE IN-TEXT-ICATED

WHO YA GONNA CALL? NOBODY. YOU'RE DRIVING

BE ON SANTA'S NICE LIST, DRIVE POLITELY

NEW YEAR. NEW YOU. USE YOUR BLINKER.

WHAT'S SCARIER—YOUR COSTUME OR YOUR DRIVING?

100 IS THE TEMPERATURE, NOT THE SPEED LIMIT

LIFE IS FRA-GEE-LAY. SLOW DOWN

VISITING IN-LAWS? SLOW DOWN. GET THERE LATE

IF YOU MISS YOUR EXIT, IT'S OK WE MADE MORE

AWWWWW SNAP! YOUR SEAT BELT!

IT'S FALL, Y'ALL. BUCKLE UP BEFORE YOU LEAF

DON'T MAKE ME STOP THIS CAR! BUCKLE UP

PEACE, LOVE, SEATBELTS

DUCK, DUCK, BUCKLE UP

TREAT YOUR KIDS LIKE A FANNY PACK: BUCKLE UP IN BACK

NOBODY PUTS BABY IN A HOT CAR

DRIVING FAST AND FURIOUS? THAT'S LUDACRIS

WE PITY THE FOOL WHO TEXTS & DRIVES

MAY THE FOURTH BE WITH YOU. TEXT YOU I WILL NOT

BABY YODA USES THE FORCE BUT STILL NEEDS A CAR SEAT

SPEEDING LEADS TO THE DARK SIDE

HOCUS POCUS. DRIVE WITH FOCUS

FANS DON'T LET FANS DRIVE BLITZED

MAKE IT TO THE END ZONE, DRIVE ALERT

PLAY BALL! STRIKE THE DISTRACTIONS

BLOW THE WHISTLE ON DISTRACTED DRIVING

KEEP RIVALRIES OFF THE ROAD, DRIVE CALM

COMMUTING ISN'T A COMPETITIVE SPORT, RELAX

MOM NEEDS YOUR HUG, NOT YOUR TEXT

LIFE IS A HIGHWAY, DRIVE SAFELY ALL DAY LONG

Invented in the Baltic region of Europe in the late 18th century, the card game solitaire was originally used for fortune-telling.

HEFTY HISTORY OF WEIGHT-LOSS CRAZES

On paper, losing weight seems straightforward, but also difficult and unpleasant—it's a matter of eating fewer calories than the body burns, achieved through exercise and through restrictive dieting of some kind. Over the centuries, numerous scientists, nutritionists, regular folks, and straight-up charlatans have tried to convince the world that they had a less painful, easier, and faster—if not magical—path to weight loss. They've gone down in history as the purveyors of briefly popular (and marginally effective) fad diets.

REGIMEN: The Immortality Diet

DETAILS: Luigi Cornaro was a wealthy nobleman who lived in Venice (now part of Italy) in the 1500s. He made his fortune developing farming equipment but found his fame spreading what he purported to be the secrets to living a very long and healthy life. In 1558, while in his eighties, Cornaro published *Discourses on a Sober and Temperate Life*. In the book, translated and printed across Europe, Cornaro explained that by the time he was 40, he felt exhausted and unhealthy. Attributing his ill health to overeating and too much alcohol consumption, he worked out a meal plan where he ate precise amounts of simple foods—just bread, broth, meat, and egg yolks—and a little wine. By following his "Immortality Diet," Cornaro lived to be 98 (or 102—sources disagree).

WHY IT FLOPPED: The diet was incredibly difficult to follow because it allows for the consumption of only 350 total grams of food each day (but 14 ounces of wine).

REGIMEN: Swamp Avoidance

DETAILS: British doctor Thomas Short was an epidemiologist, a specialist in disease theory, and he practiced in Coventry and Sheffield in England in the early 1700s. In 1728, he published one of his first works, a pamphlet called *A Discourse Concerning the Causes and Effects of Corpulency, Etc.*, a study on the causes of obesity. Short believed that some people were more predisposed to being heavyset than others. In his field research, he found that test subjects whose weights were the highest almost always lived near a swamp. So, Short posited, living near a swamp had something to do with obesity, and in his book he advised those looking to lose weight to move far away from any swamps (and then eat what they liked).

WHY IT FLOPPED: Despite Dr. Short's observations, scientists have never found a conclusive link between swamp proximity and weight.

The world's most expensive book: Leonardo da Vinci's science diary, *The Codex Leicester*, sold for $30.8 million in 1994.

REGIMEN: The Drinking Man's Diet

DETAILS: Many diets and lifestyle plans today are of the high-protein, high-fat, low-carbohydrate variety. These diets make the body lose a lot of weight quickly via ketosis—when no sugars or carbohydrates are consumed, the body converts fat into usable energy instead of relying on glucose. The best-known example of this is outlined in *Dr. Atkins' Diet Revolution*, published in 1972 by Robert C. Atkins and popularizing the "Atkins Diet." In the previous decade, the much more colorful, straightforward, and macho *The Drinking Man's Diet: How to Lose Weight with a Minimum of Willpower* hit bookstores. Within two years of its publication in 1964, the pocket-size book sold more than 2.4 million copies around the world, and in its scant 50 pages, author Robert Cameron appealed to manly men who didn't want to munch on salads and vegetables to slim down. He advocated the consumption of only alcohol and meats—steaks, ribs, hamburgers (sans buns), with cheese and with creamy and fatty sauces on top. Cameron was a cosmetics executive, not a doctor, although he claimed to have talked to a nutritionist before publishing *The Drinking Man's Diet*.

WHY IT FLOPPED: Mainstream nutritionists and the American Medical Association derided the book, but it held steady as a popular weight-loss method—particularly among men—until Dr. Atkins came along.

REGIMEN: The Sleeping Beauty Diet

DETAILS: According to the logic of this diet, you can't eat—or overeat—if you're sleeping, so you might as well sleep as much as possible and give your body a chance to just lie there and burn fat. Unlike most other diet plans, which dictate the specific foods adherents should eat or avoid, this diet is all about pills: inventors recommended consuming powerful sedatives to help users sleep for as many as 15 hours a day. The diet surfaced in 1976 when news broke that it was attempted by Elvis Presley in his later, heavier years; he even hired a doctor in Las Vegas to make sure he stayed asleep by placing him into a medically induced coma.

WHY IT FLOPPED: Any diet that involves hospitalization isn't feasible for most Americans long-term, and its popularity certainly wasn't helped when its most famous adherent, Elvis Presley, died at age 42.

REGIMEN: The Scarsdale Diet

DETAILS: In 1978, Scarsdale, New York–based cardiologist Dr. Herman Tarnower published *The Complete Scarsdale Medical Diet*, which details a weight-loss plan heavy on fruits, vegetables, and an unlimited amount of lean protein (such as eggs, fish, and chicken) so long as daily caloric intake doesn't exceed 1,000 calories a day, or about half of the recommendation for what a healthy adult ought to consume.

WHY IT FLOPPED: It was a temporary sensation that was the result of a grisly scandal. Five million copies of the book were sold after the 1980 death of Dr. Tarnower, murdered by a jilted lover, Jean Harris, who in her trial claimed to be the true inventor of the Scarsdale Diet.

REGIMEN: The Master Cleanse

DETAILS: Dietician Stanley Burroughs first marketed the Master Cleanse in 1941, and it became a phenomenon when he published the book *The Master Cleanser* in 1976, and again in 2006 when pop superstar Beyoncé claimed to have used the method to drop 20 pounds in less than two weeks. What is the Master Cleanse? For 10 days, dieters are to avoid all food whatsoever and consume only unsweetened tea along with a drink made from a mixture of water, lemon juice, a little pure maple syrup, and a dash of cayenne pepper six times a day. Supposedly, that concoction forces the body into purifying itself of toxins.

WHY IT FLOPPED: The human body needs a certain number of calories each day to function, so if someone is eating next to no calories, chances are, they're going to lose weight because the body is starved and begins to eat itself. Once they go off the Master Cleanse and start eating real food again, the weight tends to come back.

REGIMEN: The Cabbage and Urine Diet

DETAILS: Cato the Elder was a prominent figure in ancient Rome, a senator who wrote some of the oldest surviving texts in Latin, including a Roman history and guides to cooking and agriculture. Around 175 BC, both in his written works and public lectures, he extolled the benefits of cabbage, which he believed to be a miracle food of sorts. Cato claimed that a diet based entirely on cabbage could cure everything from indigestion and warts to stomach ulcers, dysentery, and alcoholism. Considering that cabbage, whether eaten raw, boiled, or prepared as a soup, has almost no calories, Cato's dietary plan also helped ancient Romans lose weight.

WHY IT FLOPPED: After his wife and one of his sons fell ill, Cato prescribed an all-cabbage diet. They still died, and that discredited the diet's efficacy. It was also hard for people to get on board with a diet that Cato said worked best if one also drank the urine of others who consumed a high-cabbage diet.

Pop singer Brandy and rapper Snoop Dogg are first cousins.

REGIMEN: The Bananas and Skimmed Milk Diet

DETAILS: Dr. George Harrop was an esteemed physician in the U.S. in the 1920s, studying, practicing, and teaching at the Johns Hopkins Hospital and Columbia University, specializing in nutrition and metabolic issues. By 1934, he'd developed an austere diet plan to help his obese patients lose large amounts of body weight, and quickly. As first published in the *Journal of the American Medical Association*, Harrop's daily meal plan recommended six whole bananas and four glasses of fat-free ("skimmed") milk, split up into three meals, one of which also included a bowl of unadorned lettuce or cabbage. After 10 days of eating that way, patients were allowed to add small amounts of fish, lean meat, and eggs. The United Fruit Company, the world's largest banana distributor, got ahold of Harrop's study and, seeing how it could trigger increased banana sales, published instructions for what it called "The Bananas and Skimmed Milk Diet."

WHY IT FLOPPED: The United Fruit Company distributed thousands of pamphlets and sold a lot of bananas in 1934, but the Bananas and Skimmed Milk Diet pretty much died out by 1935. Doctors criticized the diet because it hadn't yet been widely tested or peer reviewed. Also, the weight tended to return once adherents abandoned the diet, which reportedly left thousands with deep abdominal discomfort because of an inability to process such large amounts of fiber and dairy.

REGIMEN: The Lord Byron Diet

DETAILS: Because they almost always project an image of fitness, and thinness, celebrities are common and enduring guinea pigs for diet crazes. Whatever they do, millions of regular folks try to re-create, and this phenomenon all began in the early 1800s with the popular Romantic poet and young, handsome, roguish, and scandalous womanizer Lord Byron. Byron weighed 200 pounds in 1806, but by 1811 had shed 75 thanks to a diet of potatoes and vinegar. Because his every action was breathlessly recounted by reporters of the day (and spread by high society gossips), the details of his diet became widely known and repeated by teenagers and young adults seeking to emulate him. The 1810s Lord Byron method for maintaining an ultra-trim figure: a thin slice of bread and tea for breakfast, a small plate of cooked mixed vegetables and wine-splashed seltzer water for dinner, and, before bed, a cup of green tea.

WHY IT FLOPPED: Physicians and cultural critics sounded the alarm in newspapers, warning that starving oneself would lead to terrible health in both the short and long term. And as the flowery, emotive Romantic movement was just a passing fancy anyway, so too was the accompanying diet.

Real headline: "A parrot that was trained by drug dealers to alert them of police presence is refusing to speak after being detained."

REGIMEN: The Beverly Hills Diet

DETAILS: Judy Mazel created and popularized the Beverly Hills Diet, despite a lack of any training in medicine or nutrition. A failed actor, Mazel struggled with her weight for most of her adult life until the late 1970s, when she spent six months working with a Santa Fe nutritionist to develop an eating plan. Mazel lost 72 pounds and took what she learned back to the suburbs of Los Angeles, opening a weight loss clinic geared toward influential wealthy and celebrity clientele. In 1981, Mazel published *The Beverly Hills Diet*, detailing how she'd lost so much weight. The book sold a million copies and instructs readers how they can supposedly lose weight by eating the correct combinations of foods, or by eating them at certain times of day. For the first 10 days, dieters are instructed to eat only different types of fruit, and in a particular order. During the next eight days, they can add a little bread and butter and three ears of corn to their daily intake, and then protein on day 19 (but only from expensive, fancy sources, such as lobster and steak). All the while, dieters are to never eat carbohydrates and protein on the same day.

WHY IT FLOPPED: Nutritionists dismissed the Beverly Hills Diet as a fad, one based on unproven data. Meanwhile, doctors and emergency rooms filed numerous reports of Beverly Hills Dieters seeking aid for heart arrhythmia, potassium deficiency, muscle weakness, and severe diarrhea and dehydration.

REGIMEN: The Tapeworm Diet

DETAILS: The standard of beauty in Victorian times was to look like one was infected with tuberculosis: pale and extremely thin. To achieve the latter, women would literally poison themselves by drinking ammonia tinctures or taking arsenic pills, or by wearing corsets that squeezed and contorted their bodies to have 16-inch waists. Or they'd willingly and knowingly let a tapeworm take residence in their digestive system. Interested parties would take a pill (purchased via mail order) that consisted of little more than a tapeworm egg. The worm would theoretically hatch in the stomach and the parasite would take root; the host human could then eat whatever she wanted because the tapeworm consumed most of it. Once the desired weight loss was complete, the user would try to lure out the tapeworm by placing a glass of milk at one end or the other of her digestive tract.

WHY IT FLOPPED: The idea of putting a parasite in one's body, and then the gross ways of getting rid of it, was never going to be a feasible, long-term, mainstream weight-loss strategy.

In a 1933 *New Yorker* article called "The Waltz,"
Dorothy Parker popularized the term *scaredy-cat*.

MOUTHING OFF

WTF QUOTES

In this case, "WTF" means "weird talking famous." (In other words: celebrities.)

"If a cupcake falls from a tree, how far away will it be from down?"
—Jaden Smith

"I don't necessarily agree with everything that I say."
—Marshall McLuhan, Canadian philosopher

"I LEARN ABOUT MYSELF. THERE IS NO SELF. YOU LEARN YOU'RE NOT A SELF. YOU LEARN YOU'RE NOTHING. ULTIMATELY. HOPEFULLY."
—Harry Dean Stanton

"I'd love to live like a poor man, only with lots of money."
—Pablo Picasso

"I am on a drug. It's called Charlie Sheen. It's not available. If you try it once, you will die. Your face will melt off and your children will weep over your exploded body."
—Charlie Sheen

"I would not say that the future is necessarily less predictable than the past. I think the past was not predictable when it started."
—Donald Rumsfeld

"I don't really have a favorite player to guard. I guess somebody on the bench who doesn't play. It's easier to guard them."
—Kawhi Leonard, NBA player

"Pablo Picasso said art is a lie that tells the truth. What if you just want to tell the truth and not lie about it?"
—Nicolas Cage

"Bear suits are funny. Bears as well."
—Christopher Walken

Interviewer: *Let's talk about your Cable Ace Awards.*
Gary Busey: *Let's talk about buttered sausage.*

ROBOTS IN THE NEWS

*Get up to speed now on the exciting developments and news in the
world of robots—before they rise up and take over the planet.*

ANGRY CHESS ROBOT

In July 2022, a seven-year-old identified in news reports only as Christopher—said to
be one of Russia's best chess players under the age of nine—competed in a match in
Moscow against a chess-playing robot. At one point, Christopher got so excited to
take his next move that he went to move a piece too soon after the robot had taken its
turn. That violation in protocol caused the robot to glitch, and with its robot hand,
it reached out and grabbed one of Christopher's human fingers, squeezing it tightly
enough that it fractured.

It took four adults to jump in and release Christopher from the robot's clutches.
"There are certain safety rules and the child, apparently, violated them," said Chess
Federation of Russia vice president Sergey Smagin. "This is an extremely rare case, the
first I can recall."

DANGEROUS DRIVING ROBOTS

Because of its proximity to the booming and prosperous technology community in
Silicon Valley, and because companies including Google have thoroughly mapped
out its streets into a navigable, computerized grid, San Francisco is a virtual testing
ground for autonomous automobiles, or self-driving cars. By November 2022, the
technology had advanced to the point where the robotic cars could make the same
bad decisions as human drivers. One night, a San Francisco Police Department officer
attempted to pull over a Chevy Bolt, noticing that the car's headlights weren't turned
on—a safety violation. When the officer approached the car to investigate, the vehicle
sped up and drove another block before stopping. Then the officer couldn't confront
the driver...because there wasn't one.

SUCCESSFUL IMPREGNATION ROBOT

In 2022, a team from a company called Overture Life built and shipped off a
specialized robot to New Hope Fertility Center in New York City. There, the
engineers assembled one of the world's first fertility robots, consisting primarily of
a laptop, camera, petri dish, mechanical needle, and microscope. Then, mechanical
engineering student (and avowed nonexpert in fertility medicine) Eduard Alba
used a PlayStation 5 video game controller to manipulate a robotic needle, using
it to puncture a 0.1 mm-size egg and deliver a single sperm. In vitro fertilization is

typically done by hand, but Alba and cohorts fertilized a dozen eggs via their robot for multiple clients; two developed into healthy baby girls, both born in early 2023. It's the first known instance of fertilization by robot.

UNCANNY BIRD ROBOTS

Mechanical engineering professor Dr. Mostafa Hassanalian led a team at the New Mexico Institute of Mining and Technology to create a set of lifelike birds. Reason: to investigate the nature of aviation in a controlled study. "If we learn how these birds manage...energy between themselves, we can apply that into the future aviation industry to save more energy and save more fuel," he told reporters.

The robot birds Dr. Hassanalian and company made began as actual, biological birds—albeit dead ones, their outsides preserved via the process of taxidermy. Then the engineers outfitted them with electronics and robot parts, essentially turning them into drones that perfectly resemble birds. (Although they're technically cyborgs.) The birds can fly for only up to 20 minutes, so Dr. Hassanalian's crew is working on increasing battery life before they use them to infiltrate communities of real wild birds.

SNAKE ROBOTS

According to scientists, snakes had legs about 100 million years ago. A snake-loving YouTuber and self-described "fixer" named Allen Pan took it upon himself to restore what evolution took away. "When any other animal has deformed legs, humanity comes together to spit in God's face, and we build that animal awesome new cyborg legs," Pan said in a video titled "Giving Snakes Their Legs Back." So, after observing lizards in a pet store and snakes at a snake breeder's house, Pan developed and tested out a series of robotics-powered contraptions into which a snake can be inserted that give the slithering serpents robotic, prosthetic legs. They're able to move around slowly and without confidence, resembling dachshunds crawling.

REAR END ROBOT

To ensure that its smartphones are durable and well-made, South Korean electronics giant Samsung sends its prototypes through a rigorous testing process. Attempting to replicate real-world situations, various robots and machines drop, attack, and abuse the phones. Samsung also ensures that a phone will survive a very common problem— accidentally getting sat on after being put in its owner's back pocket. To test this, Samsung built and employs the use of a robot butt. Clad in a pair of denim jeans, the Lower Body Pressure Test is programmed to mechanically and repeatedly sit on phones, where engineers can test just how much pressure the devices can withstand.

If only it was real:
all the play money in a standard Monopoly game adds up to $15,140.

BEHIND THE HITS

Another edition of a longtime Bathroom Reader favorite—
the secret stories behind popular songs.

The Song: "How Long?" (1974)

The Artist: Ace

The Story: Before he joined the New Wave band Squeeze and sang for 1980s pop group Mike + the Mechanics, Paul Carrack's first big success was as the front man and main songwriter for Ace, a 1970s soft-rock group. Ace would record three albums, but only the first one would sell well, thanks to the inclusion of the 1974 #3 hit "How Long?" The lyrics sound like they're sung from the point of view of a person cheated on by a lover, confronting the cad with lines like, "How long has this been going on?" Carrack explained on *BBC Breakfast* 35 years after the song's release the real inspiration behind "How Long?": he wrote the song as a tearful callout of Ace bassist Terry Comer. Comer hadn't told the rest of the guys in the band that he'd been playing with other groups, including Quiver and the Sutherland Brothers. The rest of Ace found out about it, and they were mad. But the song worked—Comer swore off playing in other groups, re-devoted himself to Ace, and played bass on the tune that was about him.

The Song: "9 to 5" (1980)

The Artist: Dolly Parton

The Story: Patricia Resnick wrote the first draft of the screenplay for the workplace-based dark comedy *9 to 5*, about a trio of harassed, overworked, and underpaid female office workers who conspire to seek revenge against their male chauvinist pig of a boss. Resnick was inspired by the National Association of Working Women, founded in 1973 with the original name 9to5, advocating for equal pay and better treatment of women working in all industries. Actor and activist Jane Fonda was the first to book one of the three lead roles in the *9 to 5* film and recruited country music superstar Dolly Parton to costar. Parton didn't have much acting experience, but she agreed to be in the movie if she could also write the theme song. On the set, Parton wrote "9 to 5" during filming breaks. She wore long, hard, acrylic nails for the part, and after tapping them one day, realized they made a sound not unlike that of keys on a typewriter—a common office implement in 1980. The movie went on to make $100 million at the box office, and "9 to 5" hit #1 on the pop, country, and adult contemporary charts and earned Parton an Academy Award nomination for Best Original Song.

In Chinese, the number eight is lucky because it sounds like the word for "wealth," and four is unlucky because it sounds like the word for "death."

The Song: "Downtown" (1964)

The Artist: Petula Clark

The Story: By 1964, English singer Petula Clark had racked up a slew of top-10 hits in France and Germany but had yet to win an audience in the country of her birth, abandoning singing in her native language after her early U.K. singles flopped. Pye Records producer Tony Hatch saw Clark perform in Paris and pleaded with her to return to London with him and record new music in English. He played a number of songs for her that he'd written; one—called "Downtown," a paean to the romance of big-city life—didn't have lyrics yet, but Clark loved the melody and title enough to give a promise she'd record it, if Hatch wrote some decent lyrics. Just two weeks later, Clark headed to a London studio to record her part on "Downtown," backed by an orchestra of 40 musicians (including future Led Zeppelin guitarist Jimmy Page). As for those lyrics Hatch had told Clark he'd written? He hadn't quite finished yet. While Clark and the musicians were warming up, Hatch was finishing the lyrics in the bathroom. It took less than 20 minutes to record the song when it was finally ready; Clark and the band recorded it live, and committed three takes to tape. It hit #2 in the U.K. (Clark's first big English-language hit) and #1 in the U.S., right after Clark performed it on *The Ed Sullivan Show*.

The Song: "Jack & Diane" (1982)

The Artist: John Cougar

The Story: John Mellencamp, still contractually obligated to perform under the stage name John Cougar, wrote the lyrics and melody of "Jack & Diane," a wistful look back at first love between two teenagers, a football star and a debutante. Inspired to write a tune after watching the film version of Tennessee Williams's play *Sweet Bird of Youth*, Mellencamp didn't much use the plot about the romance between a young man and an older woman, just the love story and idea of how the guy, a movie star, was the most recognized person in his small town, like a high school football player would be. He also initially wrote "Jack & Diane" to be about an interracial couple, torn apart by others' prejudices; his label, Riva Records, urged him to change it to be less overtly about social issues. When it came time to record, Mellencamp's band had difficulty with the tempo—there are lots of abrupt starts and stops. To guide his group, Mellencamp recorded a helpful backing track of handclaps. He intended to remove it from the finished product, but so liked the way it sounded that he kept it in. In 1982, "Jack & Diane" became Mellencamp's first (and only) #1 hit.

The Spice Girls' nicknames (Posh, Scary, Baby, Ginger, and Sporty) were coined by a journalist who was too "lazy" to learn their real names.

The Song: "One Sweet Day" (1995)

The Artist: Mariah Carey and Boyz II Men

The Story: The most successful solo pop artist of the early 1990s: Mariah Carey. The most successful group of the era: Boyz II Men. In 1995, Carey cowrote a tribute song to her recently deceased friend and collaborator David Cole, who'd produced many of her songs and was half of the 1990s pop act C+C Music Factory. After listening to a rough cut, Carey thought the chorus could benefit from a four-part vocal harmony from a group like Boyz II Men. Months later, the two busy superstar acts finally got in a room together, and Boyz II Men member Nate Morris presented Carey with a song he'd written for a dead loved one. "It was basically identical to my song in the theme and melodically," Carey said. "It was like fate, so we put the two songs together and came up with 'One Sweet Day.'" The five singers could spare only an afternoon out of their schedules to record the song and the video, so the clip promoting the song is just a compilation of footage of the recording session. "One Sweet Day" went on to spend 16 weeks at #1—breaking the record set by Boyz II Men's "I'll Make Love to You."

The Song: "Don't You (Forget About Me)" (1984)

The Artist: Simple Minds

The Story: Producers of the 1985 John Hughes teen comedy *The Breakfast Club* went about compiling a soundtrack of rock and pop hits by hiring musicians Keith Forsey and Steve Schiff to write a bunch of songs, which they'd then persuade established bands and singers to perform. They wrote "Fire in the Twilight," which Wang Chung recorded, and then "Don't You (Forget About Me)," an anthemic synth-rock song thematically tied to the movie and meant to play over the credits. Forsey and Schiff asked Roxy Music singer Bryan Ferry to record the song, but he refused. Popular rockers the Fixx and Billy Idol also turned them down. So Forsey pursued one of his favorite bands of that moment, mildly successful Scottish alternative-rock group Simple Minds. The band's American label, A&M, urged them to record "Don't You (Forget About Me)" as a way to break out in the U.S., but they initially said no—as a matter of course, they did only songs they wrote themselves, and singer Jim Kerr really hated the line "I'll be alone, dancing you know it, baby." After watching a cut of the film with Hughes, Simple Minds changed their minds and recorded the song. Kerr ad-libbed the "hey hey hey" opening and the "la la la la" closing, intending to write lyrics for the latter but never getting around to it. A&M was proven correct—"Don't You (Forget About Me)" went to #1 in the U.S., the first of a long string of hit singles for the band in America.

Start charging rent: your body is host to about 1,000 species of germs.

RANDOM ORIGINS

Once again, the BRI asks—and answers—the question: where does all this stuff come from?

THONG UNDERWEAR

The thong is reminiscent of the precursor to all modern underwear: the loincloth, a minimalist garment that covers up private parts while leaving the buttocks more or less exposed. The first modern-day version of the thong, as a lacy women's undergarment, which similarly covers up very little, was the indirect result of the last person you'd expect: New York City mayor Fiorello LaGuardia. In 1939, the World's Fair was about to open in New York City, and LaGuardia wanted to class up the city's many strip clubs, so he declared that dancers could no longer perform nude. Some performers took to wearing loincloths made from very thin, lacy materials. But underwear fit for an exotic dancer would take a while to find their way into the mainstream. The thong wasn't commercially available in Europe and the United States until 1974, when fashion designer Rudi Gernreich introduced the thong bikini. Still, the panties were considered so risqué that they didn't sell well until the mid-1990s.

GOLDFISH CRACKERS

In 1937, Margaret Rudkin, who raised her children on a Connecticut farm named after its large pepperidge tree, sought to treat her son's severe allergies and asthma by changing his diet. After learning to bake, she devised a recipe for stone-ground, vitamin-rich whole wheat bread. Rudkin turned that into a reg ional baking company, and within five years, Pepperidge Farm had sold a million loaves of bread. During the 1950s, Rudkin and her husband began traveling Europe looking for specialty food products they could license and bring to the American market (one of their successes: Belgian Milano cookies). Rudkin sold the company to Campbell's Soup in 1961 but, in addition to becoming the first woman on the company's board, she also stayed on as a product scout. In 1962, she discovered a cracker made by large Swiss baker Kambly. Created four years earlier by founder Oscar J. Kambly, the bite-size orange-colored saltine crackers were shaped like fish (Kambly's wife's star sign: Pisces) and made on an industrial mass-producer created by a World War II–era Nazi code breaker. Rudkin brought the cracker back to Pepperidge Farm, who introduced the product as Goldfish Crackers in 1966. They're sold under that name in more than 40 countries, and Americans alone gobble up more than 150 billion individual crackers each year. In Switzerland, they're still produced by Kambly and called "Goldfish–The Original."

Skirts got so wide in the 1860s that women often got stuck in doorways.

ATLANTIS

According to myth and lore, the lost continent of Atlantis is a sunken landmass that once housed a grand and technologically advanced civilization. Historians and explorers alike have long argued its existence and sought proof, never to find anything conclusive. Unlike other known mythological entities, such as the pantheon of ancient Greek gods, the idea of Atlantis can be traced back to a specific person at a specific point in time. In about 360 BC, the ancient Greek philosopher Plato wrote about "the lost city of Atlantis." Claiming to have had the story of Atlantis passed down to him from his grandfather, a statesman who'd heard the story from an Egyptian priest, he came up with this bit of knowingly fake history to create an enemy for the city-state of Athens. Don't be like the Atlantans, warned Plato, or you might suffer their fate. According to Plato, the islanders had angered Zeus, Apollo, and the other gods to the extent that they banished Atlantis into the sea, killing everyone instantly.

LIFTING A TROPHY

Most any professional sports championship involves the presentation of a large trophy to the winning team or individual. It's customary, if not expected, for the athlete or a prominent member of the team to hoist the trophy high up in the air in triumph. It seems like a totally natural thing, but somebody had to be the first one to do it. In the 1958 World Cup final, Brazil's national soccer team defeated Sweden. The team mobbed the field and were handed the Jules Rimet Trophy. It made its way to captain Hilderaldo Luiz Bellini, and he held it up as high as he could. The reason: so the different TV cameras and news photographers jockeying for position could all see it. That moment became Bellini's legacy. There's a statue of the athlete holding the Jules Rimet Trophy standing outside Maracana Stadium in Rio de Janeiro, and when he died in 2014, the president of Brazil mentioned the trophy he held aloft back in 1958. "Bellini forever won a place in the heart of every Brazilian by lifting the Cup with both hands," Dilma Rousseff memorialized.

LIPOSUCTION

In 1921, a dancer wishing to achieve thinner, more shapely ankles and knees approached French surgeon Dr. Charles Dujarier. Dujarier agreed to operate, despite this being an entirely new and experimental idea, which would later be called body contouring. Dujarier removed skin and soft, fatty tissue around the ankles and knees via a large incision. However, he removed too much tissue and kept the sutures

If eaten before it's ripe, the *Monstera deliciosa* fruit causes a nasty sore throat; when ripe, it's delicious (hence the name: "delicious monster").

too constrictively tight, resulting in tissue death throughout the dancer's leg that eventually required amputation. That killed the concept of voluntary surgical fat removal for five decades, until surgeons in Europe decided subcutaneous surgery would work better—cutting into the skin with only a tiny incision and removing fat via a powered aspirator tube. The technique was perfected in 1977 by French doctor Yves-Gerard Illouz and his "Illouz Method," which introduced more-powerful suction to remove fatty tissue and fat cells along with the injection of a harmless saline solution to break up fatty deposits and make them easier to retrieve and remove, assisting doctors essentially working "blind" under the skin.

BRUNCH

Generally best and most widely enjoyed on holidays or the weekend, when 9-to-5 work schedules aren't in effect, brunch is a combination of breakfast and lunch (as well as a combination of those words) featuring foods commonly associated with both meals presented at the same time. The customary brunching time: the very late morning or very early afternoon, or right in between the time a person might normally enjoy their separate meals of breakfast and lunch. Its origins are hazy and date back hundreds of years, but the trend in the U.S. caught on just under a century ago. In the 1930s, movie stars would shuttle back and forth between the two entertainment capitals—the bustling theater scene of New York and the growing film industry in Los Angeles. It was easier and more practical to take a transcontinental train than it was to fly, and the way those trips were scheduled, it seems that the stars often found themselves in Chicago in the late morning. Utilizing a brief layover, the celebrities would hop off the train and into a nearby Chicago hotel restaurant, ordering some breakfast items—and some lunch items, too, depending on the individual's mood or preference. Hotel kitchens happily catered to the stars, particularly on Sundays, a day on which most standalone restaurants were closed in the 1930s, allowing hotels to monopolize the dining business. Also boosting weekend brunch: falling church attendance figures. After World War II, millions of Americans stopped attending weekly services, and after sleeping in late and waking up hungry, they'd go out for brunch.

* * *

BIRDS DO IT...

Pope Gelasius declared February 14 "Saint Valentine's Day" at the end of the 5th century. It was in the 1300s, however, that the holiday became associated with romance and love. Why? In France and England during the Middle Ages, it was a common belief that February 14 was the date birds started their mating season.

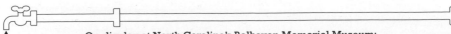

On display at North Carolina's Belhaven Memorial Museum:
a dried flea wedding, a two-headed kitten, a one-eyed fetal pig, and 30,000 buttons.

HOW TO MAKE GARBAGE

Have you ever wondered what happens to your garbage after you throw it in the can? Uncle John did, and as it turns out, it's a sophisticated, highly technological, and complicated journey for all that junk we throw away.

KEEP ON TRUCKIN'

After you take a big plastic bag of trash out to your issued can and put it on the curb, a truck from your area's sanitation department (or a private, contracted waste management company) arrives and a crane or worker dumps all the trash into an on-board hopper. A piston pushes and sweeps the trash into a holding area, instantly compacting the waste. An average side-loading truck can hold up to 15 tons (or 28 cubic yards) of garbage this way.

TRANSFER REQUEST

The first stop for the trash: a transfer station, located far from population centers on account of the tremendous smell of an entire city's garbage load and the huge plot of land required. Here, the trucks dump their loads where the trash is compacted into bricks and prepared for transfer, which means loading it onto larger trucks to be taken to its next stop. It's not always put on a truck, though—some municipalities operate rail transfer stations, or they put the trash on a barge bound for another state or an island-based processing facility.

MATERIAL WORLD

The voluminous number of compacted trash bricks next hit an MRF, or material recovery facility. Here, the debris is sorted by machines to recover useful or valuable materials from the "waste stream." When people throw away appliances or metallic objects, the sophisticated technology at the MRF can pick out the magnets, precious metals, and other such items and substances that can be cleaned and sold in bulk to manufacturers of various products.

Specialized MRFs are also used to process recycled items and pieces of trash that could and should have been recycled. Workers at "clean" facilities sort through recycling hauls by hand, looking for metals and high-quality plastics. "Dirty" MRFs sort through trash in search of recyclable material before it gets needlessly processed any further as garbage. (When you buy an expensive electronic gadget that says it's partially made from recycled materials, MRFs are where the manufacturer gets those raw materials.)

Pistachios aren't nuts—they're *drupes* (along with cherries, peaches, and olives).

🗑 THE FOUR STOPS

Following the hauling, compacting, and sorting stages, what trash remains is sent to one of four possible destinations.

- A landfill. There are more than 3,000 open-air, ever-growing trash heaps in the U.S., and a little over half of everything that's thrown away ends up in one of them. A landfill isn't designed to, or expected to, process or break down trash—it's just a storage facility for stuff that nobody wants. But a landfill isn't just a hole in the ground that turns into a mountain. It's comprised of layers of trash, each one placed atop a sheet of clay and covered in a flexible thin plastic sheet. Throughout the trash is a complicated network of pipes, and a drainage system in each layer: as it decomposes, the trash gives off a lot of liquid, which the plumbing collects and removes. When each layer fills up, landfill personnel cover it with more clay and plastic, and then some soil and plants to aid in decomposition. The garbage does eventually decompose, though it's a slow process.

- Recycling facilities. Just over a third of all solid waste generated by American homes and businesses ends up in a recycling or composting facility. Altogether, about 70 million tons of solid waste is recycled every year. These operations aim to convert what's essentially trash into new products, or to salvage what's there for reuse as is. The main materials sought after and set aside are paper, glass, plastic, and aluminum. (Two-thirds of stuff saved back is paper product, 12 percent is metal, and the rest is comprised of plastic, glass, and wood.)

- Anaerobic digesters. These large tanks, generally set up adjacent to large areas of farmland, use biological processes and microorganisms to turn organic trash into fertilizer. This is where sorted-out food waste from homes goes, along with deliveries from restaurants and industrial food operations.

- Incinerators. Landfills are a limited resource, so overburdened that they can't handle all the trash Americans generate. If there's no immediate room at a landfill, and the trash load isn't offering up any more recyclable materials, it's burned in a massive industrial furnace. About 13 percent of trash winds up here. These furnaces must get hot enough to burn most anything that's thrown in, and that's been calculated to be a temperature of about 1,800°F. "Burn" is a misnomer—the furnace incinerates materials, turning them into a fine, dusty ash. This reduces the volume of the garbage by 95 percent, and the heat generated by the incinerating garbage can be sold back to local electrical grids. This is the ultimate recycling: turning trash into energy.

The top-selling VHS tape of all time is *The Lion King*, which sold 32 million units.

HEAD-SCRATCHING HEADLINES

Do these headline writers mess with our brains on purpose? Whatever the reason, some of these are pure poetry. (And they're all real.)

Students Cook and Serve Grandparents

Driver Bribes Cop with Sweet Potato

Mimes Banned for Abusive Language

China May Be Using Sea to Hide Its Submarines

Breathing Oxygen Linked to Staying Alive

Museums Full of History

Want to Spell Like a Champ? Read Wenster's Dictionary.

School Is More Than Reading, Writing and Arithmatic

Trump Warns of "Fire and Furry"

Safety Meeting Ends in Accident

Puerto Rico Teen Named Mistress of the Universe

State Population to Double by 2040; Babies to Blame

Survey Finds Fewer Deer after Hunt

Survey Says Americans Getting Tired of Surveys

Swimmer Trapped by Beach Balls

A Nuclear Explosion Would Be a Disaster

Committee Appoints Committee to Appoint Committee

Black History Month Will Be Held Feb. 23

Think of a Headline 56 pt Bold Headline

Some Men Retain Mental Ability

Dog Saves Owner's Life after Cat Starts Fire

Weight Watchers Demonstrator Shoplifts Cupcakes

Chick-fil-A Cow to Oversee Southside Grand Opening

Cow Urine Makes for Juicy Lemons

Muddy Creek Problem: It's Too Muddy

Health Officials: Pools, Diarrhea Not Good Mix

Oreos are vegan.

ANIMALS FAMOUS FOR 15 MINUTES

When Andy Warhol said, "In the future, everyone will be famous for 15 minutes," he probably didn't have animals in mind. But even critters can't escape the relentless publicity machine.

HEADLINE: Southpaw Snail Seeks Similar Shell

The Star: Jeremy, a brown garden snail that spent its final days at the University of Nottingham in England

The Story: Unless you're really into brown garden snails, you probably haven't noticed that their shells all coil in the same direction: to the right, or clockwise. That is, except for the rare few *sinistral* brown garden snails, whose shells coil to the left. Until recently, scientists didn't know if this anomaly was caused by a genetic mutation or by some other factor. They didn't even know how lefty snails are able to mate; their reproductive organs don't line up with the righties. All snails are hermaphrodites—containing both male and female organs—so they can literally mate with themselves, but they prefer to mate with other snails to prevent inbreeding. Could that mean sinistral snails reproduce by mating with themselves? Their mating habits have never been observed, because finding one sinistral snail is hard enough. Finding *two* is nearly impossible.

But, in 2016, a farmer in London unearthed a sinistral snail, and—knowing its scientific importance—gifted it to the University of Nottingham, where it fell under the care of evolutionary geneticist Angus Davison. Davison named the snail Jeremy, after Labour party leader Jeremy Corbyn (a famous left-winger—get it?). Now, all Davison needed was a second sinistral snail for Jeremy to mate with. But it's estimated only one in 40,000 snails has this configuration, so Dr. Davison—with the aid of BBC News and England's *Today* program—asked the public to search their gardens for sinistral snails.

About a month later, the BBC reported that one had been found in Spain, and then another in Ipswich. By this point, Jeremy was something of a celebrity. (One sample headline: "Can't Hurry Love: Rare Snail Finds Romance after Global Search.") But the reporting was premature: the two new snails mated with each other. Good for the study; bad for Jeremy. As the months passed and Jeremy was approaching old age, it was looking like the gastropod was going to die a virgin. Then, in November 2017, the left-coiling snail left this *mortal coil*. But his fans could take

The Andes Mountains in South America are more than 5,000 miles long.

solace in the news that shortly before death, Jeremy mated with the Spanish lefty (named Tomeau). Of the Spanish snail's 56 offspring, about one-third were Jeremy's, allowing the famous southpaw snail to leave behind a legacy—and a few answers.

Aftermath: Three years later, Davison published his results. After three generations, all of Jeremy's snail descendants had right-coiling shells. That ruled out a genetic mutation *and* hermaphroditic mating. It's most likely that a select few snail shells turn to the left due to trauma that occurs during early development.

Jeremy's 15 minutes of fame has been bequeathed to Davison, who at last report was working on a graphic novel about his time with the sinistral snail. He says that snails' mating habits are "fantastically bizarre"; as NPR reporter Merrit Kennedy describes it, "the carnal act is known as 'traumatic insemination,' and copulation kicks off by mutually stabbing each other with 'love darts'—tiny calcium spears that transfer a hormone." It should be an interesting book.

HEADLINE: Bored Chimp Escapes Zoo, Wanders War-torn City

The Star: Chichi, a 13-year-old chimpanzee housed at the Kharkiv Zoo in Ukraine

The Story: By September of 2022, the Russian invasion of Ukraine was in its seventh month, and Kharkiv, Ukraine's second largest city, had endured nearly ceaseless shelling. It took a hard toll on everyone, including the animals at the zoo. Chichi, a friendly female chimp, was one of dozens of animals that had ended up in Kharkiv after other zoos in the country were destroyed.

Suffice it to say, the mood at Kharkiv Zoo was somber on this overcast September day. Chichi was missing her steady stream of human visitors, so she escaped from her enclosure and found her way out of the zoo and into the city. The few people who were out and about gave the powerful primate a wide berth...while recording her with their phones. She wandered into the town square, hoping to mingle, but no one got close to her. Meanwhile, videos of the forlorn chimp sauntering through the tattered city began going viral on social media.

After about two hours on the prowl, Chichi saw one of her keepers, Victoria Kozyreva, whom she'd known since she was little. Chichi gave her keeper a quick hug but promptly moved on, clearly not ready to go back to the zoo. So Kozyreva stayed close and tried to coax her back. It was only when a steady rain began to fall that Chichi ran over to her keeper, who was holding a yellow raincoat. The chimp put on the coat and gave Kozyreva another hug. Then the keeper wheeled the chimp back to the zoo on a bicycle.

Aftermath: Chichi's afternoon stroll and tender hug made for a rare feel-good story in a country that really needed it. And the world saw: major news outlets shared the video, and Chichi became an international celebrity.

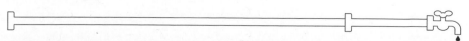

Fastest tank in the world: the Russian-built T-14 Armata. It can exceed speeds of 55 mph.

HEADLINE: Central Park Owl Brings Stir-crazy New Yorkers Outside

The Star: Barry, a barred owl

The Story: A cute little owl peers down at her reflection in Conservatory Water. This calming photograph—and several more of the Central Park Owl—went viral in late 2020, when the COVID-19 pandemic was starting to feel like it might never end. Lockdown after lockdown had left New Yorkers feeling insular and cranky.

But when word got out that an unusually unshy owl—which someone named Barry—was hanging out at various spots in the park, New Yorkers flocked there to see the bird for themselves. Ornithologists later determined that Barry was a one-year-old female, and goodness, was she photogenic. As photographer David Lei told the *New York Times*, "If there were a scientific formula for cuteness, Barry was it: fluffy and round, with those huge, expressive eyes."

Barry stretched out her 15 minutes by staying at the park through the winter instead of migrating. She inspired several fan pages on social media, and the popular Manhattan Bird Alert Twitter account kept tabs on her. Whenever Barry was spotted on one of the cams, the race was on to get there before she flew away—which wasn't that difficult because this peculiar owl didn't seem to mind being gawked at.

Aftermath: New York City can be a dangerous place; sadly, Barry learned this the hard way after she ingested some rat poison, which slowed down her senses, contributing to her being fatally struck by a park maintenance vehicle. But out of the despair that her death caused her fans came a sense of community that New Yorkers desperately needed. Some 250 people showed up at a vigil for Barry next to her favorite hemlock tree. One little girl left a note that eulogized, "You were my friend and you made me happy. Because of you, I stopped being scared to go out during the pandemic."

"RAINING CATS AND DOGS" IN OTHER LANGUAGES

Portuguese: Raining Snakes and Lizards
Romanian: Raining Frogs
Persian: Raining Jackals
French: Raining Like a Peeing Cow
Cantonese: Raining Dog's Poo

Watermelons are 92 percent water. Cucumbers are 95 percent water.

IRONIC, ISN'T IT?

There's nothing like a good dose of irony to put the problems
of day-to-day life into proper perspective.

FORGED IRONY

In 1980, Frank W. Abagnale Jr. published his memoir *Catch Me If You Can*, adapted into a hit movie by Steven Spielberg in 2002. The book and film detail the charming Abagnale's ability to talk and con his way into whatever he wanted during the 1960s, including pretending to be an airline pilot and forging millions of dollars in checks. After his capture by the FBI, Abagnale became an advisor on fraud prevention to law enforcement agencies and corporations. In 2023, investigative journalist Abby Ellin uncovered scores of evidence and interviewed numerous people from Abagnale's past to discover that the con man had substantially lied about his criminal exploits in his memoir. While he did forge checks (worth less than $1,500 total) and pose as a pilot on occasion, he never advised a Senate Judiciary Committee, and never pretended to be a college professor, doctor, or lawyer, as he claimed.

SOAKING WET IRONY

England's Buckingham and Villages Community Board was all set for an outreach program in November 2022 to provide information, tips, and instructions to locals on how to prevent property damage in case of heavy rains or flash flooding. The event, scheduled and set up to be held in an outdoor facility, had to be canceled on account of heavy rains and fear of flooding.

IRONY ON STAGE

In 1906, Sholem Asch wrote the Yiddish-language play *God of Vengeance*, about the Jewish daughter of a brothel owner who falls in love with one of her father's employees. When the play was staged in English on Broadway in 1923, authorities shut it down and arrested cast and crew on obscenity charges. In 2015, Paula Vogel wrote the Broadway hit *Indecent*, about the 1923 controversy. Douglas Anderson School of the Arts, a high school in Duval County, Florida, planned a production of *Indecent* in January 2023. But then the administration canceled the staging, calling it inappropriate—or indecent—for high school actors and audiences.

IRONY UNDER THE INFLUENCE

A Michigan State Police trooper stopped a motorist in Otsego County one night in January 2023 on suspicion of OWI, or operating a vehicle while intoxicated. The officer was correct, and, caught in the act of drunk driving, the woman behind the wheel called a friend to come pick her up. The friend she phoned was the one with whom she'd spent the whole of that night drinking. When the friend arrived at the scene in her car, the trooper arrested both women for OWI.

IRONY UNDER THE INFLUENCE, SECOND OFFENSE

Motorists on Route 601 outside Somerset, Pennsylvania, encountered a sobriety checkpoint one night in May 2015. Logan Shaulis had set up the road flares and roadblocks and forced dozens of drivers to stop, produce their licenses and registration, and prove their sobriety. Such checkpoints are commonly operated by police, but Shaulis wasn't a cop; he was a 19-year-old who was arrested by real authorities for impersonating a police officer. And the ironic twist: Shaulis was intoxicated at the time he set up the sobriety stop, and since he was behind the wheel of a car, he was arrested for drunk driving.

FLAMING IRONY

A firefighter crew in Hall County, Georgia, responded to a call on a Sunday morning in January 2023, putting out a minor house fire in the neighborhood. Other firefighters returned to the station in the town of Flowery Branch and were greeted by flames and smoke. When the emergency call had come through earlier, the firefighters had to immediately stop preparing a big hot breakfast and run to their trucks...and none of them remembered to turn off the stove. The stove suffered some minor damage from the fire in the firehouse.

IMMIGRATION IRONY

Local authorities in 2020 announced that New York City would serve as a "sanctuary city," a safe place for immigrants (legal or otherwise) and asylum seekers to stay without fear of deportation while they pursued U.S. citizenship. Over the next three years, so many thousands of people from around the world came to New York City that officials tried to relocate many to counties throughout the state, only to be rejected by the leaders of those areas, who cited overcrowding concerns. In 2023, the city of New York filed a lawsuit in the state's Supreme Court seeking to force those other counties to take in the immigrants it said it would never displace.

ENERGY IRONY

Every year, more jurisdictions around the world install wind turbines to generate virtually unlimited renewable energy, with an eye toward eventually replacing traditional, less environmentally friendly sources such as oil and gas. In November 2022, Norwegian energy company Equinor began operating an array of 11 turbines, situated about 90 miles offshore in the North Sea. Equinor has earmarked the floating turbines, providers of clean energy, to generate the electricity needed to run its North Sea–based oil drilling and gasoline processing facilities.

Apples are originally from Kazakhstan.
Seeds were brought to the New World by the Pilgrims.

WHO IS BAD MILK BLOOD ROBOT?

The covers of these illegally reproduced and sold DVDs found around the world look like they also employed a sketchy translation service to explain the plots.

Die Hard
"Reluctant hero must defeat his enemies! He has no shoes!"

Die Hard 2
"His wife is in danger! But this time he has shoes!"

Batman Begins
"When being a child, Bruce Wayne had witnessed with his own eyes the fact his parents of millionaire were killed cruelly, so affected his strong desire of revenging his parents...Following the advice of Ra\'s Al-Ghul, the chief of Ninja Group, Bruce come to Gete, which was a corrupted city filled with varlous crime groups. Bruce found a basement under his villa, in which the equpiments turned him into another person: Spiderman."

The Matrix Reloaded
"The white men wanted a stud to breed slaves."

RV
"Spend together for two weeks. Let the whole family sink into unable to cay or laugh embarrassing situation."

Harry Potter and the Chamber of Secrets
"Engaging lonely between to express himself and wanting."

Lost
"Ever since that time 815 services sink into a waste island in Pacific Ocean, luckily survive the s want to exist by hook or by crook under go to, along with time with each passing day past, the people suffered the island up many affairs of very strange."

Dexter
"The success of the day is a police forensic."

Captain America: Civil War
"Captain America in frozen a few years later, wake up. The world is not what he used to familiar appearance, various types of evil opponent to emerge in an endless stream, the whole society turbulent, sheet relies on a person's power is unable to save the world."

Red Tails
"Thank you, Noble Black Man for saving us from Hitler and the evil White Nazis!"

How I Met Your Mother
"Ted Xuan Yan and good baking friends Marshall suddenly tell the name of him, not his barrier to lazy to fry their phase agent made very long monster potato female key pal Lily bear - B - Russia."

Alien
"Space ship people get up from sleeping coffin and have eat. Computer woman find strange noising on planet and astronauts go to seeing. Astronauts find big elephant man who dead then find too many egg. Who will life to escaping? Who is bad milk blood robot? Scream not working because space make deaf."

Return of the Jedi
"Redescover the timeless film that comtinues to make entire generations afraid to go in the water"

Christmas tradition in Japan: eating KFC.

SMALL-SCREEN SONGS

Behind every great TV show—or in front of it, actually—is a great tune. Here are the stories behind the creation and composition of some of the most memorable TV theme songs ever recorded.

Show: *Laverne and Shirley* (1976)

Story: Charles Fox and Norman Gimbel wrote the faux-1950s theme song for the hit 1970s sitcom *Happy Days*, and when that show spun off *Laverne & Shirley*, they got the gig to write that show's theme song, too. Before they sat down to write, the duo attended a concert with *Happy Days* costar Anson Williams (Potsie) at the Magic Mountain theme park near Los Angeles. Singer Cyndi Greco, recently discovered singing in a pizza parlor, was also on the bill, and Fox and Gimbel liked her so much they promised they'd write a song for her should she ever record an album. Less than a year later, they needed a female vocalist to sing "Making Our Dreams Come True," the *Laverne & Shirley* theme song. Greco also recorded a full-length version of the tune that opened the #1 TV show in America, and it reached #25 on the pop chart—Greco's only hit.

Show: *Ted Lasso* (2020)

Story: For a theme song for the Emmy-winning dramedy about an American football coach who takes a job as a soccer coach in England, American star and cocreator Jason Sudeikis recruited English musician Marcus Mumford, lead singer of the popular folk-rock band Mumford & Sons. Sudeikis thought it would be an easy get— Mumford had been his friend ever since the band played on *Saturday Night Live* while Sudeikis was in the cast, and he'd later starred in the band's "Hopeless Wanderer" video. The comedian left a long voicemail message for Mumford describing the concept of *Ted Lasso*, what he needed for the theme song, and other pertinent details. Weeks and weeks passed; Mumford didn't hear the message because he was busy, out on tour with his band. "It had been in my phone for a couple of months, and he thought I was just ghosting him," Mumford said. Once he finally heard Sudeikis's message, he instantly signed on to *Ted Lasso* in part because the soccer team on the show, AFC Richmond, was a fictional riff on his favorite real team, AFC Wimbledon. "It felt like serendipity to me," Mumford said.

Show: *WKRP in Cincinnati* (1978)

Story: In 1978, TV writer Hugh Wilson created a show about the day-to-day operations of a struggling rock radio station. With the show's focus on music, Wilson knew he'd need a legitimately good, well-developed theme song and was sweating it

Research says: 12 percent of people dream in black-and-white.

when producer Ed Weinberger told him he should write the lyrics himself—because it was lucrative. "You get like 500 bucks every time it plays," Wilson later recalled. So, while on a flight, he composed some words told from the point of view of *WKRP*'s lead character (a disc jockey who'd worked on the air all over the country now settling down in Cincinnati), then hired Tom Wells, a friend who ran a studio in Atlanta, to write the melody and record it. With session singer Steve Carlisle employed for the day, they recorded a 30-second version and a three-minute one, the latter of which became an actual Top 40 hit (on the soft rock chart).

Show: *Teenage Mutant Ninja Turtles* (1987)

Story: Chuck Lorre is one of the most successful TV show creators and producers of all time, responsible for huge hit sitcoms including *Two and a Half Men*, *The Big Bang Theory*, *Mike & Molly*, and *Mom*. He started his entertainment career in the 1980s as a songwriter (he wrote Blondie singer Debbie Harry's solo hit single "French Kissing'") and scriptwriter for cartoons such as *Muppet Babies* and *Heathcliff*. When he got word in 1987 that a studio was adapting the underground comic *Teenage Mutant Ninja Turtles* into a children's cartoon, he lobbied producers to let him write the theme song. They turned Lorre down, having already performed a bit of stunt-hiring, asking the 1960s rock band the Turtles ("Happy Together") to provide an original song. Months passed; the Turtles never turned in a song. In a bind, a producer called Lorre and songwriting partner Dennis C. Brown and gave them the gig with some strict parameters—a 48-hour turnaround and a budget of $2,000. Lorre spent most of that money on *Turtles* comics (to familiarize himself with the material) and renting out a Los Angeles recording studio for a few hours. They recorded in the middle of the night because that's when the rates were lowest. Lorre and Brown turned in the demo at 5:00 a.m., with hours to spare.

Show: *Mission: Impossible* (1966)

Story: Argentina-born jazz composer and producer Lalo Schifrin came to the U.S. in the early 1960s as a standout soloist in jazz legend Dizzy Gillespie's band. He found some work scoring films and TV series, including getting an offer from Bruce Geller to make the theme to a new action-heavy spy show called *Mission: Impossible*. Geller told him, "I want you to write something that will get people's attention. Make it sound like a promise that there's going to be a little bit of action," Schifrin later said. Inspired by the exciting and secretive events in which the show's spies find themselves, Schifrin created "Burning Fuse," a hard-charging tune in an irregular, slightly unsettling 5/4 time signature based on the dashes-and-dots language of Morse code. That famous *Mission: Impossible* four-note riff is, essentially, "dash dash dot dot" or "long long, short short." It took Schifrin all of three minutes to write the full 30-second theme song, and less than 10 minutes to record it with an orchestra.

The oldest parrot (once owned by Winston Churchill) was a female named Charlie that reportedly lived for 114 years.

WHAT AM I?

Are you clever enough to solve these riddles nineteen?
Page 405 will tell you what they mean.

1. You don't want to have me, but once you do have me, you won't want to lose me.

2. I have many an ear, but I cannot hear.

3. I am easy to lift, but hard to throw.

4. I can go through glass without breaking it.

5. I have two legs that touch the ground only when I am not moving.

6. I am $3/7$ chicken, $2/3$ cat, and $1/2$ goat.

7. I have 13 hearts but no other organs.

8. I am odd. Subtract one letter and I am even.

9. If I'm walking, I must be running. If I'm running, I might be walking.

10. I am the king of school supplies.

11. I am a verb you say and do every day. Rearrange my letters and I become my own past tense.

12. I am gone the second you mention me.

13. I am the part of the bird that's not in the sky. I can swim in the ocean and yet remain dry.

14. I am always in you, occasionally on you, and, if I surround you, I can kill you.

15. Four fingers and a thumb, yet flesh and blood, I have none.

16. I am strong enough to smash ships, but I fear the sun.

17. I am six letters. Take one away and I am twelve.

18. I don't have eyes, but I once did see. I don't have thoughts, but they once came from me.

19. Different lights do make me strange, thus into different sizes, I will change.

THE UNKILLABLE CASTRO

After leading a coup that launched the Cuban Revolution and deposed military dictator Fulgencio Batista, Fidel Castro took control of Cuba. Castro ruled the country and the Communist Party of Cuba for more than 50 years, specifically as prime minister from 1959 to 1976 and president from 1976 to 2008, retiring in 2011 and dying of natural causes at age 90. Through it all, Castro survived hundreds of assassination attempts. Yes: hundreds.

BACKGROUND

During the Cold War—the long détente between the democratic U.S. and communist Soviet Union—the Central Intelligence Agency went to great lengths in an attempt to destabilize governments deemed unfriendly to American interests, particularly communist nations and ones with ties to the Soviets. Cuba, because it sat just 90 miles away from the state of Florida and had been led by Fidel Castro and his band of communist revolutionaries since the late 1950s, made for an obvious enemy for America's top espionage unit.

According to declassified government documents, Castro survived an official total of 634 assassination attempts. Of those, 467 were conspiracies uncovered and thwarted while still in the planning stage, and the other 167 were either acts of violence and near-misses intercepted by Cuban authorities, or plans that just didn't work out (such as Castro not showing up for an event he was supposed to attend and other such wrenches in the system).

All 634 of those efforts can be traced back to the CIA and its network of spies. If their agents didn't directly make the plans or hold the weapons, they trained anti-Castro organizations in Cuba and other countries to do it, paid for the operations, or sponsored the pro-democratic radio broadcasts beamed out of Florida. Nevertheless, none of their plans to kill Castro ever worked; the CIA may have infiltrated Castro's inner circle with spies, but Castro's powerful intelligence and police forces always seemed to be one step ahead—and they had inside men in American spy circles, too.

Most of the attempts on Castro's life consisted of little more than a well-placed sniper, or the idea to blow up a bridge when the leader's motorcade passed over it. Here are some of the more outlandish, audacious, and ridiculous assassination efforts, which span almost the entirety of Castro's reign as "El Presidente."

THE GIRLFRIEND EXPERIENCE (JANUARY 1960)

The CIA tracked down Marita Lorenz, a German woman with whom Castro had enjoyed a brief fling the previous year. She agreed to be the main player in a plot to kill the new Cuban dictator, seducing him and restarting the romance to gain access. The CIA provided Lorenz with poison pills—botulism toxin, which could kill within 30 seconds of consumption—that she smuggled into Cuba (and past Castro's handlers) in a jar of her cold cream. The pills dissolved into a chalky, gloopy mess and were deemed unusable.

Regardless, Castro had already correctly surmised that Lorenz had shown up out of the blue to kill him. He confronted her, handed her his own handgun, and told her that he couldn't be killed, daring her to pull the trigger. (She didn't.)

THE GREAT AMERICAN SMOKE OUT (SEPTEMBER 1960)

Castro loved to smoke cigars and was frequently photographed, and frequently delivered speeches, with one in hand. (Cuban cigars, then as now, enjoyed a reputation as the world's finest.) When Castro visited New York City to address the United Nations, the CIA derived a plan to place a box of doctored cigars in Castro's hotel room. The cigars were laced with explosives—they'd blow up when lit, theoretically killing whoever held one in his mouth. The box never got into the hotel room; NYPD officers assigned security detail wouldn't let the agents into the building.

Instead, CIA operatives attempted to sneak thallium salts into Castro's shoes, which could cause his beard to fall out right around the time he was participating in a live TV interview. They theorized that this would stress out the Cuban leader, and that he'd reach for the closest cigar to calm himself—which would've been planted by the CIA and laced with a huge dose of LSD. It wouldn't have killed him, but if he were tripping on psychedelics on live TV, it would make him appear insane, thus discrediting him and embarrassing him in front of the whole world.

Failing in their attempt to kill Castro and their attempt to destabilize his regime during an American visit, the CIA tried to import doctored cigars into Cuba after the dictator returned home. The tobacco was mixed with botulinum toxin before it was rolled into cigars: once Castro smoked one, he'd ingest the poison and die instantly. The cigars were seized by authorities before they could make their way to Castro.

A BRIDGE TOO FAR (DECEMBER 1960)

Operatives loaded the underside of a bridge on the way to Baracoa Airport in Havana on a day that Castro was scheduled to take a flight. When the vehicle carrying Castro passed over the bridge, the structure was supposed to explode. If the dynamite didn't kill him (or his driver), conspirators had plans in place to block the road nearby, thus cornering Castro, at which point he'd be attacked with sawed-off shotguns. Castro's team heard about the plan and took an alternate route to the airport.

Reason why men's suit jackets don't have to be buttoned at the bottom:
King Edward VII (1841–1910) was so fat that he couldn't button his, and started the trend.

CHINESE TAKEOUT (MARCH 1961)

Former Cuban prime minister Manuel Antonio de Varona controlled a counterrevolutionary military group in Cuba from his exile in the United States. He arranged an assassination attempt on Castro, sending his soldiers CIA-developed poison capsules. Castro regularly ate lunch at the Pekin Chinese Restaurant in Havana, and Varona persuaded the head chef there to place the poison pills in the leader's lunch, which he would unknowingly consume and then die. At the last minute, the chef panicked, abandoned the plan, and told the government about the secret plot.

THE FIRST SECOND COMING (NOVEMBER 1961)

Many Cubans are Roman Catholics, and in 1961 the CIA considered exploiting that fact to set up Castro to be killed by his own citizens. The CIA was going to stage the second coming of Jesus Christ. The agency planned to use heavy artillery to fill the sky with so much light that it appeared to be of divine origin, and then project the image of the face of Jesus on clouds above Havana. Then they'd have a guy with a microphone hooked up to a massive loudspeaker claiming to be Jesus and urging Cubans to renounce communism, and to overthrow and disarm Castro. This one never made it past the planning stage.

FUNERAL FOR A FRIEND (APRIL AND MAY 1962)

Secret CIA agent Juan Guillot was dispatched to kill high-ranking University of Havana official Juan Marinello Vidaurreta in April 1962. The big idea was that Vidaurreta and Castro were close friends, and that if the former suddenly died, the latter would attend his funeral—where CIA agents would gun him down. A month later, the CIA tried the same thing, setting up a hit on government official and Castro pal Raúl Roa García to get Castro to attend a funeral (and fall into their trap). Cuban police stopped the hit squad, armed with pistols and grenades, before they could get to García.

SUIT UP (JANUARY 1963)

One of Castro's favorite pastimes in the early 1960s: scuba diving. The CIA figured it could use that to their advantage and kill Castro via a tainted diving suit. American businessman James Donovan regularly traveled to Cuba for work and was casually acquainted with Castro. The CIA talked him into escorting their specially made diving suit into Cuba and handing it over to Castro as a gift. If Castro ever wore it, the suit would slowly poison and kill him because it was impregnated with a deadly

Boys like blue and girls like pink...these days.
A century ago, the opposite was thought to be true.

fungus that caused, among other symptoms, painful rashes. Donovan backed out of the plan before the CIA gave him the suit.

NO SHOW (1962)

High-ranking CIA officers and Varona teamed up with some Mafia figures—who wanted Castro dead or gone because they had made a fortune with casinos in the pre-communism days—to poison Castro. Employees at the Hotel Havana Libre were given poison capsules to place in Castro's food the next time he ate at the facility's restaurant, one of his favorites. The plan was called off after Castro didn't visit the Hotel Havana Libre for an entire year.

SHAKE IT UP (MARCH 1963)

The CIA staked out another popular Castro lunch haunt: the restaurant in the Havana Hilton. This time, the Mafia worked out a deal with members of the kitchen staff to place a cyanide pill in a milkshake intended to be served to Castro. One employee got as far as lacing the shake with the deadly poison—and then he spilled it on the floor.

THE SHELL GAME (MARCH 1963)

When Castro went scuba diving, he favored certain spots in the Cuba-adjacent Caribbean Sea. CIA research indicated that Castro favored one particular area of coastline that was densely populated with large-shelled Caribbean mollusks. The CIA acquired hundreds of mollusks from those waters around Cuba and sorted through them until they found one big enough to store a deadly load of waterproof explosives. Agents then painted the shell in eye-catching colors and planned to place it back in the Caribbean Sea in a spot where Castro would be sure to see it and, hopefully. pick it up. That would have triggered a fatal explosion—except the CIA never planted the bomb-filled shell because they couldn't find a good spot to do so.

THE PEN PAL (NOVEMBER 1963)

Rolando Cubela, a Cuban official secretly working with the CIA, agreed to be the trigger man in this plan—or, rather, the pen man. The CIA was supposed to give Cubela an ordinary-looking ballpoint pen. It actually housed an ultrafine needle and a syringe filled with a toxin called Black Leaf 40. Cubela, who had access to Castro, would pass security checks with the "pen," and then, when he got close to the dictator, inject him with the poison and kill him. Cubela was scheduled to execute

Seems obvious: according to 2015 studies, people who wear watches are more punctual.

the plan on November 22, 1963; when President John F. Kennedy was assassinated that same day, the CIA called off the plan and Cubela never received the pen.

TAKE HIM OUT TO THE BALLGAME (NOVEMBER 1967)

Castro loved baseball (he once played semi-professionally, before the Cuban Revolution), and in 1967 he commissioned a national baseball tournament to be held at Havana's El Cerro, the second-largest baseball park in the world. Castro watched the games from his perch in his presidential box. The CIA planned to have an operative stationed at the stadium's electrical control room. When the operative got the go-ahead, he would unplug the main cable supplying electricity to the stadium, plunging it into darkness. During that chaos, CIA-led conspirators were going to lob grenades into Castro's box.

A THREE-POINT PLAN (JUNE 1968)

With direction and funding from the CIA, four members of the Cuba-based Democratic National Front planned to ambush Castro, with several fail-safes to ensure the swift death of the dictator. First, they were going to use a convoy of vehicles to follow Castro's car, then corner it in an alley off a street in Havana. At that point, the four men would shoot Castro with ordinary .22-caliber handguns, albeit outfitted with silencers so as not to arouse too much attention. After that, they were going to fire some rockets at Castro's car—and those rockets were supposed to have been dipped in deadly, poisonous cyanide.

TAKING A STAB (MARCH 1969)

Two men associated with the anti-Castro group called the Agramonte Resistance planned to kill the leader when he was scheduled to speak at a public event in Havana. Their plan was decidedly unsophisticated: the men were going to jump up on the stage and then repeatedly stab Castro with knives. Security forces easily thwarted the duo.

FLIGHT PLAN (JANUARY 1985)

Two revolutionary groups from two different Central American countries got together in Florida to plan an audacious assassination of Castro. The Saturnino Beltran—consisting of commandos from Nicaragua opposed to new president Daniel Ortega—and anti-Castro revolutionaries from Cuba acquired surface-to-air missiles. They were going to fire them from the ground in Managua, the capital city of Nicaragua, when Castro flew in for Ortega's inauguration.

You're taller in the morning than you are at night (unless you stayed in bed all day).

MAKING THE GRADE

For anyone who's ever wondered just what makes that bag of apples "extra fancy," here's a crash course in the grading systems required of various American food manufacturers.

Milk. Grade A milk is deemed fit for universal consumption—pasteurized, pure, and cooled via mechanical or electric refrigeration. Grade B milk is dairy meant to be consumed in manufactured foods, such as in cheese. That is milk cooled in milk cans that sit in cold water taken from underground wells.

Beef. The United States Department of Agriculture ranks beef based on the extensivity of marbling (the mixture of meat and fat) present, along with the age of the cow at the time it was slaughtered—the younger the meat, the higher the score, essentially. The eight grades, from best to worst: Prime, Choice, Select, Standard, Commercial, Utility, Cutter, and Canner. The last four are generally used in processed meat products and are not sold at retail.

Eggs. Via a technique called *candling*, in which they are held up to a light source so an inspector can better determine what's happening inside the shell, eggs are graded on the thickness and firmness of their white, the purity of their yolk, and the smoothness of their shell. Grade AA eggs boast the best whites, the roundest and highest-sitting yolks, and the cleanest shells. (They're ideal for poaching and frying and are sold mostly to restaurants.) Grade A are slightly worse in every area, and are the ones usually found in supermarkets. Grade B eggs are rarely sold to the public and are used in dried, powdered, liquid, and frozen egg products.

Oranges. From best to worst, the USDA rankings for Florida oranges are Fancy, No. 1 Bright, No. 1, No. 1 Golden, No. 1 Bronze, No. 1 Russet, No. 2 Bright, No. 2, No. 2 Russet, and No. 3. Other states have different, but similar, guidelines.

Apples. Extra Fancy apples are ripe but not overripe, and they lack any signs of decay, browning, or broken skin. The more flaws, the more dings an apple gets on the USDA scorecard, sending it down through the rankings of Fancy, No. 1, No. 1 Hail, and Utility.

Butter. The top-rated kind is Grade AA sweet cream butter. It gets that ranking if it's slightly sweet, contains only a slight buttery flavor, and can easily spread at room temperature. If the butter's texture is slightly coarser and contains a pronounced butter flavor, it's going to get a Grade A. Below that is Grade B, made with sour cream instead of sweet cream, and it tends to crumble or to taste or feel watery. It's used in the creation of processed foods, where its flaws are hidden because it's just one ingredient of many.

Marilyn Monroe paid $1,440 (about $14,000 today) for the sheer, flesh-colored, rhinestone-encrusted dress she wore to sing "Happy Birthday" to JFK in 1962...

PET PRODUCTS OF THE RICH AND SILLY

Dogs and cats are wonderful, and we want to pamper our pets. Uncle John thinks some of these expensive and innovative gadgets for pets and their owners are brilliant—and some are just over-the-top.

Item: Macky Crystal Dog Poop Bag Holder

Details: It's important to clean up your dog's leavings from public areas, and many pooch owners use a little container full of small plastic poop bags that conveniently clips onto a dog leash. The Macky Crystal Dog Poop Bag Holder is just such an item, although it's made of golden leather and embedded with 20 rare and fancy Swarovski crystals.
Cost: $325

Item: Rex Specs

Details: Sunlight can hurt a human's eyes, what with its general extreme brightness and harmful UV rays. A dog can suffer the same effects, but because it would be hard to keep a pair of typical sunglasses on a dog, there's Rex Specs. Resembling miniature ski goggles, Rex Specs secure to a pet's head with an elastic strap and offer 100 percent protection from UV rays without going too dark to alter your dog's navigational abilities. And for when your dog inevitably tries to rip them off, they're shatterproof.
Cost: $84.95

Item: Petcube

Details: You may be away from home for the whole day or just a few minutes, but that doesn't mean your dog or cat has to endure that period of time without treats. The Petcube sits on any flat surface of the home or can be mounted on the wall and connects to a smartphone app. The human then uses the app to remotely deliver treats from the well-stocked Petcube at home. The device can shoot out anywhere from one to five treats in a single go, depending on treat size; users can watch their pets scramble via Petcube's built-in internet-connected webcam.
Cost: $149

Item: Swarovski Crystal Dog Bath

Details: Another ordinary product made expensive, valuable, and rare with the addition of diamond-like Swarovski glass crystals, this is little more than a small wash bin, perfect for bathing a small-to-medium dog in the yard with a hose. This one also boasts clawfoot bases made with real silver, like a 19th-century bathtub (but smaller).
Cost: $6,995

...and Ripley's Believe It or Not Museum purchased it for $4.8 million in 2016.

Item: Magniflex Gold Mattress

Details: Italian bedding company Magniflex makes handmade mattresses for humans, and also makes pet beds. The Gold Mattress is dog-sized, but like its for-humans counterpart, it's carefully stitched by hand, with thread coated in 22-karat gold.
Cost: $1,000 to $3,000 (depending on the size of the bed)

Item: Michel's VIP Parfums

Details: There's no denying that dogs can give off all kinds of foul smells. One solution: give your dog a bath. Another solution: spend a small fortune on doggie perfume. Scent maker Michel Germain offers a line of scents specially designed to neutralize that specific gross dog smell. The VIP perfumes come in two varieties: Pink Grapefruit and Mandarin Blossom.
Cost: $80 to $4,000 (depending on the size of the bottle)

Item: The World's Most Expensive Dog Collar

Details: Jeweler I Love Dogs Diamonds launched a line of gem-laden baubles for pets. The crown jewel of the collection is Amour Amour, a dog collar outfitted with 3 pendants, all of them holding a large diamond. Those account for just a few of the 1,600 diamonds (which amount to a total of 52 carats) present on the crocodile leather collar.
Cost: $3.2 million

Item: Wagner Dog Wheelchair

Details: Once they get up there in age, some senior dogs have trouble getting around on their weak little dog legs. This product restores their mobility and independence. Made of lightweight metal alloys and with a comfortable pouch that a dog can slip right into, this product allows dogs to propel themselves around the house with the aid of two large rear wheels.
Cost: $3,000

Item: Big Barker Orthopedic Dog Bed

Details: Those aged dogs don't have trouble just with walking—getting up from a reclining position is tough on them, too. The Big Barker Orthopedic Bed makes sleep more comfortable for dogs with muscle and joint issues.
Cost: $599 to $999 (depending on size)

Item: Catwine

Details: If you don't live with any other people but have cats, and hate to drink alone, you can finally turn your felines into your wine buddies. Catwine comes in two punny varietals: Meowsling (like Riesling) and Purrgundy (as in burgundy). Neither contains any actual alcohol, but they look like wine, come in wine bottles, and are flavored with salmon oil and laced with a buzz-providing infusion of catnip.
Cost: $12

Shiny, happy people: there's enough energy in our bodies
to give off a tiny, undetectable amount of light.

WHAT'S THE DIFFERENCE BETWEEN...

*Uncle John knows pretty much everything—even the subtle nuances that
separate common, similar, and frequently confused things.*

...a Novella and a Novel?

As far as writers and publishers are concerned, a novella is a work of fiction consisting of between around 20,000 and 50,000 words. More than 50,000, and up to 80,000, and the book is a short novel; 80,000 or more words constitutes a proper novel. (If it's under 20,000 words? That's a short story.)

...Hydrophobia and Aquaphobia?

While the presence of *-phobia* in both words indicates a fear or psychological distrust, *hydrophobia* concerns the body's biological aversion to water, which is a dangerous or fatal symptom of any medical condition, given that humans need water to live. An inability to process or absorb water, it's commonly associated with a rabies infection. *Aquaphobia*, on the other hand, is a psychological fear of water—or an unwillingness to swim due to a fear of drowning—usually tied to trauma.

...Corned Beef and Pastrami?

Both cured, salty, pink meats often sliced thin and stacked high on deli sandwiches, they look like similar meat products but are made from different sources. Corned beef, which originated in Ireland, begins with brined and spiced brisket, cut from the breast of a cow. Pastrami, originally from Romania or Turkey, is made in much the same way, but with deckle, a shoulder cut, or navel meat found under the cow's ribs. The only other difference is that corned beef gets a final step of boiling before serving.

...Acid Reflux and Heartburn?

Often used interchangeably to describe a feeling of extreme discomfort after eating certain foods, one is actually part of the other. The medical event in which the contents of the stomach back up into the esophagus is *acid reflux*, a symptom of an ongoing medical condition called *GERD*, or gastroesophageal reflux disease. The feeling of sharp, burning pain in the chest that results from acid reflux is called *heartburn*.

...Figure Skating and Ice Dancing?

There's a fundamental difference between these two winter sports, competition for both of which is done in pairs and at the Olympic level. Jumps are required in figure-skating events, and the more complicated they are, the higher their score. In pairs skating, those jumps usually occur when the male member of the team artfully throws his female partner into the air. In ice dancing, there are no throws, but there are lifts. But there are no jumps—they're actually forbidden. Figure skating derives from gymnastics while ice dancing is a variation of ballroom dancing done on ice.

...Perfume and Cologne?

Often gender designated—perfume marketed to women and cologne to men—the differences lay in chemistry and intent. Both are fragrances sprayed or sprinkled on the skin, with perfume containing a wider variety and higher concentration of scents and oils than cologne. Perfume has a heavier smell than cologne, meaning it's more likely worn on special occasions, with cologne being a daily-use product.

...Genius and Ingenious?

Because they're both used to describe the exceptional individuals among us, *genius* and *ingenious* are often confused. They have different (though similar) meanings and came into the English language separately. A *genius* is extremely smart or creative. Someone described as "ingenious" is a clever, original thinker or problem solver in a novel way. *Genius* is a noun or adjective that comes from a Latin word that means "greatness present at birth," while *ingenious* is an adjective only, derived from a different Latin word referring to the intellect.

...Dirt and Soil?

Dirt is a generic term that refers to whatever you dig up out of the ground—all that brown stuff and whatever it may contain. It's usually full of rocks and silt, and if it gets wet, it doesn't compact very well. Soil is carefully enriched dirt, fortified with microbes and nutrients, that packs well and is used specifically for gardening. Another big difference: worms can survive in soil, but not in dirt.

...Robbery and Burglary?

These are both crimes involving property theft, but the separation lies in the additional crimes perpetuated. If an individual uses violence or the threat of violence to coerce another into giving up cash or materials, that's a robbery. If the individual illegally enters a building with the intention of stealing things from it, that's a burglary.

...a Civil Union and a Marriage?

In the late 20th century, a handful of states introduced a legal arrangement called a civil union, which allowed same-sex couples the same rights afforded to opposite-sex married partners. Also known as a domestic partnership, a civil union allowed two people to enjoy virtually identical status from a legal standpoint as those in a marriage—but on a state level only. Outside of their home state, or on a federal level, that couple's partnership was meaningless. Civil unions aren't all that necessary since

The summer of 1893 was too hot for suspenders.
That's when belts started to take over.

the U.S. government recognized same-sex marriage at every legal level, but they're still offered in a few states.

...Farther and Further?

These are words that describe distance—albeit different lengths and in different contexts. *Farther* is the word to use for a physical, measurable distance or length. *Further* is more appropriate as a conceptual term. "The beach is farther away than the mountains," for example; or, "She wants to advance further in the company."

...Grits and Polenta?

While one is synonymous with American Southern cooking and the other with Italian cuisine, polenta and grits are both made with finely ground cornmeal. The true difference is the type of corn utilized. Southern-style grits are usually made from dent corn, and polenta from flint corn. Dent corn is better for making softer-textured grits, often similar to porridge, while polenta, frequently served as semi-solid cakes, holds its shape when made with flint corn.

...Soap and Detergent?

For agents that clean or remove stains, it's a matter of origin. Traditionally, soaps are made from the salts of fatty acids, derived from the oils of natural sources such as coconut, vegetable, pine, palm, or animal fat. Detergents are created by a long string of chemical reactions, made synthetically and in an industrial setting out of ammonia salts.

...a Territory and a Protectorate?

Territories are generally small areas around the world that fall under the claim of other, more prominent and more powerful nations. They're not fully recognized member states, so they also maintain some autonomy and are locally governed. A protectorate is almost entirely independent and isn't governed by the larger nation, relying on the superpower only for defense.

...Wizards and Warlocks?

In works in which magic is considered a real and powerful force, it's wielded for both good and evil means. Those using sorcery for the good of mankind are wizards, while the evil, tricky, and treacherous users of magic—particularly dark magic—are warlocks.

...Buffalo and Bison?

It's all about the location and the physical details. Real buffalo are indigenous only to Africa and South Asia. The animals in North America commonly called buffalo are really bison. The other way to tell the difference: bison possess a large, shelf-like hump at their shoulders and a beard on their faces, while buffalo don't sport either—but they do have much larger horns than bison.

Your right lung is about 10 percent bigger than your left lung.

OOPS!

Everyone makes outrageous blunders, so go ahead and feel superior for a few minutes.

THAT SINKING FEELING

In September 2022, after spending years on development, the Panama-based tech company Ocean Builders was finally ready to unveil the prototype of its flagship product: the SeaPod, a futuristic floating home designed for a planet with rising seas. According to the company's website, the luxury home (priced from $295,000 to $1.5 million) floats "just like an iceberg" thanks to "1,688 cubic feet of air-filled steel tubes result[ing] in so much buoyancy it is able to push the entire SeaPod up 3 meters above the water."

At the grand unveiling ceremony, everything was going swimmingly (so to speak). Then, not long after the SeaPod was deposited into the water in front of a huge crowd that included the president of Panama, it listed drastically—forcing the crew to quickly abandon house. The home of the future came to rest half-submerged at an awkward 45-degree angle. The company tried to downplay the goof, blaming it on a "ballast tank and pumping system malfunction" that flooded the Jacuzzi. They said the house would be fine after some "cosmetic touch-ups." (We'll try our luck on land.)

CLARKS*WHAT?*

Clarksville, a city in northern Tennessee, has a population of about 170,000 (and was made famous in the Monkees' 1966 hit "Last Train to Clarksville"). That's not to be confused with the tiny town of Clarksburg, also in northern Tennessee, which has fewer than 400 people (and no Monkees songs). So imagine the confusion in February 2023 when a new green highway sign was erected above I-24 near Nashville pointing drivers to "Clarksburg." The sign was supposed to say "Clarksville," but none of the state's Department of Transportation workers noticed the goof. Drivers, however, noticed it almost immediately, and the online mocking commenced: "Well I guess we all know there is a Clarksburg now? Who knew?" Transportation spokesperson Rebekah Hammonds was quick to point out that it wasn't their fault. "Even though our designs are correct, mistakes can happen in the creation of the sign by the sub contractor which then may not get noticed by the contractor." Guess that clears that up.

OF ALL THE CARS...

A six-second video and a still photo posted to a Chinese social media site in April 2023 show the aftermath of a most unfortunate accident in a parking lot. A forklift driver was carrying a large industrial oven past a line of parked cars, but the forks

Invented by ancient Greek mathematician Hero of Alexandria, the first vending machine dispensed holy water.

were positioned very close to each other so they'd fit between the oven's wheels—that resulted in a precarious load that teetered back and forth before falling onto a car's front end. Now, that's unfortunate on its own, but a quick perusal of the photo shows that the lot is mostly occupied by your typical mid-range sedans and hatchbacks. So which car did the oven fall on? A $300,000 Ferrari F8 Tributo.

DOG GONE

One of the best-known modern artists is Jeff Koons. His series of sculptures collectively referred to as *Balloon Dog* have sold for record amounts, including one that sold for $58.4 million. In February 2023, a miniature version of *Balloon Dog*, valued at "only" $42,000, was on display at a gallery in Miami. During the crowded opening, the blue porcelain sculpture stood unguarded on a pedestal, allowing patrons to walk right up to it and view it from all sides.

One patron—an art collector whose name wasn't released—was seen tapping the 16-inch-tall sculpture with her index finger. But she tapped too hard, and the porcelain pup toppled to the floor and shattered into more than 100 pieces. "It was like how a car accident draws a huge crowd on the highway," said another art collector, Stephen Gamson, who watched it happen. (He asked a gallery advisor if he could purchase the shards. The response: "For $15 million? Yeah.") The shards were swept up and placed in a box, and at last report were waiting for an insurance agent to assess them. The good news for Koons: there is now one less *Balloon Dog*, which makes the remaining pieces even *more* valuable.

SEARCH PARTYING

In October 2021, Beyhan Mutlu, a 50-year-old construction worker from Inegöl, Turkey, went out drinking with some friends. It's unclear in press reports how the evening went, but it ended up with Mutlu wandering alone into a dark forest. After a while he came across some people with flashlights who told him they were out looking for a man who had been reported missing earlier that evening. So Mutlu joined the search. Hours later, another member of the search party shouted Mutlu's name.

"Who are we looking for?" he asked. "I am here."

It was only then that it dawned on Mutlu that *he* was the subject of the search party. His wife and friends had called police when he didn't come home and failed to answer his phone. After Mutlu was "found," the police took him home after taking a statement from him. According to reports, he wasn't charged, but his friends were upset by his lack of communication. He said it's not his fault. "Basically, I am paying for my friends' mistakes. What happened is all like a joke."

What's one thing women can do faster than men? Grow hair.

WHY DO CATS...?

Meow for the next installment of our "cat-egory," wherein we explore the bizarre bond between Felis catus and Homo sapiens. (See pages 22 and 368 for "The Feline Timeline.")

BACKGROUND

Starting any question with "why do cats..." might seem futile—who really knows what a cat is thinking? Let's face it: they're weird. Also weird is why so many people love them. As science-fiction author Robert Heinlein puts it:

> Cats have no sense of humor, they have terribly inflated egos, and they are very touchy. If somebody asked me why it was worth anyone's time to cater to them I would be forced to answer that there is no logical reason. I would rather explain to someone who detests sharp cheeses why he "ought to like" Limburger. Nevertheless, I fully sympathize with the mandarin who cut off a priceless embroidered sleeve because a kitten was sleeping on it.

We couldn't verify the mandarin story, but it certainly falls in line with other accounts of feline devotion—like what happened in 50-something BC Egypt when a Roman visitor killed a cat. Even though it was an accident, a mob of angry Egyptians chased down and murdered the Roman.

Why all the fuss over a barely domesticated animal that wasn't all that crucial to survival? Sure, cats killed mice, but they were useless when it came to guarding against invaders or assisting in the hunt, like dogs; or pulling plows, like oxen; or feeding people, like cattle and poultry; or clothing people, like sheep (with the exception of the Vikings—they did wear cat pelts).

What do cats have that those other animals don't? For starters: that cute widdle face! Cat behaviorist Abigail Tucker puts it this way in her book *The Lion in the Living Room*: "House cats are blessed with a killer set of what Austrian ethnologist Konrad Lorenz calls 'baby releasers': physical traits that remind us of human young and set off a hormonal cascade...a round face, chubby cheeks, big forehead, big eyes, and a little nose." That's just one sneaky way cats have fooled us into doing their bidding (instinctively or strategically). Here are some more.

WHY DO CATS PURR?

It's long been one of the great mysteries of science—right up there with why placebos work, how birds migrate, and what dreams are made of. Here's what we know: The vocalization known as purring is a reflexive behavior (the cat doesn't do

it on purpose) that begins when a kitten is a few days old. Born deaf and blind, the kitten reacts to the vibrations of its mother's purring and instinctively purrs back. This makes sense in the wild where predators lurk: a purr is less likely to be overheard than a meow.

The purring continues throughout the cat's life—mostly when it's content, but also when it's scared or stressed. So, do cats purr to comfort themselves, emotionally or physically? Perhaps. Their purrs do have the same frequency as therapies that promote bone healing in humans (but there's no clinical evidence that a cat's purr has healing powers). Even more, some cats purr very quietly, or they don't purr at all. But this doesn't mean they're any less healthy or happy.

Another mystery is *how* cats purr. There's no single organ dedicated to the action, though researchers have discovered its source: the larynx (a.k.a. the voice box). The cat's neural oscillators (a.k.a. brainwaves) travel through the central nervous system to activate the laryngeal muscles (which open and close the glottis) to make purring happen. But unlike meowing, which occurs only on the exhale, purring is independent of breathing. Cats can purr even while they're eating. And because the action is reflexive, cats don't necessarily purr to get us to do what they want. Rather, they dig in to their "bag of tricks" to get themselves into the perfect position to make the purring commence (like jumping on your lap while you're trying to read a *Bathroom Reader* article).

WHY DO CATS MAKE THE "PURR-CRY"?

Another "baby releaser" trigger (like the cat's round face), this vocalization is exactly what it sounds like—a short purr mixed with a cry—and is most typically heard when the cat wants to be fed. In 2009, biologist Karen McComb of the University of Sussex in England conducted a study of how people react to these urgent-sounding calls. Result: "The embedding of a cry within a call that we normally associate with contentment is quite a subtle means of eliciting a response." This type of communication is innate to all cats, but they "learn to dramatically exaggerate it when it proves effective in generating a response from humans." Not surprisingly, the purr-cry elicited responses from the test subjects similar to a baby's cry. Clever cats figure out that this cry is much harder for us to ignore than a regular meow.

WHY DO CATS MEOW AT HUMANS BUT RARELY AT ONE ANOTHER?

Because we can't understand their main means of communication: scent and body language. Cats talk with other cats via physical cues such as pheromone exchanges, posture, eye contact, ear position, and tail-flicking. But when they try to talk to us this way, those cues are rarely understood. Result: the cat resorts to meowing—not unlike raising your voice to a non-English speaker: *"I am talking to you!"* But this doesn't necessarily mean that cats think humans are stupid. Actually, they think we're large, strange cats.

That's right: *Felis catus* is under the impression that *Homo sapiens* is indeed *Felis catus*. That differs from dogs, who act differently with humans than they do with one another. According to cat-behavior expert John Bradshaw of the University of Bristol, "We've yet to discover anything about cat behavior that suggests they have a separate box they put us in when they're socializing with us. They obviously know we're bigger than them, but they don't seem to have adapted their social behavior much. Putting their tails up in the air, rubbing around our legs, and sitting beside us and grooming us are exactly what cats do to each other." Bradshaw adds that cats don't look down on us. In fact, they treat the humans they like with great respect. However, "They do think we're clumsy: Not many cats trip over people, but we trip over cats. But I don't think they think of us as being dumb and stupid, since cats don't rub on another cat that's inferior to them." (That we shelter, feed, and pet them no doubt helps.)

WHY DO CATS MEOW LOUDLY IN AN EMPTY ROOM?

Even when they're not with you, they're talking to you. According to Bradshaw: "Cats learn specifically how their owners react when they make particular noises. So if the cat thinks, 'I want to get my owner from the other room,' it works to vocalize. They use straightforward learning."

That's just one of the ways that the cat's meow has changed since African wildcats became domesticated. The aforementioned purr-cry developed because cats learned that people respond to it quicker than to a regular meow. And kitty-cat meows in general are higher-pitched than their wild counterparts.

WHY DO CATS RUB AGAINST YOUR LEG?

According to PetMD, "If your cat decides that they want to leave their pheromone on you, it should be considered a badge of honor, as it is one step closer to being accepted into their feline world." Cats rely on their sense of smell nearly as much as dogs do. But they don't spray to mark their territory (except in extreme cases). Rather, cats have glands on their heads, feet, and tails that—when rubbed on surfaces—release chemical substances known as pheromones; their scent triggers a response in members of the same species. Cats do this a lot. Reason: to keep the smell fresh, which keeps the animals free from stress. That's why, if you leave your cat for a while, it'll rub you a lot when you come home. This pheromone exchange is one reason why cats enjoy being petted. (The other is because it feels good on their skin.)

In ancient Rome, a *carrus* was a two-wheeled wagon.
That's how we got the word *car*.

Cat behaviorists are quick to point out that this activity doesn't mean the cat "owns you," but that you (and your stuff) are a safe part of its territory. When other cats come across cat pheromones on a person or an object, they'll sniff it for clues about that cat's sex, age, health, and mating status. So if a kitty you've never met smells you and then rubs you, it's gathering info before leaving some its own (like exchanging business cards...on your leg).

One other reason cats rub up against you is to communicate that they want something. If that doesn't do it, they'll meow, "Hey, I want something!"

WHY DO CATS LIKE SHOWING OFF THEIR BUTTHOLES?

It might seem like they do (that thing is hard to ignore!), but they're actually showing you their tails. Like rubbing your leg, cats stick their tails straight up in the air to signal that all is well. Interestingly, this behavior is not shared by the African wildcat, the species that humans (somewhat) domesticated thousands of years ago.

That's because *Felis catus* isn't the solitary animal that *Felis lybica* was and still is. House cats have developed to become social creatures; even feral cats form social groups, or clowders. Tigers, leopards, jaguars, panthers, bobcats, and lynx are all solitary. However, there is one group of big cats that, like the house cat, band together to hunt and raise young: a pride of African lions. That explains why lions are the only other feline species that raise their tails as a greeting (although the lion's tail is curved).

Other Signs Your Cat Likes You: It sleeps on you, which shows that it trusts you when it is most vulnerable. It brings you presents (don't judge the gross ones—it's the thought that counts). It follows you around, bumps you with its head, tries to get in your way, or jumps onto your keyboard. The cutest way is called a *blep*—when the tongue hangs out just a bit. The ultimate sign of cat respect: exposing its vulnerable underside. But this is not always an invitation for a belly rub, so proceed with caution.

These just scratch the surface. To find out why your cat scratches the furniture, pounce on over to page 195.

* * *

A TALE IN THREE HEADLINES

"Beloved Cat Fired from His Job at Local Public Library"

"Beloved Cat Will Keep His Job after International Backlash"

"Library Cat Outlasts Councilman That Wanted Him Gone"

In 2014, Alan Eustace skydived from a world record altitude of nearly 26 miles. It took him 4.5 minutes to deploy his chute, and another 9.5 minutes to reach the ground.

TALKING CATS

While it's impossible to know what your house cat is really thinking (see
"Why Do Cats...?" on page 124), these fictional kitties—as channeled
by human writers—shed a little light on the feline condition.

"I am a predator, hear me roar!... *Meowww.*" —**Gumball,** *The Amazing World of Gumball*

"I don't wanna get kicked out of my house! I'm not a street cat, I'm a house cat! I don't wanna lose my furry basket or my tinkle-ball that I push along the floor with my nose!" —**Snowbell,** *Stuart Little*

"Oh no! I overslept! I'm late! For my nap." —**Garfield,** *Garfield*

"Listen, Cujo, I got some pretty wicked claws under these mitts. Do not, I beg of you, do not make me bring out these bad boys! It gets ugly!" —**Mittens (to Bolt),** *Bolt*

"I am not crazy; my reality is just different from yours." —**Cheshire Cat,** *Alice's Adventures in Wonderland*

"I know it is wet and the sun is not sunny, but we can have lots of good fun that is funny." —**Cat in the Hat,** *The Cat in the Hat*

"Cats the world over prefer to discover things they like on their own and rarely go for anything that's been provided for them." —**Nana,** *The Travelling Cat Chronicles*

"One little bird. Just one. Just one! No one will know the difference. No one. Just one. Then I'll quit. I'll quit after one. Just one. Ha ha! One little bird. One! One!" —**Sylvester the Cat,** *The Looney, Looney, Looney Bugs Bunny Movie*

"Before you start screaming, remember that I'm being honest with everything now, and so yes, Robert, I did break this. In fact, I plan on breaking something else later, but I'm going to wait until you're not looking." —**Bucky B. Katt,** *Get Fuzzy*

"See, we are nice to the mice because it is intelligent to be so. If we act sweetly, they will come in droves. If we hiss, they will run and we will have to chase after them, an unnecessary expenditure of calories." —**Cat R. Waul,** *An American Tail: Fievel Goes West*

"Through the years, I have been known by many names: Diablo Gato, the Furry Lover, Chupacabra, Friskie Two-Times, and the Ginger Hit Man. But to most, I am Puss in Boots...outlaw." —**Puss,** *Puss in Boots*

"Living as I do with human beings, the more that I observe them, the more I am forced to conclude that they are selfish." —**Cat,** *I Am a Cat*

"I would tell you what you want to know if I could, mum, but I be a cat. And no cat anywhere, ever gave anyone a straight answer." —**The Cat,** *The Last Unicorn*

What's limestone made of? Dead sea organisms.

BUSTING WEATHER MYTHS

We're at the mercy of the heavens, and so we've come up with a lot of explanations for why the weather does what it does. However, a lot of those so-called scientific "facts" we've all heard just aren't true.

MYTH: A forecast calling for a 50 percent chance of rain means that it's just as likely to rain as not.

TRUTH: Meteorologists and weather forecasters use a formula called Probability of Precipitation (PoP) to determine the chance of rainfall for a set period. It's derived by multiplying "C," the level of confidence that rain will happen somewhere in the forecast area, by "A," the percent of the area where the rainfall may occur. They aren't predicting the likelihood of rain, but how much of a particular area will receive some kind of precipitation.

MYTH: The deadliest kinds of weather are extreme storms that bring massive rain and winds, such as tornadoes and hurricanes.

TRUTH: According to the CDC, only about 6 percent of deaths caused by weather are from storms and floods. Exposure is the real killer: extreme cold is responsible for nearly two-thirds of weather deaths, and extreme heat about 30 percent.

MYTH: Lightning doesn't strike the same place twice.

TRUTH: It can, does, and will. Some areas are more prone to lightning storms than others, thus increasing the possibility that a bolt will strike in the same spot again. Also, this is why skyscrapers are outfitted with lightning rods—to absorb the predicted electrical shock. The Empire State Building is struck by lightning more than 100 times each year.

MYTH: If you find yourself in a tornado, open some windows in whatever building in which you're taking shelter—it equalizes pressure with the tornado, preventing the storm from tearing through and shattering the panes.

TRUTH: A couple of windows aren't going to change the pressure patterns or buildup from a huge tornado. A tornado could very well break some windows, or it might not; at any rate, stay away from the windows.

Good news: if you discover a cave in most U.S. states, you're allowed to name it.

MYTH: Tornadoes touch down only in sparsely populated, mildly developed areas—big buildings and dense growth slows them down.

TRUTH: Tornadoes hit everywhere; it's just that cities take up a relatively small portion of the overall landscape, so it doesn't seem like they get hit as often. There's nothing scientific about them being able to resist or withstand such a storm.

MYTH: If you hear thunder in the distance, but the sky overhead looks clear, you're safe from lightning strikes.

TRUTH: Lightning can hit as far as 15 miles away from the center of a thunderstorm.

MYTH: If you can't get into a building during a storm, get in a car—the rubber tires "ground" the vehicle, so if it's struck by lightning, the bolts are safely absorbed.

TRUTH: It's safer inside a car during a lightning storm than it is outdoors, but it's not the tires saving you from electrocution—it's the thick walls and roof made of metal protecting you, diverting electricity to the surrounding earth.

MYTH: Pass a field and see a bunch of cows sitting down? That portends a rainstorm.

TRUTH: The logic goes that rain brings with it cold air, and to keep warm, the cows snuggle into themselves on the ground. But it doesn't always get cold before a rainstorm, and cows have plenty of other reasons to take a rest—such as being tired.

MYTH: A lightning "bolt" is a physical object.

TRUTH: Just because you can see, hear, and even feel it (though hopefully not), that doesn't mean it's a tangible object. Lightning is an occurrence or event. As air warms up to 54,000°F in a fraction of a second, positive and negative ions collide and unleash a massive electrical discharge of around a billion volts. That manifests visually as a jagged bolt of light.

* * *

EVERYONE GETS AN EMMY

In television history, only eight TV shows have had all the members of their main cast nominated for an Emmy Award at some point in their run.

All in the Family (4 actors; 4 won)   *Will and Grace* (4 actors; 4 won)

The Golden Girls (4 actors; 4 won)   *Sex and the City* (4 actors; 2 won)

Cheers (10 actors; 6 won)   *Schitt's Creek* (4 actors; 4 won)

Seinfeld (4 actors; 2 won)   *Ted Lasso* (8 actors; 3 won)

Only two of the 16 songs on Alicia Keys's 2001 album, *Songs in A Minor*, are in A minor (but it still won five Grammy Awards).

ODD ODDS

*The odds that we were going to write this page about the specific
likelihood of certain events: 1 in 1 (Uncle John asked us to).*

**That you'll get called for jury duty
this year:** 1 in 50

**That your commercial airplane pilot
is drunk:** 1 in 117

That you'll bowl a perfect game:
1 in 460 (if you're a pro); 1 in 11,500
(if you're an amateur)

**That you'll get a hole in one while
golfing:** 1 in 3,000 (if you're on the
PGA Tour); 1 in 12,000 (if you're
an amateur)

**That you'll seriously injure yourself
the next time you operate a
chainsaw:** 1 in 4,464

**That you'll find a four-leaf clover in
a field of clover:** 1 in 10,000

That you'll find a pearl in an oyster:
1 in 12,000

**That you'll be struck by errant
fireworks and it will kill you:**
1 in 340,733

**That you'll win an Olympic medal in
your lifetime:** 1 in 662,000

**That you'll contract a flesh-eating
bacteria and then die:** 1 in 1 million

**That you'll make it in Hollywood
and become a big movie star:**
1 in 1.5 million

**That you'll be attacked by a shark
and die, if you live within 100 miles
of a beach:** 1 in 3.7 million

**That you'll die as the result of
an injury incurred while using
a tool or appliance designed for
a right-handed person, when you
are left-handed:** 1 in 4.4 million

**That your life will be so remarkable
you warrant a mention in a future
history book:** 1 in 6 million

**That if you become pregnant, you'll
give birth to identical quadruplets:**
1 in 15 million

**That you'll be canonized as a saint
by the Roman Catholic Church:**
1 in 20 million

**That you'll be killed by a toppled
vending machine:** 1 in 112 million

That you'll live past the age of 115:
1 in 2 billion

**That you'll be killed today by a plane
falling out of the sky:** 1 in 7 trillion

There are approximately 450 languages spoken in
South America—the majority by indigenous peoples.

SPEAK OF THE DONKEY

The language nerds over at the Language Nerds website asked their "multilingual followers" to share their languages' version of the English idiom "speak of the Devil"—said when you're talking about someone and they suddenly appear. Here are some submissions from their list, along with some that we found.

Albanian: Speak of the dog, prepare the cane.

Arabic: When you mention the cat, it comes out jumping.

Bulgarian: Speak of the wolf and he's in the sheepfold.

Chinese: Speak of Cao Cao and he'll arrive.

Czech: Speak of the wolf.

Danish: When you mention the sun.

Finnish: When the evil is mentioned, it appears.

French: Speak of the wolf and he's out of the woods.

German: Talk about the Devil, see a pair of horns growing.

Greek: Speak of the donkey.

Hebrew: It's a pity we didn't speak about the Messiah.

Hungarian: Don't paint the Devil on the wall, or it will manifest.

Italian: Speak of the Devil, and its horns shall appear.

Irish Gaelic: Speak of the angels, and you'll hear their wings.

Japanese: Speak of the Devil and its shadow will appear.

Korean: Even a tiger appears when he is spoken about.

Maltese: Look what the sea has brought up.

Moroccan Arabic: Mention the wolf and prepare a bat.

Norwegian: Speak of the sun, and it is shining.

Polish: Speak of the wolf, and here it is.

Romanian: You speak about the wolf, and it is right at the door.

Russian: Remember the s***, and here it comes!

Scottish: Shout sh*te and it comes flying.

Spanish: Speak of the king of Rome, through the door he appears.

Swedish: When you speak of the trolls, they are standing in the hallway.

Thai: Die Hard!

Tunisian Arabic: Mention the lion, he eats you.

Turkish: Speak of the dog and make your stick ready.

Ukrainian: Speaking of the wolf.

Yiddish: If one speaks of the angel, the priest comes.

Indiana's John Q. Benham owns a world record 1.5 million books.
(We wonder if any of them is a *Bathroom Reader*.)

RIDICULOUS RACES

Last one to finish reading the article has to eat this book!

KRISPY KREME CHALLENGE

When and Where: Every February at North Carolina State University

Story: This charity race (not affiliated with the Krispy Kreme Donuts chain) has everything a running race should have, with the delicious addition of donuts. Testing "physical fitness and gastrointestinal fortitude," the runners run a 2.5-mile course from the Memorial Belltower on campus to a Krispy Kreme downtown. Then they have to eat 12 donuts before running the 2.5 miles back. They must do all this within an hour.

The first race was held in 2004 (as a dare) and has been growing ever since—thanks in no small part to appearing on *Sports Illustrated*'s "102 More Things You Gotta Do Before You Graduate" list. Runners often wear costumes (pirates, wizards, bears), and the fastest times come in at around half an hour—not bad for 5 miles and 12 donuts. The real winners are the kids at UNC Children's Hospital, for which the races have raised more than $2 million over the years. (And not surprisingly, several other schools—including the University of Kansas and Florida State University—now hold their own donut-eating races.)

T. REX RACES

When and Where: Every summer at Emerald Downs, a horse-racing track owned by the Muckleshoot Tribe in Auburn, Washington

Story: Until *Jurassic Park*–style genetic engineering becomes a reality, this is as close as we'll get to a real T. Rex race—and it's not that close. This particular contest features runners dressed in oversized inflatable T. Rex costumes running partway around a horse-racing track. The first race took place in 2017 and consisted of salespeople at TriGuard, a local pest control company, which now sponsors the event.

The funniest part is when the "dinosaurs" are running, their inflated heads flopping around wildly, while track announcer Tom Harris is calling it just like a horse race: "About a hundred T. Rexes come down the stretch. And it's Dino-mite, Ramblin' Rex, along the inside. And it's Sexy Rexy and Deeno, Sexy Rexy and Deeno, and it's Sexy Rexy, by a nose!" At last report, the T. Rexes were multiplying: copycat races are being held at county fairs across the country.

BACKWARD CAR RACING

When and Where: In the 1980s in the Netherlands

Story: If you tense up at the thought of backing into a parking space, this is not the race for you. But it sure is fun to watch as a dozen souped-up 1960s Dutch DAF cars—which resemble Volvo sedans, but more boxy—race in reverse. Once drivers began to notice that DAF cars could go as fast backward as they could forward, not to mention that they had better-than-average handling, backward racing was inevitable. The tracks are full of sharp turns, with various obstacles and even ramps. And there were no rearview cameras back then, so the race car drivers had to use their mirrors and manually look behind them. And they drove as *fast* as they possibly could.

Needless to say, there were lots of wrecks. Many of the cars ended up upside down, and the few that crossed the finish line never did so without suffering a few dents.

The Dutch races are long gone, but the reverse-racing tradition continues on many American tracks—including at the Beech Ridge Motor Speedway in Maine, a defunct NASCAR track that hosted the Day of Destruction until 2021. Included in the festivities were dozens of souped-up cars and trucks of all makes and models that raced backward around the track. (Or, at least they started out racing backward. Pretty soon, it just turned into a smash-up derby.)

THE ANTARCTIC ICE MARATHON

When and Where: Every December in Union Glacier, Antarctica, only a few hundred miles from the South Pole

Story: Like any regulation marathon, this race is 26.2 miles long. Unlike any other marathon, the race is on a frozen course, and there are neither spectators nor fanfare. Proving how tough this race is, the record time for the Antarctica Ice Marathon is 3:34:47, compared to the record time for a typical marathon, which is 2:00:25. Of course, the world-record runner wasn't dressed to deal with below-freezing temps, nor did he withstand 20-mph winds. And unlike most other races in "Antarctica," this one is on the mainland—at an elevation of 2,300 feet, and not on an island close to South America.

This race is not for the faint of heart—or for the faint of wallet, as the entrance fee is $20,500 (which includes airfare to and from Punta Arenas, Chile). But it's a must-do for hardcore runners who want to join the exclusive 7 Continents Marathon Club (this southernmost marathon has a sister race at—you guessed it—the North Pole).

If you're reading this on a commercial airliner flying at 30,000 feet, you're about 7 percent of the way to space.

AUSTRALIA DAY COCKROACH RACE

When and Where: Every Australia Day (January 26) at the Story Bridge Hotel in Brisbane, Australia

Story: Bring your own "cocky," or, for only $5, you can buy one at the hotel and then enter it into "the greatest gathering of thoroughbred cockroaches in the world."

The cockroaches—with names like Cocky Dundee and Kim Car Squashian—don't race around a track. Instead, they start in the middle of a 20-foot-wide gaming ring (a vinyl circle in the parking lot), and after a glass jar is lifted off them, the first bug to scuttle out of the ring and into the hands of its "steward" is the winner. (This is after a procession of bagpipers serenades the carrier of the jar on the way to the starting position.) Judging from videos of past races, it seems like not all the cockies are caught; a few escape into the crowd. But they're all hand-painted so their stewards can pick them out. And any cockroach that flies is immediately disqualified.

This race goes back to 1982, when a couple of barflies decided to test the theory that Brisbane cockroaches are indeed the fastest. They're not wrong, as these little guys run an equivalent (if they were human-sized) of 200 mph.

The event has spurred many copycat roach races, so maybe there's one near you. A good place to start looking: local entomologists (including Madagascar Madness: The Running of the Roaches, held by the entomology department at Loyola University). There's also one held every four years in New Jersey—the winner supposedly predicts who will win the Democratic presidential primary.

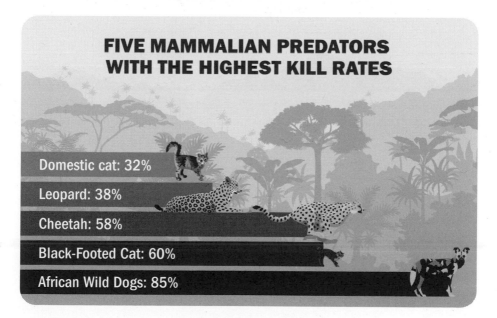

FIVE MAMMALIAN PREDATORS WITH THE HIGHEST KILL RATES

Domestic cat: 32%

Leopard: 38%

Cheetah: 58%

Black-Footed Cat: 60%

African Wild Dogs: 85%

What's the Roman numeral for zero? There isn't one.

THRIFT STORE SCORES

You never know what you might find at a thrift store, charity shop, or secondhand store—maybe a treasure, work of art, or a priceless historical artifact.

A JACKSON POLLOCK PAINTING

In the early 1990s, Teri Horton of Costa Mesa, California, spent $5 on a 66"-by-48" painting at a local thrift shop, a work of abstract expressionism—a bunch of seemingly random splotches of paint on a canvas. Horton quickly tried to make a few bucks on the painting, offering it up at a yard sale in 1992. An art teacher browsing Horton's items saw the picture and believed that it could be an obscure work by the most famous abstract expressionist of them all: Jackson Pollock. Horton had no idea who that was, but she decided to have the painting authenticated and appraised, because it might be worth millions if it's a true Pollock original. Forensic art expert Paul Biro confirmed that it was a Pollock painting, but the International Foundation for Art Research wasn't convinced—it wasn't signed, and there's no reference in any of Pollock's personal records of him painting such a work. Nevertheless, an art dealer offered Horton $2 million for the piece, and a private collector was willing to pay $9 million. Horton turned them both down, believing the artwork to be worth $50 million. She died in 2019 at age 86, still holding on to the maybe-probably Pollock piece.

A RARE PHOTO OF BILLY THE KID

William Bonney was better known by his nickname, Billy the Kid. The Wild West outlaw was a real person and the stuff of legend because of his daring criminal escapades but also because for more than a century, there was only one known photo of the 19th-century figure in existence. Flash forward to 2010, when old photo collector Randy Guijarro browsed the sale items at an antique store in Fresno, California. "I had just a couple of bucks left, and I found three photographs I liked, and of the three, the oldest tintype, I actually kind of chucked it back in the box," he told reporters. Urged by the voice in his head to buy that last photo after all, he said, Guijarro and his wife, Linda, thought that this photo may have some historical significance. They spent five years researching, and persuaded auction house and authenticator Kagin's to take a look. After utilizing the services of an NSA-affiliated facial recognition expert, Kagin's announced that the photo dated to 1878, and depicted Billy the Kid and his accomplices in a gang called the Regulators, hanging around after a wedding in Lincoln County, New Mexico. Guijarro paid $2 for a total of three photos; the Billy the Kid picture went to auction at a price of $5 million.

"Execution by elephant" was practiced in ancient Asia.

AN ANDY WARHOL HANDBAG

In the U.K., nonprofit organizations like Oxfam run their own "charity shops" and generate proceeds by selling donated, secondhand items. A retired man named John Richard spent $30 on a handbag at an Oxfam store in Kingston. He liked how it was constructed from a print featuring a campy image of Elvis Presley, done in a pop-art style that reminded Richard of Andy Warhol. Thinking it might be worth a little bit more than $30, Richard took the bag to a Philip Treacy boutique in London. Treacy usually designs and sells expensive hats, but he also once made a line of handbags out of authentic Warhol prints. Richard's find was the real deal, one of only 10 ever produced. "It is definitely one of our originals," manager Gee Brunet told reporters. "I was surprised he found it in a charity shop." Richard sold the bag, worth an estimated $500,000, and used the money to help his partner open a hair salon business.

A RARE VINTAGE WATCH

In 2014, Arizona resident and watch collector Zach Norris was in a Phoenix Goodwill in search of a deal on a push golf cart. He ended up with a better deal than any watch aficionado could have hoped for. While in the store, Norris sorted through a bin of used watches, because "I'm always on the watch hunt." Among the mundane contents (mostly low-end pieces with dead batteries), he spotted something that caught his attention: one watch that read LeCoultre Deep Sea Alarm on the dial. Norris knew the timepiece was worth more than the $5.99 the store was charging—he was "familiar with the Jaeger-LeCoultre name [and] knew their early pieces, especially divers, were worth a lot of money"—but he didn't know just how much.

After purchasing the watch, he headed to an authorized Jaeger-LeCoultre retailer in nearby Scottsdale. It was there that he learned the watch he'd just scored was one of the most desirable ever made by the company. This particular watch was a rare version from 1959, the first year the model was made, and was one of only about 900 manufactured. The watch was also among the first timepieces designed to feature an alarm for use by divers, adding to its desirability among collectors. After his discovery, Norris posted the watch on a "Vintage Watches" Facebook page and listed it for sale on another collectors' website. He was soon bombarded with offers from across the globe. Eventually, he settled on an offer of $35,000 from a collector in San Francisco. Also part of the deal? In addition to the cash, the collector threw in an Omega Speedmaster Professional—Norris's "dream watch." Not bad for an investment of only six bucks. With the money he made, Norris fixed his truck and paid for his wedding.

Cherokee, Alabama, is home to the world's only coon dog cemetery.

HOW TO BE HAPPY

As Pharrell Williams joyfully sings, "Clap along if you know what happiness is to you / (Because I'm happy) / Clap along if you feel like that's what you wanna do." If only it was that easy! Or maybe it is. Here we present some findings and advice from the world's leading happiness experts, including psychologists, behavior scientists, and more. We don't personally vouch for any of these (Uncle John is happy enough already), but let us know if one of these suggestions works for you!

Some Things, Money Can't Buy

According to Yale University psychologist Laurie Santos, "There's a misconception that happiness is built-in and that we can't change it. The science shows that our circumstances—how rich we are, what job we have, what material possessions we own—these things matter less for happiness than we think." Sure, having loads of cash could help things along, but research has found that you're only slightly more likely to be happy with money than without it. The good news is that these tips and tricks for leading a happier life won't break your bank.

Meditate. It can sound hokey, and you might feel self-conscious when first trying it, but the experts agree that taking time out of your day to dim the lights, turn off everything, and sit and relax for 10 minutes while breathing slowly can make a world of difference toward your overall outlook. You can also add in repeating a positive mantra during this time.

Count to 10. Or count "one Mississippi, two Mississippi, three Mississippi, four" before you respond to something—or someone—with anger. Or take four deep breaths. Whatever you decide on, stick to it, and then whenever you feel yourself about to lash out and make everyone's day worse, pause and reset.

Find a new hobby, and, with it, new friends. No offense to your existing friends (unless they deserve it), but if you're in a rut, a change of activities could do you wonders. Embark on an activity you've always wanted to try—like geocaching or pickleball or deejaying—and join a local group/team/whatever.

Unplug. If you're a serious gamer, serial scroller, or habitual Netflix binger, get outside at least once a day—even if it's just a walk around your block—and look around at things. Listen to the real world...without taking your phone out. Multiple studies have shown that people who spend a few minutes in nature (and unplugged from technology) every day are happier than people who don't.

In Idaho, it's against the law for snakes to bite people on Sundays...unless it's snowing.

Free yourself from Facebook. Or TikTok, or Instagram, or whichever social media platform you find yourself "doomscrolling," making you feel envious of friends who look a lot more happy than you are. Remember that social media gives a very limited, and rarely accurate, depiction of the world around you. So, if you're bummed out all the time, and mindlessly scrolling indefinitely, try giving yourself 24- to 48-hour breaks from your feed and see if that makes you less bummed out. The same goes with the news: if it makes your blood boil every time you turn it on, limit your intake.

Take stock of what you've got. It's easy to fall into the trap of focusing only on the negative. Try to focus on what's positive in your life. If it helps, make a list at the end of the day of three things that went well, even it's as simple as, "I pet the dog and he liked it."

Pet a pet. Don't have a pet? Get one if it's feasible. A dog or cat or turtle won't make your troubles go away, but psychologists have confirmed that spending a little time with your animal friend lowers stress levels and helps you keep things in perspective.

Embrace your pessimism. Pretending everything is hunky-dory isn't the way. Pessimism is a survival instinct that kept our prehistoric ancestors prepared for bad weather and anticipated wolf attacks (and the like). The experts advise that you shouldn't say to yourself, "Self, I have to stop thinking about how much I hate my job." Instead, reframe it into something like, "Self, I am having trouble at work, and I need to come up with coping mechanisms, or find a new job." Acknowledging your problem gives you power, but trying to hide from your problem gives it power.

Listen to what you say about yourself. Or, as the experts put it, practice self-compassion. It's easy to be your own worst critic: "I'm so fat." "Nothing ever goes my way." "FML." When the way you describe yourself is harsher than anything your friends and family are saying about you, you're getting in your own way. A good way to start a change: keep track of every time you begin a thought with "I should be doing..." or "I'll never be able to...."

Be your own friend. How? Pretend you're someone else for a moment. What advice would you give to someone going through what you're going through? We're always more objective when it comes to other people, so if you manage to view your own self as that "other person," you can see your problems—and their potential solutions—a lot more clearly.

Keep a journal. This helps you "be your own friend" by putting a layer of separation between you and your thoughts. Researchers suggest that getting them out there

Rats laugh when tickled.

on paper or on a screen, instead of just seeing them inside your head, can give you perspective you wouldn't get otherwise. If you find that journaling is for you, look up methods to do it effectively and bring positive change to your life.

Don't sweat the small stuff. Easier said than done, but it's important to keep in mind that a lot of what sets us off on a daily basis are the minor issues that wouldn't bother us so much if we were happier. That's where the counting-to-10 trick comes in—it gives you a moment to decide whether whatever is bothering you is really worth the emotional toil in the long run. Everyone knows a drama magnet that's always making mountains out of molehills; if that drama magnet is you, look for some ways to change your perspective.

Let bygones be bygones. We love this comparison: "holding a grudge is like drinking poison and waiting for the other person to die." Letting go of grudges is a surprisingly effective way to allow yourself to stay in the moment. This doesn't mean pretending you were never wronged; it's allowing yourself to drop the bitterness that you've been hanging on to for far too long, instead of continuing to let it affect your emotional well-being.

Shed the external toxins. This is a big one—and for many people, the most difficult. Unhappiness may very well be linked to a toxic relationship. If there's someone in your life that brings you nothing but stress, let them go if at all feasible. Yale scientists have determined that spending time with happy people makes you happier, too.

Eat better. Millions of Americans have the kind of diets that make nutritionists' toes curl. Exceeding the recommended daily allowances of sugar, salt, and trans fats taxes your energy levels, leaving you lethargic and short-tempered. Experts agree that a happiness diet includes less processed food and fast food, and more homemade meals with fruits and vegetables. It might seem like a steep hill to climb, but you'll start feeling better sooner than you think if you do nothing but cut out the fast food.

Sleep better. Are you unhappy because of sleepless nights? Or are you suffering sleepless nights because of your unhappiness? Finding out is crucial. You might have sleep apnea or another condition that makes it hard to sleep well. There are lots of resources to help you find out, some of them free of charge depending on what state you live in. You can also go online and search "How do I sleep better?" to get started. (Use medication as a last resort.)

Treat yo' self. Maybe all you need to pull yourself out of the doldrums is treating yourself to a spa day or a movie day or a hike in the woods at least once each month.

Some zookeepers wear a patterned "zebra jacket." Why? Because orphaned zebra foals imprint on the stripes, just like they would imprint on their mothers' unique stripes.

Granted, for some (especially parents), this can seem next to impossible, so it's important to schedule that day well in advance and tell everyone they'll need to find their own rides/make their own meals/finish their own science projects that day. Because you won't be available.

Learn to say no. Already-busy people who suffer from "yes-itis" add to their own stress when they take on new things at the behest of others. This doesn't apply to everyone, and it's not an excuse to become selfish, but if you never seem to be able to tell someone else "no," set some boundaries in your life. It might upset some people in the short term, but it should make things better in the long run.

Declutter. If you're miserable in your mess, get rid of the mess. Whether you do it in 10-minute chunks or all at once, psychologists and organization experts agree that cleaning up your space can turn it back into your happy place.

Make a list. Another small task that can make a big impact when you're overwhelmed with all the "to-dos"? Make a life list, or plan your week out, or put all your bills on a spreadsheet. Then, every time you complete a task and cross it off that list, you give yourself a little dopamine boost. Here's a tip: if you accomplish something that wasn't on the list, put it on the list and cross it off anyway, and you still get the same dopamine boost!

Seek professional help. As Abraham Lincoln so succinctly put it, "Most folks are about as happy as they make up their minds to be." Notice he said "most" people. Because there's being unhappy, and there's clinical depression. The line between the two can be confusing, and knowing which side of it you fall on can be the key to achieving happiness. Going to therapy or getting other mental health assistance is a lot harder for some than others, but it could be the only way. If you have health insurance, you can usually get sessions partially or fully covered; if you don't have insurance, look up free local resources or support groups. There are people out there, right now, ready to help you.

Be nicer to others. Study after study has shown that performing random acts of kindness makes you feel happier. Sure, you'll save a minute or two by leaving the shopping cart in your parking space, but it'll niggle at you as you drive away, knowing that you've made someone else's day a little bit harder. Contrast that with the triumphant feeling you get when you roll the cart back to its proper place! Heck, even the simple act of smiling at somebody or giving a sincere compliment is rewarded with a dopamine boost, both for you and the recipient. For some tips on how to be nicer, turn to the next page.

A sense of humor is partly genetic.

JUST BE NICER

Following up on the previous article, "How to Be Happy," it might seem like there are more mean people than ever, but there really aren't. They tend to get amplified more—especially in this age of over-information—but most humans are decent folks if given a chance.

"Human kindness has never weakened the stamina or softened the figure of a free people. A nation does not have to be cruel to be tough."
—Franklin Delano Roosevelt

"You can lie to anyone in the world and even get away with it, perhaps, but when you are alone and look into your own eyes in the mirror, you can't sidestep the truth. Always be sure you can meet those eyes directly."
—Betty White

"It is not enough to be nice; you have to be good. We are attracted by nice people; but only on the assumption that their niceness is a sign of goodness."
—Roger Scruton

"Be kind whenever possible. It is always possible."
—Dalai Lama

"A part of kindness consists in loving people more than they deserve."
–Joseph Joubert

"Carry out a random act of kindness, with no expectation of reward, safe in the knowledge that one day someone might do the same for you."
—Princess Diana

"To err on the side of kindness is seldom an error."
—Liz Armbruster

"Don't mistake niceness for weakness."
—Jennifer Granholm

"Niceness is a decision, a strategy of social interaction; it is not a character trait."
—Gavin de Becker

"I think probably kindness is my number one attribute in a human being. I'll put it before any of the things like courage or bravery or generosity or anything else."
—Roald Dahl

"You cannot do a kindness too soon, for you never know how soon it will be too late."
—Ralph Waldo Emerson

"Be nice to nerds. Chances are you'll end up working for one."
—Bill Gates

"Too often we underestimate the power of a touch, a smile, a kind word, a listening ear, an honest compliment, or the smallest act of caring, all of which have the potential to turn a life around."
—Leo Buscaglia

A traditional chef's hat has 100 folds, representing the 100 ways to cook an egg.

GHOSTS IN THE NEWS

People commit weird acts that make headlines all the time—and ghosts are people, too. Well, they used to be, at least.

THE GHOST OF DALE EARNHARDT

In January 2022, police in Las Vegas responded to a call of a man driving the wrong way on the city's 215 crosstown highway, with callers saying that he'd struck several other vehicles and nearly hit some bicyclists, seemingly with intent and purpose to do so. Authorities arrested the driver, 51-year-old Daniel Asseff, and he shortly appeared in court facing charges of attempted murder, driving under the influence, and battery with a deadly weapon, for using his car with the intent to harm. Asseff, who tested positive for heroin and methamphetamine just after the incident, admitted to the judge that he had in fact driven the wrong way on purpose. But he'd had an excuse—he was just following orders. Asseff claimed that the ghost of Dale Earnhardt, Sr., the champion NASCAR driver who died near the end of the Daytona 500 race in 2001, had told him to do it to get the mayor's attention. Judge Ann Zimmerman didn't take that defense into consideration when setting the defendant's bail at $500,000 and ordered him to undergo a competency evaluation.

THE GHOSTS OF LADIES OF THE NIGHT

Linda Hill runs Hill House Manor, a large vacation rental home in Gainesville, Texas. Several renters told her it was haunted, but she didn't think much of it until she was taking a shower one day in 2022 when she heard someone quip, "Looking good!" "I thought it was my husband. I mean, he and I were the only ones in the house," Hill told reporters. But her husband was on the other side of the house, so Hill realized it was probably one of the ghosts her renters had mentioned. Hill, on the lookout since the shower incident, claims to have identified several different kinds of ghosts in Hill House Manor, including old people, children, and spectral prostitutes. Several male renters have reported waking up in the middle of the night to feel something they can't see caressing their faces, arms, or shoulders. That, Hill said, is the prostitutes trying to attract a client. "They try to stir up business, but they can't figure out a way to conclude the transaction, so nothing ever happens." On one occasion, Hill said, one of her ghosts followed a renter home, but apparently got bored and came back to the manor.

THE GHOST OF AN UNDERAGE VANDAL

In March 2023, Coby Todd left his job at a Dallas-area grocery store and returned to his just-purchased Ford Mustang. That's when he says he saw it all go down: a shopping cart, without being pushed by a living person or the forces of gravity and on a windless day, plowed into his car. Security footage backs up Todd's story—there's nothing and no one around that could have made the cart move all the way across the parking lot. Todd's conclusion: A ghost did it. He'd been ghost-hunting at a home in the Frontier Village area the previous day, and he said he felt the presence of a "little boy" ghost. Todd figures the ghost followed him home, and then to work at the supermarket. "Maybe he was trying to play with me," Todd told reporters. "Maybe he's not at peace yet and he was trying to let me know something."

THE GHOST OF A HOTEL PEEPER

Police in Daytona Beach, Florida, arrived at the scene of a reported shooting one night in May 2023. Upon closer investigation, the incident was instead thought to be a botched burglary. Officers discovered 38-year-old Andrew George on his back, screaming in pain, and covered in his own blood, while his companion, 36-year-old Natasha Kachuroi, watched over him. The couple had rented a room at a Travel Inn motel nearby, until they heard what they thought was someone trying to enter through their bathroom window. They asked for a refund from the front desk, only to run away when they felt a "shadow" approaching. The ghostly figure gave chase, and after George fell into a marina and Kachuroi fished him out, the two took cover in a local business, to which they gained entry by smashing a window. When a neighbor heard the kerfuffle and went to investigate, the pair chased her back to her home and tried to break in. George was charged with two counts of burglary; Kachuroi was booked on principal to a burglary and drug possession. The shadowy ghost was never apprehended.

THE GHOST OF A JUDGMENTAL STEPMOTHER

In September 2022, flyers began appearing on signposts and bulletin boards around London offering a free refrigerator to anyone who wanted it, provided that they could haul it away and also didn't mind that it's haunted. In the poster, the annoyed owner of a "cursed fridge" wrote about the "soul within" the appliance. "My stepmother had a heart attack on our kitchen floor in the middle of an electrical storm, and her soul was transferred into the computer unit of our smart fridge." The owner claimed the fridge is judging her eating and food storage habits, such as "how many slices of cheese I've eaten or whether I've properly put the lid back on something."

"Pawtisserie" pastries and "dogguccinos" are on the menu at
Dogue in San Francisco, a gourmet restaurant for dogs.

UNAMUSED

*For every popular theme park like Universal Studios or Disney World, where millions
of people each year pay a lot of money and wait in long lines to experience state-of-the-
art rides and attractions, there are plenty more that quickly flop and disappear. Here
are some amusement parks that failed to become popular vacation destinations.*

Park: The Wooz
Location: Vacaville, California
Story: Navigating big mazes—concocted out of wooden panels and situated outdoors—
was a major fad activity in Japan in the 1980s. So Japanese company Sun Creative
System announced that they'd open 60 maze parks across the United States, with the
first situated in Vacaville, about an hour's drive from San Francisco, selected because
of the area's large Japanese population and significant Japanese tourism. Sun gave
the park a nonsensical acronymic name: the Wooz, or "wild and original object with
zoom." Unlike other amusement parks of the day, with their dozens of rides and
attractions, the Wooz had just three activities—all of them mazes. The park included a
Mini-Wooz for kids under five, the regular Wooz for anyone five and up, and the Super-
Wooz, an extra-challenging maze reserved only for those who finished the normal
Wooz in under 40 minutes. The whole point of the Wooz was to finish the mazes in as
little time as possible—which didn't really justify a car trip or high admission prices.

Not only was there nothing else to do, but visitors found the mazes themselves
tedious, difficult, and unbearable in the hot California sun. A full quarter of maze-
goers gave up and used an emergency exit or squeezed under the partitions just to
get out and get it over with. After a lackluster launch in August 1988, and a monthly
changing of the mazes to encourage repeat business, attendance dropped off and the
Wooz closed in 1992. Those 59 other planned Wooz parks never opened.

Park: Hard Rock Park/Freestyle Music Park
Location: Myrtle Beach, South Carolina
Story: Adjacent to a massive outlet mall complex and accessible by car and boat in
the Myrtle Beach tourism hub, Hard Rock Park was a brand extension of Hard Rock
Cafe, the classic rock–celebrating theme restaurant chain. Like the eateries, Hard
Rock Park set its sights on Baby Boomers—and *only* Baby Boomers. Playing up 1960s
and 1970s music, the opening day concert in April 2008 featured the Moody Blues
and the Eagles, while the park was split up into several themed "rock environs,"
including Rock & Roll Heaven, British Invasion, Lost in the 70s, Born in the U.S.,

and Cool Country. While there were playgrounds for kids and a small water park section, Hard Rock Park plastered old rock memorabilia on walls, held concerts from aging rock stars at a 10,000-seat amphitheater, and presented rides about rock bands, notably a Moody Blues–themed attraction called Nights in White Satin: The Trip and a rollercoaster called Led Zeppelin the Ride.

Hard Rock Park opened in the middle of an economic collapse. Operators couldn't secure the credit line needed to mount a massive advertising campaign, so very few people outside Myrtle Beach even knew the park existed. Hard Rock Park sunk deeper into debt with too few paying customers, and after closing down early in September 2008, operators filed for bankruptcy. FPI MB Entertainment bought the area out of bankruptcy court and renamed it Freestyle Music Park. In addition to revamped environs (Rock & Roll Heaven became Myrtle's Beach, a campy tiki-themed area), Freestyle Music Park offered a brand-new children's section with four rides based on songs few kids in 2009 knew, including Journey's "Wheel in the Sky" and the Steve Miller Band's "Get Off My Cloud." The changes didn't save the park financially, particularly when old, unpaid creditors sued. Hard Rock Park/Freestyle Music Park closed for good in the fall of 2009.

Park: The World of Sid and Marty Krofft

Location: Atlanta, Georgia

Story: Puppeteer and producer brothers Sid and Marty Krofft dominated Saturday morning TV in the 1970s with their shabby, surreal, even psychedelic live-action shows featuring puppets and creatures, including *H. R. Pufnstuf*, *The Banana Splits*, and *Sigmund and the Sea Monsters*. The Krofft shows had a certain look and feel, and they formed a loose franchise—one well-known enough that investors thought it could sustain an amusement park. In 1972, the Omni International Complex opened in Atlanta; it was an entertainment complex containing multiple sports arenas, convention space, and, as of May 1976, the World of Sid and Marty Krofft, an indoor, six-story amusement park that could serve a maximum of 6,000 guests. In the months leading up to opening weekend, Krofft TV shows aggressively promoted the park, offering glimpses of the attractions that awaited, such as the world's longest escalator, a carousel decorated with crystal animals, a live Krofft character theatrical show, and a ride where guests bounced around a pinball machine inside a big round pod.

The World of Sid and Marty Krofft closed in November 1976, just six months after opening. The Kroffts theorized that it was hard to draw people to downtown Atlanta during an attempt at gentrification (via the construction of the Omni). Also, word spread that a family could do everything there was to do at the park in under two hours—but at admission prices (unfavorably) comparable to those of the much vaster Six Flags over Georgia just 10 minutes down the road.

There are more lighthouses in the U.S. (779) than any other country, and more in Michigan (129) than any other state.

Park: Goosebumps HorrorLand Fright Show and Funhouse
Location: Orlando, Florida
Story: Initially a series of mildly scary horror novels written for grade-schoolers and teens, R. L. Stine's *Goosebumps* books grew into a franchise in the 1990s, with a top-rated TV series adaptation and, in 1997, a mini land housed inside of Disney-MGM Studios, part of the Walt Disney World Resort. One of the flagship offerings of the enormously named Goosebumps HorrorLand Fright Show and Funhouse was the Goosebumps HorrorLand Fright Show. It was a staged and scripted magic show featuring *Goosebumps* book characters, including Amaz-O the Magician (who would temporarily misplace a kid volunteer from the audience), Curly the Skeleton, the Lord High Executioner, and snarling monsters. After that, the audience was shuffled into the other big attraction, the Funhouse. It was little more than a maze crossed with a hall of mirrors that ended in a *Goosebumps* gift shop.

Disney received so many visitor complaints that they revamped the land a few months after its October 1997 launch. The renamed Goosebumps HorrorLand Fright Show still had the maze, but it required more time and more skill to get through, and the characters from the stage show haunted the halls. Unfortunately for all parties involved, all fads die. The Goosebumps attractions opened right around the time when *Goosebumps* book sales started to drop. Disney shut down the operation just after Halloween 1998.

* * *

MUSICAL GENRE NAME ORIGINS

Ska. It began in Jamaica in the late 1950s, meshing traditional local musical forms with rock 'n' roll. Cluett Johnson fronted a band called Clue J and His Blues Blasters, and he reportedly asked his guitarist to play in a way that sounded like "ska-ska-ska."

Reggae. A smoother, laid-back outgrowth of ska, one of the first internationally popular songs in the genre was 1968's "Do the Reggay" by Toots and the Maytals. Songwriter Toots Hibbert came up with the slang term to describe a rough individual.

Shoegaze. Moody, dreamy, and full of hazy guitar feedback, the band Moose was dubbed a "shoegaze" act by a writer for British music magazine *Sounds* because its members rarely looked up from the floor (because that's where all their guitar feedback and effects pedals sat).

Jazz. *Jasm* was a 19th-century slang term meaning "energetic," and when a new kind of peppy instrumental music started gaining popularity in the 1910s, *jasm* became *jass*, and then *jazz*.

Potato Parcel will print any message on a potato and send it to someone. (Profanity's allowed, but no "hateful, harmful, or threatening messages.")

THE FILTHIEST PAGE IN THE BOOK

If you're already a germaphobe, just skip this article. If you aren't, you will be by the time you get to the end.

Plastic Payment. Credit and debit cards tend to get handled a lot, fished out of a wallet or purse, and used in ATMs or point-of-sale machines at stores. Dirty hands touch those cards, which leave their germs behind for the next person's card to pick up. Studies show that cards actually harbor far more germs than paper money and coins.

Dish Cleaners. Used to scrub away food on dishes—laden with bacteria from germ-filled human diners—and then usually put away a little wet, kitchen sponges and rags absorb bad stuff as a matter of course. Three out of every four sponges may be laced with harmful germs like E. coli or salmonella.

Pillows. Millions of dust mites live on your face and in your hair. They eat your skin and whatever else they can find on you, and poop where they stand. Then you shed those mites and feces onto your pillow each night. That all makes its way through the pillowcase, making about one-third of the weight of a pillow comprised of dust mites, mite poop, and dead skin.

Keyboards. Germ-carrying bacteria are measured in colony-forming units, or CFU, and the keyboard for a computer in the average office is home to about 3.5 million CFU—in just one square inch. (A toilet seat packs just 172 CFU per square inch.)

Gas Pumps. Not many people wash their hands before they fill up their car's tank. So many people touch that pump handle each day, and leave their germs behind, that scientists estimate that the average handle is thousands of times dirtier than a public toilet seat—to be precise, it's covered in nearly 12,000 times as much bacteria.

Toothbrushes. We brush our teeth in part to get rid of the swarms of bacteria and other nasties hanging out in there. Rinsing off the toothbrush afterward doesn't get rid of all of them, so they're left to fester. Then, the brush is likely sprayed with microscopic fecal matter several times a day: if you flush the toilet with the lid up, the force sends an invisible spray of particles a few feet away—like to the bathroom counter where a toothbrush sits.

Menus. You walk into a restaurant, get handed a menu, hand it back to the server, and they hand it to someone else. That's a lot of opportunities to absorb germs. One study found that the average menu harbors 185,000 bacteria. Yum!

Crocodiles can't stick out their tongues.

A PUZZLING PAGE OF SLANG

Every subculture, community, and hobbyist group has its own shorthand, in-the-know terms and phrases used to describe the unique aspects of its members' common interest. Even jigsaw-puzzle enthusiasts are a collective, and they have their own vernacular.

Whimsy piece: a puzzle piece that resembles an object or figure, such as a human or an animal. It's either a twist of luck or purposely done by the puzzle maker.

Anti-whimsy piece: literally any puzzle piece that takes a random shape, what with its jutting knobs, rounded rectangles, and indentations, and located next to a whimsy piece.

Innies: the small inlets or holes in a puzzle piece. Some puzzle people also call them *blanks*, *sockets*, and *slots*.

Outies: the rounded parts of the piece that jut out, which connect to other pieces' innies. They're also widely called *tabs*.

Interjambs: the formal name for *outies*, although puzzlers may also call them *knobs*, *narps*, *nerps*, or *nubbins*.

Edge pieces: the straight-sided pieces that form the outer "frame" of the puzzle. Puzzlers also refer to them as *flat sides*, *outside pieces*, and *side pieces*.

Dancing man: not quite a whimsy piece, but a randomly cut one that vaguely resembles a human in movement, with an outie on top (like a head) and blanks all around that make the rest look like a body.

Dissectologist: the technical term for a jigsaw puzzle enthusiast.

Dissected maps: a now obscure name, this is what jigsaw puzzles were called in the 19th century. Puzzles began as maps, printed on wood, and then cut into pieces, or "dissected."

Pre-production: setting up to make a puzzle. It involves separating out all the pieces into edge pieces and others, turning them all face up, and sorting by color.

Anchoring: that magical moment, deep into a puzzle construction, when you locate that one piece that allows you to connect a big chunk of completed middle to an edge piece.

Hole in one: a piece that a puzzler spots that they think will fit with another, and the first combination of innie and outie goes together without any spinning around or reconfiguration required.

Working blind: putting together a puzzle while refusing to refer to the image of the completed build printed on the box.

Alaska is the only state name that can be typed on one row of the QWERTY keyboard.

WEIRD ANIMAL NEWS

This year's herd of strange creatures includes a friendly scavenger, a reverse Goldilocks scenario, a dog pretending to be a cat, and cows that talk to space.

HI

As of this writing, there are no accounts of a cow jumping over the moon (we'd have written about it). But the bovines in this story did manage to send a message beyond the biosphere, with a little help from a Kansas farmer named Derek Klingenberg. He subscribes to a satellite-imaging system called FarmersEdge, which helps farmers monitor their crops from orbit. Klingenberg studied the images of his farm, and then—using the angles of the shadows—he was able to determine when the satellite flies over each day. With that information, he used his feed truck to arrange 300 head of cattle into this formation:

Hi

He checked the satellite photo later that day and said, "Holy cow. It worked."

But Klingenberg's cows weren't just saying hello to a satellite. This was in March 2018, when tech company Tesla sent an electric car into orbit with a mannequin in the driver's seat. To sum up, a farmer on Earth helped the cows in his field say hi to a dummy in orbit.

HIS BARK IS BIGGER THAN HIS BITE

Liu Wen, a mom in Henan, China, took her young son to the People's Park of Luohe zoo in 2013. They didn't just want to see the animals, they wanted to hear them, too. The two arrived at the enclosure marked "African lion" and waited for the big, brown, furry beast to roar. When it finally did, it barked. Like a dog—which, in fact, it was.

After the woman complained, a zoo administrator confirmed that the caged "lion" was actually a Tibetan mastiff. He said the real lion was away at a breeding facility, and the dog belonged to a staffer; it was staying at the zoo "over safety concerns" (he didn't elaborate). According to the *Beijing Youth Daily*, this wasn't an isolated incident: "Three other species housed incorrectly included two coypu rodents in a snake's cage, a white fox in a leopard's den, and another dog in a wolf pen." Liu Wen was livid: "The zoo is absolutely cheating us!"

NOTHING TO SEE HERE, CARRION

If you live in Somerset, England, and you see perched above your garden an enormous vulture, his name is Gilbert, and he likes to visit his neighbors and say "hello." That's according to Alan Wells, who manages the nearby Pitcombe Rock Falconry in Bruton. Known as a turkey vulture and usually found in North America, this friendly

The first LEGO bricks were made of wood.

scavenger with a six-foot wingspan and featherless red head ended up in Wells's care after the Prague Zoo closed during the COVID-19 pandemic. Wells had tried to train the bird to fly freely, but Gilbert, it seems, would rather visit people in their gardens.

The affection isn't always mutual, as Wells has received a bevvy of complaints. But "a turkey vulture only eats dead stuff," he told the BBC, "so if your pet, guinea pig, or rabbits are running around your garden, they're perfectly safe. He's not interested in anything that lives." (That last sentence makes it a bit unsettling that the vulture likes to sit on people's fences and just watch them.)

COME OUT, COME OUT, WHOEVER YOU ARE

All through the winter of 2022, residents in a South Lake Tahoe, California, home heard "rumbling, snoring-like" noises coming from under the house. They ignored the sounds at first, but as the noises got progressively louder—and the house started vibrating—they suspected it might be one hibernating bear. So they called in the BEAR League, a nonprofit group dedicated to helping people coexist with bears in peace.

The professional handlers made loud noises in an attempt to scare the animal. It worked! An adult brown bear emerged from the crawl space opening. But that still didn't explain why the noises were so loud. Then another bear emerged. Then another. Then another. Then another. That's right—the unsuspecting residents had *five* bears sleeping beneath them all winter: a mama and four cubs (one of whom she'd adopted). BEAR League executive director Ann Bryant explained to HuffPost, "Each winter, about 100 to 150 of our bears attempt to hibernate under homes here at Tahoe. The BEAR League is kept very busy moving bears out of these crawl spaces, often several bears each day." But not usually several out of the same house.

SERVES THEM RIGHT FOR SCARING US

Imagine that you're walking in a narrow walkway and all of a sudden, there's a huge, scary spider right in front of you! Most people's reaction plays out like this: "So they saw [the spider] and really quickly...they stop walking...They freeze...They look at it, and then within a couple seconds, they run away." It might surprise you to know who "they" are in this scenario: spiders. Harvard researcher Daniela Roessler told NPR the odd experiment came about by accident when she placed a 3D-printed spider next to a real jumping spider, and the real spider jumped away. So she set up a study nicknamed "Arachno-Arachnophobia" to determine if spiders are indeed afraid of other spiders.

First, she placed a 3D-printed sphere in front of the jumping spiders. No reaction. Then she tried the 3D-printed spider, and then an actual spider corpse. Result: the jumping spiders (which do eat their own, and get preyed upon by many larger arachnid species) were most afraid of the spider models with eyes. The takeaway, says Roessler, is that spiders are just as scared of one another as we are of them. "For all arachnophobes out there, we found a thing you have in common with spiders. Time to reconsider and sympathize."

After Chris Carter read an article reporting that 3.7 million people claimed they had been abducted by aliens, he created *The X-Files*.

YOU COLLECT...WHAT NOW?

We salute odd people who collect odd things! Here are some of the oddest examples. We didn't include any details—suffice it to say that the sizes of these collections range from the dozens (celebrity hair locks) to the hundreds (Big Mouth Billy Bass singing wall fish) to the thousands (fossilized feces).

traffic cones

airplane barf bags

celebrity hair locks

doll eyes

garden gnomes

vacuum cleaners

full vacuum cleaner bags

nails

bras

dice

dust

Spam

coprolite
(fossilized feces)

antique mousetraps

paper clips

napkins

napkin rings

moist towelettes

toilet paper

back scratchers with
little hands

fortune cookie fortunes

coffee cup lids

Super Soakers

Troll dolls

Monopoly board games

Pringles potato chip
containers

Slinkies

tiny chairs

oversized novelty items

ChapStick

surfboards

mammal wieners

bowling balls

road maps

marbles

PEZ dispensers

IBM laptop computers

computer
microprocessors

novelty pens

condoms

bricks

tin boxes

toasters

brainteaser puzzles

film projectors

pizza boxes

vintage photos of men
posed in a row

bad taxidermy

bagpipes

shoe treads

toenail clippings

umbrella sleeves

belly button lint

cellphones

hot sauce

sugar packets

banana stickers

Joker playing cards

water bottle labels

hotel "Do Not Disturb"
door signs

talking clocks

Big Mouth Billy Bass
singing wall fish

toothbrushes

police hats

stuffed toy cows

haunted dolls

rubber duckies

human teeth

Thinking of attending a video game design school?
There are more than 2,000 of them worldwide.

FOUNDING FATHERS

You know the names.
Here's a look at the real people behind them.

EDWARD KINGSFORD

Henry Ford, one of the world's most successful and wealthy early automakers, was as much of an environmentalist as he was an enterprising industrialist. While hundreds of thousands of cars rolled off his assembly line, he hated how his business left a lot of waste in its wake. He owned a sawmill in Iron Mountain, Michigan, that supplied his factories with all the wood it needed (in the early 20th century, automotive bodies and other car parts were made mostly from wood). While camping with inventor Thomas Edison and his cousin-in-law Edward Kingsford in 1919, Ford pondered if there existed a way to use the scrap wood and sawdust from his Iron Mountain facility. Someone suggested charcoal briquettes, compressed coal-like bricks used as a slow-burning fuel source, patented in 1895 by W. P. Taggart but not widely used. Ford asked Kingsford, who operated a Ford dealership in Iron Mountain, about acquiring 313,000 acres of forest land in the area—for use in auto parts *and* briquettes. Kingsford brokered the deal, and, with Ford, put a charcoal-making process into action. Scrap wood was collected, dried, burned, and then mixed with starch and compressed into nuggets, later sold in Ford dealerships alongside cheap charcoal grills. Private investors bought the briquette division from Ford in 1951 and named it after its originator, then started selling Kingsford charcoal briquettes in giant blue-and-white bags at hardware stores.

JULIUS RICHARD PETRI

The Petri dish is standard laboratory equipment, and it's very simple in design. It's basically a glass nesting dish, with a glass cover that fits smoothly on top. It was designed by a scientist assisting another famous and pioneering scientist at the time (whose name isn't nearly as widely known today as Petri's).

In 1877, German army doctor Julius Richard Petri was assigned to work at Berlin's Imperial Health Office for Dr. Robert Koch. A major figure in bacteriology, Koch discovered the root causes of cholera, anthrax, and tuberculosis, and his lab grew lots of bacteria for study. That required a controlled, sterile environment; leaving samples exposed to the air quickly and easily led to contamination. Bell jars didn't work—they were too heavy, prone to breakage, and didn't accommodate microscopic examination. Tired of making do with pieces that didn't quite work, Petri forged his own dish: flat, made of glass, and accompanied by a specially made airtight lid. It prevented airflow, encouraged bacterial growth, and could be easily slid under a microscope. Petri dishes used by scientists today are pretty much exactly like the first ones, although they're more commonly made from plastic or acrylic instead of glass.

ROSE TOTINO

The American food scene in the wake of World War II presented a unique opportunity. Countless soldiers who fought in or near Italy developed a taste for a local dish consisting of baked dough topped with tomato sauce, cheese, and various meats and vegetables. It was called pizza, and it was still such a novelty in the U.S. in 1951 that when Rose Totino met with a bank loan application board to get $1,500 to open a restaurant serving the dish, she had to bring samples so the moneymen would know what she was talking about. With the loan in place, Totino opened Totino's Italian Kitchen in northeastern Minneapolis. Meant to be a simple takeout counter, crowds of people wishing to sample this "pizza" thing congregated to such a degree that Totino made her establishment a sit-down restaurant.

The eatery was so successful that when the frozen food industry developed and exploded in the early 1960s, Totino got involved, adapting her signature pizza recipes into one of the first pizzas to be nationally distributed to supermarket freezers. So many full-size, authentic (but frozen) pizzas sold that Totino sold the frozen food business to Pillsbury in 1975 for $22 million. Pillsbury would go on to launch a line of inexpensive, rectangular "Party Pizzas" and mini calzones called "Pizza Rolls" under the Totino's brand name. Totino became a vice president at Pillsbury (the first female one in the company's history) and kept operating her restaurant until 1987, when she sold it to her grandson.

RUSSELL KELLY

The post–World War II economic boom created a surplus of office work. Women had entered the workforce during the war, and afterward were widely employed in secretarial and clerical positions. Even so, Detroit's business community couldn't keep up with the workload, so William Russell Kelly created Russell Kelly Office Service. Companies outsourced their typing work to him—he'd pick up documents, take them to his home office, and type up what needed to be typed. That, or he'd delegate the work to one of his two employees.

Before long, Kelly's clients started inquiring about the need for more help, wondering if he could send someone to cover a day's work for a secretary who called

The first toy fad created by TV commercials: the Hula-Hoop in the 1950s.

out sick or didn't show up. Kelly sent his employees out on those jobs, deciding to offer and advertise such "temporary employment" services—creating the first-ever temp agency. He renamed the company Kelly Girl Service, Inc. in 1957, after the nickname his employees had coined for themselves in order to easily identify themselves when reporting to a new gig for the first time. As Kelly Girl moved into other industries, and hired more men, the company changed names again, in 1966, to Kelly Services.

KLAUS MARTENS

During a furlough in 1943, 25-year-old German army doctor Klaus Martens took a ski trip to the Bavarian Alps, not far from his hometown of Seeshaupt, outside of Munich. He suffered a crash and badly broke a foot. Recovering at home, and unable to find an orthopedic shoe that offered ample support and pain relief, he endeavored to build his own footwear—like the boots worn by him and so many other troops on every side of the fighting, but actually comfortable. He was still getting his designs together two years later when World War II ended and countless Germans looted stores. Martens stole cobbler tools, leather, needles, and thread from a Munich shoe store and fashioned himself a comfy pair of boots somewhat resembling what he'd had in mind. Months later, while in Munich meeting with investors, Martens ran into college friend Herbert Funck, now a mechanical engineer.

Funck became fascinated with Martens's odd-looking but practical shoes, and he asked to become his friend's partner in the business of boot making. Funck redesigned everything, using epaulets off his army uniform as eyelets and buying a Nazi uniform for its leather leggings, which he repurposed into the bulk of the boot. For the soles, bounce and comfort were key, and Martens decided he should make them like tires...or *out* of tires. Because he was a German national, he couldn't trade with the American military presence stationed in Munich, but Funck, born in Luxembourg, could, and he negotiated the purchase of a major rubber store in the form of tires from disused Nazi warplanes. To make them even bouncier, Martens and Funck injected the soles with air bubbles; to make them more durable, they sealed the leather directly to the sole.

Handmade shoe production of "Doc Martens" began in 1947 in Seeshaupt. The shoes sold so well that Martens and Funck had to open a Munich factory in 1952, and by decade's end, Doc Martens offered more than 200 styles. In 1960, production moved to Northamptonshire, England, the most industrious shoemaking region in Europe. The new factory opened for business on the first day of April 1960, inspiring the model name of the company's most famous offering: the 1460, the yellow-stitched boot adopted by numerous countercultural groups—including hippies, mods, punks, and Seattle grunge scenesters—in the decades following.

Geologists believe there are undiscovered caves large enough to house entire cities.

STRANGE CRIME

Some true crime stories are tough to categorize. They're just...strange.
(Shameless plug: for more stories of bizarre criminal capers,
check out the Portable Press book Strange Crime.)

MAKE YOURSELF AT HOME

Early one morning in September 2021, at around 4:00 a.m., Raymond Pearson left his Canton, Ohio, home to go to work. While pulling out of the driveway, he saw a shirtless man walking down the sidewalk. Pearson stuck around and waited for the man to get beyond his house before continuing. "When I left, my family was sound asleep," he told the Canton *Repository*. "My family was safe." Thankfully, no harm came to his wife, son, or brother, who were all sleeping inside. But the same can't be said for their leftover chicken. The shirtless man doubled back, broke in through a window on the front porch, and raided Pearson's fridge. He was just getting started.

More than two hours later, Pearson's wife, Stacy Steadman, rose to wake their teenage son for school and noticed that the light was on in the guest bedroom. When she peeked in, there was the man, sound asleep on the bed. Steadman woke up Pearson's brother, Bryant, who subsequently chased the man out of the house.

It was later determined that while the family members were sleeping, the intruder lit candles in the bathroom, swam in the pool (where he left behind his soggy pants), and stole a pair of their son's underwear before going to sleep in the guest room. Police found the man down the street and arrested him. He was reportedly under the influence of several substances. Steadman still can't believe what happened. "He just helped himself to everything in our house."

MY PRECIOUS

When Ian Campbell saw the diamond ring, he "fell into a trance" (as he later explained during his trial). The 54-year-old Irishman was vacationing in the Mediterranean resort city of Marmaris, Turkey, in 2018 when he wandered into a swanky jewelry store. When the jeweler wasn't looking, Campbell pocketed the "brilliant 2.5 carat weight [ring] with a market value of $40,000 (€35,000)." When confronted, Campbell turned around and swallowed the ring, and then denied it. He stuck to his story...until an ultrasound revealed the ring in his belly. Police gave him the option of passing it naturally, or else he would undergo surgery to retrieve it from his abdomen. After 36 hours with no outward motion, Campbell consented to having the diamond ring surgically removed. At his trial, he explained that he was still

Experts say: shuffle a deck of cards seven times to make sure it's sufficiently mixed.

mourning the tragic loss of his wife, along with her diamond wedding ring. When he saw the ring in the store, "The jeweler was telling me something, but I couldn't even hear him because I was in a trance...I feel a strong urge to take those rings, especially the ones with higher carat diamonds." Campbell was found guilty and sentenced to eight years in prison, and at last report plans to appeal.

A NIGHTMARE ON THE RIVER

At a riverfront park in Huntington, West Virginia, in August 2021, Jonathan Ascencio was having dinner with his two-year-old daughter and five-year-old son when a strange woman wandered up and sat down at their picnic table. "I know, as a father, that this person's on drugs," he told WSAZ News. "I start packing up the stuff to leave, and she...told [the kids] to 'go get in the boat,'" Ascencio recalled while fighting back tears. Ascencio's son, who has autism and is nonverbal, and his daughter both started following the woman toward the water. Ascencio leapt up and was able to retrieve the two-year-old, but the woman had gotten ahold of the five-year-old's hand and led him to the riverbank, where she then threw him in the water! Ascencio was still holding his daughter, and, "I felt kind of powerless. I could jump in and get him," but that would leave the toddler alone "with that crazy lady." Right then, the "crazy lady" jumped into the river and started swimming toward the boy. Ascencio yelled for help. Thankfully, a nearby woman ran over and was able to get the boy out of the water. He was mostly unharmed (there were scratches on his arm), and it was a good thing that he'd recently been taught how to swim.

Police later arrived to find the woman still treading water. They ordered her to come out and were met with the response, "That's not going to happen." Then she claimed that they had no jurisdiction because she was in "international waters" (she wasn't). By the time firefighters retrieved her in a boat, she'd been treading water for 40 minutes. Later identified as 41-year-old Kimberly Maxwell of Ashland, Kentucky, she was charged with "kidnapping, malicious assault, and child neglect creating the risk of death or injury." Ascencio said that the only reason he took his kids to the river was because KFC was closed inside, and that his son liked to look at the lights on the bridge reflecting on the water. But then, "It turned into a nightmare."

THEY ONLY FLY AT NIGHT

In April 2023, a 26-year-old man from Chicago (identity not released) was detained at a security checkpoint at Boston's Logan International Airport. For what? A straw. At least, what looked like a straw. Upon closer examination, TSA agents determined that it's actually a "self-defense weapon" made of titanium, a light but strong metal. The man was arrested, since not even pocketknives are allowed to be carried on to planes. And this was no mere pocketknife. "It's super tough and long enough to be used like a dagger," says the manufacturer's website. "Its chiseled tip is sharp enough to puncture most synthetic materials." And non-synthetic materials, too, such as human skin—which is presumably how this "hidden in plain sight" weapon got its name: the "vampire straw."

THE STUFF OF LEGENDS

In July 2022, police in Manchester, England, were searching the home of a suspected car thief named Joshua Dobson, 18, but they couldn't find him anywhere. Then an officer noticed something strange: a very large stuffed teddy bear seemed to be "breathing." Reason: Dobson was hiding inside it...but not for long. He removed himself from the bear and was taken into custody. He was later sentenced to nine months in a young offender's institution. A police spokesman later confirmed that Dobson was "stuffed behind bars," adding, "Hopefully, he has a bearable time inside."

* * *

PACKING IT IN

Alfred Packer could tell a tall tale better than anyone, so it's no surprise that he was able to convince 20 men that he knew well the hills around Breckenridge, Colorado (he may or may not have). Under Packer's directive, the group left for the Colorado Territory in early November 1873 on a search for gold.

By late January, the men were bedraggled, hungry, and stumbling through heavy snow when the chief of the Ute took pity on them and told the would-be miners they could stay with his people until the snow melted. Five of the miners were determined to strike it rich, though, and paid Packer to set off with them to Breckenridge in early February, carrying a 10-day supply of food.

Two months later, Alfred Packer arrived alone at the Los Piños Indian Reservation in Colorado, claiming to have been abandoned by his companions. He said they had left him, one by one, and he'd spent the waning winter alone, hungry, and frightened. But the men who had remained with the Ute were suspicious of Packer's obviously nourished physique and reported him to authorities. In May 1874, Packer admitted that he'd actually been with the five men until their ends: after being stranded in the snowy wilderness, they'd died one by one of disease, starvation, accidents, and, in one case, self-defense. And as the miners died, he'd eaten pieces of them, and had even carried some of their flesh around for weeks to stave off starvation. No one knew what to make of the story. Then, in August 1874, the bodies of the five miners were found...laid out together at a campsite in the mountains. It appeared that they'd all been killed (one even showed defensive wounds as though he'd fought back). Packer was eventually convicted of murder and sent to prison.

Medieval knights rarely wore suits of armor—
only when it was absolutely necessary for battle.

COMMON HOUSEHOLD APPLIANCE TRIVIA

The other day we were standing by the BRI microwave when somebody asked Uncle
John for an article idea. He stood there for a minute, then said, "appliance trivia."

Gas stoves were fairly commonplace in homes by the mid-19th century, while the electric range didn't come on the scene until 1893. It made its public debut in a Chicago World's Fair exhibition showcasing electricity in the kitchen. But it took so long for American communities to adopt electricity that the cost of electric stoves couldn't compete with gas; electric stoves weren't regularly installed in home kitchens until the early 1930s.

Why is a stove sometimes called a "range," anyway? It's a marketing term, highlighting for catalog shoppers an all-in-one appliance consisting of burners for stovetop cooking combined with an oven for baking and roasting, which offered a "range" of possibilities in a single unit.

An electric dishwasher is more or less a steam machine, and the combination of heat and hot air can be used to cook food. Give it a try when making couscous, soft-boiled eggs, or steamed fish. (Just don't put any other dishes in there—or soap.)

Truly a labor-saving device, the first electric clothes washer was marketed in 1908 by the Hurley Machine Company. Consisting of a heavy moving drum and a galvanized tub, it was called the Thor. A user still had to hang their clothes to dry—the first practical electric dryer wasn't invented until 1938.

Inventors attempted a dryer before 1938. In 1892, the first patent on a clothes dryer went to George T. Sampson, who funneled heat from a gas stove into a drying chamber. It didn't catch on. In the 1900s, J. Ross Moore hung wet clothes in a drying shack where he installed a small stove; the hot air inside slowly dried the clothes. He'd refine the concept repeatedly until 1938, when the Hamilton Manufacturing Company would market an appliance based on his design.

Microwaves weren't widely adopted until the late 1970s and early 1980s, when the price and size of the quick-cooking gadgets came down. When weapons-maker

Raytheon introduced the first microwave oven in 1947, the Raytheon RadaRange, the thing resembled a refrigerator, standing six feet tall and weighing 750 pounds. The cost: $2,000 to $3,000 (about $41,000 in 2023 money).

Before the invention of the odorless, nontoxic freezing chemical Freon in 1928, which enabled "deep freezers" (as they were called upon launch in the 1940s), Americans made their own freezing chambers. Provided they lived in a cold enough climate, they'd make an ice pit in the yard—a dug-out hole lined with straw.

One of the most popular new kitchen gadgets of the last decade: the air fryer, an all-purpose cooker that uses rapidly circulating hot air to cook food to oven quality at microwave speeds. It's an old idea. Inventor William Maxson developed a similar device in the 1940s and sold his Whirlwind Oven (developed during the war to feed hot meals to military servicemembers during flights) to commercial airlines. That made airplane meals—premade and frozen, then heated up in the air at the time of consumption—a reality. Those ovens were the standard method for making airplane food until the adoption of the microwave.

Ever noticed your Wi-Fi stops working for a minute, or the movie you're streaming on your phone becomes momentarily garbled, when you throw a Hot Pocket in the microwave? It's because Wi-Fi and microwaves operate on the same frequencies and can get in each other's way.

In the 1920s, many city garbage dispersal plants used incinerators to burn food waste—which uses more energy than it generates. Inventor John W. Hammes was inspired to create the garbage disposal, processing and liquifying food waste at its point of origin (the home, in the sink) and then sending it into the sewage network. In 1940, Hammes sold the first models via his company, InSinkErator, still in business today.

It can be used for all kinds of things, but Stephen Poplawski intended his device—the electric blender, consisting of a motorized container with a spinning blade inside—to be used for shakes and malts in restaurants. The blender also helped save the world. In the 1950s, when Dr. Jonas Salk developed the vaccine that would eradicate polio worldwide, he used a Waring brand blender. He pureed samples of the dead polio virus to make it into an injectable solution in which the medicine was evenly distributed.

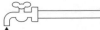

Clapback, defined as "a vicious retort to an insult," was coined by Ja Rule in his 2003 diss-track, "Clap Back."

GHOSTWATCH

On Halloween night in 1992, the UK's BBC One aired a "live" haunted-house investigation that blurred the lines between reality and horror—and made a lot of Brits extremely cross. This could actually be a funny story...if not for all the traumatized kids. Instead, the cautionary tale that is Ghostwatch provides a fascinating look into the nature of fear and the limits of trust in entertainment.

Found Footage

Sure, you might get frightened watching a scary movie, but not *that* frightened. That's because, no matter how well it's done, you know you're watching actors who are pretending. But what if you were to watch a similar story unfold, only you weren't at all sure that the terrified people on the screen *were* pretending? Now *that* would be scary.

Take the infamous 1938 *War of the Worlds* radio broadcast—with its convincing fake news bulletins, realistic sound effects, and skilled actors including Orson Welles. Thousands of radio listeners really thought that martians were invading New Jersey (at least, the listeners who hadn't read H. G. Wells's classic novel thought that). Similarly, by the time *The Blair Witch Project* hit movie theaters in 1999, the filmmakers had spent months fueling rumors (by posting fake news stories on the nascent Internet and distributing "missing" posters) that three young filmmakers had been murdered by witches in a Maryland forest. Then, did you hear? *Someone found their footage and edited it into a movie!* As time passed, and social media made us all more savvy, *Blair Witch* became just another horror movie. But that summer, before everyone knew for sure that it wasn't real, it was scary as heck.

Ghostwatch pulled a similar stunt in 1992—and viewers really fell for it. Back then, people mostly trusted the BBC—lovingly nicknamed "Auntie" (from the phrase, "Auntie knows best"). This "reality show that went too far" did not help maintain that trust.

Cast of Characters

"We're going to investigate one of the fascinating and baffling areas of human experience: the supernatural," says Michael Parkinson, a well-respected, silver-haired BBC presenter (what the Brits call a "host") near the start of the 90-minute broadcast. It's airing on Halloween night—on a Saturday, no less—right after the evening news. Parkinson is hosting from a TV studio set with two leather chairs, a roaring fireplace, and a framed wall painting of a ghost wearing a bedsheet. Sitting opposite him is paranormal expert Dr. Lin Pascoe, a true believer who's been part of the team investigating "the most haunted house in Britain" for months.

First singer to wear a wireless microphone on stage:
Kate Bush, on her first tour in 1990.

On the far side of the studio, BBC presenter Mike Smith is emceeing from the phone bank, which is just like the phone bank on the BBC's *Crimewatch*. Only here, the people manning the phones aren't cops, but "paranormalists." Smith's wife, a Saturday morning kids' show host named Sarah Greene, is stationed inside the haunted house with a camera crew. Outside in the street, Craig Charles—whom viewers know from the sci-fi sitcom *Red Dwarf*—is joking around with the curious but skeptical neighbors.

Recipe for Disaster

Parkinson, Smith, Greene, and Charles were all appearing as themselves. For Americans in 1992, it would have been the equivalent of, say, Mike Wallace from *60 Minutes* as host, with LeVar Burton from *Star Trek: The Next Generation* as the reporter in the street, talk show stalwart Regis Philbin manning the phone bank, and his cohost Kathie Lee Gifford in the haunted house.

All those factors—the star power, the Saturday night holiday, and the enigmatic nature of the well-publicized show—brought in upward of 11 million viewers, including plenty of children whose parents assumed the show would be innocuous fun.

"Mum, Dad, can we stay up for this Halloween special on the telly? It's got Sarah Greene!"

"It's past your bedtime."

"But it's Halloween!"

"Well, it does have Michael Parkinson, so how scary could it be?"

Slow Burn

The whole affair might seem passé now, but at the time, viewers were hooked from the beginning, even though not a lot happens for the first 45 minutes. This was a decade before *Ghost Hunters* launched the era of paranormal reality shows. No one had really watched investigators with infrared cameras and other gadgets following strange noises through a dark house.

During the program, viewers are informed that this particular house is located on Foxhill Drive in Northolt, a town in West London, and is inhabited by a recently divorced mother and her two young daughters. Dr. Pascoe tells Parkinson that her team was first called there months ago to determine why the water pipes were banging. The youngest daughter had named the ghost "Pipes."

As we learn more of the situation's backstory, Parkinson does his best to give the investigators and the frightened, giggly mother the benefit of the doubt, but it becomes apparent that he's a skeptic when one of the daughters is caught banging on a pipe. "We set out to catch a ghost," Parkinson barks, "and what we have captured instead is the remarkable instance of a hoax."

The real hoax was just getting going.

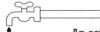

An estimated five billion photographs were taken in the year 1990, the same amount that are taken *every day* in the 2020s.

Trigger Warnings

Just when it's starting to look like the Auntie's live ghost-hunting experiment is a bust, all hell breaks loose. (Warning: spoilers are ahead. If you want to watch *Ghostwatch* before you finish reading, it's usually available to stream, and it's on DVD.) The show takes a turn and becomes decidedly kid-unfriendly. There's no gore, per say, but there are some horrific descriptions of gore (including face-eating cats and a dead pregnant dog). And Pipes turns out to be the ghost of a possessed child molester, who appears in the little girls' bedroom as a scary bald man wearing a dress. The possessed molester possesses the girls—*Exorcist*-style—and leaves scratches all over their bodies (OK, that's a bit gory—Uncle John had to cover his eyes). It gets even worse when the sisters are left alone in the house with the ghost and the TV crew while Mom watches from a news van parked out front. One of the sisters disappears, so Greene (the wholesome kids' show host) goes searching for her. Then Pipes goes after Greene. She's running for her life as the lights flicker. Meanwhile, her husband Mike watches helplessly from the studio.

The last ten minutes of *Ghostwatch* become truly chaotic as viewers are informed that the collective energy of all the people watching across Britain has manifested a "national séance" that makes Pipes more powerful than ever. Then it all goes off the rails when Greene—who never did find the missing sister—gets sucked into the "glory hole," a cupboard under the stairs where Pipes resides. The door slams shut and there's a blood-curdling scream. And then, silence. The picture scrambles and then cuts to Parkinson, all alone in the destroyed TV studio, muttering a nursery rhyme and speaking like he's possessed. The screen fades to black. And then...credits.

Breaching the Trust

Viewers were *not* OK with *Ghostwatch*. While the cast and crew—who had filmed the show months earlier in July—celebrated their "success" at a viewing party, the BBC's switchboard was overcome by tens of thousands of angry callers. The few who got through to the number displayed on the screen during the broadcast got a recorded message telling them the show is fictitious. Most people got a busy signal. Little did they know that the "callers" featured on the show were all actors—so were the mom and her two daughters, the ghost, the paranormalist, and the American skeptic who shared his skepticism via satellite (and who sounds just like Jeff Goldblum). Everyone was working from a script.

There were some clues that *Ghostwatch* was fake: Foxhill Drive didn't exist. And at one point, the camera cuts to a close-up of a cup right before it flies off a table. That couldn't have happened live. The viewers who noticed these inconsistencies were angry because it really seemed like the network was presenting these events as real. And the people who got genuinely frightened were angry when they realized they'd

Time away: 81 percent of American workers get fewer than four weeks of paid time off per year, while 70 percent of Europeans get four weeks or more.

been duped. There were three reports of pregnant women getting so scared that they went into labor.

Traumatized

Ghostwatch was hardest on the children who got to stay up late and watch it. It joined those few other prime-time TV specials that scared and scarred a generation—including 1983's *The Day After*, which did a really good job showing how a nuclear war would affect a typical American family. (Hint: very badly.)

The *BMJ* (formerly known as the *British Medical Journal*) reported that *Ghostwatch* caused two confirmed cases of children with PTSD (including one child who had to be admitted to a hospital). Countless more suspected cases went unconfirmed. The big problem was that most of the younger viewers didn't make it to the end of the broadcast, so they went to bed thinking it was real...and then got scared by their curtains. (That's where the *Ghostwatch* cameras had picked up the dark figure of Pipes, watching the little girls as they slept.) "About half the people I know of my age saw *Ghostwatch* and no one who did forgot it," writes the *New Statesman*'s Kate Mossman in one of many articles and documentaries looking back on the special. "It lingers in the communal memory like an urban legend, along with playground rumors of a suicide, which we didn't think could be true."

Sadly, it was true. Martin Denham was 18, but he had learning disabilities that gave him a mental age of 13. That didn't make him any less happy than other kids, said his mother...until *Ghostwatch*. She described the sensitive teen as "hypnotized," convinced that ghosts were causing his house's banging water pipes, just like in the show. Five days after the broadcast, Martin hanged himself. In his pocket was a note: "If there is ghosts I will now be one and I will always be with you as one."

What Were They Thinking?

"I wanted the whole nation to be terrified," said *Ghostwatch* writer Stephen Volk, who remains unrepentant. He didn't necessarily intend to *fool* the nation—at least, not at first. When BBC One hired Volk to pen a ghost story for the network's Drama Series, he'd written movie screenplays for only macabre tales such as *Gothic* and *The Guardian*. Because this would be on TV, Volk decided to make it about TV. He began by asking what would have scared him as a 12-year-old—like a ghost hiding behind the bedroom curtain—and then he added bits and pieces from *The Exorcist*, *Psycho*, and *A Nightmare on Elm Street*. He also took inspiration from a famous case known as the Enfield poltergeist, which also affected a tween girl.

Volk submitted his six-part docudrama chronicling a monthslong investigation, filmed like a documentary. Producer Ruth Baumgarten told him they had one night—and she was trying to get Halloween—so he had to truncate it to 90 minutes.

Top three causes of accidental deaths in the U.S.:
1) poisoning; 2) motor vehicle accident; 3) fall.

They decided to make only the final episode of Volk's proposed series—the live investigation—and use fake callers and fake experts to fill in the backstory.

From there, the ideas started snowballing. Volk had the thought that they should present *Ghostwatch* as if it were live. And instead of the usual 16-mm film cameras, they'd shoot it on video to really make it look newsy. Then they'd cast the four leads with trusted BBC personalities. Director Lesley Manning then added deliberate bloopers and technical glitches to make the broadcast seem even more real. "We never used the word 'hoax'," recalled Manning. "We were unpicking the language of television."

At a meeting shortly before airing, some of the network brass, and some people associated with the show, voiced their concerns about the subterfuge. Volk and the producers reluctantly agreed to add a "BBC *Screen One* Drama Series" title card at the beginning (but only for one second), and then credits at the end. "What about those who've tuned in late and think it's live?" offered Sarah Greene. She was one of the few people involved who anticipated "a s***storm."

The S***storm

Martin Denham's parents blamed their son's suicide on the BBC and filed for a judicial review, leading the Broadcasting Standards Commission to launch an investigation. Conclusion: *Ghostwatch* was a "deliberate attempt to cultivate a sense of menace," and the network "has a duty to do more than simply hint at the deception."

In its defense, the BBC insisted that they more than "hinted" at it. In addition to the title card and end credits, throughout October, there were commercials advertising *Ghostwatch* as part of its drama series. A week before Halloween, *Radio Times* magazine's cover story was about Michael Parkinson making his "acting debut."

The other line of defense: *Ghostwatch* aired after 9:00 p.m., when children should have been in bed. Even so, Greene quickly appeared on the network to reassure kids that it was all made up and she was never in any real danger. Then the BBC issued a formal apology.

But it didn't matter. Trust had been breached, and the Auntie's reputation took a big hit. "Part of the whole reaction to *Ghostwatch*, in a way, was because it was the BBC. It is the voice of the nation, it tells you when wars break out, it tells you who's the next prime minister," said Volk on the special's 30th anniversary. "That people felt so affronted when the BBC wasn't telling them the truth and...Michael Parkinson...is shown to be fallible, if not, downright lying to you, was part of the game we were playing."

About a week after the broadcast, the BBC said "game over" and urged everyone associated with the show to never speak of it again. And the network has no plans to ever air it again. It was only when *Ghostwatch* was released on DVD ten years later that all those scarred children—now entering adulthood—were finally able to revisit that fateful Halloween night that made them all afraid of their own bedrooms.

INSTANT EEL AND UNDERWEAR!

In Japan, much of the retail economy business is conducted through self-service vending machines. Simply insert the correct amount of yen into a vending machine—found in hundreds of thousands of locations—and you can buy virtually anything in a fully automated fashion. And we mean anything.

Raw goat meat

Minced horse meat

Bear meat

Cooked sweet potatoes

Canned bread

Pigs' feet

20-pound bags of rice

Umbrellas

Sriracha hot sauce

Guns

Socks

Cooked eel

Face masks

Breast milk

Sausage and bacon

Hamburgers

Edible insects

Nylon stockings

Origami

Corn

Shots of sake

Prayer cards

Religious charms and relics

T-shirts

Cigarettes

Fresh-cut flowers

Herbs

Raw vegetables

Kerosene

Worms (for bait)

Fresh fish

Goldfish (in plastic bags)

Incense (at graveyards)

Underwear

Canned coffee

Halloween costumes

Earbuds

Hot noodles

Crepes

Live beetles

Popcorn

Board games

Souvenirs of the 2021 Tokyo Olympics

Movie tickets

Pokémon cards

Wigs for dogs

False eyelashes

Cartons of fresh eggs

Soup stock

Neckties

Disposable cameras

Tomatoes

Batteries

Electricity (to charge a cell phone)

Single-use paper cups

Fortunes

CBD

Banana bunches

Fermented soybeans

COVID-19 tests

Books

Toilet paper

Cake in a can

Which part of your skeletal system isn't counted as bones? Your teeth.

BIRD UP!

With their beautiful singing voices, gift of flight, and ability to imitate human speech (parrots only), birds have long fascinated humans. Still, they're odd little creatures, and they've inspired a lot of amusement—and bemusement.

"I bought myself a parrot, but it did not say 'I'm hungry,' and so it died."
—**Mitch Hedberg**

"Birds are a miracle because they prove to us there is a finer, simpler state of being which we may strive to attain."
—**Douglas Coupland**

"The sound of birds stops the noise in my mind." —**Carly Simon**

"The hawk's cry is as sharp as its beak."
—**Edward Abbey**

"Parrots are a thousand times less miserable than we are." —**Voltaire**

"Sometimes I see a bird fly by and I feel jealous. But then other times I see a bird fly into a closed window and I feel laughing." —**Demetri Martin**

"I bet the sparrow looks at the parrot and thinks, yes, you can talk, but listen to yourself." —**Jack Handey**

"I think penguins are the most human of all the birds, which may be why people love them. They're cute, they stand upright, and they look like they're wearing tuxedos." —**Shia LaBeouf**

"Remember that the most beautiful things in the world are the most useless; peacocks and lilies for instance."
—**John Ruskin**

"I once had a sparrow alight upon my shoulder for a moment, while I was hoeing in a village garden, and I felt that I was more distinguished by that circumstance that I should have been by any epaulet I could have worn."
—**Henry David Thoreau**

"People who count their chickens before they are hatched act very wisely because chickens run about so absurdly that it is impossible to count them accurately."
—**Oscar Wilde**

"Here are the instructions for being a pigeon: (1) Walk around aimlessly for a while, pecking at cigarette butts and other inappropriate items. (2) Take fright at someone walking along the platform and fly off to a girder. (3) Have a s***. (4) Repeat." —**Bill Bryson**

"Essentially, a parrot is a monkey with wings." —**Joseph Garner**

"Parrots typically operate on one volume, loud. Sometimes they will vary this with extra loud and unbearably loud."
—**Shannon Cutts**

"Birds are the most accomplished aeronauts the world has ever seen. They fly high and low, at great speeds, and very slowly. And always with extraordinary precision and control."
—**David Attenborough**

If you slept with a teddy bear or security blanket when you were a kid, there's a 34 percent chance that you still do as a "grown-up."

FAILED FOURTH NETWORKS

Until the arrival of the Fox network in 1987 (and the emergence of The WB and UPN in the 1990s, which would later merge into The CW), American broadcast television consisted of little more than three over-the-air networks. This wasn't for a lack of trying. Here are some notable attempts to bring another channel to the airwaves...none of which panned out.

Mutual Television

Of the "Big Four" national broadcasters that dominated radio's golden age of the 1930s and 1940s, only one didn't successfully move into television—the Mutual Broadcasting System, home of such hits (and future early TV favorites) as *The Lone Ranger* and *Adventures of Superman.* In the late 1940s, as its radio competitors launched television ventures, Mutual also gave TV a try. Upstart TV stations WOR in New York and WOIC in Washington, D.C., agreed to be Mutual Television providers while the parent company entered talks with big movie studio MGM to produce shows starring its stable of actors. Forever trailing NBC and CBS in radio advertising dollars, Mutual didn't have the substantial funding necessary to build a network of TV affiliates, and it continued to lose money (and audience share) into the 1950s as shows jumped to rivals' still-thriving radio networks and burgeoning TV outlets. In 1952, General Tire bought out Mutual, and by the end of the decade it was in bankruptcy. Mutual lived on as a radio content provider until the 1990s, while some of its more prominent affiliates opened TV stations that carried programming for NBC, CBS, and ABC.

United Network

In 1966, Daniel Overmyer, an industrialist who owned dozens of warehouses and a handful of low-wattage UHF TV stations, decided that he'd put his wealth from the former into expanding the latter with the launch of what he planned to call the Overmyer Network. The businessman said the service would broadcast original programming for eight hours a day, seven days a week, including a news show produced by print syndicate United Press International. Overmyer would eventually sign up 35 stations around the U.S. to be affiliates, though in name only. Along with a few independent stations, most Overmyer carriers were CBS affiliates who wanted the rights to broadcast the network's first program: *The Las Vegas Show*, a nightly late-night talk and variety show broadcast live from Las Vegas. Hosted by popular comic Bill Dana, the show was seen as a viable competitor to NBC's stalwart *The Tonight Show Starring Johnny Carson.* The service, renamed the United Network before its launch, debuted in May 1967 with *The Las Vegas Show*. The United Network spent more money than it brought in via advertising for its one and only show—it cost so much to lease transmission lines and equipment from AT&T that the business ran out of money after only a month. In June 1967, *The Las Vegas Show*—and the United Network—went off the air.

Pat Weaver Prime Time Network

With the creation of *Today* and *The Tonight Show*, NBC executive Pat Weaver invented two television formats that persist to this day: the morning magazine and the late-night variety program. In 1956, after resigning his position as NBC's chairman, Weaver set out to create an entirely new TV network from scratch. After the demise of the DuMont Network, Weaver claimed to have pulled together 40 affiliates suddenly and unwillingly left independent and without content. Not quite ready to call his endeavor a full-fledged network, Weaver told reporters that he had a "programming service" in mind from which stations could pick and choose the programs they thought would best fit their audiences and communities. Only one show was publicly announced for the venture, tentatively titled the Pat Weaver Prime Time Network: a national expansion of a local New York children's educational program called *Ding Dong School*. The programming service never hit the air.

NTA Film Network

While TV networks in the 1950s provided affiliates with programming for prime time and daytime, the affiliates were largely left on their own to fill overnights and weekends. The solution for affiliate stations looking to close the gaps, and independent stations needing to fill their entire schedules: old movies, syndicated by the big Hollywood movie studios. Twentieth Century Fox's National Telefilm Associates subsidiary was making so much money leasing its catalog to TV stations that it announced it would form a network out of them. In 1956, the NTA Film Network launched, selling movies to TV stations as well as programming suitable for daytime, including the original courtroom show, *Divorce Court*. As the TV industry grew, with other syndicators and networks providing more content that was newer and more attractive than black-and-white movies, the NFA Film Network faded out and closed shop by 1962.

MetroNet

Metromedia Broadcasting was among the biggest and most important players in the TV industry from the 1950s to the 1970s, despite never having a network of its own. Initially a string of a few independent television stations situated around the U.S., Metromedia also produced syndicated content, notably the long-running daytime talk series *The Merv Griffin Show*, the kids' magazine show *Wonderama*, and the hit game show *Truth or Consequences*. By the mid-1970s, Metromedia controlled almost as many stations as a proper network, and in 1976, they attempted to create one. Announced as MetroNet, its de facto affiliates were promised a Sunday night lineup of family-friendly programming, two soap operas airing in prime time five nights a week, and a variety show hosted by Charo on Saturday evenings. It had the network and shows in place, but what doomed MetroNet before it got started was its advertising...or lack thereof. Despite being an unknown quantity as a national network, MetroNet planned to charge ad rates equivalent to what ABC, CBS, and NBC were charging at the time. So many big airtime buyers balked that MetroNet never made it to broadcast.

Prime Time Entertainment Network

By the early 1990s, most major American cities could support a half dozen or so television stations. Even with channels affiliated with ABC, CBS, NBC, and Fox, there remained spots on the dial that needed programming to fill the day, and they relied on syndication—programs produced by TV studios and sold to individual stations (as opposed to being part of a network feed). Warner Bros., a major provider of syndicated series, created a virtual network in January 1993 out of 177 of its TV station clients. It launched the Prime Time Entertainment Network, a service providing hour-long prime-time dramas for as many as four nights a week. At launch, PTEN aired space show *Babylon 5*, the 1970s reboot *Kung Fu: The Legend Continues*, the sci-fi series *Time Trax*, and the crime drama *Pointman*. Viewership figures for PTEN were competitive—*Babylon 5* proved particularly popular—but then the affiliates started to drop out. Another division of Warner Bros. and Paramount Pictures also recognized the need for programming on independent stations, and in late 1993, they individually announced that they'd launch their own networks: The WB and UPN, respectively. So many PTEN affiliates signed up with The WB and UPN that the service ran out of outlets and shut down by 1995.

* * *

BASEBALL, FINLAND STYLE

Pesapello, also known as *boboll*, *pesis*, and Finnish baseball, translates to "nest ball," and it's the national sport of Finland. Inspired by baseball and created in the 1920s by Finnish baseball fan Tahko Ohkala, the ball is pitched vertically, the base patches are zig-zags, the manager tells the offense what to do by waving a color-coded fan, the defense uses hand signals, and it's played in two halves of four innings in which the final score is tallied by number of innings won (the winner of an inning being the team that scores more runs in their offensive part). It was introduced to the rest of the world as a demonstration sport at the 1952 Olympics in Helsinki, Finland, but it didn't catch on outside of Europe (and northern Ontario in Canada).

One of the designers of the Volkswagen Beetle: Adolf Hitler.

DAY JOBS OF THE LITERATI

Unfortunately, creating timeless and influential works of literature, music, and art doesn't always bring excessive wealth. For that reason and others, many of history's most important creators held on to their bill-paying 9-to-5 gigs.

Lewis Carroll. The author of *Alice's Adventures in Wonderland* and *Jabberwocky* wrote under a pen name to keep his literary life separate from his much more serious career of mathematics instructor at Oxford University, and deacon in the Church of England.

T. S. Eliot. The American-British poet invented the modernist style with his long works "The Love Song of J. Alfred Prufrock" and *The Waste Land*. The latter was published to wide acclaim in 1925, at which point Eliot left his job working in Lloyds Bank in London to be an editor at publisher Faber and Faber. He'd stay there until the mid-1960s, two decades after he won the 1948 Nobel Prize for Literature.

Alice Munro. Regarded as a master of the short story, Munro has won almost every major writing award, including the Man Booker International Prize, multiple Governor General's Awards, and the Nobel Prize for Literature. She published her first major works in 1968, five years after she and her husband opened and began operating Munro's Books in Victoria, British Columbia.

Anthony Trollope. The British author published 47 novels, 42 short stories, and 5 travelogues during his life. Between 1837 and 1867, he was a postal surveyor of the English government. (One of his on-the-job accomplishments was introducing free-standing drop-off mailboxes.) He did much of his writing during an allotted three-hour period before he went to work each day.

William Carlos Williams. The poet behind simple popular works such as "This Is Just to Say" and "The Red Wheelbarrow" didn't want to have to compromise his artistic vision by writing commercially minded works, so he went to medical school and opened a practice in Rutherford, New Jersey. Williams worked as a full-time pediatrician for 40 years.

Herman Melville. Melville wrote a series of seafaring adventure novels in the 1840s, but when he aimed for something heavily literary in 1851 with *Moby-Dick*, it flopped and nearly killed his career. After suffering a mental health break, he found a job as a customs inspector at the ports in New York City. He worked there for nearly 20 years. After his 1891 death, *Moby-Dick* began to earn a reappraisal.

Solar winds travel through space at speeds exceeding 1 million mph.

Antonio Vivaldi. The Italian composer is synonymous with the Baroque era of music in the early 1700s, and his violin concertos *The Four Seasons* are among the most widely performed classical pieces of all time. Vivaldi was ordained into the Roman Catholic priesthood at age 25, and it left him enough free time to teach violin lessons to orphans and to compose.

John Cage. A highly experimental and modernist composer, Cage played with the ideas of sound and nontraditional instruments to stretch the definition of music in the 20th century; his most notorious piece is "4'33"," a work consisting of the "absence of sound" (otherwise known as silence). Pushing the envelope in music wasn't particularly lucrative, so Cage worked for New York advertising agencies as a graphic designer, creating business cards, campaigns, fonts, and letterheads.

Philip Glass. Another New York–based, experimental, atonal, avant-garde composer and musician (he was producer for a New Wave band called Polyrock), the heralded Glass didn't exactly rake in the dough with his music, so he supplemented his income by working variously as a furniture mover, a taxi driver, and a plumber. His jobs included installing dishwashers.

Charles Ives. Twentieth-century American composer Charles Ives toiled away for decades, writing music and trying with little success to get others to perform or publish it. In 1947, he won the Pulitzer Prize for music with "Symphony No. 3." Ives was 73 years old and on the other end of a long career in insurance and finance. After working at Mutual Life as a clerk, he cofounded the insurance company Ives & Myrick, where he's credited with introducing estate planning to the modern middle class.

Robert Pollard. The only permanent member of the influential and foundational indie rock band Guided by Voices, since its inception in 1983, is singer and main songwriter Pollard. The band has released more than 35 albums and Pollard has written almost 3,000 songs. Guided by Voices never moved beyond cult popularity, and so, beginning in the mid-1980s, Pollard became a public-school instructor in Ohio. He taught multiple subjects at the junior high and high school levels before focusing on being a fourth-grade teacher.

Wallace Stevens. The winner of two National Book Awards, Stevens garnered a Pulitzer Prize in 1955 for his compilation of masterworks, *Collected Poems*. Launched into a new level of fame and influence, Stevens was offered a teaching position by Harvard University. He turned it down because he didn't want to leave his well-paid position as a vice president at the Hartford, a major insurance company. (It gave him ample time to write—he'd compose poems in his head while he walked to work, then jot them down when he got to the office.)

Guinea pig is considered a delicacy in Peru, Ecuador, and Bolivia.

IT'S A CONSPIRACY!

Uncle John and his friend, a humanoid lizard man who is President of Earth and lives in a mountain near BRI headquarters, agree that it's utterly mind-boggling how people believe the wildest things—like these conspiracy theories.

In 2003, U.S. armed forces led an invasion of Iraq to stop an alien invasion. Iraqi dictator Saddam Hussein had come into possession of a portal, or stargate, allowing for instantaneous interstellar travel and for extraterrestrials to come to Earth. It had supposedly been left in Iraq by the Anunnaki gods thousands of years ago.

The sinking of the Titanic was an inside job. The Federal Reserve was secretly established by the powerful Jesuit order of Roman Catholic priests to take over all world banking. Fed opponents John Jacob Astor, Isidor Straus, and Benjamin Guggenheim all happened to take a trip on the *Titanic*'s maiden voyage in 1912, and so the ship's captain, a secret Jesuit, sank the ship to silence their criticisms.

Yuri Gagarin wasn't the first man in space. In 1961, the Russian cosmonaut successfully orbited the planet and returned safely to Earth—unlike the many other space travelers his government sent into space before him who died in explosions and failed attempts.

Robert Kardashian faked his death. After the expensive attorney helped client O. J. Simpson earn an acquittal of murder charges in 1995, he pretended to die, got plastic surgery, changed his name, moved to Texas, and rose through the ranks of local politics until he won a U.S. Senate seat under the name "Ted Cruz." The reason: to get away from his family, the Kardashians of reality-television fame.

Finland doesn't exist. It's a plot hatched by Japan and the former Soviet Union. They invented a fake landmass to hide a prime fishing spot in the Baltic Sea; Japanese boats can fish as much as they want in those waters without any nod to environmental law or limits, and the Russian government gets a cut. All other countries in the area signed a treaty to keep the whole operation secret.

Michael Jackson was murdered by Iranian secret operatives. The King of Pop died in June 2009, amid widespread anti-government protests in Iran. Hardline ruler Mahmoud Ahmadinejad had Jackson murdered and made it look like a drug overdose to distract protestors. It worked, and the government wasn't overthrown after all.

Online retailer Wayfair sells housewares as a front for a human trafficking operation. If you know which specific cabinet or piece of furniture to order, it comes with a child or young woman inside.

The Internet is populated almost entirely by robots. From about 2016 on, with the rise of algorithms, bots, and artificial intelligence, nearly all online activity is carried out by content-generating machines communicating with one another, posing as humans.

Little Caesars is cheating. How does the cut-rate pizza chain sell large pizzas for $6 each and turn a profit? Because it secretly uses frozen DiGiorno pizzas, heats them up, and sells them as their own.

Miley Cyrus is a clone. During the run of *Hannah Montana* in the 2000s, Cyrus tried to quit the Disney Channel series and stop recording tie-in albums. She wanted to have a normal childhood, but Disney was making too much money—so they killed Cyrus and replaced her with a more compliant replicant.

There's a deadly portal inside CERN. The statue of the Hindu deity Shiva in front of the CERN building hints at the true nature of the machinery inside. The Large Hadron Collider is being used to create a portal to summon Shiva, known as the Destroyer, and bring about Armageddon.

Bigfoot is real, and he's an alien, and there are lots of him. Sightings of the monster reportedly peak around the times and locations of UFO sightings. That's because Bigfoot is an alien, a criminal from another planet and exiled to this one. Back in the 1970s, the Soviet Union captured one and made 2,000 to act as agents of chaos around the world.

Britney Spears was a secret asset. In 2008, Spears made headlines when she ended her tumultuous marriage to husband Kevin Federline. That was all by design— the George W. Bush administration hired her to do just that, to distract people from voting against Bush's party and cronies in the 2008 election.

Hitler and the aliens were in cahoots. During World War II, Nazi scientists invented a bell that when struck, allowed for time travel. Nazi German dictator Adolf Hitler used the bell to go back in time to ancient Egypt, offering the Egyptians secrets of modern technology with which to build the pyramids as a communication device to contact aliens, who would then use their advanced weapons to help Hitler win World War II. When the Allied Forces found out, they made a deal with the aliens: they'd share *their* high-tech weaponry and, in return, the aliens could abduct humans to study.

Queen Elizabeth II was a cannibal. She ate human flesh—it's how she lived into her nineties. She turned on the entire royal family to her unique lifestyle, too.

Birds aren't real. They're surveillance drones controlled by the government.

First evidence of people wearing hats: a 15,000-year-old cave painting in France.

GRAVE STYLES OF THE RICH AND FAMOUS

What's the point of being rich, famous, important, and successful in life if you can't show off after death with an over-the-top burial monument?

PRINCESS DIANA

The British royal's final resting place is in a single-occupancy mausoleum on an island surrounded by a man-made lake on her family's country estate in Althorp. The public isn't permitted to visit the site, but they can see another, smaller memorial built on the shores.

JULES VERNE

In 1907, two years after the death of the French author of *Journey to the Center of the Earth* and other early science-fiction classics, a marker made by sculptor Albert Roze was installed. Roze used a cast of Verne's head made upon his death to design a statue of the author himself, wrapped in a shroud and violently breaking through his own tombstone, as if risen from the dead.

BUCK OWENS

Country music legend Buck Owens rests in the family plot in Bakersfield, California. Bearing two plaques—"The Buck Owens Family" and "Buck's Place"— the classical-style building is supported by huge pillars that flank two heavy, metal doors, each adorned with a full-size guitar.

OSCAR WILDE

The author and playwright rests in the Père Lachaise cemetery In Paris. His modernist tomb is decorated with a carved limestone figure, bearing wings. The supernatural being's male genitals were in full view, which caused a scandal when the memorial was revealed in 1912. In 1961, the genitalia were removed in an act of vandalism. The entire monument now sits behind a glass barrier to protect the stone.

JOHNNY RAMONE

The Ramones helped usher in punk rock and its stripped-down, no-frills sound. The grave of Ramones guitarist Johnny Ramone is more elaborate than any of his music—it's adorned with a life-size statue of the musician playing his instrument.

HARRY THORNTON

A classical pianist popular in England in the early 20th century, Thornton died in the influenza epidemic of 1918 and was buried in London's Highgate Cemetery under a full-scale and completely accurate stone replica of a grand piano (with the lid propped open).

NICOLAS CAGE

As of this writing, Oscar-winning actor Nicolas Cage isn't dead. Nevertheless, he's already built the site of his future interment. He bought a plot in New Orleans's oldest cemetery, St. Louis Cemetery No. 1, and commissioned a nine-foot-tall stone pyramid. It's inscribed with the Latin phrase "Omni Ab Uno," or "Everything from One."

Glee star Lea Michele goes by her first and middle names. Why?
She was made fun of in school for her last name: Safarti.

SINGLE-HANDEDLY RESPONSIBLE

Big changes and new, universal preferences generally don't come about right away. Most things evolve over time, as technology and tastes change. But once in a while, just one action or person comes along and, virtually overnight, changes everything.

THE MCNUGGET CHANGED CHICKEN CONSUMPTION

In 1980, beef was overwhelmingly the most popular meat sold in U.S. grocery stores and consumed in restaurants. That year, Americans' per-capita consumption of beef was 76.4 pounds, compared to 47.4 pounds of chicken. And of that chicken produced and sold, almost all of it was sold whole or on the bone (an entire bird suitable for roasting, or a package of drumsticks or split breasts, for example).

In 1992, chicken consumption surpassed that of beef for the first time, with 66.5 pounds of chicken per person versus 65.9 of beef, and the gap continued to grow in the following years. What happened? The ascendance of processed, boneless, fried, bite-size chicken pieces—"nuggets" or "strips." Back in 1980, McDonald's, the most frequented fast-food restaurant in the country, introduced the first widely available boneless chicken product: the Chicken McNugget. Sold in servings of 6, 10, or 20, they were fried-and-breaded chunks of chicken without the bones. McNuggets were also the most successful new product in the chain's history. Today, Americans eat about twice as much chicken as they do beef; 90 percent of that chicken is sold with the bones removed, as fresh or frozen filets and cutlets, or as breaded, precooked nuggets and strips.

A SKETCH-COMEDY SHOW CHANGED THE SUPER BOWL HALFTIME SHOW

Despite the Super Bowl being a widely anticipated, holiday-level annual event with its late-winter broadcast ranking as the single-most-watched thing on TV all year, organizers considered the halftime show an afterthought. They just wanted to cheaply entertain the live spectators filing in and out of their seats as they retrieved beers or used the restroom. From Super Bowl I in 1967 until Super Bowl XXVI in 1992, the performers were almost always some combination of a college marching band, a drill team, and a past-their-prime musician, such as 1950s star Chubby Checker (in 1988) or 1970s pop choir Up with People (in 1986).

The Super Bowl halftime performance had earned its reputation as a dire, dated, cheesy break in the action. So, when the official CBS broadcast of the 1992

The longest recorded flight of a chicken: 13 seconds.

Super Bowl cut to "Winter Magic," a salute to the Winter Olympics that featured figure skaters, a marching band, and the 1980 U.S. Men's Olympic hockey team waving, 20 million people changed the channel to Fox, the upstart network airing a special live episode of its hit satirical sketch-comedy show *In Living Color*, starring Jim Carrey, Jamie Foxx, and the Wayans brothers.

Nobody had ever dared to counter-program against the Super Bowl before. Fox spooked Super Bowl organizers into elevating the production values of their halftime show. In 1993, Michael Jackson, arguably the most popular entertainer in the world, was booked to play the mid-game break, and he'd be followed in the years to come by other ultra-famous musicians including Stevie Wonder, Aerosmith, U2, Janet Jackson, Paul McCartney, Justin Timberlake, and Prince.

A LITTLE BOY CHANGED BASEBALL'S FOUL BALL POSSESSION RULE

In the average Major League Baseball game today, the teams go through about 100 baseballs, discarding them when they start to show wear-and-tear or accepting the loss when they get hit out of the park or into the stands. In the early decades of baseball, the National League and the American League didn't have billions of dollars to work with like they do now, so they had to make the balls—much more expensive to produce then—last as long as possible. It was an unwritten rule that one ball would be used for an entire game.

In polls of fans in the late 19th century, the most common complaint was that games took too long to play, with the length extended by umpires walking up into the stands to get the ball back every time it was hit out of play and force the fans who grabbed them to return them. By 1904, the leagues passed a rule in which ushers had to wrestle the ball back; if a spectator refused to return that ball, they'd be escorted off the premises and arrested.

It would take a child standing up to the big leaguers—and an unforced public relations error—for the national pastime to be a bit looser with its balls. While attending a Philadelphia Phillies home game in 1922, 11-year-old Robert Cotter snagged a foul ball hit his way. As expected, an usher came by to reclaim it. Cotter refused to hand it over, and team management decided to make an example of him—they had the boy arrested, and he ended up spending the night in jail. The next morning, at the little boy's arraignment, the judge threw out the case and chastised the Phillies, earning the team a lot of bad hometown press...and a league-wide policy change.

A HITCHCOCK ACTRESS INSPIRED IMMIGRANTS TO OPEN NAIL SALONS

More than 125,000 refugees came to the United States, primarily to California, in 1975 following the end of the 20-year-long Vietnam War. Tippi Hedren, the actress

Stale urine was used as mouthwash in ancient Rome.

best known for starring in Alfred Hitchcock's *The Birds*, helped out at a refugee camp in Northern California, planning to sponsor and help resettle 20 single, displaced Vietnamese women. At the camp, so many women complimented her elaborately manicured nails that she had her personal manicurist, Dusty Coots, flown up from Beverly Hills to the camp to do the women's nails and then teach them how to do a Hollywood-worthy manicure.

Those women dispersed throughout the country (mostly California), got their nail technician licenses (with Hedren's help), and opened small salon businesses in strip malls, just beginning to take hold as a retail outlet. By the mid-1980s, owning or working in a nail salon became a quintessential part of the Vietnamese American experience for many women. Today, American nail salons generate about $8 billion of revenue each year. All those manicures and treatments are performed primarily at individually owned stores or small chains, and the majority are operated by first- or second-generation immigrants from Vietnam who came to the U.S. following the Vietnam War. Nationwide, 50 percent of nail salon owners are Vietnamese; in California, that number is above 80 percent.

A POISONING SPREE IN CHICAGO LED TO THE ADOPTION OF SAFETY SEALS

It's standard packaging and operating practice in the U.S., and it has been for decades: all over-the-counter medications, including pain relievers and vitamins, are sold encased in a bottle that's factory-sealed and topped with a foil disc that must be punctured or cut out to access the product inside. That's called a safety seal—and if it's broken or absent, it indicates that the medicine inside may have been tampered with and is not safe to ingest. Medication producers didn't even think about this consumer protection until they absolutely had to, forced into it by a public health crisis and resultant mass hysteria.

In September 1982, 12-year-old suburban Chicago child Mary Kellerman told her parents she thought that she was coming down with a cold. She died about an hour later. A few miles away in another Chicago suburb, 27-year-old Adam Janus died of what looked like a heart attack. His brother and sister-in-law died later that week. Three more mysterious deaths occurred in Chicagoland in the coming days, with authorities finding a connecting point: every dead person had taken a dose of extra-strength Tylenol shortly before their passing. And their autopsies all indicated ingestion of cyanide. In other words, the Tylenol had been laced with a fatal poison.

Within weeks of the deaths, Tylenol manufacturer McNeil Consumer Products issued a complete recall, taking back 31 million bottles of the pain reliever and urging all Americans to not use it. A few more tainted bottles were found in Chicago, indicating that the unidentified culprit was operating there. When Tylenol returned to store shelves nationwide by the end of 1982, the bottles came packaged

Strawberries aren't berries, but bananas are.

with a safety seal, a standard quickly adopted by every other major pharmaceutical manufacturer. (And authorities never found the person or persons who poisoned the pills in Chicago.)

KOBE BRYANT CHANGED THE STYLE OF SHOE BASKETBALL PLAYERS WEAR

Since the popularity of basketball emerged in the early 20th century, professional and elite players wore "high-tops," with the sides of the shoe completely encasing the ankles (and then some), thought to offer balance and support, along with protection from all-too-frequent ankle injuries. The perennially popular high-cut Converse All Stars (also known as "Chuck Taylors," after the player who helped redesign them in the 1920s) were the go-to basketball shoe; Converse controlled 80 percent of the basketball shoe market until the 1980s.

What changed? Signature shoes designed for and marketed by famous basketball players, particularly the first wave of Michael Jordan's signature Nike "Air Jordans." Big, bulky, puffy, and packed with all sorts of tech and design elements that would supposedly make for a better basketball player, millions of people wanted to wear the same shoes their favorite pros wore, both on and off the court.

Following Jordan's retirement, the next generationally dominant NBA player was Kobe Bryant, who played for the Los Angeles Lakers from 1996 to 2016, winning an MVP award and five league championships in that time. Early in his career, he signed a deal with Nike to produce a line of Nike Zoom Kobe shoes. In 2008, when planning the fourth entry in the series, Bryant asked for something new. "I want the lowest, lightest-weight basketball shoe ever," he reportedly told Nike designers. "I want to prove to people that you can wear a low-top basketball shoe."

Bryant was raised in Italy (his father played pro basketball there) and he was a soccer nut. If you don't count jumping, Bryant noticed, a soccer player moves much like a basketball player, with sudden movement changes and having to mix up the speed of their running. Soccer players always wore low-top cleats, which inspired Bryant to introduce the idea for basketball shoes. The Zoom Kobe IVs were released later in 2008, and Bryant wore them in games to give himself a winning edge. And within a few years, everybody else in the NBA, wanting to be like Bryant, started wearing low-tops, too. A high-cut signature shoe hasn't been widely produced since the early 2010s.

* * *

"The real problem of humanity is the following: We have Paleolithic emotions, medieval institutions and godlike technology. And it is terrifically dangerous, and it is now approaching a point of crisis overall."
—Edward O. Wilson

In 1918, during WWI, the U.S. Marine Corps Reserve recruited 305 women, mostly for clerical duties. After the war, they were all discharged.

ALL ZUCCHINIS ARE SQUASH...

...But not all squash are zucchinis. We often see these kind of comparisons when trying to explain the difference between two similar things and one encompasses the other. To our knowledge, there is no term for this, so let's come up with our own neologism, shall we? How about...an "allbutnotall"? (That's the best we can come up with at the BRI. Send us your better idea and maybe we can coin a new word!)

All tangerines are mandarins, but not all mandarins are tangerines.

All bourbon is whiskey, but not all whiskey is bourbon.

All tequila is mezcal, but not all mezcal is tequila.

All champagne is sparkling wine, but not all sparkling wine is champagne.

All liquids are fluids, but not all fluids are liquids.

All barrels are casks, but not all casks are barrels.

All crystal is glass, but not all glass is crystal.

All enzymes are catalysts, but not all catalysts are enzymes.

All strains are variants, but not all variants are strains.

All murders are homicides, but not all homicides are murders.

All emotions are feelings, but not all feelings are emotions.

All applications are software, but not all software is an application.

All bugs are insects, but not all insects are bugs.

All tortoises are turtles, but not all turtles are tortoises.

All toads are frogs, but not all frogs are toads.

All locusts are grasshoppers, but not all grasshoppers are locusts.

All fascists are populists, but not all populists are fascist.

All attorneys are lawyers, but not all lawyers are attorneys.

All advertising is marketing, but not all marketing is advertising.

All graphs are charts, but not all charts are graphs.

All CPAs are accountants, but not all accountants are CPAs.

All acronyms are abbreviations, but not all abbreviations are acronyms.

All similes are metaphors, but not all metaphors are similes.

All statements are sentences, but not all sentences are statements.

Better go west: jet lag is worse when you travel east.

LOLLAPALOOZA!

The story of the biggest and silliest name in rock 'n' roll festival-style concerts.

BREAKING THE ADDICTION

After the breakthrough of "college rock" in the early 1980s with bands such as R.E.M., but before the emergence of Seattle-based "grunge" as the definitive guitar sound of the 1990s, the most important "alternative rock" came from Los Angeles. Leading the scene: Jane's Addiction, whose second album *Ritual de lo Habitual* sold more than a million copies within a year of its 1990 release and got tons of radio and MTV airplay for the single "Been Caught Stealing." At the same time, the band was coming undone. The members weren't getting along, and bassist Eric Avery informed the group that he'd be leaving the band at the end of its 1990 tour.

One of the tour's last dates was the Reading Festival, an annual extravaganza in the U.K. featuring dozens of bands on the bill, dating back to the 1960s and routinely attracting more than half a million fans. Jane's Addiction was supposed to headline the 1990 iteration. A dream gig, it didn't happen—lead singer Perry Farrell blew out his voice while playing a warm-up show at a small London club the night before. A doctor told him not to sing, but bandmembers went to the Reading Festival anyway and hung out with other bands backstage and mingled with the crowd. Drummer Stephen Perkins wondered aloud to Farrell why the U.S. didn't have anything like the Reading Festival. Indeed, the most famous multi-act concerts were usually limited-time affairs, such as the one-weekend Woodstock in 1969, or the US Festival, staged in 1982 and 1983.

PLANS IN MOTION

Farrell liked the idea of a festival stateside, one that Jane's Addiction could headline as their last show ever. He and Perkins floated the idea to their booking agent, Marc Geiger, and after chatting, they had a more ambitious idea. What if instead of a one-time-only, destination-style concert like Reading, the festival took to the road, playing large, open-air stadiums and parks in multiple American cities over the course of a summer? Geiger had sent bills of three or four bands out on the road, but nothing like the seven-, eight-, or nine-act bill that Farrell envisioned. It was possible, he said, but not probable.

Meanwhile, Farrell took to planning the tour—which would ideally hit the road in the summer of 1991, less than a year away. First, he needed a name, and flipped through a dictionary to see if anything struck him. He found a contender in *lollapalooza*, a disused 19th-century slang term that meant "something great or wonderful" as well as "giant swirling lollipop." Farrell had also been watching an old

Three Stooges short on late-night TV, and one of the stooges compared something to a "lollapalooza." That was a sign—he called up Geiger in the middle of the night to tell him that the Lollapalooza festival was officially underway.

FITS THE BILL

Because Lollapalooza was first conceived as a tribute and send-off to Jane's Addiction, the bands approached to appear on the first festival's lineup were all selected by the members of that group. Jane's Addiction's musicians had eclectic taste, represented in the bill of acts that signed on: U.K. goth rock band Siouxsie and the Banshees, industrial-electronic act Nine Inch Nails, weird Los Angeles joke-punkers Butthole Surfers, funk-metal collective Living Colour, ska band Fishbone, rapper Ice-T's heavy metal side project Body Count, and Rollins Band, the new punk project by former Black Flag leader Henry Rollins.

What would make Lollapalooza different from other festivals and other multi-band tours? It would boast a festival atmosphere and be localized for each stop. Farrell wanted to provide an all-encompassing, stimulating experience beyond just entertaining crowds with music they already liked. The politically minded singer wanted to expose young concertgoers to social issues and start debates, and so organizers reached out to charities, causes, and nonprofit organizations—from all over the political spectrum—to put up information booths at every Lollapalooza tour stop. (The League of Women Voters and Handgun Control Inc. said yes. The National Rifle Association and U.S. military recruiters said no.)

In addition to the bands on stage and the outreach area, Lollapalooza would feature other activities and entertainment. Body piercing and tattoo booths agreed to participate, local art (personally picked by Farrell) was displayed in makeshift galleries, and spoken word and open mic tents were available for attendees to perform in.

ON THE ROAD

Despite the significant logistical challenges of arranging venues, accommodations, bands, sideshow performers, art, and educational resources—all in just a few months—the first Lollapalooza tour began in July 1991. The festival would play 26 shows in 21 American cities in just 40 days. A novelty well-covered by the press, Lollapalooza captured the zeitgeist of American youth in the early 1990s, spreading and popularizing the music and associated culture of alternative rock.

Just a few months after Lollapalooza wrapped up, the grunge movement exploded out of Seattle. Bands including Pearl Jam, Nirvana, and Alice in Chains all sold millions of albums, inspiring young people to fully embody the culture presented at Lollapalooza. That also meant that a second Lollapalooza would be a much higher-profile and highly scrutinized event, relative to its first outing. And Lollapalooza number two was just plain bigger. This time, the tour comprised 36 shows in 29 cities (in the U.S. and Canada). The headliners were superstars: Pearl Jam, Soundgarden, and the Red Hot Chili Peppers. So many bands wanted to be a part of Lollapalooza that organizers added a second stage for lesser-known acts (some of which went on to become bigger names than that year's headliners); in subsequent years, they'd add a third for local and unsigned bands.

THE END IS NEAR

As the 1990s wore on, Lollapalooza became a reflection of pop culture rather than a place where lesser-known bands got exposure, and it was bringing in tens of millions of dollars. Nirvana was offered $10 million to headline the 1994 tour; they pulled out of the show one day before lead singer Kurt Cobain committed suicide in April 1994. Smashing Pumpkins played in their stead, with frontman Billy Corgan bringing Cobain's widow, Hole singer Courtney Love, onstage each day to discuss Cobain (the so-called "voice of a generation" to the Lollapalooza target audience) and play a few songs.

The sixth Lollapalooza would prove to be the last one for a while. The alternative rock counterculture openly eschewed anything macho and mainstream, and past Lollapalooza fans were baffled when the tour booked blockbuster-selling, aggressive heavy metal band Metallica to headline the 1996 tour. That prompted founder and organizer Perry Farrell to walk away and form his own new festival, ENIT, which sought to embrace the spirit of the early Lollapalooza tours. After the music press declared electronic dance music to be the "new grunge," Lollapalooza organizers booked those kinds of bands for the 1997 tour. Acts like The Orb and The Prodigy failed to attract huge crowds, and after a decent headliner couldn't be signed for 1998, organizers announced that Lollapalooza was over.

ENCORE

Jane's Addiction reunited in 2003, prompting Farrell to stage a new Lollapalooza with his band at the forefront. A series of 30 festivals proved popular, and a 2004 Lollapalooza with the Pixies, Morrissey, Sonic Youth, and the Killers was announced, but low advance ticket sales prompted Farrell and other organizers to call it off months before it began.

Unlikely as it was, Lollapalooza returned in 2005—completely reformulated. What had once set Lollapalooza apart was taken out of the equation: it wouldn't tour anymore but would take place in a single location over one weekend—like its inspiration, the Reading Festival. In August 2006, Lollapalooza played Grant Park in Chicago. (International one-offs with different organizers and different acts would also be staged in Europe and South America.) In recent years, the festival is no longer centered around alternative rock, with rappers such as Kendrick Lamar and Tyler, the Creator headlining, as have pop singers Dua Lipa, Doja Cat, and Billie Eilish. Even Metallica returned to Lollapalooza in 2022.

In a single day, one germ can multiply into eight million germs.

PRESIDENTIAL COINAGES, PART II

On page 51, we showed you the Oval Office origins of game plan, gag rule, fake news, *and more. Here are more presidential additions to the lexicon.*

IFFY

Coined by: Franklin D. Roosevelt (1933–45)

Meaning: Full of uncertainty

Origin: Many of the words we take for granted were originally met with scorn because, as the age-old cry goes, "That's not a word!" Such is the case with *iffy*, which wasn't a word until FDR said, "Well, it's pretty iffy as to where the Supreme Court stands on this." Despite all the wailing about turning a conjunction into an adjective, Roosevelt insisted on using *iffy*, and now we all do—albeit a little differently: his original meaning was "imagine a hypothetical situation," and now it's used to describe an endeavor that has a less-than-stellar chance of succeeding.

Bonus Words: FDR also changed the boring "Message to Congress" to the more dramatic "State of the Union." He's also been credited with coining *cheerleader*.

LUNATIC FRINGE

Coined by: Theodore Roosevelt (1901–1909)

Meaning: A political or social movement with views that are considered extreme

Origin: Roosevelt enjoyed rugged activities such as horseback riding, hiking, and hunting. Modern art? Not so much. He wrote this in 1913 (shortly after he lost the presidential election):

> It is vitally necessary to move forward and to shake off the dead hand, often the fossilized dead hand, of the reactionaries; and yet we have to face the fact that there is apt to be a lunatic fringe among the votaries of any forward movement. In this recent art exhibition, the lunatic fringe was fully in evidence, especially in the rooms devoted to the Cubists and the Futurists, or Near-Impressionists.

Roosevelt didn't come up with the phrase, but until he used it in this context, a *lunatic fringe* was the name of a shocking lady's hairstyle fad from the 1880s. (The hairstyle still exists today, but it's now called *bangs*.)

First city to win a championship in all five professional team sports: Chicago. (Baseball: 1906; hockey: 1934; football: 1986; basketball: 1991; soccer: 1998.)

Bonus Words: Roosevelt has also been given credit for *loose cannon*, *bully pulpit*, and *muckraker*.

MALAISE

Coined by: Jimmy Carter (1977–81)

Meaning: Medically, it's a general feeling of discomfort that could mark the beginning of a more serious affliction; metaphorically, it's a state of worry that the worst might be yet to come.

Origin: We have President Carter to thank for the broader meaning of this French word. In July 1979, when the U.S. was mired in economic upheaval, record inflation, and an energy crisis that caused long lines for gas, Carter gave what the press dubbed "the Malaise Speech," even though he didn't use *malaise* in the speech itself. He urged Americans to do their part by being less wasteful and materialistic, and that didn't sit well with a lot of people. It was in a press conference a few days later when Carter described the nation's plight as a "malaise." The figurative meaning took hold quickly; not long after, Carter's political opponent, Senator Ted Kennedy, complained, "Now, the people are blamed for every national ill, scolded as greedy, wasteful, and mired in malaise."

MILITARY-INDUSTRIAL COMPLEX

Coined by: Dwight D. Eisenhower (1953–61)

Meaning: A country's armed forces and the private defense contractors that supply them

Origin: On January 17, 1961, President Eisenhower said in his Farewell Address to the Nation, "In the councils of government, we must guard against the acquisition of unwarranted influence, whether sought or unsought, by the military-industrial complex. The potential for the disastrous rise of misplaced power exists, and will persist." The speech was drafted by Ike's speechwriters, Ralph E. Williams and Malcolm Moos, and in early versions it was "war-based–industrial complex," but the president changed it to "military."

Bonus Words: Eisenhower has also been credited with "more bang for the buck" (when asking the Pentagon to reduce its spending), but that phrase originated with his Secretary of Defense, Charles Erwin Wilson. And according to lexicographer Paul Dickson, Ike drew ire from language purists for verbing *final* into *finalize*: "There were editorials in the major papers that the president shouldn't use a word like *finalize*. It wasn't proper English." It became "proper" English once the president said it.

Americans spent nearly $137 billion on their pets in 2022—
up 11 percent from the previous, pandemic-mired year of 2021.

MISUNDERESTIMATE

Coined by: George W. Bush (2001–2009)

Meaning: To underestimate by mistake

Origin: Known for his peculiar relationship with the English language, Dubya made his most lasting contribution to it at a campaign rally the day before the 2000 presidential election, boasting that he won the primary because "they misunderstimated me."

The press had a field day with the malapropism. The *National Review* wrote, "Bush gave his standard stump speech, although he unveiled a new word: *misunderestimated*, which is apparently what the Democrats did vis-à-vis his campaign."

Beyond all the fun people have had with the word, British journalist and author Philip Hensher counts it among Bush's "most memorable additions to the language, and an incidentally expressive one: it may be that we rather needed a word for 'to underestimate by mistake.'"

Bonus Words: "Most people don't realize this," Bush once joked, "but Thomas Jefferson and I share a hobby. We both like to make up words." For example, when he declared, "I am the decider," he gave us all permission to be the decider in our lives (or at least use that word). (Bush is also sometimes credited with coining *strategery*, but that actually came from a Will Ferrell impression of the president on *Saturday Night Live*.)

NORMALCY

Coined by: Warren G. Harding (1921–23)

Meaning: The state of being usual, typical, or expected

Origin: Harding is credited with coining this word during a campaign speech, but it's uncertain if he said it on purpose, or if he misread *normality*. Here's the quote: "America's present need is not heroics but healing; not nostrums but normalcy; not revolution but restoration." People and the press were puzzled, as *normalcy* wasn't really a word.

Or was it? It did happen to be an obscure variation of *normality* that was used by clergy during Harding's Baptist upbringing in Ohio. (It had also been used in mathematics since the 1850s.) Nevertheless, after Harding said it, his opponents pounced on it. Harding's campaign insisted he meant to say *normalcy*, and to prove it, they adopted a new campaign slogan: "Return to Normalcy."

What is normalcy, anyway?
More presidential coinages on page 313.

Total number of moons in this solar system: 290.

SORRY, MR. PRESIDENT

Apparently, it's very hard to be the president of the United States, as these former presidents of the United States will readily, hilariously admit.

"Being president is like running a cemetery: you've got a lot of people under you and nobody's listening."
—**Bill Clinton**

"Scrubbing floors and emptying bedpans has as much dignity as the presidency."
—**Richard Nixon**

"My esteem in this country has gone up substantially. It is very nice now when people wave at me, they use all their fingers." —**Jimmy Carter**

"Politics is supposed to be the second oldest profession. I have come to realize that it bears a very close resemblance to the first." —**Ronald Reagan**

"Mothers may still want their favorite sons to grow up to be president, but, according to a famous Gallup poll of some years ago, they do not want them to become politicians in the process."
—**John F. Kennedy**

"All the president is, is a glorified public relations man who spends his time flattering, kissing, and kicking people to get them to do what they are supposed to do anyway." —**Harry S. Truman**

"No man who ever held the office of president would congratulate a friend on obtaining it." —**John Adams**

"Any man who wants to be president is either an egomaniac or crazy."
—**Dwight D. Eisenhower**

"The two happiest days of my life were those of my entrance upon the office and my surrender of it."
—**Martin Van Buren**

"If you could kick the person in the pants responsible for most of your trouble, you wouldn't sit for a month."
—**Theodore Roosevelt**

"It is the duty of the President to propose and it is the privilege of the Congress to dispose." —**Franklin D. Roosevelt**

"Being president is like being a jackass in a hailstorm. There's nothing to do but to stand there and take it."
—**Lyndon Johnson**

"No man will ever bring out of that office the reputation which carries him into it." —**Thomas Jefferson**

"I'll be damned if I am not getting tired of this. It seems to be the profession of a President simply to hear other people talk." —**William Howard Taft**

"I am not fit for this office and should never have been here."
—**Warren G. Harding**

For 18 days in 1998, Lake Champlain was designated the sixth Great Lake.

TWINS IN THE NEWS

Twins—whether identical or fraternal—are an amusing, miraculous anomaly.
As positively strange and rare as these biological clones may be, it gets even
weirder when they make headlines for doing weird twin stuff.

SPOT THE DIFFERENCE

Some identical twins look so much alike that strangers can't tell them apart—and
sometimes even their own mother isn't able to differentiate. In 2023, Argentinian
mother of newborn twin boys Sofia Rodriguez went viral on Twitter after confessing
that she can't naturally tell her sons apart, and it got so bad that she required the
assistance of authorities. "Tomorrow I have to go to the police station so they can take
my twins' fingerprints and tell me which one is which," Rodriguez tweeted. "I win the
award for mother of the year." But after getting prints taken for Lorenzo and Valentin,
at the time just 45 days old, Rodriguez didn't find herself unburdened by confusion: the
fingerprints weren't in the computer system. Meanwhile, she was able to tell that one of
the twins—she isn't sure which—got his infancy vaccines twice (and the other got none)
because he had a rapidly disappeared syringe mark on his shoulder.

LONG-LOST TWIN

Through childhood and well into his adult life, Indian farmer Sanju Bhagat lived with
a large and swollen belly. He was embarrassed by it, but nothing seemed to alleviate
it. Bhagat realized the problem was medical when his belly swelled so severely that he
looked like he had a full-term pregnancy and was having difficulty breathing. After
taking an ambulance to Tata Memorial Hospital in Mumbai, doctors immediately
operated, believing a tumor lay in Bhagat's stomach, so large that it was pressing
against his respiratory system and causing the breathing troubles. As Dr. Ajay Mehta
cut into Bhagat's abdomen, gallons of fluid spilled out—and then the doctor saw a
tiny arm. Mehta then discovered another limb, plus genitals, hair, fingernails, and
a jaw. Mehta eventually removed a strange half-formed being. The diagnosis: *fetus in
fetu*. When Bhagat was growing in his mother's womb 36 years earlier, he devoured
his not-yet-developed twin brother, who continued on as a kind of parasite inside
Bhagat's body after birth. Fewer than 90 cases have ever been documented.

DOCTOR, DOCTOR

Identical twins Kayla and Kellie Bingham both attended the Medical University of
South Carolina, both studying to become doctors. And on an eight-hour final exam
in May 2016, both twins wound up with the same result—Kayla and Kellie answered

the same 296 questions out of 307, with the same 54 answered incorrectly. University officials didn't think that was any kind of twin-coincidence; leveling charges of academic dishonesty, the school accused the sisters of cheating and launched an investigation. The evidence was scant; officials believed the twins must have been sharing information and sending one another secret signals somehow. "We exhibited normal test-taking behavior," Kayla Bingham told reporters. The sisters appealed and then sued the university, citing their perfect academic records. A jury ruled that MUSC had defamed the Bingham twins and awarded them $1.5 million in damages (or $750,000 each).

WHICH ONE ARE YOU AGAIN?

Zhao Xin and Zhao Xun are identical twin brothers from the Shanxi province in China. They married Yun Fei and Yun Yang—a pair of identical twin sisters—on the same day. All four members of the group had such difficulty determining which member of the opposite sex was their spouse and which was their in-law that they experienced several embarrassing and awkward mix-ups. "They don't just look alike, but speak with similar voices and facial expressions," the China News Service said. Seeking to put an end to the confusion, the foursome met with surgeons at Hongkang Hospital in Shanghai and came up with a solution—everyone underwent minor facial plastic surgery, so they'd all have a distinctive, unmistakable, and singular appearance. Doctors felt so bad for the couples that they performed the surgeries for free.

DIPLOMA, DIPLOMA

Twins account for around one out of every 250 births in the United States. In a large high school, like the 2,600-student Mansfield High School outside Dallas, there'd be about 10 sets of twins, statistically speaking. However, Mansfield's class of 2022 alone quadrupled that average. That year, a total of 73 multiples graduated from the school—35 pairs of twins, and one set of triplets. There were so many twins (and triplets) that the district even held a special graduation ceremony for them.

JIM, THIS IS JIM. JIM, THIS IS JIM.

Not only do identical twins look alike—but sometimes they live nearly identical lives, even without each other's influence. Jim Lewis and Jim Springer were adopted at birth and raised by different families 40 miles apart—both of whom named their new baby Jim. They tracked each other down as adults and as they caught up, they uncovered numerous similarities. Both grew up with a brother named Larry and had dogs named Toy, and both loved math and hated spelling in school. When they grew up, they both married and divorced women named Linda, and then both married women named Betty and fathered sons named James Allan. They also realized they frequently vacationed at the same Florida beach at the same time—but never saw each other.

Pace requires 25 million pounds of jalapeños annually to make its jarred salsas.

MYTH-CONCEPTIONS

*"Common knowledge" is frequently wrong. Here are some examples of things
that many people believe...but, according to our sources, just aren't true.*

MYTH: Amish communities avoid electricity—the most notable way that they reject
decadent modern life and its conveniences.

TRUTH: Amish communities don't consider electricity to be sinful or wrong. They
strongly believe in self-sufficiency, and to use electricity would mean being relying
on the electrical grid, run and governed by outsiders and others. Many Amish areas
in Pennsylvania have introduced electricity over the past few decades in the form of
independently managed solar panels.

MYTH: You shouldn't throw rice at a just-married couple leaving their ceremony
because birds eat that rice, and it absorbs water from their bodies, causing the birds to
swell up and die.

TRUTH: Rice is very safe for birds, and many species around the world eat it regularly.
Uncooked rice doesn't really absorb moisture until it's halfway cooked, and besides,
by the time that rice ends up in a bird's belly, it's already been ground up and is in
the early stages of digestion. The myth circulated for years but became false common
knowledge when Ann Landers published the anti-rice warning in a 1988 column.

MYTH: George Washington was unanimously voted the first president of the United
States in the election of 1789—every state chose him in the electoral college.

TRUTH: Washington carried 10 states, defeating John Adams in all of them. New York
failed to choose its electors by the deadline while North Carolina and Rhode Island didn't
participate in the electoral college because they hadn't yet ratified the Constitution.

MYTH: The expression "time immemorial" has always been synonymous with "before
the dawn of time," or "before time was measured."

TRUTH: The term originated in English common law, and it refers to historical events
that occurred before a very specific day: July 6, 1189. That's the date of the death of
King Henry II and the taking of the throne by his successor Richard the Lionheart.

MYTH: A Meyer lemon is a particularly sweet, flavorful, and brightly colored variety
of lemon.

Segregation-era law in Alabama: it was illegal for people of
two different races to play checkers together.

TRUTH: Imported to the U.S. in 1908 by U.S. Department of Agriculture employee Frank Meyer, the Meyer is a naturally occurring hybrid, a result of a citron mixed with another hybrid, that of a pomelo and citron. The Meyer is a citrus fruit, but it only looks and tastes like a lemon.

MYTH: Drowning occurs when someone dies by inhaling water, which floods their lungs and leaves them fatally unable to breathe.

TRUTH: Scientifically speaking, drowning is a neurological phenomenon. The brain automatically issues a panic response when submerged in water. A person can be said to have drowned if they experienced that moment of shock—drowning may not even include the inhalation of water, or even result in death.

MYTH: When a human woman is pregnant, her body creates a placenta, an in utero organ that delivers oxygen and nutrients to the growing fetus.

TRUTH: The placenta grows out of the same sperm-fertilized egg from which the baby grows, and its growth is driven by genes from the father.

MYTH: Ninjas wore all black.

TRUTH: In modern theatrical productions, stagehands wear all black to appear as "invisible" as possible when they're moving sets and props between scenes in order to maintain illusion and disbelief. This custom was borrowed from Japanese Kabuki theater, where kuroko (stagehands) wore all black as far back as 400 years ago. When Kabuki plays about legendary ninja warriors and assassins started being performed, directors dressed them like the kuroko, so the audience would understand instantly that the ninjas were supposed to blend into the night and be virtually invisible. In reality, ninjas blended in with their surroundings by dressing just like everyone else did in the communities they were tasked with infiltrating.

MYTH: Mother birds feed their babies by eating food, processing it, and then barfing it back up directly into the mouths of their youth.

TRUTH: Near a bird's throat is a chamber called a crop, or a craw. It's used to store food safely, and no digestion occurs inside it. When a mother bird looks like she's vomiting, she's just retrieving the food she was saving to share with her babies.

MYTH: A contingent who left England on the Mayflower and settled in Plymouth Rock, Massachusetts, in 1620 were called the Pilgrims.

Longest ever lightning bolt: 477.2 miles (in 2022).

TRUTH: We call them Pilgrims today because that's what they were—pilgrims, or travelers motivated by religion. At the time, those who set sail on the Mayflower were part of a Church of England separatist group called the Brownists, named after their leader, Robert Browne.

MYTH: George Washington Carver developed and invented dozens of things in the early 20th century, with most of his innovations revolving around peanuts.

TRUTH: George Carver did that stuff. The myth regards his name. He was born into slavery in the 1860s and wasn't given a middle name. He adopted W for a middle initial as an adult to make sure he received the correct mail. A reporter asked if the W stood for Washington, and Carver replied, "Why not?" It stuck.

MYTH: The British Empire got a big idea in the late 1700s: ship off its convicts and prisoners halfway around the world to its new colony of Australia.

TRUTH: Between 1788 and 1868, the British sent more than 160,000 people to Australian penal colonies. That wasn't an original idea, but a shift—prior to that, England sent its prisoners to its colonies in America. They did it from 1718 until they couldn't anymore—when the American Revolution ended British rule in what soon became the United States.

MYTH: In science, there are three states of matter. A substance can take the form of a solid, liquid, or gas.

TRUTH: There are four states of matter that can be observed in daily life: solid, liquid, gas, and plasma. Many others—such as superfluid, degenerate, fermionic condensate, Bose-Einstein condensate, and time crystals—can be manufactured in a lab under extreme and rare conditions.

MYTH: Only sparkling wine produced in Champagne, France, can legally call itself "champagne."

TRUTH: In the Treaty of Versailles, which set out the parameters for ending World War I and rebuilding postwar, Article 275 prevented signatories from producing sparkling wine and calling it "champagne"—only product bottled in the Champagne region of France could be called by that name. This was primarily done to prevent German winemakers from creating imitation champagne. But only European nations signed the Treaty of Versailles, not the United States. That means that companies in the American wine industry, which developed long after World War I, can call their sparkling wine "champagne" if they like.

Aw, 'chucks! Nunchucks are illegal to own in Massachusetts.

JURY DUTY STORIES

"We, the Jury" (page 41) tells the history of the jury system, and why it remains a benchmark of a free society. Most juries work exactly as they're intended to. It's only when things get screwy that they become newsworthy. And it's our civic duty to tell you about them.

CALLING IN SOME HELP

When a British insurance broker named Stephen Young was on trial in 1994 for double homicide, the jury was sequestered—meaning they had to stay at a hotel and avoid all contact with the outside world. Four of the jurors violated the last part in an unusual way when they used a wineglass and a Ouija board to ask a ghost if the defendant was guilty. The ghost reportedly said yes, so the four jurors told the rest of the jurors...and they found Young guilty. Upon appeal—after news of the séance came to light—Young was still found guilty by the second jury.

CONTEMPT OF COSMETICS

In June 2011, Susan Cole, a 57-year-old cosmetologist, showed up for jury duty in Denver, Colorado. If you were there, perhaps you saw her; she was the one with "makeup [that] looked like something you would wear during a theater performance," curlers in her hair, a long skirt over her mismatched socks and shoes, and a T-shirt that said, "Ask me about my best-seller." When the judged questioned whether anyone in the jury panel had a mental illness, Cole told Judge Anne Mansfield that she has PTSD and gets "very confused in the morning when I try to get ready." She was dismissed.

As luck would have it, a few months later, Judge Mansfield was listening to the "Dave Logan Show" on local radio when Cole called in and bragged about getting out of jury duty by dressing like a clown and pretending to be crazy: "I got up and said, 'Yeah, I have some mental issues.' Then the judge said, 'Does anyone care if she leaves?' And everybody else said all at once in a great big voice, 'No!'" Judge Mansfield didn't find it funny. After Cole was unable to provide proof of a PTSD diagnosis, she was charged on felony charges of first-degree perjury and attempt to influence a public servant. She was sentenced to probation and 40 hours of community service.

WHAT'S A JURY DUTY?

In 2012, Jacob Clark of Cape Cod, Massachusetts, received a jury duty summons in the mail. But he had a pretty good excuse for getting out of it: he was only nine years old. As the third grader recalled to the *Cape Cod Times*, "I was like, 'What's a jury duty?'" The goof was blamed on a typo, and a court spokesperson said mistakes like this do happen from time to time. (In another case, a cat was summoned in Boston.)

Before Julius Caesar invaded Britain in 55 BC, most Romans didn't believe Britain existed.

THE MOST FAMOUS GRAND JUROR OF ALL TIME

The phrase "famous juror" should be an oxymoron, given that anonymity is the key to keeping juries tamper-proof. Apparently no one told that to Emily Kohrs, the forewoman of the special grand jury that convened in Fulton County, Georgia, in 2022 to determine whether former president Donald Trump should be charged for interfering with the state's 2020 election.

After the grand jurors were released, Kohrs, 30, booked interviews in publications and on cable news and then shared details about the proceedings, along with her own opinions. For example, she gave the duration of a phone call between Trump and an election official ("I would have lost my voice if I had talked that long"). She also gushed about the famous people she met, such as Lindsay Graham, adding, "My coolest moment was shaking Rudy Giuliani's hand." As both of those men were witnesses, she shouldn't have been talking to them.

Because Georgia's laws are less stringent than federal laws, the "most famous grand juror in the history of jurisprudence" (as MSNBC described her) technically didn't break the law. But, as the *New York Times* wrote, "what Kohrs did break, flagrantly, were the unwritten rules. Grand juries are supposed to be affairs of the utmost solemnity and discretion. Kohrs possessed neither." A Fox News legal analyst compared her to a "vapid immature high school teenager."

THE JUDGE-AND-JURY "STALL OF SHAME"

And the award for the most Bathroom Reader–worthy jury duty incident comes to us from a Buzzfeed article that asked for people's oddest jury duty stories: "One juror had a bowel condition and terrible gas, but the judge wouldn't exempt him. At one point, the juror's gut made a noise so loud that the lawyers asked to remove him. The judge refused, but soon this guy let out the most vile fart. The judge turned a shade of green only seen in cartoons and puked all over the stand. A lawyer fainted. The bailiff had to carry the puke-covered lawyer to the chambers, and we were all dismissed."

*   *   *

5 GROSS SHOTS AND SHOOTERS

- **Smoker's Cough.** Black licorice–flavored Jägermeister and mayonnaise.
- **Prairie Oyster.** Cognac, Worcestershire sauce, salt, pepper, vinegar, tomato juice, Tabasco sauce, and egg yolk.
- **Motor Oil.** Jägermeister, peppermint schnapps, cinnamon-flavored Goldschläger, and coconut rum.
- **Infected Whitehead.** Vodka, Bloody Mary mix, and a dollop of cottage cheese.
- **Black Death.** Vodka and soy sauce.

Bulking up: every second, the Earth gets one pound heavier
by absorbing space debris and meteorites.

AND WHY DO CATS...?

On page 124, you learned why cats purr, why they rub your leg, what their meows mean, and more. Here are some more insights into the secret language of Felis catus.

WHY DO CATS RUIN YOUR FAVORITE THINGS?

If you'd pay more attention to me, hypothetically thinks the house cat, *I wouldn't have to resort to breaking your mug on the kitchen floor.* That's the main reason for this annoying behavior: to get your goat. Your cat watches you closely—your patterns, your preferences, and, most crucially, what behaviors get the most rise out of you. Dinner not out on time? Clawing the curtain. Still not out? Mug on the floor.

These attention-seeking measures are rooted in instinct. A hunting cat will "toy" with its prey—be it a real mouse or a toy mouse—by pawing and swatting at it to see how it reacts and whether it's worth hunting. If you're a cat, a broken glass might not provide much fun in and of itself, but having your owner stop what they're doing and yell gibberish at you while carrying you to the next room is the most attention you've had in hours! *I should break more stuff!*

Similarly, cats scratch things—instinctively—to stretch their legs, to release pheromones, to shed used claws, and to indicate happiness (or, if scratching too much, to communicate stress). Yet despite the five scratching posts conveniently placed around the house, the only "scratcher" that gets your attention is the sofa.

WHY ARE CATS SO KNEADY?

It's an odd feeling to have your cat (somewhat) gently poke its claws into your chest—left, right, left, right, and so on. It's even odder knowing that this behavior began during kittenhood to stimulate the mother's teats to give milk. As cat-behavior expert John Bradshaw explains, "All the behavior they show toward us is derived in some way from the mother-kitten relationship." This behavior worked well enough for them as newborns that it has stuck around into adulthood. Because cats don't have a lot of communication behaviors (perhaps "half a dozen," says Bradshaw), they go with what they know. As such, kneading could indicate an array of cat emotions:

- Kneading your chest is most often a sign of affection—as evidenced by the purring and "slow blinking" (another contentment signal). However, excessive kneading—without the other friendly cues—could indicate a problem that requires a vet visit.

About 90 percent of American homes have air conditioning;
only 20 percent of European homes do.

- Cats will also knead cushions, beds, and other soft surfaces. They do this to either get your attention, to mark territory, or to indicate that they're stressed. If that's the case, you'll notice other stressful symptoms such as harder scratching, flicking the tail (or holding it close to the body), pinning the ears back, and a lower meow.

- Cats will also knead in order to stretch their muscles, soften their bedding for a nap (like cats in the wild do to tall grasses), or to indicate that they're ready to mate. (If that's the case, there will be plenty of other clues.)

WHY DO CATS OFTEN IGNORE YOU WHEN YOU CALL THEM BY NAME?

Some people believe that cats don't come when you call because they don't know their names. They do. This was proven by Atsuko Saito, a psychologist at Sophia University in Tokyo. She conducted an experiment throughout Japan, where volunteers in homes and in a cat café recorded their cats' reactions when their names were called by both friends and strangers. All the cats in the study perked up at the sound of their name; they were also clever enough to know the difference between their name and a similar-sounding word. A separate study showed that cats even know when you're talking *about* them to other people. So if cats do know their names, why don't they always come when you call?

There are a few possible reasons for this. Cats, unlike dogs and humans, are not social animals; humans have kind of forced cats into that predicament. One reason your cat might not be taking your calls is because it doesn't need you as much as you need it. When it wants you, you'll know. Also, all cats have their own personalities, and some are less sociable than others.

It also comes down to early development. Kittens that grow up around people are more likely to respond to their names than cats that had little human contact early on. Many of those cats will try to avoid people. Even social cats need their owners to monitor this behavior; if your cat suddenly starts ignoring you, it might be ill, or, if it's an older cat, its senses may be waning.

WHY DO CATS SLEEP SO MUCH?

An adult cat sleeps 12 to 16 hours per day; a kitten, up to 20. A cat doesn't sleep this much all at once, mind you—it sleeps in short 15- to 30-minute bursts conveniently called catnaps. Doing so prevents the animal from ever falling into a deep sleep, which is harder to wake from. This is how it works with all felines: as predators, they need to be alert, so short naps conserve energy. Like vampires, your

If you're average, you'll produce four pint glasses of spit today.

cat is most active from dusk until dawn, so it sleeps the day away. (Unlike vampires, though, cats seek out sunny spots to sleep in.)

There are other reasons your cat might be sleeping a lot, according to PetMD. One is boredom. "While sleeping might not seem like a big deal, boredom can lead to other problematic behaviors in cats, such as destruction, constant meowing, and over-grooming. To stay engaged…cats need stimulation throughout the day in the form of vertical territory (cat trees, scratching posts, and cat shelves), puzzle feeders, and regular playtime with the family." An overly sleepy cat could be stressed, sick, or injured, so keep an eye on your cat's sleeping habits.

WHY DO CATS ALWAYS LAND ON THEIR FEET?

In 2012, a cat named Sugar fell between 150 and 200 feet from a Boston high-rise, landed on her feet, and suffered no broken bones. This feline superpower kicks in immediately after the cat begins to fall. An organ in the ear called the vestibular apparatus activates the "righting reflex." Then the cat's uniquely flexible backbone allows it to swiftly position its feet beneath it. It spreads out—not unlike a flying squirrel—and its low body-to-weight ratio slows the descent. When the cat finally lands on its feet, the front paws are protecting the face, and its weight is evenly distributed, lessening the force of the impact.

But the righting reflex doesn't happen instantly. A cat that falls from only a few stories might not turn around in time and could be seriously injured or killed.

WHY DO CATS BITE AND LICK PEOPLE?

Good news: Your cat isn't checking to see if you taste good (it already knows your salty sweat is delicious). The licking behavior is simply grooming—because it still hasn't figured out that you're not a cat. The biting behavior is likely play, which begins in kittenhood; cats play-bite one another while learning how to defend themselves. If your usually mellow cat resorts to biting, it's likely that you haven't picked up on other clues—hiding, hunching over, hissing, swatting, and folding the ears back. Or, possibly, the cat has gotten overstimulated and is saying, "I've had enough." This most commonly occurs in the midst of a belly rub. If the biting gets really bad, see a vet.

According to PetHelpful.com, "Yelling at your cat for biting is never a smart idea. If they bite you hard while you're playing, firmly exclaim 'ow' and then leave. They will discover that biting forcefully puts an end to playtime. Punishing or yelling at them will only make them fearful and more likely to respond negatively." So, worry not: an aggressive cat bite doesn't mean your house cat is hunting you, because they don't hunt humans. That being said…

WILL YOUR CAT EAT YOU IF YOU DIE?

Yes. Yes, it will. If the circumstances are grim enough—you've been dead for days and all the food is gone—your cat (or dog!) will resort to feeding on your flesh in order to survive. They are predators, after all. In 2020, *The Journal of Forensic Sciences* reported the grisly findings of a study where human corpses were left outside a research facility. The local wild bobcats preferred the meat of the arms and thighs, while the local feral cats (the same species as your domestic cat) preferred the meat of the face.

DOES YOUR CAT LOVE YOU?

Now that you know just how manipulative your kitty can be, does that mean that showing "affection" is just another cat trick to get a full belly and a warm place to sleep? Good news: your cat really does like you, mostly because you do feed and shelter it. That makes sense, evolutionarily, in that the first friendly wildcats to bond with humans were more likely to reproduce kittens that were similarly amicable. Then the ancient Egyptians further bred them for these positive traits. And because cats truly are independent animals that don't require constant companionship (like dogs), a cat that comes to you does so of its own accord.

But is this *love*? "While there's no scientific way to measure love in regard to cats," posits Samantha Bell, a cat-behavior expert at Best Friends Animal Society, "I do believe they can feel great affection towards humans and each other. I can say with certainty that we can help them feel safe and comfortable. And we can tell they enjoy being around us when they sit on our laps, stick around and don't leave, purr, etc."

THE FUTURE OF THE HOUSE CAT

The most dramatic change in *Felis catus* took hold very recently—between 1950 and 2000—when house cats started spending more of their lives inside. Today, nearly half of all cats live indoors full-time, and those numbers are rising rapidly. The main reason is safety: indoor cats live 15 to 17 years, while outdoor cats live as few as 2 to 5 years (according to a University of California, Davis, study). Then there's the growing movement to protect threatened avian species—outdoor cats are responsible for an estimated 2.4 billion bird deaths per year in the U.S. alone.

How will staying inside alter cats? They'll become even more like us. A 2018 study of 3,000 cat owners concluded that cats not only take on the personality traits of their owners, but owners are treating their cats more and more like human children. How this all might play out is detailed in Abigail Tucker's book *The Lion in the Living Room*.

Tequila is made from agave, which botanically is a type of asparagus.

- There will be more strange-looking "one-off" cats with genetic conditions like Grumpy Cat (a viral sensation with feline dwarfism). While not adapted to thrive in the Darwinian sense, these genetic anomalies will remain safe at home. And thanks to the Internet, they'll become famous.

- Selectively breeding hybrid species will make some cats very large and wild-looking. Take the Bengal cat, created in the early 20th century by crossing domestic felines with Asian leopard cats. Or more recently, the wrinkly, hairless Dwelf cat, which *Parade Pets* describes as "a cross between the Munchkin, American Curl, and Sphynx breeds [with] shorter legs...so they tend to develop achondroplastic dwarfism," but "are very loving."

- Feral cats—the outdoor descendants of domestic cats—will become truly wild again as they grow larger than bobcats and form big colonies that should be avoided.

Those are just three possibilities. Whatever happens with our world, cats will do what they've always done: figure out how to transform it into *their* world.

OK, that's a whole lot about cats, but if you're curious for more (like how they got nine lives, or how to spell the sound they make), go to page 294.

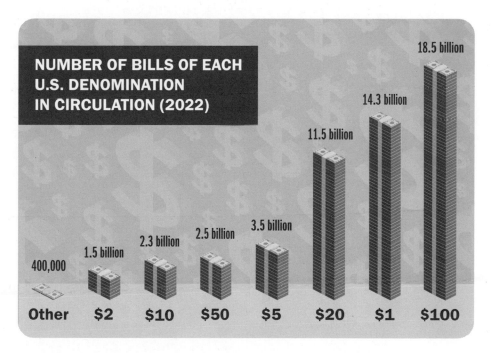

NUMBER OF BILLS OF EACH U.S. DENOMINATION IN CIRCULATION (2022)

Other	$2	$10	$50	$5	$20	$1	$100
400,000	1.5 billion	2.3 billion	2.5 billion	3.5 billion	11.5 billion	14.3 billion	18.5 billion

GLADIATORS VS. TRUCKS

In the late 1980s and early 1990s, the athletic TV game show American Gladiators pitted regular people against a stock team of tough, muscle-bound competitors. The Gladiators usually rolled over the average folks like they were monster trucks, another popular and raucous entertainment of the day. That's not all the Gladiators and trucks had in common— they also shared similar names. Of those listed below, can you determine which belong to American Gladiators and which were given to gigantic trucks? (Answers are on page 405.)

1) Titan

2) Brutus

3) Dragon

4) Tower

5) Bulldozer

6) Siren

7) Earth Shaker

8) Bronco

9) Thunder

10) RAGE

11) Turbo

12) Whiplash

13) Zombie

14) Blaze

15) Avenger

16) Viper

17) Axe

18) Tank

19) The Destroyer

20) Vendetta

21) Nitro

22) Predator

23) Hawk

24) Megalodon

25) Atlas

26) Cyclone

27) Raminator

28) Stone Crusher

29) Madusa

30) Grinder

31) Havoc

32) Rebel

Real name of Chinese checkers? Sternhalma. It was created in 1892 in Germany.

HICCUP!

They're probably the weirdest and most unnerving thing the human body does (that doesn't involve a bathroom). Here's the how, why, and what of a surprisingly still-mysterious phenomenon: hiccups.

Take a Breath. The muscle that controls breathing, an involuntary and automatic function, is the diaphragm. Every intake of breath contracts the diaphragm and expands the chest. In its simplest terms, a hiccup is a muscle spasm—of the diaphragm specifically. When it happens, an electrical message travels on a neural pathway, or a reflex arc, up to the brain, which tells the body to temporarily malfunction. The spasm is continuous, so it repeatedly sends the message over and over, resulting in the repetitive opening and closing of the flap that covers the vocal cords in the throat (the glottis). That rush of forced, escaping air creates the familiar "hic!" sound.

Cause and Effect. A wide variety of stimuli cause hiccups. Among the most common hiccup creators: consumption of spicy food, alcohol, or carbonated drinks; eating too quickly; acid reflux; stress, extreme nervousness, or excitement; and sudden temperature changes. Hiccups are also a noted side effect of some steroids, tranquilizers, and surgical-grade anesthesia. Scientists aren't certain of the connecting thread between all those situations. Hiccups could feasibly be the result of different, unrelated irritations. Spicy food, for example, irritates the stomach, and since it's so close to the diaphragm, the unsettled organ pushes up against the diaphragm, causing it to spasm.

Getting Technical. The medical term for hiccups is *singultus*, a word originally used to denote a hiccup-like phenomenon: quick intakes of frantic breath during crying.

So Speedy. The forceful contraction of the diaphragm—a hiccup, in other words—involves the opening and closing of the vocal cords, and it takes just 35 milliseconds. The rate of hiccups during an episode averages anywhere from 4 to 60 per minute, the body keeping up the pace in a rhythmic fashion until it slows down, before finally stopping.

Animal Instinct. Humans aren't alone in their suffering. Most mammals are subject to hiccups, which have been studied or observed in cats, rats, rabbits, horses, and dogs.

A Feature Nobody Asked For. One of the prevailing scientific theories about why we hiccup is that it's a relic of an earlier stage of human evolution. According to this theory, when proto-humans evolved enough to get out of the ocean and onto land, they developed the hiccup as a failsafe to prevent water from entering the lungs.

Second Opinion. Rejecting the vestigial response theory, Dr. Daniel Howes published a new theory in 2012: hiccups are a burp reflex. Howes says that the

Say hello to your little friends: there are 67 species of bacteria residing in your belly button.

presence of air in the stomach leads to hiccups. Studying babies who drank milk too fast, he found that the body quickly responds to that unwanted gas in the stomach by forcing sharp intakes of breath, moving the swallowed air out...causing hiccups.

A Youthful Concern. The older you get, the less common hiccups are in your age group. And those age brackets include the unborn, too. Hiccups are very common in the womb, a fact that goes against all the other reasoning about why they happen—because babies' lungs aren't yet developed fully, and they're not breathing the same way as those of us already born. Scientists think prenatal hiccups are a baby's body's way of training the breathing muscles for when they begin breathing air (and not amniotic fluid). The training seemingly continues after birth—newborns spend as much as 2.5 percent of their waking hours hiccupping.

In Search of a Cure. There are dozens of so-called hiccup remedies that have persisted over the years. They don't necessarily work, because they were never based in science, but they've lasted this long because they inadvertently hit on some solid logic. Holding your breath, getting startled, or drinking water all can reset or trick the diaphragm, the lynchpin in a hiccuping spell. The only surefire cure for hiccups (most of the time): waiting. They generally subsist on their own in under 15 minutes.

Straw Pole. Taking into consideration that pressure on the diaphragm is involved in hiccups, and that drinking water can quell a hiccup attack, Texas neurosurgeon Dr. Ali Seifi invented HiccAway. Launched in 2021, it's essentially a plastic straw, but thicker. The tube increases pressure on the diaphragm while it's used to sip liquid, a one-two punch that Dr. Seifi says can stop hiccups.

Too Much? Doctors consider a normal, nonproblematic episode of hiccups one that lasts for up to 48 hours. Longer than that, and the hiccups could indicate a central nervous system disease (such as meningitis or encephalitis) or a metabolic issue (kidney failure or diabetes).

Poor Charles. History's most prolific hiccuper: a Nebraska farm worker named Charles Osborne. While handling a hog on June 13, 1922, he started hiccuping for some reason...and didn't stop for nearly 68 years. He repeatedly saw doctors who tried a number of mainstream and experimental techniques, including having him breathe a mixture of carbon dioxide and oxygen (but that just suffocated him). Osborne ultimately learned a special breathing technique to minimize the frequency and intensity of the hiccups. They stopped on their own in February 1990; he died a little over a year later, having hiccuped an estimated 430 million times.

Elephants can hear rain clouds gathering.

CHARLES'S BARKINGS

In the 1980s and 1990s, Charles Barkley—a.k.a. Sir Charles, a.k.a. the Round Mound of Rebound—was an NBA legend, and an aggressive big man who protested in commercials, "I am not a role model." He later became a jovial sportscaster and basketball analyst. Through it all, he's made some very funny (and controversial) remarks.

"You got to believe in yourself. Hell, I believe I'm the best-looking guy in the world and I might be right."

"I don't care what people think. People are stupid."

"Sometimes that light at the end of the tunnel is a train."

"People say I eat a lot. I really don't. More or less I just eat all the time."

"I heard Tonya Harding is calling herself the Charles Barkley of figure skating. I was going to sue her for defamation of character, but then I realized I have no character."

"I love everybody. Some I love to be around, some I love to avoid, and others I'd love to punch in the face."

"I think that the team that wins game five will win the series. Unless we lose game five."

"The older I get, the faster I was."

"I read that heavy drinking is bad for your health. I decided I better stop reading."

"If all babies are so cute, how the hell do we have so many ugly people in the world?"

"Kids are great. That's one of the best things about our business, all the kids you get to meet. It's a shame they have to grow up to be regular people and come to the games and call you names."

"You can't start a diet in the middle of the week, that's just stupid."

"The only difference between a good shot and a bad shot is if it goes in or not."

"Golf is fun—until you hit somebody in the head."

"Every time I think about changing a diaper, I run a little bit harder and a little bit faster to make sure I can afford a nanny until my daughter's old enough to take care of that herself."

"These are my new shoes. They're good shoes. They won't make you rich like me, they won't make you rebound like me, they definitely won't make you handsome like me. They'll only make you have shoes like me."

Each year, about 569 million Slim Jim sticks are made.

GREATEST (IMAGINARY) HITS

Have you ever seen these famous movies or heard these hit songs? Probably not, because—contrary to the insistence of many—they don't exist and never did.

Film: *Dracula* (1920)

Story: Bram Stoker's 1897 novel *Dracula* has been adapted into dozens of movies and is largely credited with stoking popular vampire mythology. The very first time Count Dracula appeared on a movie screen was in *Dracula*, a 1920 film produced in Russia. That's according to *The Vampire Book: The Encyclopedia of the Undead* by J. Gordon Melton, purported to be a complete omnibus of all vampire fiction and media. No print, frames, or stills of the movie, supposedly directed by Victor Tourjansky, exist in the present day. In 2013, Russian news agencies reported that a print was found in Serbia, and it was uploaded to YouTube.

Unreal: Experts quickly debunked the newly discovered movie as a hoax—it was a modern film designed to look like a 1920s silent black-and-white film. Considering the lack of existing materials, a hoax print, and how it would've been hard to make a major film smack in the middle of Russia's devastating civil war, film historians don't think the 1920 *Dracula* ever existed.

Songs: "Ready N' Steady," "The Song of Love," and "Drag You Down"

Story: From 1970 until his death in 2022, Joel Whitburn was the preeminent pop chart historian in the United States. Studying old *Billboard* data, he wrote dozens of books cataloging American popular music. Whitburn also claimed to own a copy of every single to ever appear on a *Billboard* chart, except for one—"Ready N' Steady," a 1979 release by a band called The D.A.

Unreal: Whitburn didn't have a 45 of the song because he made it up. He fabricated the entry in his chart books as a trap, to keep track of who might cite his works without proper credit. Whitburn repeated the ruse twice with the fake songs "The Song of Love" (supposedly a #84 hit in 1955 by real bandleader Ralph Marterie) and "Drag You Down" (a not-real 1986 rock chart hit from a not-real band called Cysterz).

Film: *Goncharov*

Story: In the early 2020s, movie buffs and film writers got very excited when evidence of a long-lost early work by Oscar-winning filmmaker Martin Scorsese was uncovered. In 1973, before he made classics such as *Mean Streets* and *Taxi Driver*, Scorsese directed *Goncharov*. The plot: a man named Goncharov (Robert De Niro) flees the Soviet Union for Italy and gets caught up with the Mafia. The film also stars

Al Pacino, Gene Hackman, Cybill Shepherd, and Harvey Keitel. First a poster for the never-released, long-buried *Goncharov* surfaced, then claims of the discovery of a print. Social media sites including X (Twitter) and Tumblr erupted over *Goncharov,* with thousands clamoring to see the early work by a master filmmaker, with others, who claimed to have already seen it, giving it praise.

Unreal: It was all an elaborate joke. Overzealous Scorsese fans failed to notice that the poster included a 1980s-era shot of Shepherd and attributed its screenplay to the clearly fake "Matteo JWHJ 0715"—the Tumblr username of the hoax's originator and perpetrator.

TV Series: *Operation: Aliens*

Story: After the release of the sci-fi horror movie *Aliens* in 1986, and before the release of *Alien 3* in 1992, Kenner Toys launched "Operation: Aliens," a line of action figures featuring the characters from the films (mostly space marines and horrific extraterrestrial monsters called xenomorphs). The line was also a tie-in with *Operation: Aliens,* an animated series the Fox network ordered and produced for its Saturday-morning lineup, scheduled to air in 1992 around the time that *Alien 3* would hit theaters. Fox Kids then refused to air the show—full of violence and gore, just like the *Aliens* movie—citing its inappropriateness for its target audience of little kids.

Unreal: Stills purporting to stem from *Operation: Aliens* were widely distributed online in the 2010s, supposedly taken from a South Korean animation studio. A Fox Kids executive debunked the story for *Aliens vs. Predator Galaxy* magazine, saying that the network had merely thought about an *Aliens* series, but never so much as ordered one. The animated stills? Those came from a never-aired advertising campaign for the "Operation: Aliens" toys.

* * *

3 SHORT STORIES ABOUT VERY LONG THINGS

World's longest constitution. The sixth state constitution of Alabama, adopted in 1901, was 388,882 words, the lengthiest legal document ever in use. It was more than 50 times as long as the U.S. Constitution and 12 times as long as an average American state constitution. (It was replaced in 2022 by a shorter document.)

World's longest sniper kill. In November 2023, a Ukrainian fighter in Special Group "Alpha" reported a kill at a distance of 3,800 meters, or 2.36 miles. If confirmed, that would beat the previous record of 3,539 meters (2.2 miles), belonging to a Canadian marksman fighting in Iraq in June 2017.

World's longest wedding veil. For her wedding in Cyprus in 2018, Maria Paraskeva wore a veil slightly more than 22,843 feet long. It took a year to make and 20 people to carry it.

Last victim of the Spanish Inquisition: Cayetano Ripoll, executed
in 1826 for teaching his students about deism.

WEIRD DEATHS

When you think about it, death itself is weird—one moment you're alive and then the next, you're not anymore. But these ways in which people shuffled off this mortal coil are among the most baffling and unexpected.

DEATH BY MAGNET

In January 2023, Leandro Mathias de Novaes accompanied his mother to a hospital in São Paulo, Brazil, where she needed to receive an MRI scan. A lawyer by trade, de Novaes carried a handgun for personal protection, and entered the MRI room with a pistol concealed in his waistband. Before he went into the room with the powerful magnet-based machine, staff told de Novaes to remove any metal from his person. He kept the gun on him and didn't disclose it to staff; the machine's magnetic field was so strong that it ripped the firearm from the lawyer's waistband, causing it to fire. A discharged bullet lodged in de Novaes's abdomen, and three weeks later he died of internal injuries.

DEATH BY PROTEIN POWDER

A 28-year-old man (unnamed in news reports) was driving his Lexus just before dawn one morning in February 2022 in a San Diego suburb. The vehicle, traveling at a high speed in a residential area, suddenly veered right and forcefully crashed into a parked car. The motorist died later that day in a hospital of injuries suffered in the accident. An investigation theorized that the cause of the crash was driver distraction: the man had been stirring protein powder into a container of water with a knife, and when he struck the parked car that he didn't immediately see, the force of the impact drove the knife into his neck.

DEATH BY EPOXY

Indian man Salman Mirza and his former fiancée rekindled their romance in June 2021. After a night of partying, the couple checked into a hotel room to take things to a physical level. Evidently without a condom but wanting to practice safe sex and guard against an accidental pregnancy, Mirza turned to the epoxy adhesive he was known to carry for the purposes of inhaling it to get high. He slathered the epoxy on his sensitive areas, apparently thinking that sealing everything up down there would prevent any unwanted secretions. A day later, Mizra was dead from multiple organ failure, possibly caused by the large amounts of toxic glue applied to his skin.

Airplane toilets are coated in Teflon.

DEATH BY POTATO

In the small town of Laishevo in the Russian region of Tatarstan, Mikhail Chelyshev entered the root cellar of his family home, where there was food being stored. According to authorities, he fainted from toxic fumes in the cellar and died soon afterward. Curious as to her husband's whereabouts, his wife, Anastasia, entered the cellar, and she too passed out and died upon inhaling the fumes. Their teenage son and Anastasia's mother, Iraida, both suffered the same fate. Iraida left the door open, unlike the others, allowing the fumes to dissipate, which is how eight-year-old Maria Chelysheva was able to discover the bodies of her family members in the cellar without passing out herself. The cause of death: accumulated toxic gas released by a large quantity of rotten potatoes.

DEATH BY FLYING COW

Very few deaths involve cows or answering the call of nature, and even fewer involve both at the same time. A strange sequence of events in April 2023 left 82-year-old Indian man Shivdayal Sharma dead. Sharma urinated near a train track located in the Alwar region of India. As he did so, a Vande Bharat express train came speeding through on a track adjacent to where Sharma was relieving himself. However, a cow was hanging out on that track, snacking on garbage and weeds. And the express train smashed into it, sending the cow flying into the air. It landed about 100 feet away—on top of Sharma, crushing him and killing him instantly. To add an ironic twist, Sharma worked for India's national railway system until his retirement in 2000.

DEATH BY DOG

In January 2023, 30-year-old Wichita, Kansas, plumber Joseph Smith was in the passenger seat of a friend's pickup truck. In the backseat sat some hunting gear, including a rifle, and a dog belonging to the owner of the truck. And then a bullet from the loaded, ready-to-fire gun struck Smith in the back, killing him instantly. An investigation by the local sheriff's office determined that the dog had stepped on the rifle, inadvertently pressing down on the trigger, firing the gun, and sending a bullet into Smith, who happened to be close by.

DEATH BY PIG

Butchers are supposed to kill animals, but the order was reversed during an incident at the Sheung Shui Slaughterhouse in Hong Kong in January 2023. A 61-year-old butcher identified in news reports only as Cai was doing his job as he'd done thousands of times before, about to embark on the process of butchering into sellable pork products a pig he'd already hit with an electric stun gun. The pig wouldn't go down without a

What's the only organ that can regenerate itself? The liver.

fight, however. The animal regained consciousness and wiggled around so much that it knocked Cai to the ground. That caused the man to endure severe wounds to his hand and foot, apparently caused by his meat cleaver, leading to blood loss.

DEATH BY SOCCER

Norbert Tóth served as a player-coach to Juta, his semi-professional soccer team in Somogy County, Hungary. In May 2023, while playing in the championship game, Tóth scored a goal that put his team in the lead. After kicking it through and celebrating wildly, Tóth told his teammates that he felt unwell and asked for a substitution. He retired to the locker room and the game continued. When a teammate went to check on Tóth a few minutes later, he was unresponsive. After nearly an hour of revival attempts, Tóth was taken to a hospital where he was pronounced dead. Doctors believe the 53-year-old athlete suffered a fatal heart attack, triggered by excessive post-goal celebration.

DEATH BY HOLE

In July 2022, Klil Kimhi attended a work retreat at a vacation rental home in the Isreali town of Karmi Yosef. A half dozen coworkers, including Kimhi, were enjoying the large swimming pool on the premises when, extremely suddenly, the bottom gave out and everything—water, pool toys, the pool itself—began sinking into the ground. A sinkhole had developed and spontaneously cracked open. Five swimmers escaped, but not Kimhi, who couldn't resist the powerful, sucking pull of the sinkhole. He died in the tragedy, which was later revealed to be entirely preventable because the owner of the home had never applied for a pool-building permit—which wouldn't have been granted because of infrastructure problems common in that area.

DEATH BY TOAD

After the 2022 Russian invasion of Ukraine, several executives at Russian oil company Lukoil publicly came out against the war. Some of them later died under mysterious circumstances, including Aleksandr Subbotin—but not from any foul play. Subbotin was a heavy drinker, and to treat his frequent hangovers, he'd go to the home of a man who called himself Magua, a self-proclaimed shaman. Magua would administer doses of poison extracted from the sac of a toad. After ingesting the poison, Magua's clients, including Subbotin, would vomit, and subsequently feel cured of their day-after-drinking symptoms. Subbotin had submitted to the procedure numerous times; in May 2022, he complained of the toxin causing heart palpitations. Instead of seeking medical assistance, Magua instructed Subbotin to go lie down in the basement. Subbotin died in there, of a heart attack.

Shortest-serving monarch: King Vira Bahu I of Polonnaruwa (modern-day Sri Lanka) was crowned the night his father died in 1196, then assassinated the next morning.

RICH, FAMOUS, AND INVENTIVE

Celebrities: is there anything they can't do? In addition to being generally talented,
good looking, charismatic, and powerful, several famous people also harnessed
enough ingenuity and smarts to invent something and receive a patent for it.

Celebrity: Julie Newmar

Invention: Today, compression undergarments that slim the silhouette, such as Spanx, are known as shapewear. One of the first forms of it was invented by the actress best known for playing Catwoman on the 1960s *Batman* TV series. In 1974, Newmar took the bottom half of her old skintight, curve-hugging Catwoman costume, combined it with compression pantyhose and elastic fabric, and filed for a patent on "Pantyhose with shaping band for cheeky derriere relief." The very tight leggings fit around the body in such a way that lifted a woman's rear end and made it appear smaller, or, as Newmar said in her application, "look like an apple instead of a ham sandwich."

Celebrity: Eddie Van Halen

Invention: Van Halen played the electric guitar with extreme speed and precision because he picked all over his instrument's fretboard with two hands, rather than one. That left it difficult to hold up his guitar, so he created and patented the "musical instrument support" in 1985. It attaches to the back of the guitar (or any other stringed instrument), flips out, and holds up and steadies it.

Celebrity: Steve McQueen

Invention: In the 1960s and 1970s, the action star frequently performed his own driving stunts in movies such as *Bullitt*, and he also participated in auto races. He so hated sitting on bench-style seats that in 1970 he earned a patent on an early bucket seat that kept the driver safely in place, especially when they were driving fast.

Celebrity: Hedy Lamarr

Invention: The Austrian actress and "most beautiful woman in the world" was one of Hollywood's biggest draws in the 1930s and 1940s. When World War II broke out, she wanted to help the Allies defeat the Nazis, and she had an interest in communications and radio technology. With composer George Antheil, Lamarr created a way for the military to securely transmit radio messages via the patented "secret communication system" or "frequency hopping." Rather than sending out

Before it made fancy cars, the Lamborghini company was a tractor manufacturer.

messages on a single frequency that could easily be intercepted, Lamarr's technology allowed for messages to move between different channels in a pattern agreed to ahead of time. Lamarr gave her patent to the U.S. Navy in 1942, but they didn't have the technology needed to make it work. However, her method later became the basis for cellular phone transmission, communications satellites, and Wi-Fi.

Celebrity: Albert Einstein

Invention: The guy who devised the theory of relativity knew some things about science, and it's no surprise that he held 50 patents for inventions including hearing devices and cameras. But he also held a patent for...a shirt? His "new, original, and ornamental blouse," patented in 1936, featured side openings that also served as arm holes, and a central panel in the back that could expand into a suit jacket.

Celebrity: Roald Dahl

Invention: In addition to writing classic children's books including *James and the Giant Peach,* Dahl took an interest in neuroscience after a 1960 car accident gave his infant son hydrocephalus, a painful and damaging condition also known as water on the brain. Working with neurosurgeon Kenneth Till and engineer Stanley Wade, Dahl built a shunt that could efficiently drain unnecessary brain fluid. The Wade-Dahl-Till Valve helped save the lives of thousands of children around the world.

Celebrity: Jamie Lee Curtis

Invention: The *Halloween* star and *Everything Everywhere All at Once* Academy Award winner raised a few children and changed so many diapers that she figured the process could be improved. In 1988, Curtis was awarded a patent on her "Unitary Disposable Diaper with Integrated Soilage-Management Structure, Including Disposal Container." It's a disposable, single-use-style diaper constructed with a pocket into which fluids or solid waste cannot enter that can be used to store much-needed baby wipes. (Her patent expired without being marketed because she refused to work with any company that wouldn't make biodegradable, more environmentally friendly diapers.)

Celebrity: Lawrence Welk

Invention: The host of *The Lawrence Welk Show* brought cheery and cheesy dance numbers and old-fashioned big band tunes (which he called "champagne music") into Americans' homes from 1951 to 1982. That era is also when smoking peaked—about half of American adults regularly smoked cigarettes. In 1953, Welk received a patent for an intricate decorative ashtray designed to look like an accordion (his signature instrument). Made of glass, and totally square, its sides were ridged to allow easy placement of a burning cigarette. At the bottom was a stylish illustration—of a glass of champagne expelling musical notes and bubbles, just like on *The Lawrence Welk Show.*

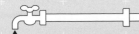

In 1971, the NFL's Atlanta Falcons drafted 63-year-old John Wayne. (He didn't play.)

GREAT MOMENTS IN JESTERISM

While they probably didn't wear floppy hats with bells on the end, court jesters
were a real thing. These comedians, singers, and storytellers entertained
European monarchs and their courts for centuries. Here
are some of the most notable among them.

Lord Minimus

His real name was Jeffrey Hudson, but Queen Henrietta Maria of France gave her
jester and official "Queen's dwarf" this moniker in order to playfully indicate his
stature as a royally beloved person who stood about two feet tall. After he was
abandoned in 1625 at age six, when he was the size of a baby, the Duchess of
Buckingham took him in, and he lived in her household until he was given away as
a gift to Henrietta Maria—the duchess "served" him to the queen as part of the final
dish at a banquet, when he crawled out of a large pie dressed in a suit of armor. The
queen put Lord Minimus to work entertaining: in one popular bit, another member
of court would set out sandwich-making materials, then pull Lord Minimus out of
his pocket and make the jester the "meat."

Roland the Farter

The official jester to King Henry II of England in the late 12th century, Roland's
primary talent was farting—loudly and emphatically. He'd fart to punctuate jokes, as
a part of a routine, or simply on command. His signature move (Henry II's favorite)
was executing a jump, a whistle, and a fart, all at the same time. Roland was the
prime attraction at the king's annual Christmas extravaganza. When he wasn't
entertaining, he lived in the stately Hemingstone Manor upon 30 acres of land,
gifted to him by Henry.

Borra

In 1410, King Martin I of Aragon was bedridden with a fatal illness. To lighten
his mood, he called to his sickbed his long-serving jester, Borra. The entertainer
was miles from the royal palace when summoned, and it took him hours to arrive.
When the king asked why he'd taken so long, Borra joked, "In the next vineyard,
I saw a young deer hanging by his tail from a tree, as if someone had punished
him for stealing figs." Likening an animal to an executed thief was so outrageously

hilarious to King Martin I that he reportedly laughed for three hours straight… and then died.

Perkeo

"Perché no?" is an Italian phrase that means "why not?" Often uttered in response to the offer of another glass of wine, the phrase morphed into *Perkeo*, the nickname of a jester who loved to drink alcohol. He imbibed so much that it was his talent, and apparently quite a marvel to watch. Perkeo served Charles III Philip, Count of Palatinate-Neuburg (a territory of the Holy Roman Empire) in the early 18th century. Perkeo was a jester, but his title was a goof: "Knight of the Royal Vat." Perkeo was the guardian of the world's largest barrel of wine, which made sense because he entertainingly drank as many as eight gallons of the stuff for an audience every day. (Perkeo reportedly died the day after drinking—for the first time—water instead of wine.)

Triboulet

The jester born Nicolas Ferrial entertained French kings Louis XII and Francis I in the 16th century. Triboulet (literally "jester dressed in red") was born with very short arms and very short legs, likely a result of undiagnosed microencephaly, and royals and members of court likened him to a monkey, ordering him to run around and dance like that animal. Triboulet once so offended King Francis I in his jests that it nearly led to his execution: he slapped the king on the rear end, and, ordered to explain himself, said, "I'm sorry, I didn't recognize you. I mistook you for the Queen." Francis at least let Triboulet choose his method of execution, to which the jester replied, "old age." The king thought that was so funny he let Triboulet live (and fired him instead).

Richard Tarlton

Tarlton did double duty in what were two of the highest-profile jobs for a comedian in the late 1500s: he was a member of the highly regarded acting troupe Queen Anne's Men, and he served as jester to Queen Elizabeth I. Tarlton played the small comic roles in numerous plays and improvised a lot (much to playwrights' annoyance), and William Shakespeare likely based the deceased but fondly remembered character Yorick in *Hamlet* on him. (Tarlton died of the plague in 1588.) But as jester for the queen, he would fence, tell jokes off the top of his head, and dare to insult high-ranking officials, including Sir Walter Raleigh and the Earl of Leicester, in front of them. Why? Because it made Elizabeth, prone to fits of melancholy, laugh. Tarlton could be counted on to cheer her up, usually by honestly and brutally pointing out Her Majesty's faults.

Year Austrian-born Adolf Hitler became a German citizen: 1932.
Year Hitler took control of Germany: 1933.

Stańczyk

Just as the acts of comedians today run the gamut from lowbrow to erudite, so too did the comedy of jesters. Stańczyk's wit was intellectual, caustic, and satirical. A jester for three Polish kings in the mid-16th century, Stańczyk was known as a "wise fool," more likely to offer insights into the dark nature of man and opinions on political matters than he was to crack a simple joke. In 1533, King Sigismund I invited Stańczyk on an expedition to hunt a bear he'd imported from Lithuania. The bear attacked the queen and knocked her off her horse. During the chaos, Stańczyk ran away rather than fight. When taken to task by the king, Stańczyk quipped, "It is a greater folly to let out a bear that was already locked in a cage." The king understood the jester's intent—he was reportedly (and obliquely) criticizing the monarch's mishandling of Prussia, a land conquered by, but not annexed into, Poland.

Claus Narr

Narr is the German word for "fool," so this jester's name translates to "Claus the Fool." He was discovered, according to legend, in the village of Ranstadt in the 15th century when a representative of the king of Saxony saw Claus tending to his geese. The official's horses had startled the birds, and Claus had to carry a flock of them under his arms and tuck a few dead ones under his belt. That was so funny, the official hired him to be a jester. Once sent to court, Claus liked to set up pranks and pull practical jokes on top-ranking members of the court, much to the king's liking.

Twisty Pole

Roles similar to the jester existed long before and far away from medieval Europe. In China in the 3rd century BC, there was no specific word for a jester, though *you* (the Chinese character denoting someone who used humor to mock and joke) was used to describe the court entertainers that served rulers. Twisty Pole was an example of a *you*, employed by the first and second emperors of the Qin dynasty, the first to rule over a unified China. While *you* specialized in music or physical comedy, Twisty Pole was a master of sarcasm, which he utilized in his role as one of his bosses' most trusted advisors. Emperor Qin Shi Huang could have brought major financial ruin to China had he carried out his plan to build a massive game preserve. Twisty Pole stopped him by telling him it was a great idea, because in the event of an invasion, the deer and gazelles could be trained to charge the enemies with their horns. That embarrassed the emperor into canceling the plan. Twisty Pole similarly put to rest Emperor Qin Er Shi's idea to paint the Great Wall of China, calling the plan a "splendid idea" because the wall would then be too slick for invading hordes to climb over.

The average prisoner in Brazil reads nine times as many books as the average Brazilian.

THE BEST PIRATE NICKNAMES

Yes, they were bad guys (and gals), pillaging and killing and waging terror on the high seas from the 16th to 18th centuries (or thereabouts). But they sure had cool nicknames.

Black Caesar	Captain Jackman
Red Legs Greaves	Billy One Hands
Flora Burn	Redbeard
Long Ben	Samuel Axe
Black Sam	Blueskin
Diabolito	Simon the Dancer
Turn Joe Ireland	Colonel Plug
Calico Jack	Bully Hayes
Black Bart	Roaring Dan Seavey
Old Captain Crackers	Bone
Sadie the Goat	Jack the Bachelor
Callus Meg	Big Brew
Half Butt	Yankee Jim
The Wolf of Badenoch	Wild Wolf
Blackbeard	Wild Tiger
Whip of the East Sea	Bluetooth
The Buzzard	Red Legs

In 1720, slaves comprised two-thirds of the population of South Carolina.

IT'S SERENDIPITY

Call it a happy accident. Call it a twist of fate. English writer Horace Walpole called it "serendipity." His inspiration: an old fairy tale called "The Three Princes of Serendip," in which the heroes are always "making discoveries they are not in quest of." Enjoy these true stories of serendipity from all walks of life.

PENICILLIN

The most celebrated case of serendipity took place in a petri dish. Actually, in two petri dishes, seven years apart. The first was in 1921, when Scottish scientist Alexander Fleming was leaning over a petri dish containing a culture of bacteria when a drop of nasal mucus (or a tear drop, depending on the telling) dripped from his face into the dish...and killed the bacteria. He'd discovered *lysozyme*, a natural substance the body uses to fight off minor infections. That serendipitous drop set Fleming on a mission to find stronger compounds to create a "miracle drug"—one that can kill harmful bacteria without harming the human body.

Fast forward to 1928. Fleming returned to his lab from a two-week summer vacation to find that a petri dish containing *Staphylococcus aureus* had been ruined. The culture had been tainted from an open window, or possibly from a nearby lab that was culturing molds; Fleming added the petri dish to a pile of others to be cleaned. Later, when he was complaining to an assistant about the mess, he picked up a dish from the top of the pile and noticed something odd. It was the contaminated dish in which the *Staphylococcus* bacteria had been growing, and an invading mold spore had killed the bacteria. A few weeks later, with the help of a mycologist, he identified the fungus as belonging to the genus *Penicillium*. It was powerful enough to kill bacteria but nontoxic to humans.

Twelve years later, two chemists (Ernst Chain and Howard Florey) turned Fleming's discovery into an antibiotic called penicillin that has since saved millions of lives. All three scientists were awarded the Nobel Prize. Fleming reflected on the serendipitous nature of his discoveries: "But for the previous experience [the mucus in 1921], I would have thrown the plates away as many bacteriologists have done before."

VIAGRA

In the 1990s, drug company Pfizer was conducting clinical trials with a compound called sildenafil that they were hoping would ease cardiovascular problems by opening the blood vessels near the heart. But the experimental drug wasn't working. Then a

Only 4 percent of the planet's mammal "biomass" consists of wildlife; 34 percent is human and 62 percent is livestock.

nurse noticed that some of the male test subjects, who were lying on their stomachs, were too embarrassed to get up: the compound was opening up blood vessels... someplace else. In 1998, the USDA approved Viagra as an erectile-dysfunction drug.

THE DEATH STAR TRENCH

The final space battle in the original 1977 *Star Wars* film saw the Rebel fighters attacking the Death Star, a moon-sized space station with a narrow trench along its equator. As the good guys approach their target, they fly their spaceships through the trench at breakneck speeds while enemy ships are firing on them. Audiences had never seen anything like it.

But the space station's model builder, Colin Cantwell, "didn't originally plan for the Death Star to have a trench," he wrote on Reddit. "When I was working with the mold, I noticed the two halves had shrunk at the point where they met across the middle." It would take Cantwell a week to repair. "So, to save me the labor, I went to [writer-director George Lucas] and suggested a trench. He liked the idea so much that it became one of the most iconic moments in the film!"

LOUIS ARMSTRONG'S SINGING

Louis Armstrong (1901–71) was one of the most beloved entertainers of the 20th century. Though he originally rose to prominence in the 1920s as a jazz trumpeter, he's best known today for his gravelly singing voice on classics such as "What a Wonderful World." But "Satchmo" never set out to be a singer; his "aggressive" method of playing the trumpet forced him into it by wreaking havoc on his lips—once keeping him from blowing his horn for a whole year. At first Armstrong started singing to give his lips a rest. But it turned out that he was pretty good at it. However, it was the trumpet-caused damage to his throat that gave his voice its distinctive gravel.

Serendipity and Louis Armstrong also helped popularize scat singing. The syncopated, gibberish singing style had been around for a few years, but few people outside of nightclubs had heard it. According to Armstrong, when he was recording the vocals for the song "Heebie Jeebies" in 1926, the sheet music slipped off the stand. As he recalled, "When I dropped the paper, I immediately...started to scatting. Just as nothing had happened. When I finished the record I just knew the recording people would throw it out. And to my surprise they all came running out of the controlling booth and said 'Leave that in.'"

MICROWAVE OVENS

Born in 1894, Percy Spencer was orphaned as a small boy and quit grade school to

First Beatle with a solo #1 song: George Harrison, "My Sweet Lord" (1970).
Last Beatle with a solo #1 song: Harrison, "Got My Mind Set on You" (1987).

work in a factory. Intrigued by the nascent technology of electricity, he read books on the emerging field and taught himself trigonometry, calculus, chemistry, physics, and metallurgy. During World War II, Spencer was working at Raytheon, experimenting with microwave tubes to increase the effectiveness of microwaves by using heated cathodes. His improvements drastically improved radar capabilities, giving the Allies a huge advantage in the war and earning him a Distinguished Public Service Award, the highest civilian honor granted by the U.S. Navy.

But one day at the lab, something odd happened. Spencer was standing next to a magnetron when he noticed a candy bar in his pocket was melting, but his clothes weren't hot. Curious whether the energy could cook food, Spencer placed a cup of popcorn kernels next to the magnetron and was soon enjoying the world's first microwave popcorn. After a few years in development, in 1947, Raytheon introduced the RadarRange, the world's first (non-accidental) microwave oven. Not bad for an engineer who never finished grade school—which, according to a colleague at MIT, Spencer used to his advantage: "The educated scientist knows many things won't work. Percy doesn't know what can't be done." It also shows that serendipity isn't worth diddly-squat unless someone notices happy coincidences and acts on them.

STAND BY ME

This 1986 drama, directed by Rob Reiner, originally had the same title as the Stephen King book it was based on: *The Body*. But the suits at Columbia Pictures weren't comfortable with that title, as described by screenwriter Raynold Gideon: "It sounded like either a sex film, a bodybuilding film, or another Stephen King horror film." Problem was, shooting was well underway and the suits didn't like any of the other title ideas, either.

One day on set, Kiefer Sutherland, who plays the older bully that terrorizes four younger boys, was teaching his young costar River Phoenix how to play the guitar. Sutherland started with one of the few songs he could play and sing, "Stand by Me," a 1961 Motown hit by Ben E. King. According to Sutherland, Reiner must have overheard the two young actors playing and singing the song, and felt inspired to suggest it as a title for the film; said Gideon, "It ended up being the least unpopular option." The movie was an enormous hit, and it revived Ben E. King's career.

It was also serendipitous that King even sang the song in the first place—he had no intention of recording it. Based on an early 20th-century hymn called "Stand by Me," later popular with gospel singers as "Stand by Me Lord," King wrote the song for his former group, the Drifters, to perform. They weren't interested, so he reluctantly did it himself. Good thing, too. It reached #4 in 1961, and then #1 in 1987, thanks to the popularity of the movie.

In 1936, New York State legalized toplessness—for men.

THE FASTEST...

*Here's a quick article about all the stuff and things that
went faster than all the other stuff and things.*

Tortoise. Tortoises and turtles are famously slow-moving, so Bertie really made a name for himself. In an event at the Adventure Valley theme park in the U.K. in 2014, Bertie was clocked walking at a record-setting pace of 0.92 feet per second.

Hockey goal. Five seconds into a game in December 1981, Doug Small of the Winnipeg Jets scored a goal against the St. Louis Blues. Bryan John Trottier of the New York Islanders repeated the feat in a game against the Boston Bruins in 1984, then Alexander Mogilny of the Buffalo Sabers did it against the Toronto Maple Leafs in 1991.

Touchdown. In a 2003 NFL game, the Philadelphia Eagles started with an onside kick. Dallas Cowboys receiver Randal Williams caught it on the Philadelphia 37-yard line, midair, and ran it in for a touchdown. Total amount of time taken off the game clock: three seconds.

Rapper. In the third verse of his 2020 hit "Godzilla," Eminem was clocked rapping 224 words in about 30 seconds, a world-record pace of 10.65 syllables per second.

Knockout. In a 1947 Golden Gloves tournament in Minneapolis, boxer Mike Collins opened his bout with one powerful punch that sent Pat Brownson to the mat. Refs ruled it a knockout just four seconds into the contest.

Landmass. Every year, Australia moves seven centimeters in a northeastern direction, making it the quickest-moving continent on Earth.

Space object. Haumea is classified as a dwarf planet, and it orbits the Kuiper Belt in the outer reaches of the solar system, past Neptune. It makes a complete rotation on its axis in just four hours, making it the fastest-spinning thing in the solar system. The spin is fast enough to distort the planet's shape, making it look like a football.

Surgeon. Before general anesthesia made surgery easier for doctors and less painful for patients, surgeons operated as quickly as possible to reduce agony and the possibility of infection. British surgeon Robert Liston was the fastest of them all: in the 1840s, he could amputate an entire leg in two and a half minutes.

Heartbeat. In 2012, *Indian Pacing and Electrophysiology Journal* published a study about a patient with an extreme heart defect that made his heart thump at 600 beats per minute.

Metabolism. The ruby-throated hummingbird is the smallest bird on the planet and processes food so quickly that it must eat at least three times its weight daily or it dies.

The sun has an official name: sol. (It's Latin for "sun.")

MARIO VS. PAC-MAN VS. SEQUEL-ITIS

The most successful video game characters of all time: Mario and Pac-Man. The plumber and the round yellow thing have each starred in well over 100 different games since the early 1980s. A lot of those sequels, spin-offs, offshoots, and derivations—see below—aren't very good.

SUPER MARIO BROS. 2 (1988)

Super Mario Bros. came bundled with the Nintendo Entertainment System console in the 1980s, so the game was instantly popular. Nintendo's programmers in Japan cranked out a sequel that looked and played exactly like the original—but with an extremely high level of difficulty. For the American market, programmers inserted Mario into an obscure Japanese-exclusive game called *Doki Doki Panic* and called it *Super Mario Bros. 2*. No longer jumping on enemies to kill them, Mario is tasked with plucking vegetables from the ground and throwing them at bad guys. And when Mario defeats the final villain—a giant frog king—it's all revealed to have been just a dream.

MS. PAC-MAN (1981)

Arcade denizens pumped $1 billion worth of quarters into *Pac-Man* machines in 1980, prompting publishers Namco and Midway to come up with a sequel, but one that would attract a demographic *Pac-Man* failed to charm in huge numbers: women. *Ms. Pac-Man* is virtually the same game as *Pac-Man*, with some minor changes including the shape of the pellet-filled maze and the order of the fruits the main character eats, and it stars Pac-Man's wife—who sports a pink bow on her head.

SUPER MARIO BROS. & FRIENDS: WHEN I GROW UP (1992)

Available solely for home computers, *When I Grow Up* isn't a game so much as it is a slideshow and virtual activity book for kids, intended to give them ideas about careers they could pursue someday. Children click through various static images of Mario, his brother, Luigi, and other *Super Mario Bros.* characters at work as nurses, mail carriers, and hairdressers. The game came with an "electric crayon" a user could employ to color in the images—selecting colors being about the only actual activity.

PROFESSOR PAC-MAN (1983)

Originally a straightforward, generic quiz game called *Quiz Ms.*, *Pac-Man* publisher Midway decided to brand it with their global phenomenon. *Professor Pac-Man* features the title character (Pac-Man wearing an academic mortar board and half-spectacles)

Percentage of U.S. companies that are classified as a
"small business" (500 employees or fewer): 99.7.

asking a series of questions with visual clues. It was so unpopular in arcades that it was never developed into a version for home gaming consoles.

MARIO TEACHES TYPING (1992)

Kids didn't need to have a Nintendo system to play this game, so long as they had a home computer. *Mario Teaches Typing* replicates scenes from previous Mario games while also purporting to teach players keyboarding skills. Speech bubbles from Mario pop up on the screen and he instructs what words need to be typed quickly and properly—or else Mario can't clear obstacles and enemies.

PAC-MAN 2: THE NEW ADVENTURES (1994)

Even though dozens of other Pac-Man games had been released already, this game was marketed as a direct sequel to the original. It plays completely differently. Gone are the maze and dots in favor of Pac-Man wandering around a town in search of specific objects (a milk bottle, a flower). And instead of directly controlling Pac-Man, players operate a slingshot to fire a projectile to hit the area they want the yellow man to investigate (or to hit Pac-Man himself).

DANCE DANCE REVOLUTION: MARIO MIX (2005)

A best-selling game series in the 2000s, *Dance Dance Revolution* invites players to replicate on-screen dance moves on a floor mat, accompanied by pop hits of the day. *Mario Mix* is a *Dance Dance Revolution* spinoff in which players dance to the computerized music from classic Mario games.

PAC-MAN VR (1996)

It's a remake of the original *Pac-Man* from the early 1980s, with the player controlling the yellow round creature as he acquires white pellets and runs away from ghosts through a maze. Except that this time, the Pac-Man character isn't seen from above, but from the player's first-person point of view. It wasn't really VR, or "virtual reality"—that was just a buzzword at the time. Interest was so low in arcades that every *Pac-Man VR* was recalled by manufacturer Virtuality and destroyed.

MARIO & LUIGI: PARTNERS IN TIME (2005)

The object of many Mario games is to rescue the Mushroom Kingdom's Princess Peach from the clutches of danger or from bad guys. In *Partners in Time*, Peach uses a time machine that runs on bits of a star to travel back decades. She's then abducted; Mario and Luigi must also travel back in time to save Peach and save the Mushroom Kingdom from invading aliens called the Shroobs. To repel these villains, the brothers team up with baby versions of themselves.

Number of times Sweden's King Carl Gustaf XVI has worn his crown: 0.

WORD ORIGINS

Ever wonder where certain words came from?
Here are the interesting stories behind some of them.

POINDEXTER

Meaning: A nerd, or a socially awkward smart person

Origin: "Poindexter is a common surname, but the slang term comes from a character, a child genius, named Poindexter in the animated television series *Felix the Cat*, which started airing in 1959...The slang use of *poindexter* is first recorded in 1981, but it is almost certainly older in oral use. The slang use of *poindexter* may also be influenced by an older slang term for a nerd or intellectual, *pointy-head*...In its early days, poindexter was associated with 'Valley Girl' slang, which was all the rage c.1982." (From Wordorigins.org, by Dave Wilton)

PUPPY

Meaning: A young, small dog

Origin: "From Old French *poupee*, 'doll, plaything,' which is related to *poppet* and *puppet*. To 'sell someone a pup' is to swindle them, especially by selling them something that is worth far less than they expect. This dates from the early 20th century and was presumably based on the idea of dishonestly selling someone a young and inexperienced dog when they were expecting an older, trained animal." (From *Oxford Dictionary of Word Origins*, by Julia Creswell)

MUSTACHE

Meaning: A carefully trimmed and shaped bar of hair above the upper lip

Origin: "It came into English from French, but other languages have a similar word, for example the Italian *mostaccio* and Spanish *mostacho*. All these come from the Greek word *mastax*, meaning 'jaw.'" (From *Word Origins*, by George Beal)

SOY SAUCE

Meaning: A salty sauce served with East Asian foods

Origin: "The basic name for soy sauce in China is *jiangyou*, written with characters meaning 'the liquid extracted from *jiang* [soybeans]'...The Japanese word for 'soy sauce' is *shoyu*; it derives from and is written with the same characters as *jiangyou*. The various early English words for soy sauce, soy and soya, came from *shoyu*...It is interesting to note that the present American and British terms 'soy' and 'soya,' now generally used to refer to soybeans, were originally derived from the Japanese word for soy sauce (*shoyu*) and the German word *soja*." (From "History of Soy Sauce, Shoyu, and Tamari," by William Shurtleff and Akiko Aoyagi)

PLACEBO

Meaning: A purposely noneffective medicine substitute meant as a control in studies, or to test psychological effects of medicines

Origin: "Placebos were originally intended for hypochondriacs who insisted that the doctor prescribe *something* for their perceived pains. This is reflected in the history of the term because the Latin word *placebo* means, 'I will please.'" (From *The Complete Idiot's Guide to Weird Word Origins*, by Paul McFedries)

JUNGLE

Meaning: A dense, tropical forest

Origin: "'Jungle' is derived from the Hindi (and thus also from Sanskrit) words. There are no tropical forests in India, and the definitive text on the derivation of the word...makes a good case for saying that 'jangala' really meant an open savannah-like terrain, very suitable for the Indian lion. How 'jungle' came to be understood in British English as a thick tropical forest with creepers etc. is still somewhat unclear; the Hindi word 'jungle' in rural north India is a term still very much in use to describe the fields and the margins of cultivated lands such as common grazing lands." (From *The Guardian*)

CANDID

Meaning: To speak with frankness and honesty

Origin: "One of the symbols of a young man's progress to full citizenship was the right to wear the plain toga, the *toga virilis*. Meanwhile, the *toga candida* of political candidates was bleached using sulfur to make it much whiter than the usual cream version. From *candida* we have the modern word 'candid' as these candidates were meant to be honest and true." (From *World History Encyclopedia*)

GUY

Meaning: A man

Origin: "The word has surprisingly black roots: It's derived, etymologists believe, from the name Guy Fawkes, one of the leaders of the Gunpowder Plot that attempted

So should we launder it? American cash money is 75 percent cotton and 25 percent linen.

to assassinate King James I in 1605. Years after Fawkes's plan was foiled, British children paraded his effigy around on Nov. 5—a custom that, over the course of decades, made 'guy' a sort of slang, first for a poorly dressed person, and then more generally for a man (of any wardrobe)." (From *The Washington Post*)

LADY

Meaning: A woman

Origin: "In Anglo-Saxon times most families were quite large, so there was much work to be done around the household. Custom decreed that special tasks should be allotted to various female members of the group. Unmarried girls usually looked after such matters as milking and spinning. But the privilege of making bread, one of the most important items of their diet, was reserved by the housewife herself. She was called the *lae-dige*, meaning 'the bread kneader.' Later centuries modified the term to *lady*." (From *445 Fascinating Word Origins*, by Webb Garrison)

APOLOGY

Meaning: Expression of regret or of being sorry for an offense

Origin: "The original meaning of *apology* was 'formal self-justification,' often used as the title of a piece of writing rebutting criticism. This is indicative of the word's origins in Greek *apologia*, a derivative of the verb *apologeisthai*, 'speak in one's defense,' formed from the prefix *apo-*, 'away, off,' and *logos*, 'speech.' The meaning 'expression of regret for offense given' developed in the late 16th century." (From *Dictionary of Word Origins*, by John Ayto)

GOSSIP

Meaning: Discussing salacious news about a not-present party, or the kind of person who engages in such chatter

Origin: "Gossip derives from Old English *godsibb*, a compound noun made up of *god* and *sibb*. While *god* is readily understood in modern English, *sibb* meant 'kinsman, relative' and is apart today in the word *sibling*. The word was composed in the eleventh century to denote a 'godparent.' Since friends would be invited to enter into this special relationship, it is not surprising that, by the fourteenth century, *godsib* had come to mean a 'familiar friend.' Friends generally enjoy a good chat in each other's company and so by the second half of the sixteenth century a *gossip* also denoted 'someone who indulges in tittle-tattle.'" (From *Dictionary of Word Origins*, by Linda & Roger Flavell)

Divorce is illegal in two countries: the Philippines and Vatican City.

THE WORST AND WEIRDEST TV VARIETY SHOWS

The variety show ruled TV in the 1970s and early 1980s. Invariably a mixture of celebrity hosts and guests, singing, dancing, and cheesy comedy sketches, fare such as The Sonny & Cher Show *and* Donny & Marie *delighted audiences. So much so that the dial was lousy with variety shows—and lousy with particularly lousy ones.*

The Bay City Rollers Show (1978–79)

Sid and Marty Krofft—brothers and TV producers responsible for several live-action, grotesque, and fantastical Saturday morning TV shows in the 1970s such as *Sigmund and the Sea Monsters* and *The Banana Splits*—created a variety show for kids in 1976, *The Kroft Supershow.* Consisting of serials and sketches, it was retooled in 1978 into *The Bay City Rollers Show.* Starring the briefly popular Scottish pop-rock band and teen idols (best known for the hit "Saturday Night"), the musicians with impenetrable Scottish accents participated in comedy sketches, played songs, and interacted with a cranky monster named Mr. Munchy. It lasted 31 episodes.

The Starland Vocal Band Show (1977)

Consisting of two middle-aged married couples who harmonized their way through vocal-driven soft rock tunes, the Starland Vocal Band only ever had one hit: 1976's "Afternoon Delight." It reached #1, and it propelled the band to the Grammy Award for Best New Artist, along with, in 1977, six episodes of a TV variety show on CBS. *The Starland Vocal Band Show* featured the group singing both standards and their own songs, the political musical comedy of Mark Russell, and comedy sketches written by and starring a young David Letterman.

Saturday Night Live with Howard Cosell (1975–76)

The show now known as *Saturday Night Live* went on the air in 1975 as NBC's *Saturday Night* because there was another series on the air featuring the phrase "Saturday night live." Broadcasting in prime time on ABC, *Saturday Night Live* starred abrasive, polarizing, slow-talking sportscaster Howard Cosell as its master of ceremonies. While the repertory cast featured comedians that would go on to appear on the other *SNL*—Bill Murray, Brian Doyle-Murray, and Christopher Guest—this one also had acts such as tennis player Jimmy Connors singing, Siegfried & Roy and their exotic tigers, and decidedly old-school singers Paul Anka, Shirley Bassey, and Frank Sinatra. It was canceled after 18

Hottest man-made temperature: 7.2 trillion degrees F.
(That's 250,000 times hotter than the sun.)

little-watched episodes of the wooden and out-of-his-element Cosell trying to bring order to the technical-gaffe-prone live show that critics found chaotic and messy.

The Chuck Barris Rah-Rah Show (1978)

After creating the innuendo-laden game shows *The Dating Game* and *The Newlywed Game*, Chuck Barris devised the tongue-in-cheek talent competition *The Gong Show*. That show—in which bad singers, bad comedians, and other woeful acts competed to win $516.32 (if they didn't get interrupted mid-performance by a B-list celebrity judge ringing a gong)—inspired NBC's prime-time revue, *The Chuck Barris Rah-Rah Show*. It was exactly like *The Gong Show*, combining unwatchable acts and Barris's teasing banter, but with the element of competition removed. It lasted just three months on the air.

3 Girls 3 (1977)

What do choreographer and TV legend Debbie Allen, Meat Loaf's duet partner and *Night Court* star Ellen Foley, and *Dharma & Greg* supporting player Mimi Kennedy have in common? Absolutely nothing, and that was the point of the 1977 NBC variety show *3 Girls 3*. The show aggressively pushed and promised that the three just-starting-out performers were the superstars of tomorrow, placing them in bland musical numbers and comedy sketches. Creators Kenny Solms and Gail Parent had tried since 1973 to get a show on the air exploring the weirdness of overnight stardom, with both ABC and CBS missing the point; the former wanted to cast three established performers and CBS wanted it as a vehicle for Diahann Carroll. Those other networks may have been on to something, because *3 Girls 3*—with its stars picked from 300 women who auditioned—fared so poorly that NBC pulled it after one episode.

The Hanna-Barbera Happy Hour (1978)

Animation studio Hanna-Barbera was the first name in television cartoons from the 1960s on, churning out dozens of hit shows including *The Flintstones*, *The Jetsons*, and *Scooby-Doo, Where Are You!* It was such a brand name in entertainment that NBC commissioned the prime-time live-action variety show *The Hanna-Barbera Happy Hour*. Airing for just five weeks in the spring of 1978, two puppets (operated by puppeteers in full-size suits) named Honey and Sis—one woefully untalented and the other very talented—performed in song-and-dance numbers and acted in recurring comedy skits. Those skits included the disco-set soap opera spoof "The Disco of Life" and "The Truth Tub," where Honey and Sis hung out and talked. They also sparred with guests including Betty White, Tony Randall, and Charo, and Hanna-Barbera costumed characters including Yogi Bear and Snagglepuss.

European capital city with the most trees: London.

COFFEE, EAST GERMANY–STYLE

From the "dustbin of history" comes the story of how a coffee-loving communist nation's inability to enjoy its favorite beverage transformed the global coffee industry and planted the seeds for revolution.

A CRISIS LOOMS

Certain countries are associated with coffee, either for growing it, consuming a lot of it, or building a rich and robust culture around it. Brazil and Colombia produce the stuff, while France loves its cafés and Italy introduced espresso-fueled drinks to the world. In the early 20th century, Germany was as coffee-mad as its European counterparts and had one of the highest consumption rates in the world. The average German sucked down gallons annually, both in cafés and at home.

The quintessentially German enthusiasm for the hot, brown, caffeinated liquid continued past World War II, even when Germany split into politically opposed nations in 1949—democratic West Germany and communist, Soviet-aligned German Democratic Republic, known as East Germany. West Germany's private businesses continued to import coffee for its citizens, the supply meeting demand and the market weathering price fluctuations as they came and went. In communist East Germany, the government controlled everything, so the state had to figure out how to get coffee to the people. Essentially a satellite branch of the communist superpower that was the Soviet Union, East Germany got most of its coffee from its political big brother.

A LITTLE SHORT

Coffee-producing countries tended to prefer to do business with democratic, capitalist countries, because they'd pay market price (or more) for as much coffee as they wanted. The perpetually extremely cashed-strapped Soviet Union could afford to acquire only a finite amount of coffee to distribute to its own states; whatever was left went to East Germany. Almost immediately after the communist takeover, coffee shortages were common in East Germany.

This was bad news for the fledgling government, because the supply of coffee was essential to persuading the citizens that their political system was a success. Coffee, as a luxury item, was relatively affordable for the government to provide to the people compared to, say, functional automobiles.

First athlete disqualification from the Olympics under drug testing: Hans-Gunnar Liljenwall of Sweden tested positive for excessive alcohol in 1968.

Unfortunately, Cold War hostilities ramped up in 1955 with the adoption of the Hallstein Doctrine. The multinational agreement among democratic powers sought to kill trade and imports into communist countries. Under the doctrine, countries that actively engaged in business with East Germany would be barred from trade activity with wealthy West Germany. This meant that the Soviet Union couldn't provide much coffee to East Germany anymore, and East Germany was cut off from what supply it could get on its own.

So many German families were split apart and kept that way when the country divided into two that family members would send care packages to each other. West Germans routinely mailed coffee to their East German relatives—up to 25 percent of the coffee in East Germany was acquired this way. (Those in East Germany return the favor by sending back stollen, a fruit-and-nut cake traditionally eaten at holidays; it was widely available, and better made, in their country.) But all that below-board trading with the west upset the East German government—not only did it subvert its authority, but it exposed big, embarrassing flaws in the communist system as it was trying to take root.

In 1954, the East German government imposed limits on mailed coffee shipments, capping them at 250 grams (about eight ounces). For the duration of the enforcement of the Hallstein Doctrine, from 1955 to 1970, East Germans simply had to make do with a very low stock of coffee, consuming far less but with their passion never truly disappearing.

A FROSTY RECEPTION

In July 1975, a strange natural disaster took place, one that would affect the price and consumption of coffee worldwide—not just in East Germany. Over a span of four days, an unseasonal and severe cold snap hit Brazil. Snow fell for the first time in recorded history in some areas of the nation that was, by a wide margin, the world's biggest coffee producer, farming around a third of the global supply. As a result of the extreme and unexpected freeze, about half of Brazil's coffee trees (about 1.5 billion in all) died virtually overnight, killed off by becoming frozen all the way through, inside and out. The dead coffee trees took on an eerie dark shade, giving the catastrophe its nickname: the "Black Frost."

The coffee harvest for 1975 had already happened, so the effects of the Black Frost wouldn't be felt for a year. From 1976 until 1980, world coffee production dropped by more than 50 percent. The Black Frost was largely responsible, but so was politics. Significant coffee-producing African countries Ethiopia and Angola were engaged in long, brutal civil wars in the 1970s, and couldn't and wouldn't participate in global trade at a high level. Just after the Black Frost, the industry-controlling, price-setting International Coffee Organization (ICO) quadrupled the wholesale price of the commodity, from 20 cents to 80 cents. In 1977, with the shortage underway, the ICO tripled the price, with coffee skyrocketing to $2.29 a pound.

INTERNATIONAL INCIDENT

The availability of coffee was critical to the East German government's propaganda machine. To meet demand, the government got into the coffee business itself...sort of. All coffee still going into the country was gathered at its point of origin, collected, and processed at industrial facilities. At those factories, workers packaged Kaffee Mix, vacuum-sealed 125-gram packages of a pre-ground product ready for use in coffee makers and percolators.

Kaffee Mix was designed to make a little coffee go a long way, which is to say that the brew contained very little actual coffee. There was enough ground coffee in a packet to give it a coffee flavor and color, but it consisted primarily of cheap, readily available fillers that tasted nothing like coffee—chicory, pea flour, rye flour, various types of beans, or dried and dehydrated sugar beets. What did it taste like? Chicory, pea flour, rye flour, beans, and beets.

A BAD COMBINATION

Not only did the brew reportedly taste awful, but it messed up coffee machines. Coffee makers are designed to brew coffee; when the appliances pushed water through that mixture of flours and other materials, it clumped and turned into a mushy glop—clogging and breaking coffee makers. So if thousands of East Germans even wanted Kaffee Mix (it was better than nothing), they couldn't make it without having to acquire a new coffee maker, a prohibitively expensive notion in the poor country and one that might take years—coffee makers were as scarce in East Germany as coffee.

Kaffee Mix was supposed to be the big solution to a big problem. The East German government had counted on the faux-brew to easily and cheaply comprise 80 percent of its national coffee supply. That quickly backfired.

TAKING IT TO THE STREETS

Despite living under the totalitarian, iron-fisted Iron Curtain regime, where protesting and speaking out in any way against the government was not tolerated and could be severely punished, East Germans absolutely refused to drink their state-issued packets of bad-tasting, barely caffeinated, poor excuse for a coffee substitute. And thousands of people decided to do something about it. In the mid-1970s, with national morale low and social unrest beginning to stir, more than 14,000 people—representing the signatures of hundreds of thousands of East Germans—sent petitions of complaint

More dragon than fly: when hunting prey, dragonflies have a 97 percent success rate.

to the government regarding Kaffee Mix. A few peaceful, pointed street protests took place, with outraged coffee aficionados taking aim at and placing blame on high-ranking official Chairman of the Council of State Erich Honecker. Signs mockingly referred to Kaffee Mix as Erichs Krönung, combining the leader's name with that of West German coffee brand Jacobs Krönung.

The East German government grew desperate. As of 1977, it didn't have enough operating capital in its coffers to buy more coffee from nations willing to ignore the Hallstein Doctrine. But given the universal hatred of Kaffee Mix among the people and the government's reliance on coffee to prove the success of their political system, the nation needed to act.

ROGUES UNITE

The wealthiest nations of the developed, capitalist world—most of Western Europe and the United States, for example—dealt with the shortage and steep prices the way they always did: they paid more for the required and desired goods and absorbed the blow as a quirk of the open market. In communist East Germany, things were even more dire than before.

But East Germany's not-so-favored nation status put it in a unique position. Since it was already outside the global club of preferred trade partners, it could freely do business with other anti-democratic nations that had pulled out of the coffee business—such as war-torn Ethiopia and Angola. Government agents flew to those coffee-rich nations and bartered deals that would ensure East Germans would finally have enough to drink.

- One of the biggest industries in East Germany in the 1970s: artillery and munitions manufacturing. The country armed Ethiopian dictator Mengistu Haile Mariam's troops, the Derg, for the country's looming war with neighboring Somalia.

- East Germany also manufactured W50 trucks, one of the few successful products ever made behind the Iron Curtain. East Germany found a major market in Angola, exchanging lots of trucks for lots of coffee.

BACK TO SQUARE ONE

By 1978, coffee imports from Ethiopia and Angola comprised just under half of East Germany's supply. Again, the state controlled its production and made a coffee brand called Rondo, consisting entirely of actual coffee.

But the success was short-lived, and not without consequences. Immediately after the East German weapon shipments arrived, the Derg violently purged Ethiopia of its

There are 950 trillion invasive quagga mussels in Lake Michigan.

perceived enemies, slaughtering more than 100,000 people it accused of conspiracy. The East German government, undeterred, tried to renew its weapons-for-coffee contract in 1979. Mengistu refused to negotiate—he'd gotten what he wanted, and the coffee he controlled could fetch more money than the cash-strapped East Germans (in debt to the equivalent of tens of millions of dollars) could pay.

GOOD MORNING, VIETNAM

Left with another large-scale, potentially long-term coffee shortage, East Germany looked east, to another communist ally: Vietnam. In the four years since the end of the Vietnam War in 1975, the government there had aggressively acquired and repurposed farmland for a cash crop that had suddenly and recently increased in global value by tenfold: coffee.

The two countries—neither a member of the ICO and both hamstrung by a lack of funds and limited in their ability to buy and sell goods around the globe—worked out a deal in 1979: East Germany would provide farming equipment to Vietnam to grow coffee, as well as assist in building the infrastructure to house and educate coffee farm workers. In exchange, half of Vietnam's resulting coffee crop would be shipped back to East Germany.

The one problem with this plan? Coffee trees take about 10 years to fully mature and reach their peak production rates. According to the agreement, yes, East Germany would get half of all Vietnamese coffee—but they wouldn't see a massive yield until 1990.

VIETNAM RISING

Vietnam's coffee plantations began to fruit in 1986, and East Germany insisted on an early harvest. That resulted in East Germany receiving about 5,000 tons of coffee beans, with similar amounts in the following years. Finally, 1990 arrived, and with it, a predicted record coffee crop in Vietnam. But it didn't go to East Germany—because the country no longer existed. Following the fall of the Berlin Wall in 1989, Germany reunified as one democratic nation in 1990, eliminating communism and the concept of East Germany entirely. That meant Vietnam could keep 100 percent of its coffee yield.

But one thing that stuck around after two Germanys became one: an insatiable desire for coffee. The new German government looked to Vietnam to meet its needs for the stuff, and Vietnam provided. The repeated influx of German money bolstered and expanded the Vietnamese coffee industry. Today, it's the second-biggest producer of coffee on the planet, trailing only Brazil. And the country that imports the most coffee from Vietnam, a robust 13 percent of it? Germany.

A 9-volt battery is made from six LR61 batteries.

TOO MUCH TITLE

Back in the 18th and 19th centuries, novels took off as a popular form of entertainment. They were "novel" in the sense that long-form storytelling was new, leading publishers and authors to promote and get attention for their books by giving them long, salacious, and, in retrospect, silly titles that often spoil the plot entirely. Here are some 1700s and 1800s books you probably know, and their full titles that dissipated over the years.

Then: *The Personal History, Adventures, Experience and Observation of David Copperfield the Younger of Blunderstone Rookery*
Now: *David Copperfield* (Charles Dickens)

Then: *Vanity Fair, Pen and Pencil Sketches of English Society*
Now: *Vanity Fair* (William Makepeace Thackeray)

Then: *Frankenstein; or, The Modern Prometheus*
Now: *Frankenstein* (Mary Shelley)

Then: *Tess of the D'Urbervilles: A Pure Woman*
Now: *Tess of the D'Urbervilles* (Thomas Hardy)

Then: *Uncle Tom's Cabin; or, Life Among the Lowly*
Now: *Uncle Tom's Cabin* (Harriet Beecher Stowe)

Then: *Little Women, or Meg, Jo, Beth and Amy*
Now: *Little Women* (Louisa May Alcott)

Then: *Through the Looking-Glass, and What Alice Found There*
Now: *Through the Looking-Glass* (Lewis Carroll)

Then: *A Christmas Carol. In Prose. Being a Ghost Story of Christmas*
Now: *A Christmas Carol* (Charles Dickens)

Then: *The Life and Strange Surprizing Adventures of Robinson Crusoe, of York, Mariner: Who lived Eight and Twenty Years, all alone in an un-inhabited Island on the Coast of America, near the Mouth of the Great River of Oroonoque; Having been cast on Shore by Shipwreck, wherein all the Men perished but himself. With An Account how he was at last as strangely deliver'd by Pyrates. Written by Himself.*
Now: *Robinson Crusoe* (Daniel Defoe)

Then: *Gulliver's Travels, or Travels into Several Remote Nations of the World. In Four Parts. By Lemuel Gulliver, First a Surgeon, and then a Captain of Several Ships*
Now: *Gulliver's Travels* (Jonathan Swift)

Then: *Silas Marner: The Weaver of Raveloe*
Now: *Silas Marner* (George Eliot)

Then: *Treasure Island, or The Sea Cook: A Story for Boys*
Now: *Treasure Island* (Robert Louis Stevenson)

Then: *The Mayor of Casterbridge: The Life and Death of a Man of Character*
Now: *The Mayor of Casterbridge* (Thomas Hardy)

Then: *The History of Tom Jones, a Foundling*
Now: *Tom Jones* (Henry Fielding)

Then: *The Deerslayer, or The First War-Path*
Now: *The Deerslayer* (James Fenimore Cooper)

Only two Olympic gold medals for Chile: both in men's tennis in 2004.

CREATIVE TEACHING AWARDS

At the Bathroom Readers' Institute, we love teachers—without them, none of us would have become writers! These teachers, however, should have stuck to the subject matter.

Subject: Civics

Winner: Mona Lisa Tello, 61, a science teacher at Manhattan's High School of Graphic Communication Arts

Creative Approach: In 2011, Tello forged a jury-duty summons and presented it to the principal as an explanation for why she'd taken two separate (paid) leaves of absence, totaling 15 days, in the past two years. Suspicious, the principal took a closer look at the jury summons and found more spelling goofs than any teacher should make—*trail* instead of *trial, manger* instead of *manager,* and *sited* instead of *cited*—and the wrong address and phone number for the New Jersey courthouse named on the form.

What Happened: Tello, who appeared in court wrapped in a giant blanket, "agreed to retire," then pled guilty to felony forgery. She didn't receive jail time, but she got 10 days' community service and had to pay back her salary for those 15 days—more than $3,300. She claims the principal left her no choice in taking time off after she allegedly fell down the school's escalator and wasn't allowed to submit an accident report.

Subject: Student Relations

Winner: Iowa Middle School and Iowa High School in Iowa, Louisiana

Creative Approach: In what may have seemed like a great idea during planning conversations, the homecoming committee came up with a "stoplight day" theme for part of 2018's spirit week: any single students should wear green to school, those who were in a relationship should wear red, and kids should wear yellow if "it's complicated."

What Happened: That *all* proved to be "complicated," especially for the tween-aged kids on the shared campus. And their parents let the school, and local news stations, know it. "Sure, some middle school kids are going to have boyfriends and girlfriends and crushes," said one dad, "but I don't think we need the school to play matchmaker for a 10- to 14-year-old." School board officials wouldn't comment on who came up with the idea, but they promised never to do it again.

Subject: Ethics

Winner: Amy Robertson, principal of Pittsburg High School in southeastern Kansas

Creative Approach: Becoming a high school principal is a highly competitive

endeavor: only those with extensive experience and squeaky-clean backgrounds are offered positions following a thorough hiring process. But after Robertson took over as principal in March 2017, some students sensed something fishy going on—and those students happened to work on the school's newspaper, the *Booster Redux*. The five juniors and one senior started snooping, and, a few weeks later, issued a bombshell report: Robertson received her master's and doctorate degrees from one Corllins University, which the employment screening firm MGO has classified as a "diploma mill" where you can purchase a degree. Corllins was not accredited, and had numerous complaints lodged against it with the Better Business Bureau; it didn't even have a working website. When the students questioned Robertson about her "flimsy" past teaching experience, she gave conflicting answers. She also failed to provide proof of her bachelor of fine arts degree from University of Tulsa.

What Happened: After the story was published, Robertson resigned in disgrace. The six students were lauded by professional journalists all over the nation, and personally thanked by the superintendent. "Everybody kept telling them, 'stop poking your nose where it doesn't belong,'" said their newspaper adviser, Emily Smith. It does beg the question: how could these teenagers perform a better background check than the pros in charge of hiring? "All of the shining reviews did not have these crucial pieces of information," student reporter Connor Balthazor, 17, told the *Washington Post*. "You would expect your authority figures to find this."

Subject: Driver's Ed

Winner: Russell Cohen, 58, a substitute driving instructor at Suffolk Auto Driving School in Long Island, New York

Creative Approach: During a Saturday morning driving session in October 2018, Cohen had four teenagers in his car; he was in the passenger seat while one of the teens, Matt McGeough, drove. The students noticed from the start that something was amiss. Cohen was making "inappropriate comments" to the female students in the back. Then he told McGeough to drive them to a diner, where he'd buy them food. The instructor went inside while the students waited in the car, but when Cohen returned, it was without any food.

Cohen then told McGeough to get out of the driver's seat so he could drive himself, and he was so erratic that at one point he hit a curb while going 50 mph. The teens begged Cohen to drop them off at a McDonald's; after the kids got out of the car, Cohen sped away. The McDonald's manager called police, who captured Cohen a short time later...after he rear-ended a car. Thus endeth the driving lesson.

What Happened: Cohen was arrested and charged with aggravated driving while intoxicated and endangering the welfare of a child.

History's only successful slave revolt: the Haitian Revolution (1791–1804).

REST NOT IN PEACE

Ready for the most disturbing article of the book?
It's about dead bodies and the people that kept them around
for way too long. Don't say we didn't warn you.

FLORIDA'S FRANKENSTEIN

Born Georg Carl Tänzler in Germany in 1877, when Carl Tanzler (a.k.a. Count Carl von Cosel, Dr. Death, and Florida's Frankenstein) was a boy, he claimed that the ghost of a dead ancestor showed him the face of his "one true love." When Tanzler was in his early 50s, he met that face. It belonged to 22-year-old Maria Elena "Helen" Milagro de Hoyos, a Cuban American tuberculosis patient at the Key West, Florida, hospital where he was working as a radiology tech. Tanzler fell in love with Hoyos, but he couldn't cure her, so in 1931 (as he admitted in a letter found in his home after his death), he poisoned her so she would die "mercifully." With the blessing of her family, Tanzler paid for a mausoleum and visited her almost every night for two years. Then he stole her body and brought it home. After removing the maggots from the corpse, Tanzler used piano wire to hold what was left of it together. Then he replaced the skin with cloth that had been soaked in wax and placed a pair of glass eyes in the eye sockets. Finally, he gave Hoyos her own "death mask" (made from a plaster mold he'd taken at the time of her death) to wear.

Then Tanzler lived in secret with the heavily perfumed corpse, which spent most of its time lying in bed, but not always: one evening, seven years after Hoyos moved in, a little boy reported seeing Tanzler dancing with a "life-sized doll" in the living room. Hoyos's family was already suspicious. Her sister went to the house, where Tanzler let her see his "one true love." The horrified sister called police, and the jig was up.

Tanzler claimed that he wasn't abusing Hoyos; he was performing experiments, trying to bring her back to life. Somehow, he was able to skirt prosecution, much to the dismay of her family. The public was sympathetic toward "Florida's Frankenstein," and thousands of people showed up to a public viewing of the body. Then Tanzler had the gall to ask for it back. Request denied. So he used the death mask to top off a life-sized effigy that he'd said he made—but to this day, some people suspect him of stealing the corpse a second time. He lived with that effigy until he died, (otherwise) alone, at the age of 75. His body wasn't found for three weeks.

There are only six major types of corn. Popcorn, a type
of flint corn, is the only one that "pops."

DAD'S NOT HERE

For years, cousins Janet Carroll and Stephani Blubaugh had been wondering where their Uncle Mike was. From their out-of-state homes, they would call his house in Overland Park, Kansas, where he supposedly lived with his daughter and her family, and they kept being told that the octogenarian "was sleeping" or "didn't feel good." In October 2022, police responded to the rundown home and discovered Mike Carroll's corpse lying on a bed. It was later determined that his pacemaker had stopped working July 1, 2016, meaning the family had lived with their deceased dad for six years. It wasn't until his daughter, Lynn Ritter, suffered a heart attack and ended up in the hospital that her husband, Kirk, called the police about his father-in-law's body. Janet Carroll, and the rest of the now-estranged family, has questions: "Just so confused about the whole thing. How can he lay there for that many years and nobody reported?" At last report, Carroll's nieces were trying to get their uncle a proper burial next to the grave of his wife. And because Carroll died naturally and there was no desecration of the corpse, the Ritters weren't guilty of breaking any Kansas laws regarding the body— but they are under investigation for Social Security fraud.

CLOSET CASE

In late July 2023, Beverly Ma's mother and sister stopped by her Las Vegas home to check in on her, motivated by concern for her well-being after they hadn't heard from her "for some time"—the last text they'd gotten from her was on June 22, and she hadn't responded to texts sent to her since then. When the family members reached the home, Ma's roommate, George Bone, told them that Ma "was in the closet and had been there for two months." One of the family members called 911, and Bone got on the phone and—while he was brushing his teeth—told the dispatcher that Ma had committed suicide and he'd found her body in the closet. He later told police that Ma had died at some point in May; when questioned about why he hadn't reported it, he blamed his avoidance on his being "afraid of going back to jail...for being found with a dead body." In the two months since Ma's death, Bone hadn't just sent the family texts from Ma's phone to make them believe she was still alive, but he'd also made a few changes around their shared home. He'd hung up a number of fly traps to fight off a new insect infestation, set the thermostat to 60°F (in an attempt to slow decomposition), and placed a cooler in the master bedroom, near the closet containing Ma's body, so that he'd be alerted if "she rose from the dead like in the movie *The Grudge*." He may have ordered the fly traps and cooler from Amazon— investigators later discovered that Bone had used Ma's Amazon account (and her money) to make online purchases of 171 items totaling $10,000. Police noted a number of holes in Bone's story, and he was eventually charged with Ma's homicide (along with three theft-related charges).

THE BODY THAT WOULDN'T GIVE UP

In 1976, a TV crew was filming an episode of *The Six Million Dollar Man* in an amusement park fun house in Long Beach, California. Hanging from a rope was a creepy red mannequin that had been part of the decor for a few years. When a crewmember accidentally hit the mannequin, its arm fell off. When the tech tried to reattach the arm, he took a closer look and—wait, is that...bone? He called the police.

The cadaver was taken to the coroner, where they deduced that it was a young man, about five foot three, who—judging by the bullet found in his chest from a discontinued type of ammunition and the now-illegal arsenic-based embalming fluid—died sometime in the early 1900s.

It was 1911, to be exact. That was the year that notorious outlaw Elmer J. McCurdy robbed a train in Oklahoma and was cornered by police in a nearby barn. After a hail of gunfire from law enforcement, the outlaw was dead at 31. His corpse was taken to a funeral home in Pawhuska where he was embalmed and propped up in the parlor, waiting for family members to come retrieve him. No one showed up for several years, and he became something of a curiosity, with the undertaker dubbing him "The Bandit Who Wouldn't Give Up." (One nearby merchant even sold postcards of the corpse.) In 1916, two men claiming to be McCurdy's brothers appeared and took his body away.

However, the men weren't his brothers, but carnival owners. After that, the body spent the next two decades on the sideshow circuit, transforming into a leathery mummy. At some point he was covered in wax and made part of a "villains" sideshow. Starting in the 1940s, McCurdy spent a few decades in storage, and then changed ownership a few more times before landing in the Hollywood Wax Museum, and finally at that Long Beach fun house, where he was painted fluorescent red and strung up as a prop. At some point along the line, not only was McCurdy's identity lost, but so was the fact that he was a former living human. After the gruesome discovery at the fun house, it took some digging to verify it was McCurdy (the first clue was the gunshot wound to the chest). After no family came forward, the Bandit Who Wouldn't Give Up was sent back to Oklahoma and buried beneath two feet of concrete, to make sure he stays put this time.

* * *

"I had a lot more fun being 20 in the '70s than I'm having being 70 in the '20s."
—**Joe Walsh**

Earth averages one volcanic eruption a week.

JUST PLANE FACTS

Welcome on board Bathroom Reader Airlines flight 37. This is your captain,
Uncle John, speaking. Our sitting time is approximately a few minutes.
That's just enough time for you folks in the main cabin to read these
interesting tidbits about big metal things that zoom through the sky.

✈ Bring lip balm: commercial airplane cabins are literally drier than a desert, with less than 20 percent humidity. (The Sahara Desert has about 25 percent humidity.)

✈ There's a reason that airplane food has a reputation for tasting bland: your sense of smell and sense of taste are diminished by as much as 30 percent in a high-altitude plane. That's due to the aforementioned low humidity as well as a drop in air pressure.

✈ Speaking of air pressure, it's so much higher outside the plane that it's virtually impossible to open a plane door from the inside during flight.

✈ You fart more on a plane. That's also due to the pressure—as it drops, the air inside you expands and runs out of space until that diminished sense of smell comes in handy. This phenomenon is especially taxing on pilots, who don't move around as much as the rest of the flight crew. Because of this, more than 60 percent of pilots report abdominal bloating.

✈ That inflight oxygen mask above your head has only 10–15 minutes' worth of oxygen (12 minutes on a 737).

✈ True or false? The dirtiest, most bacteria-laden part of the plane is the lavatory. False: it's the tray table right in front of you.

✈ True or false? Those always-a-bit-too-small airplane blankets are washed after every flight. False: they're sometimes washed only once a month.

✈ Commercial air travel is safer than it's ever been, and it's getting safer each year. According to the International Civil Aviation Organization, in 2022, "the aviation industry saw a 9.8 percent decrease in accidents compared to 2020. Furthermore, fatalities resulting from aircraft accidents dropped by a factor of 66 percent." And this same time period saw an 11 percent increase in scheduled flights.

✈ The leading cause of airplane crashes is pilot error, followed by mechanical error, inclement weather, and air traffic control error. Then come those unfortunate birds who fly into a flight path and cause a plane to crash (and turn Captain Sully into a hero). To test the strength of planes' windshields and engines, airlines shoot real

Unlike with most other birds, males and females of many parrot species look almost identical.

chickens out of a "chicken gun" to simulate birds strikes. (Not to worry, the chickens are already dead when they're tested.)

At the moment we're writing this, there are approximately half a million people flying on 8,000 aircraft. By the end of the day, six million people will have flown somewhere.

Planes are most likely to crash in the final eight minutes of the flight. These crashes also result in the most fatalities. To increase your chances of survival, sit in the rear few rows of the plane, and keep your seatbelt on.

When a plane is getting ready to land, the flight crew doesn't dim the cabin lights to create mood lighting—they do it as a safety precaution. Because the final moments of a flight are the ones in which a crash is most likely to occur, passengers need to be ready for an emergency situation—at night, that means being able to see in darkness. The cabin lights are dimmed so everyone's eyes are adjusted to the dark, just in case.

Why are most planes white? Because white paint weighs less than dark paint (the difference is the weight of up to eight passengers). White paint is also cheaper over time (it requires repainting less frequently), it keeps the plane cooler, and it makes it easier for maintenance crews to spot problems.

A commercial jet gets only about 0.2 miles per gallon, whereas cars get anywhere from the high teens to over 40 mpg. However, when factoring in that jets carry more people than cars, they're actually much more fuel efficient, getting 100 miles per gallon per passenger.

"The life of everyone on board depends upon just one thing: finding someone back there who can not only fly this plane, but who didn't have fish for dinner," says Dr. Rumack (Leslie Nielsen) in *Airplane!* after the pilot and copilots all get food poisoning. That's no joke. It's for this exact reason that pilot and copilot are almost never fed the same meal.

On February 25, 1990, smoking was permanently banned on all U.S. domestic flights. So why are there still ashtrays in the lavatories? So that if someone does try to light up in there, they'll have a place to put their butt that won't damage the plastic paneling or clog the toilet.

Anyone who does try to smoke in the lavatory (or do other things) should know that when they switch the little tab inside the door from "Vacant" to "Occupied," it doesn't completely lock the door. Other passengers can't open it, but in the event of an emergency, flight attendants know where to find a secret button. (It's located beneath the metal "lavatory" sign outside. Proceed with caution.)

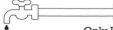

Only U.S. senator with a star on the Hollywood Walk of Fame:
actor-turned-politician George Murphy.

BEHIND THE LINES: AD-LIBS

Most famous movie lines come from the writer (see page 15), but not all of them. Every so often, an actor or director will come up with a different phrasing—or something new that the writer never thought of—and those become lines we remember.

FAMOUS LINE: "I AM IRON MAN."

Said by: Tony Stark (Robert Downey Jr.) in *Iron Man* (2008)

Story: From the dawn of the superhero comic book in 1938 (when Clark Kent first donned his Superman suit), the most sacred superhero trope has been the secret identity—and that trope stayed firmly in place when superheroes took to the big screen in the 1970s. That's why it was such a big shock at the end of *Iron Man*, when industrialist Tony Stark is giving a press conference after a mysterious man in a metal suit has just saved the world, and he declares: "I am Iron Man."

No one expected it in the theaters, and no one expected it on set that day. Why? Because that line wasn't in the script. Downey Jr. just said it to see how it would land. Of course, that wasn't the only improvised line in the movie. The actor said that he and director Jon Favreau improvised a lot during filming. "Sometimes it's very self-indulgent to come in, and you know hand out new pages or say, 'oh I'm not saying that, so feed me that.'" But because Downey Jr. had that freedom, he really went with it and tried things.

According to producer Kevin Feige, they were going to have Tony reveal his secret identity in a future movie (as eventually happened in the Iron Man comic books), but that ad-lib changed everything. Thanks to that surprise ending, the hit movie launched the Marvel Cinematic Universe on a high note. And more important, said Feige, "That success inspired us to go further in the trusting ourselves to find balance of staying true to...the spirit of the comics but not being afraid to adapt and evolve... If you're changing something for no reason, that's one thing, but if you're changing something because you want to double-down on the spirit of who the character is? That's a change we'll make. Tony Stark not reading off the card and not sticking with the fixed story? Him just blurting out, 'I am Iron Man'? That seems very much in keeping with who that character is."

FAMOUS LINE: "I'M HEARING THIS, AND I WANT TO HEAR *THIS*."

Said by: Emily (Emily Blunt) in *The Devil Wears Prada* (2006)

Story: Blunt's delivery makes this line so quotable. The character of Emily, an

Watch out: Australia is the fastest moving continent
on Earth, traveling 2.7 inches north each year.

overambitious editor's assistant at a fashion magazine, is at her desk with her face in her left hand, her right hand sticking up, speaking with puppet gestures: "I'm hearing this, and I want to hear *this*."

That line wasn't in Lauren Weisberger's 2003 novel, nor was it in Aline Brosh McKenna's screenplay. Blunt added it herself (thanks to director David Frankel, who urged the cast to improvise). But Blunt didn't come up with it, either. "I like to soak up people on the street," she explained. "Like, I saw a mother speaking to her child in a supermarket when we were shooting that film. She yelled at her kid and she kind of opened and closed her hand [makes puppet gestures] and she goes, 'Yeah, I'm hearing this, and I want to hear *this*.'"

FAMOUS LINE: "YOU CAN'T HANDLE THE TRUTH!"

Said by: Col. Nathan Jessup (Jack Nicholson) in *A Few Good Men* (1992)

Story: Nicholson didn't so much improvise this line as revise it, which is quite the feat considering the line was penned by one of the all-time great dialogue writers, Aaron Sorkin (*The West Wing*, *Moneyball*). But it was Sorkin's first movie, and Nicholson was already a Hollywood legend when he played Col. Jessup, whose fiery witness-stand monologue in the military drama became as well-known as the movie itself. After Col. Jessup calls the brash young prosecutor (Tom Cruise) a "cocky little bastard," Cruise's character then demands, "I want the truth!," to which Jessup was originally supposed to respond, "You already have the truth!"

While prepping for the scene, Nicholson suggested to director Rob Reiner that changing "already have" to "can't handle" would be more in line with what the proud veteran would say to the cocky young prosecutor. Reiner went with the instincts of Nicholson, who performed his iconic monologue in one take, and in doing so earned his 10th Oscar nomination.

FAMOUS LINE: "YOU SHALL NOT PASS!"

Said by: Gandalf the Grey (Ian McKellan) in *The Lord of the Rings: The Fellowship of the Ring* (2001)

Story: Standing on the Bridge of Khazad-dûm, deep in the mines of Moria, Gandalf turns and confronts the Balrog, giving the Fellowship the chance to escape. He yells to the massive, flaming beast, "I am a servant of the Secret Fire, wielder of the flame of Anor. The dark fire will not avail you, flame of Udûn!" A moment later he raises his staff, and, as he slams it onto the stone bridge, he yells, *"You shall not pass!"* (Then Gandalf and the Balrog fall into the chasm.)

Research says: college men who join a fraternity will lower their GPA by 0.25 points but increase their average future income by 36 percent.

It's one of the most powerful lines—and moments—from Peter Jackson's Oscar-slaying trilogy, but it's not what J. R. R. Tolkien had Gandalf say in the 1954 novel. The original line was "You cannot pass!" It's well-known that Jackson and the trilogy's two other screenwriters, Philippa Boyens and Fran Walsh, changed lots of lines and introduced new ones. (One example: "Nobody tosses a Dwarf!" was all Jackson.) But this seemingly innocuous change alters the entire meaning of Gandalf's command.

How so? It's more explained in the books than in the movies that Gandalf is not an old man, but rather an angel sent by the gods to protect Middle-earth. The Balrog is also a magical being. What the book's Gandalf essentially says is, "I'm going to call forth the powers of these other gods, who will make it so you *cannot* pass." Then Gandalf becomes an observer as the gods hold back the creature. Changing "cannot" to "shall not" puts the power back in Gandalf's hands—which makes it more dramatic for the moviegoing public.

In the movie, Gandalf does say, "You cannot pass," *before* reciting the "servant of the Secret Fire" spell. That's repeated word for word from the source material. But then, in the book, Tolkien writes, "At that moment Gandalf lifted his staff, and crying aloud he smote the bridge before him."

To add a dramatic beat, instead of "crying aloud," Jackson directed McKellen to repeat the "cannot pass" line. But it's unclear exactly whose idea it was to change it. Some sources say it was an ad-lib by McKellen; McKellen himself, in an interview on *The Graham Norton Show*, referred to it as a blooper. "I got [the catchphrase] wrong. I'm rather stuck with it now."

But very little was left to chance on those movies, and even though Jackson and company haven't addressed the change, he did say that McKellen had a "nightmarish time" filming that scene. The trained stage actor had never worked on a special-effects movie, so instead of acting opposite another actor, McKellen had to deliver his lines to a ping-pong ball. "We were in a little studio right beside the airport," said Jackson. "Planes were taking off at the time, and Ian had to, kind of, do his Balrog confrontation, and it was tough." Whether "You shall not pass" was a flub or an ad-lib, Jackson ultimately decided to keep it.

FAMOUS LINE: "I KNOW."

Said by: Han Solo (Harrison Ford) in *Star Wars: Episode V–The Empire Strikes Back* (1980)

Story: Harrison Ford made it no secret that he wasn't enamored with George Lucas's *Star Wars* script, or his directing style (which began and ended with "faster and more intense"). Lucas stayed out of the director's chair for the sequel after persuading a reluctant USC film school teacher named Irvin Kershner to take over, because Kershner was better at character development. That gave the actors the chance to work with a more collaborative director, and Ford took full advantage.

During a dramatic scene where Darth Vader is about to freeze Han Solo in carbonite, Princess Leia (Carrie Fisher) tells Han she loves him. Neither Ford nor Kershner liked Lucas's original written response from Han: "I love you, too." As Kershner recalled, "We tried take after take after take. Nothing satisfied me."

Ford argued that Han would say something more "badass." So he came up with the line, "I know." Kershner liked it, and he and Ford lobbied for the change. "[Lucas] had not written the scene with a laugh," recalled Ford. "But that laugh opens you up emotionally. You don't have another emotional outlet in that scene. The kiss, as the Princess and I are pulled back, is visually strong, and there'll never be a payoff for the scene without a laugh."

They filmed several takes of "I know" before Kershner finally said, "Yeah, that's Han Solo." But as Ford recalled, Lucas *still* wasn't convinced. "He thought it was horrible and that it would get a bad laugh. So I was obliged to sit next to him when he tested it for the first screening. There was a laugh, but it was a laugh of recognition. And so, he generously let it stay in the movie."

FAMOUS LINE: "YIPPEE-KI-YAY, MOTHER [YOU KNOW THE REST]."

Said by: Detective John McClane (Bruce Willis) in *Die Hard* (1988)

Story: Call this one a collaborative ad-lib. On the set of the movie that made Willis an action star, he bonded with screenwriter Steven E. de Souza over their mutual love of cowboys. "Bruce and I grew up watching the same TV shows," recalled de Souza. "Roy Rogers used to say 'Yippee-ki-yay, kids.'" So de Souza used it for a line at a pivotal moment when McClane, via a walkie-talkie, is taunting the evil mastermind Hans Gruber (Alan Rickman), who asks, "Do you really think you have a chance against us, Mr. Cowboy?" The response that de Souza wrote: "Yippee-ki-yay, a**hole."

While filming the scene, Willis kept changing the "ki" to "ti"—which de Souza insisted wasn't right. After a bit of back and forth, director John McTiernan sided with the writer, and "ki" it was. On the final take, just for fun, Willis changed *a**hole* to the epithet that ended up on screen. "The studio nervously left it in for the first test screening," said de Souza, "and the reaction made it permanent."

Why did Willis change it? "I was just trying to crack up the crew. I never thought it was going to be allowed to stay in the film."

FAMOUS LINE: "I DON'T WANT TO GO."

Said by: Peter Parker (Tom Holland) in *Avengers: Infinity War* (2018)

Story: Spoiler alert: Thanos (Josh Brolin) disintegrates half the universe at the end

Only country with wild tigers and wild lions: India.

of *Infinity War*. One of the about-to-be-disintegrated characters is Spider-Man. By his side is his mentor, Tony "Iron Man" Stark (Robert Downey Jr.), who's not going to disintegrate. The line in the screenplay by Christopher Markus and Stephen McFeely was, "I don't feel too good," to which Tony replies, "I'm sorry," as Peter disappears.

But directors Joe and Anthony Russo didn't feel like the scene packed enough of an emotional punch, so Joe told Holland to improvise and stretch it out until the director was brought to tears. Unsure of what to say, Holland asked what his motivation is. Russo's answer: "You don't want to go."

So Holland went with that exact phrase, and kept repeating it. He later revealed that that's an acting technique he uses: "I'll say a phrase over and over again," until the waterworks get going. So he said, "I don't want to go," over and over, but it still wasn't hitting hard enough.

That's when Holland's seasoned costar, Downey Jr., stepped in and offered his own direction: "You don't want to go because you're a child. And you're using your strength as Spider-Man to fight this." Anthony Russo said that was the key that sparked "a pretty spectacular performance for a 21-year-old actor."

Holland added that "I don't want to go" is the Spider-Man line that still gets quoted to him more than any other. And despite the fact that it's one of the saddest moments in the history of superhero movies, he also said it was one of the most fun times he's ever had on a set. "People tell me they imagine that scene must have been horrendous to shoot, but I look back on it with nothing but happiness. It was amazing. I loved it. I got to hug Robert Downey Jr., like, 60 times, and cry on his shoulder. What's not to love?"

*   *   *

OBEY THE CODE

Marvel Studios attempts to defer leaks about movies in
production by shooting them under code names.

The Avengers: "Group Hug"

Thor: The Dark World: "Thursday Mourning"

Captain America: The Winter Soldier: "Freezer Burn"

Ant-Man: "Big Foot"

Spider-Man 3: "Serenity Now"

Spider-Man: Far from Home: "Fall of George"

Spider-Man: Homecoming: "Summer of George"

TIME TRAVEL IN THE NEWS

Are time machines real? Probably not—but just because something doesn't actually exist doesn't necessarily prevent it from making headlines. Here are some recent news stories where (or when?) time travel somehow came into play.

TIME-TRAVELING BURGLAR

In May 2023, police in Ocala, Florida, were investigating a burglary at a local residence, where someone had thrown a brick through the window, left behind a book, and gone swimming in the pool. They spoke to nearby resident Daniel Robert Dinkins, who (sort of) admitted to the crime, stating, "That may have been me." Dinkins then revealed that he lived near the house in question and had wanted to use their swimming pool but also wanted to "share [the book] with them." As to why he threw the brick, where a baby was sleeping, Dinkins said he didn't know about the infant. However, he also said that he was a time traveler who had come back in time and descended upon the house in order to "save the baby from something way in the future when the child is much older." Despite the time-travel defense, Dinkins was charged with felony burglary.

TIME-TRAVELING DRUNK GUY

Police arrested a man in Casper, Wyoming, for public intoxication in 2017. The individual (unnamed in news reports) offered a different perspective on the events: he seemed so out of sorts, he claims, because he was a time traveler from the year 2048 who traveled three decades into the past to warn the people of Wyoming of an upcoming and deadly alien invasion. The man, who asked to speak to the "president" of Casper, said that he came to help people get prepared for the impending apocalypse, and that his ability to time travel was made possible by the aliens filling him with alcohol. (His defense was rejected.)

TIME-TRAVELING OYSTER LOVER

One afternoon in July 2019, 42-year-old Jason Kolb went up to a group of his neighbors in Conewago Township in Lancaster County, Pennsylvania, and announced that it was the year 2015. The reason: he had a time machine back in his trailer and had sent himself four years into the past. His proof of his excursion

In the Old West, 25 percent of cowboys were Black.

through time: he showed off a can of oysters with the date "2019" stamped on it—the expiration date, which Kolb interpreted as the packing date. Suspecting intoxication, the neighbors called police, who soon thereafter busted Kolb on a drunk driving charge and also found a small bag of unidentified white powder on his person.

TIME-TRAVELING MEAT PIE KING

King Henry VIII ruled England and its empire from 1509 to 1541, and during that time he stood for many official portraits. In one of the most famous renderings, painted sometime between 1537 and 1541 and heavily reproduced and reprinted in English history books, the monarch wears a pair of slippers with a rectangular toe box and featuring plenty of small decorative slits.

In February 2023, an X (Twitter) user identified only as Luke from Manchester posted the famous portrait with the declaration that the shoes point to the royal being a time traveler who got the design from a present-day English snack. "Why do Henry VIII's shoes look like a Greggs Steak Bake?" Luke from Manchester tweeted. Indeed, the shoes do resemble a Greggs Steak Bake, a meat-stuffed pastry sold by a major British bakery chain. Like the monarch's shoes, they're rectangular and are covered in slits. The tweet went viral and opened up a serious conversation about whether King Henry VIII really did travel through time for fashion inspiration from a meat pie; another X user responded, "On another note—ciabatta (bread) translates to slipper. This has been going on a long time."

TIME-TRAVELING HUMANITY ENCOURAGER

The year 2023 was supposed to be a breakthrough year for science and human accomplishment, according to a man who calls himself Eno Alaric. This individual (whose name is an anagram for "once a liar"), isn't a psychic or prognosticator, but a time traveler from the year 2671 who came back to the 21st century to tell humanity what was in store.

According to Eno Alaric, the following things were supposed to happen in 2023: aliens would choose 8,000 humans to form a coalition to save the planet from destruction (March), a tsunami would destroy San Francisco (May), seven people would mysteriously drop out of the sky simultaneously (June), scientists would cure skin cancer (August), and a disease-curing crystal would be discovered (December). Eno Alaric's predictions went viral on social media in early 2023, but attention dropped off significantly as the year passed with none of those events coming to pass.

One of the funders of the Smithsonian's dinosaur exhibit: Guns N' Roses guitarist Slash.

WHATEVER HAPPENED TO...?

*Almost nothing sticks around forever, even common or popular institutions
(and annoyances). Here's how and why some of them disappeared.*

...White Dog Poop on the Ground?

In the 1970s and 1980s, chalky, white-colored dog poop was a common sight on
sidewalks and in parks. By the 1990s, it was rare, and today it's virtually gone. Vintage
dog waste was white because dog poop used to include too much calcium. Pet-food
manufacturers bulked up their products with calcium-rich meat and bone meal. It
delivered more calcium than a dog could use, so the extra got eliminated. As wet poop
dried in the sun, the white calcium deposits emerged. With more knowledge about
proper dog nutrition, dog food companies stopped using bone meal as filler, thus
lowering the calcium count—and making for dog poop that's usually just brown.

...Tunnel of Love Rides at Fairs, Carnivals, and Amusement Parks?

In the early 20th century, when small and local amusement parks sprouted up all
over the U.S., a common attraction was a "Tunnel of Love" or "Old Mill" ride.
Couples would board a little boat and take a slow, easy ride through a dark tunnel.
Sometimes the rides were decorated with images of Cupid and hearts, other
times with murals featuring mythical creatures, faux-geological features, or unused
Halloween decorations replicating haunted houses. It didn't really matter what a
ride looked like—it offered an excuse for couples to get a moment alone together in
the dark, where they could snuggle and share physical contact. Chaperoned dates
were commonplace in the U.S. until the mid-1950s, and when the sexual revolution
arrived in the 1960s and 1970s, they went away—as did the Tunnel of Love. In 1950,
about 700 rides were in operation in the U.S. By 2020, there were fewer than 10.

...Pictures of Missing Kids on Milk Cartons?

After a slew of high-profile (and tragically concluded) child disappearance cases in
the late 1970s and early 1980s, a national grassroots movement developed to raise
awareness and offer parents and kids tools against potential kidnappers. Photos of
missing kids, captioned "Have you seen me?" appeared on flyers, grocery bags, pizza
boxes, and, most famously, milk cartons. By 1985, 700 independent dairies around
the U.S. participated in the program. Pictures stopped showing up by the mid-1990s:
more effective preventative and case-solving practices had developed, including
organizations fingerprinting children, and kids and parents being encouraged to have
a shared safety code word to discourage strangers from lying to kids about having
been sent to pick them up. Police networks offered better communications, too, all of

If you're average, you forget 95 to 99 percent of your dreams.

which made milk cartons an ineffective tool in the fight against kidnapping. Famous pediatrician Benjamin Spock also noted that the pictures of missing children on milk tended to frighten kids when having their morning cereal.

...1-900 Numbers?

A lot of entertainment companies made a lot of money in the 1980s and 1990s with heavily advertised telephone hotlines promising jokes, stories, advice, sexy conversation, and contact with celebrities. All you had to do was dial a particular phone number with a 1-900 or 1-976 prefix—which cost around $2 a minute at the very least. In 1992, the 1-900 number industry peaked with annual revenues of $3 billion. A lot of that came from adult-oriented lines, and that same year, the Supreme Court ruled that 1-900 numbers couldn't legally provide such services. In 1993, the Federal Trade Commission ordered operators to state prices upfront during the phone calls—when people found out that they might spend a small fortune, thousands hung up immediately. Revenues declined, and the industry certainly wasn't helped by the Internet making information and communication instantaneous and virtually free, or by AT&T's refusal in 2002 to provide billing services for 1-900 lines.

...Toys in Cereal Boxes?

Excitedly tearing into a big box of sugary cereal to find a free action figure, whistle, or ball began to slip into the past in 1988 when Kellogg's issued a massive recall of plastic toys when they realized they could break apart, get into the cereal, and present a choking hazard. Although just one choking instance was reported, cereal brands got spooked and put the toys in sealed plastic bags. Cereal makers phased out toys in the 2000s, which shaved a few cents from the price per unit of their products, adding up to millions. And with the rise of smartphones and tablets, kids don't buy as many toys as they used to; market research by cereal companies suggested kids prefer premiums such as codes they can scan to play games online or enter to win prizes.

...Flushing a Toilet Sending a Blast of Scalding Hot Water on the Person Taking a Shower Nearby?

Home plumbing systems are set up in a more sophisticated way than they were in the mid-20th century. The trunk-and-branch system used to be the industry standard. Water entered the home through a main pipe, or "trunk," then went to where it was summoned—by taps, faucets, and toilet valves—through narrower pipes called branches. If the water system was already employed in the use of the shower, delivering warm-to-hot water, the flushing toilet confused the plumbing with its request for a fresh batch of cold water. That diverted any cold water from the just-right temperature of the shower to the toilet, leaving nothing but the hottest of hot stuff to rain down on the shower occupant...until the toilet refilled and the system corrected itself.

Each year, the ants in New York City eat about 60,000 hot dogs' worth of food waste.

MAILBOX MAYHEM

It's always a bit unnerving when you go through your mail and find a letter addressed to someone else. Just imagine how unnerving it is to open your mailbox and find a doll...or a sausage...or a hand grenade...

NEW NEIGHBORS

Not long after Don and Nancy Powell bought their house in Orchard Lake, Michigan, in 2018, they bought a specialty mailbox that resembles their new home. At a foot high and two feet deep, it's larger than most mailboxes, and it even has little windows and a solar light making it appear as if someone's home, at least at night.

Four years later, on a late summer day, Don Powell, 72, went to get his mail and discovered something else inside: two handmade wooden dolls, sitting on a little couch. With them was a handwritten note: "We've decided to live here. Mary and Shelley."

Was it a mistake? Or a prank? Powell asked his neighbors (including one named Shelly) if the dolls belonged to them. No one fessed up. Because the mailbox was large enough to fit the dolls *and* the mail, Powell just pushed Mary and Shelley to the back and got on with his life.

A few weeks later, he opened the mailbox to find that Mary and Shelley had gotten a dog, a rug, and some wall art. A few weeks later came a bed. Then came another note explaining that the dolls' previous abode was a "two-story Dutch-style doll house" but the Powells' mailbox was a better fit for accommodating their cousin Shirley—a third doll, with a broken leg—who liked to visit.

Determined to find the culprit, Powell posted on the social media site Nextdoor and pleaded with the doll squatters to reveal themselves. Again, no one fessed up, despite Powell's joking warning that he'd asked the police to keep an eye on the mailbox. But fellow Nextdoor users were clearly entertained by Powell's predicament, as one commenter alluded to: "This is so much fun to read, I was ready to get off of Nextdoor, but this makes me want to stay."

Powell eventually decided he wasn't sure he wanted to learn who was responsible for the doll escapades, saying he was "enjoying the mystery." His wife Nancy said the dolls are "cute" and "a good positive thing, especially during these crazy times." As of this writing, the dolls' benefactors were still at large. Powell said that he's most baffled by their motives, but considering that he's a psychologist by trade, and a pretty well-known one at that, it's likely that somebody's just messing with his head.

First person to write about tofu in the English language: Benjamin Franklin.

THE SURFDALE SAUSAGER

"I sent a picture to my friend group and some of them had been sausaged as well," said Jacob Coetzee. "That's when we realized we had a serial sausager on the island." The island in question is Waiheke, New Zealand, a 30-minute boat ride from Auckland. According to an exposé in the New Zealand website Stuff, the first sausage appeared in a mailbox on the upscale island in the summer of 2021: it was barbecued, wrapped in buttered bread, and smothered with tomato sauce.

More sausages followed. Then they began showing up in more mailboxes throughout the suburb of Surfdale (though the breads and sauces sometimes changed). Neighbors began throwing around wild accusations. "It's ripping us apart; we can't trust one another," said one resident. "I've been accused; my brother's been accused. It's a witch hunt."

But most residents, living in a place known for its quirky art scene, seemed to take it in stride—though it's unclear if any of them ate their free snacks. (Would you?) According to Stuff, it's not against the law in New Zealand to put a sausage (or other objects) in a stranger's mailbox, and the police didn't receive any complaints.

"[The culprit] is someone with a bit of time and money, access to a barbecue, probably not a vegetarian and not particularly health-conscious hence the white bread," posited clinical psychologist Dougal Sutherland. "We're looking at someone reasonably intelligent and good at hiding...Only a male would put a sausage in a letterbox. Freud would have a field day." There were no further reports stating if the Surfdale Sausager was ever identified, but if there are, we'll let you know in a future Bathroom Reader just how accurate Sutherland's profiling turned out to be.

A TASTELESS PRANK

As of last report, "The motives of the perpetrator remain unclear." See if you can figure it out: The perpetrator stuffed Blenheim, New Zealand, mailboxes with what looked like free samples of Weight Watchers low-fat muesli bars. However, when residents opened the packaging, instead of a bar, there was a rolled-up piece of cardboard. This started in early 2016 and went on for more than a year, affecting dozens of mailboxes. "As a psychologist...I would say it's more likely to be some form of elaborate prank instead of any kind of psychological disturbance, although that can't be ruled out," said Martin Sellbom from the University of Otago's Department of Psychology.

One thing's for certain: the perpetrator(s) put a lot of effort into obtaining dozens of actual Weight Watchers muesli bars—either by buying or stealing them—and then using razor blades to cut the wrappers just enough to remove the real bars and replace them with cardboard doppelgängers before discreetly gluing the wrappers back together.

First Lady Edith Bolling Wilson was directly descended from Pocahontas.

"I picked it up from the letterbox and thought, 'Sweet, a free muesli bar,' but when I opened it up it looked weird," said one bummed resident, who "thought it was an advertisement for a muesli bar or a gift, but it was just cardboard." None of the local grocery stores reported any significant purchases of the bars, or thefts, and a Weight Watchers spokesperson said the company is just as flummoxed as the residents. "Although it certainly exposes people to the brand, we think that they might like the bars more if they got to experience the deliciousness that's normally inside."

RANDOM ACTS OF CASH-NESS

There was a serial do-gooder on the loose in Nottingham, England, in December 2022. Two days before Christmas, the anonymous benefactor visited dozens of mailboxes, and in each one placed £100 in cash. "Is it from Santa?" That's what resident Sarah Lynne's son asked about the mysterious envelope. As she told the *Mirror*, she was as stunned as her son. "Things like this never really happen for me." Included in each envelope was a note of encouragement requesting that the receiver some day "pay it forward" by doing something nice for a stranger. One of the lucky mailbox owners witnessed when "a girl walk[ed] to the door and post[ed] the envelope" before leaving in an unfamiliar car; who that girl was, and who she was working with, remain a mystery. But whoever it was gave away several thousand pounds. "With everything happening in the world right now," said Lynne, "it's just nice to know there are still good people." Proving herself to be one of them, she used some of the money on donations to local food banks.

This wasn't a one-off event, it seems. Other residents of the area had received similar deliveries the past two years. Residents in Avon and Somerset were also recipients of anonymous donations, when a man was spotted slipping money through people's doors...leading to a police investigation. The department was the target of online mockery for "going after" one of the benefactors. They released a statement in their defense: "We were contacted by a resident in Frome who had received cash and a note through her letterbox from an unknown man, which she was not expecting and was not addressed specifically to her. Amid concern the money had been wrongly delivered, we appealed for information to discover who the cash had belonged to. A man has since come forward and has confirmed it was a 'generous act of kindness.'" Good for him!

LLEAVE MY MAILLBOX ALLONE!

In October 2018, Staci Tinney's home surveillance camera recorded a couple in a black pickup truck pull up to the mailbox in front of her house in Charleston, West Virginia. "A woman was hanging out of the passenger's side," Tinney said. After

the woman stole items from inside, "it looked like she was putting something in my mailbox." Tinney investigated and found a laminated photograph of a llama wearing sunglasses. According to police, several other neighborhood mailboxes' contents were replaced with similarly strange pictures. Police had no lleads.

RETURN TO SENDER

In March 2023, a postal employee discovered something that looked a lot like a hand grenade in the mailbox outside a coffee shop in Fort Mitchell, Kentucky. Police evacuated Biggby Coffee and the surrounding area and called in the bomb squad. Sure enough, it was a real grenade—but, luckily, it was inert. The "gift" did not come with a letter of explanation, but the case was turned over to federal authorities for investigation.

DID YOU KNOW?

Do you know what to do if a bird builds its nest in your mailbox? It does happen. Ornithologists recommend that, if possible, you let the birds stay there until their eggs hatch and the young can fly off on their own. If a nest with eggs in it is disturbed, the parents will abandon it and the eggs will die. If you are forced to relocate a nest because it presents a safety hazard, call the local animal authorities. Why? Some bird species are protected, so their nests can't legally be moved. Good luck!

If it's OK to move a nest containing hatchlings, experts recommend building a makeshift alternative out of twigs and a plastic milk container, basket, or birdhouse before carefully moving—with gloves on—the babies. Then place the new nest as close as you can to the old nest in a safe, shady spot. If you can move the original nest to that spot, do so, but only if the move won't damage it. Either way, make sure you completely remove the old nest, so Mr. and Mrs. Bird don't try to move right back in.

THE WORLD POPULATION OF REGISTERED MOTOR VEHICLES

1950: 127 million

1976: 342 million

1996: 670 million

2016: 1.3 billion

2036: 2.8 billion (estimated)

Next time you bite into a fast-food burger, you might be eating meat from up to 100 different cows.

WEIRD CANADA

Canada—the land of Mounted Police, poutine, Wayne Gretzky,
Celine Dion...and some really strange news stories.

 ## Middle Ground

In May 2021, police in Beaconsfield, Quebec, arrested Neall Epstein on a charge of criminal harassment. In addition to uttering death threats, the citation came for "flipping the bird"—or displaying an extended middle finger, a vulgar and aggressive gesture—toward a neighbor over a dispute involving a drill. In 2023, the criminal case against Epstein was dismissed by Judge Dennis Galiatsatos. In a 26-page ruling, Galiatsatos wrote that while what Epstein did was rude, it qualified as freedom of expression, guaranteed under Canada's constitution. "To be abundantly clear, it is not a crime to give someone the finger," the judge wrote. "Flipping the proverbial bird is a God-given, charter-enshrined right that belongs to every red-blooded Canadian."

Not Toying Around

A word that begins with an *E*, once used as an umbrella term to describe indigenous people who lived in the far northern parts of Canada (also formerly used in the brand name of an ice-cream bar now known as Edy's Pie), is now considered a slur. Depictions of such people (now more properly known as Inuit or Inuks) with fur coats and living in igloos is equally distasteful and offensive, which is why Toronto mother Teresa Miller was so surprised when her daughter's Kinder Surprise—a chocolate egg with a small toy inside—contained a plastic Inuk emerging from an igloo. "It's just disrespectful and unnecessary," Miller said. "We're sorry that this toy caused offense," chocolate company Ferrero Rocher told reporters, but they wouldn't commit to removing the toy from distribution.

Pop Culture

Early one morning in April 2023, Sharon Rosel of Earls Cove, British Columbia, awoke to the sound of her dog barking in response to a noise outside her home. She went to investigate and found a black bear, which had broken into her Suzuki SUV. Rosel operates a food truck and is careful to not leave any food in her vehicle, where a bear could get it, but she didn't think one would be able to smell consumables through aluminum. But by the time she was able to scare off the bear, it had drunk nearly six 12-packs of soda. Of the 72 cans in Rosel's vehicle, the bear drank 69, leaving behind

First British sovereign to graduate from college: King Charles III.

only three diet sodas and dripping residue from Orange Crush on the car's white leather seats. "Do not underestimate their sense of smell," Rosel told reporters.

How to Steele an Election

On October 24, 2022, the Ontario city of Port Colborne (population: 20,000) was set for municipal elections. Incumbent Bill Steele looked set to cruise to reelection, running unopposed. But then one day before Election Day, another candidate entered the race: Charles Steele, the mayor's brother. The two Steeles hadn't spoken to each other in about 30 years. Charles Steele told reporters he believes "in democracy," adding that if he hadn't run, his brother would have been "acclaimed," or remain mayor automatically. In the end, Bill Steele easily defeated Charles Steele by 3,054 votes to 1,806. (And the brothers still aren't on speaking terms.)

Cheesy Does It

About 100 people live in Cheadle, a town near Calgary in southern Alberta. As of November 2022, it's also home to the world's largest (and probably only) statue to commemorate the experience of getting bright orange dust on one's fingers while eating Cheetos, Frito-Lay's messy, cheese-flavored corn-based snack food. The monument stands 17 feet tall and consists of massive lifelike fingers, painted silver, holding aloft a huge Cheeto, as orange as the dust it has left on the digits below it. The Canadian division of PepsiCo, Frito-Lay's parent company, decided to place the statue in Cheadle because its name sounds so much like "Cheeto," and to give that infamous Cheeto residue a proper name as a publicity stunt. "Cheetos fans have always known that the delicious, cheesy dust on their fingertips is an unmistakably delicious part of the Cheetos experience, but now it officially has a name: Cheetle," said PepsiCo senior marketing director Lisa Allie.

Barking Up No Tree Whatsoever

In May 2023, visitors to the unnamed park at the corner of Provencher Boulevard and Jean-Talon Street in Montreal noticed a freshly posted sign warning that fines of between $500 and $2,000 could be issued for those guilty of violating a rule: "It is forbidden to let your dog bark, whine, or howl," the sign read. Even more absurd: the park where this sign was posted is a dog park. Montreal city officials confirmed to media outlets that the sign was new, but the bylaw relating to domestic-animal control had been on the books for decades. "The sign was intended to help reduce the nuisance experienced by the neighborhood of this dog park," a spokesperson said. Two months earlier, a similar anti-dog sign posted in a Toronto dog park came down after public backlash; the sign at the Montreal park remained in place.

FUNERAL FOODS

Mourning is one of the hardest things to do in life. But everyone must do it, and every culture honors its dead in some way, with many utilizing food as part of the rituals of grief. Here are some "funeral foods" from around the world.

Koliva. In a Greek Orthodox Christian tradition, wheat berries are boiled until soft and then flavored with honey, raisins, nuts, or pomegranate. The mushy substance is then shaped into a mound to resemble a gravesite, then covered in powdered sugar, into which a cross and the initials of the deceased are traced.

Halva. A traditional dessert in the Middle East and Mediterranean, *halva* is dense, crumbly, and very sweet, made from sugar, sesame paste, and rosewater. It's a funeral or mourning dish especially prevalent in Armenia, Turkey, and Iran.

Yukgaejang. During a Korean funeral, the dead is offered bowls of rice, and spoonfuls are fed to the deceased. The living will often eat *yukgaejang*, a spicy beef soup made with bean sprouts, garlic, scallions, sweet potatoes, and hot chili, along with rice and kimchi.

Irish wake cake. At a traditional Irish wake, the family spends time with the body and with one another in the days before the funeral to mourn and share food, such as an Irish wake cake. It's a dry, pound cake–style dish made with cream cheese and dried fruits.

Cabbage rolls. In Estonia, mourners eat pastries at the grave site immediately after the funeral and then gather in the home of a relative for a reception to eat cabbage rolls, leaves stuffed with ground veal and rice, and cooked in a flavored broth.

Mannish water. In Jamaica, the wake takes the form of "Nine-Nights," a nine-day party. One food almost always served at the final event is mannish water, a soup made from the head, entrails, and testicles of a goat in a broth of carrots, potatoes, green bananas, white rum, and habanero peppers. It's paired with *bammy*, a cake made from cassava flour.

Borsok. In a Muslim ritual in Kyrgyzstan called *jyt chygaruu*, or "releasing the smell," these yeasty ball doughnuts made from flour, salt, sugar, and butter are deep fried until fragrant—their scent is said to aid the spirit on its journey. The *borsok* are strewn on a table and verses from the Koran are read before eating.

Funeral pie. Introduced a century ago by Amish and Mennonite communities in Pennsylvania, a funeral pie is a simple dessert made on short notice from pantry staples—usually flour, eggs, sugar, and raisins—to deliver to the family of the dead.

Only place in the solar system with fire: Earth. (Nowhere else has enough oxygen.)

STAR WARS STUFF

Uncle John keeps reminding a certain writer, "Not everyone likes Star Wars."
That certain writer's response? "Then I'll find some Star Wars
trivia even non-fans might find interesting." Here it is!

MAY NEW YORK BE WITH YOU

After Luke Skywalker (Mark Hamill) is captured by a monster in 1980's *Star Wars: Episode V–The Empire Strikes Back*, his feet are frozen to the ceiling of an ice cave, and his lightsaber is just beyond reach. Luke closes his eyes and uses the Force...the music swells...and the handle of the lightsaber starts shaking! And if you look closely at the base of the lightsaber handle, you'll see the words "Made in New York." That's because the prop was simply an antique camera's flashbulb handle, made by Graflex in Rochester, with some buttons glued to it.

STARFACE

When it came time to cast the swashbuckling, smuggling freighter pilot, Han Solo, the studio courted Al Pacino, one of the 1970s biggest draws thanks to *The Godfather* and *Dog Day Afternoon*. "They offered me so much money," Pacino recalled. After reading the script, "I didn't understand it...so I said I couldn't do it. I gave Harrison Ford a career." (And Pacino went on to do *Scarface*.) But it was really casting director Fred Roos who managed to get the small-time actor's foot in the door...literally. In early 1976, Roos hired Ford, a carpenter by trade, to install a door at American Zoetrope, the location where writer-director George Lucas was casting the original *Star Wars*. Until that point, Ford had had only small parts, including one in Lucas's previous hit, *American Graffiti*, but Lucas insisted he didn't want to reuse actors from that movie. So, when Lucas saw Ford installing the door, they chatted and he asked Ford if he wouldn't mind feeding lines to the hopefuls auditioning for other roles. Even then, Lucas had no plans of casting him. Some of the other actors who tried out for the Han Solo role: Burt Reynolds, Kurt Russell, Nick Nolte, and Christopher Walken. "But when I played the screen tests of Harrison playing the role against the other actors playing the role, there was no question that he was the best," Lucas recalled later.

FLYING SOLO

In *Star Wars*, Harrison Ford plays one of the best pilots in the galaxy. He's a pilot in this galaxy, too, though not quite the best. In 1999, Ford totaled a helicopter in a

It's the angle and direction a hair shaft takes as it emerges from the
follicle that determines whether it'll be straight, wavy, or curly.

riverbed. A year later, his six-seater plane was blown off a runway. In 2015, he crashed a World War II plane on a golf course and barely made it out alive. In 2017, he landed on a taxiway instead of a runway and nearly clipped a 737. And in 2020, after being told to wait for another small aircraft to land, Ford touched down first and got berated by air traffic control.

He hasn't had the best of luck on movie sets with things that fly, either: While filming *Raiders of the Lost Ark* in 1980, a Flying Wing plane rolled over his knee and tore his ACL. On the *Stars Wars: Episode VII–The Force Awakens* set in 2014, Ford suffered a broken leg and other significant injuries after he was pinned beneath a *Millennium Falcon* door.

But we'd be remiss if we didn't mention the time he aided in a search-and-rescue mission and saved a missing 13-year-old Boy Scout. As the Scout later told reporters, when he boarded the helicopter that had just landed, "The pilot turned round and said, 'Good morning'...then I was like, 'Oh my God, Han Solo has just rescued me, how cool is that?'"

JAR JAR JACKSON

Two music stars who were almost in 1999's *Star Wars: Episode I–The Phantom Menace*: Michael Jackson and Tupac Shakur. Shakur, one of the most popular rappers of the decade, wanted to break into acting, so he read for the part of Mace Windu, the Jedi Master. But not long after that, Shakur was shot and killed, and the part ultimately went to Samuel L. Jackson. And the King of Pop, Michael Jackson himself, reportedly wanted to play the amphibious alien Jar Jar Binks. But Jackson wanted to do the part in prosthetic makeup, whereas Lucas wanted the character to be CGI. According to Ahmed Best, who did get the part of Jar Jar, his best guess about the real reason Lucas said no was that "Ultimately, Michael Jackson would have been bigger than the movie, and I don't think George wanted that."

MAD FOR STAR WARS

The January 1981 edition of *Mad* magazine featured a parody of *The Empire Strikes Back* that follows the adventures of Fluke Skystalker, Hands Solow, and Princess Leotard. No, wait, that was *Cracked* magazine's December 1980 parody. The *Mad* parody featured Lube, Ham Yoyo, and Princess Laidup. Anyway, the lawyers at Lucasfilm sent *Mad* a cease-and-desist letter demanding they hand over all the profits from the issue. The folks at *Mad* put a quick end to the matter by sending the lawyers a copy of a separate letter they had recently received from George Lucas himself, who *loved* their parody: "Your sequel to my sequel was sheer galactic madness."

Largest parking lot in the world: the West Edmonton Mall in Alberta, Canada (20,000 spaces).

WHEN IN ROME

The strangest attempt to cash in on *Star Wars* was *Starcrash*, a so-bad-it's-good "space fantasy" filmed in Rome and released in the U.S. in 1979. Cowriter and director Luigi Cozzi insists it's not a *Star Wars* rip-off...completely. He never saw *Star Wars*, but he did read the novelization. He says his movie is more inspired by the schlocky *Flash Gordon* serials and the sexy sci-fi hit *Barbarella* than the original *Star Wars* film. The plot certainly veers from *Star Wars*, but it's got a lot of similar elements: spaceship battles, smugglers, laser-sword fights, mystical powers, an "imperial space force," an "emperor of the galaxy," and a funny robot. Just how bad is *Starcrash*? Imagine if Ed Wood filmed a low-budget sci-fi spaghetti Western. The movie does feature a pre–*Knight Rider* David Hasselhoff and venerated thespian Christopher Plummer, who had this to say about his time in Italy filming *Starcrash*: "Give me Rome any day. I'll do porno in Rome, as long as I can get to Rome."

* * *

STAGECOACH RULES

In the 1800s, travel by stagecoach was common. Up to nine passengers shared the coach; second-class passengers rode on top with the luggage. To keep things friendly, Wells Fargo posted rules of etiquette in each of their coaches.

1. Abstinence from liquor is requested, but if you must drink, share the bottle. To do otherwise makes you appear selfish and unneighborly.

2. If ladies are present, gentlemen are urged to forego smoking cigars and pipes as the odor of same is repugnant to the Gentle Sex. Chewing tobacco is permitted but spit WITH the wind, not against it.

3. Gentlemen must refrain from the use of rough language in the presence of ladies and children.

4. Buffalo robes are provided for your comfort during cold weather. Hogging robes will not be tolerated and the offender will be made to ride with the driver.

5. Don't snore loudly while sleeping or use your fellow passenger's shoulder for a pillow; he or she may not understand and friction may result.

6. Firearms may be kept on your person for use in emergencies. Do not fire them for pleasure or shoot at wild animals as the sound riles the horses.

7. In the event of runaway horses, remain calm. Leaping from the coach in panic will leave you injured, at the mercy of the elements, hostile Indians, and hungry coyotes.

8. Forbidden topics of discussion are stagecoach robberies and Indian uprisings.

9. Gents guilty of unchivalrous behavior toward lady passengers will be put off the stage. It's a long walk back. A word to the wise is sufficient.

That feeling when you say a word over and over until it loses meaning?
That's called semantic satiation.

UNCLE JOHN'S STALL OF FAME

Uncle John is continuously amazed—and pleased—by the unusual ways people get involved with bathrooms, toilets, and so on. That's why he created the "Stall of Fame."

Honoree: Truck Yard, a bar in The Colony, Texas
Notable Achievement: Preserving a one-of-a-kind collection of toilet seat art
True Story: Way back in our *Absolutely Absorbing Bathroom Reader*, we honored Barney Smith of San Antonio, Texas, for creating the world's first and only Toilet Seat Art Museum. That was 2002, and by that point, the master plumber had painted designs and illustrations on to more than 400 toilet seats (that would have otherwise been thrown away) and displayed them on the walls of his garage. By 2017, Smith had painted 1,400 seats, but he was 97 years old and ready to sell his collection—on one condition: "I don't care whether it goes to New York or Kalamazoo...they've got to keep it together."

Clorox helped launch an online campaign to find a buyer. Happily, the toilet seats all got to stay in Texas thanks to Truck Yard, a "dive-ish bar garden with a huge backyard, live music, food trucks, and booze where everyone's invited, especially your dog." And now you and your dog can view the entire collection at Barney Smith's Toilet Seat Art Museum housed in a barn on the Truck Yard lot. Don't let the commodious medium dissuade you—this is some fine (folk) art: brightly colored renderings of Texas landmarks, portraits of birds and other wildlife, and multimedia seats adorned with road signs, license plates, and cacti are just some of what the museum has on offer.

Honoree: Shigeru Ban, a renowned Japanese architect
Notable Achievement: Letting you see where you will pee
True Story: Walking into a public restroom can be a crapshoot (in the worst-case scenario, literally). Who, or what, might be in there? In 2020, Ban came up with a solution to this conundrum: a restroom with see-through walls. When a stall is unoccupied, the prospective user can inspect the premises without having to venture in. Once inside, a "new technology" incorporated by Ban clouds up the walls for complete privacy. Best of all: "At night, the facility lights up the park like a beautiful lantern."

This restroom is part of the Nippon Foundation's Tokyo Toilet Project, which has tasked the best architects (and even a fashion designer) from Tokyo and around the

Q: What do Neil Patrick Harris, Jason Priestley, and Jennifer Aniston have in common?
A: They all made appearances on *Quantum Leap* (1989–93).

world to redesign 17 public restrooms in the busy Shibuya ward of the world's most populous city. And Ban's transparent restroom is just the beginning. "We invite you to take a look at the uniqueness of each of these facilities."

Honoree: Waldron Island, a "limited development district" in northern Washington
Notable Achievement: Coming up with an ingenious way to keep that small-town feeling
True Story: If you want to move to Waldron Island, you'll have to abide by its weird bylaw: no more than two bathrooms per home. But what if you want to add a third one? No deal. While the rule might seem harsh, it keeps this picturesque island in pristine condition. Despite being located in the rainy Pacific Northwest, there's not a whole lot of fresh water available for the unincorporated community. The two-toilet-max rule makes prospective residents who have grander toilet aspirations or like to have each bedroom in a home accompanied by its own bathroom look elsewhere, and helps preserve available potable water. The bylaw has kept the population of the island—which also lacks ferry service and electricity—at around 100 people since its founding in 1890.

Honoree: Cintas, an Ohio-based company that supplies workplace apparel and restroom supplies
Notable Achievement: Making public restrooms better by publicizing the best of them
True Story: With a workforce of 40,000, this nearly century-old company knows a thing or two about places to go. As they say, "How a business maintains its facilities is a reflection of a business's commitment to customer service." In that spirit, in 2002, Cintas launched America's Best Restroom contest. Each year, the company invites its clients and the general public to nominate a "unique, impressive restroom. Maybe it's elegant, eclectic, or downright quirky." That, the thinking goes, motivates businesses to "go the extra mile" in creating unique experiences—which benefits us all.

You can nominate any restroom (with the owner's permission), and businesses are urged to nominate their own, as the winners receive a ton of free publicity and $2,500 worth of Cintas's products and services.

Two of our favorites: The 2021 winner was Two Cities Pizza in Cincinnati, Ohio, where the restrooms are "fully outfitted with a subway platform, train car, station stops playing over the speaker, authentic subway handles above the sinks, and even graffiti on the walls."

And the 2019 winner: "Nashville Zoo's Expedition Peru women's restroom offers a floor-to-ceiling glass window, perfect for viewing the family of cotton-top tamarins. This lush indoor exhibit features these critically endangered primates and all their antics."

Most bombed nation in world history: Laos.

MOUTHING OFF

SILLY SOCCER QUOTES

These star soccer players ("footballers" outside the U.S.) prove that the ability to run and kick a ball is completely independent of the ability to talk and make sense.

"If we played like this every week, we wouldn't be so inconsistent."

—Bryan Robson

"WHEN YOU ARE 4–0 UP YOU SHOULD NEVER LOSE 7–1."

—Lawrie McMenemy

"I don't have any tattoos, but that's mainly because none of my limbs are wide enough to support a visible image."

—Peter Crouch

"Our chances to get to the next round are 50–50, maybe 60–60."

—Rudi Völler

"We lost because we didn't win."

—Cristiano Ronaldo

"The last six games of the Invincibles season were the most pressurized, because we were under pressure."

—Ray Parlour

"Football is a game of skill, we kicked them a bit and they kicked us a bit."

—Graham Roberts

"I would not be bothered if we lost every game, as long as we won the league."

—Mark Viduka

"I'm as happy as I can be, but I've been happier."

—Ugo Ehiogu

"Leeds is a great club and it's been my home for years, even though I live in Middlesbrough."

—Jonathan Woodgate

"Everything in our favor was against us."

—Danny Blanchflower

"I can see the carrot at the end of the tunnel."

—Stuart Pearce

"MY PARENTS HAVE BEEN THERE FOR ME, EVER SINCE I WAS ABOUT 7."

—David Beckham

"THEY'RE THE SECOND BEST TEAM IN THE WORLD, AND THERE'S NO HIGHER PRAISE THAN THAT."

—Kevin Keegan

HOW TO SPEAK AUSTRALIAN

G'day, mates! Oz (the ripper way to refer to Australia) is kind of equal parts U.K. and U.S. The culture is very American—in that Aussies are big into the outdoors, surfing, and barbecuing. But the former British colony has retained a lot more of the Queen's English (and her slang), so you get that mixed in with some surfer talk and some Cockney rhyming slang, for a language unique to the land down under.

Bruces & Sheilas

Mate: a friend

Cobber: a very good friend

Bruce: an Aussie man

Sheila: an Aussie woman

Happy little Vegemite: a happy Aussie

Tall poppy: a conspicuously successful person

Postie: a mail carrier

Bikie: a member of a motorcycle club

Ankle biter: a child

Shark biscuits: kids on the beach

Rellie: a relative

Dags & Wankers

Bludger: a lazy person

Bogan: an uneducated person

Dag: an out-of-style nerd

Pom: a derogatory term for a British person

Wanker: a jerk; also **whacker, dipstick, ratbag**

Drongo: fool

Galah: (after a not-so-bright Australian cockatoo) a stupid person

Up yourself!: conceited

Have a Squizz

How ya goin'?: "How are you?"

Good on ya!: "Well done!"

You beauty!: "You rock!"

Reckon!: "Absolutely"

Fair dinkum?: "Honestly?"

It's gone walkabout: "It's lost."

Bloody oath: "Yes."

Give it a burl: "Give it a try."

Have a squizz: "Have a look."

No drama: "No problem"; also **no wuckas**

Defo: "Definitely."

Dardy!: "Cool!" (adopted from South West Australian Aboriginal peoples)

Crikey!: "Holy s***!"

Blimey!: "No way!"

Rack off!: "Get lost!"

Sick Adjectives (Adjies?)

Bloody: very

Grouse: very good

Ripper: great

Sick: great

Corker: something excellent

Gnarly: awesome (surfer lingo)

Piece of piss: easy

True blue: patriotic

Crook: ill

Cactus: dead; broken

Lollies & Stubbies

Bog in: start eating

Not as flat as you think: according to astronomers, the Milky Way galaxy is bent like a "warped vinyl record."

Tucker: food
Sanger: a sandwich; also **cut lunch**
Snag: sausage
Avo: avocado
Lollies: candy
Bikkie: cookie
Esky: insulated container for cold beers
Barbie: barbecue
Brekky: breakfast
Tea: dinner
Ciggie: cigarette
Tinny: a can of beer
Stubby: a bottle of beer
Slab: a carton of beers
Goon: cheap, boxed wine

The Bush & the Big Smoke

Down Under: Australia and New Zealand
Big smoke: a big city, especially Sydney or Melbourne
Billabong: a pond in a dry riverbed
Out in the Bush: in the country
Outback: the desolate interior of Australia
Woop Woop: the middle of nowhere
Bush telly: campfire
Mozzie: mosquito
Aussie salute: brushing flies away with your hand

Thongs & Ugg Boots

Daks: pants
Tracky daks: sweatpants
Knickers: ladies' underwear
Bathers: a swimsuit; also **togs**
Budgie smugglers: Speedos
Runners: sneakers
Thongs: flip-flops
Ugg boots: Australian sheepskin boots

Sunnies: sunglasses
Brolly: an umbrella

Having a Winge

Buggered: exhausted; also **rooted**
Devo: devastate
Chockablock: crowded (**"It's chockers in here"**)
Veg out: relax in front of the telly (TV)
Sprung: caught doing something wrong
Knock: to criticize
Full: drunk
Heaps: a lot
Prezzy: a present
Pash: a long, passionate kiss
Bun in the oven: pregnant (or **preggers**)
Furphy: an absurd rumor
Earbashing: nagging
Whinge: complain
Drop a clanger: say something awkward or inappropriate
Nuddy: naked

Yakka & Accadacca

Yakka: work
Pull a sickie: call in sick to work when you're not sick
Uni: college (short for "university," as the Brits call it)
Arvo: afternoon
Facey: Facebook
Accadacca: the rock band AC/DC
Maccas: McDonald's
Footy: Australian rules football
Servo: a service station
Ute: a pickup truck
Chunder: vomit (verb and noun)
Dunny: outside toilet
Lappy: laptop

Just four countries in Africa have McDonald's restaurants.

LI'L HEROES

If you're the type who's always going on about how kids "don't pull their own weight," well, if one of those good-for-nothing kids ever saved your life, then maybe you'd change your tune.

EMERGENCY STOP

In April 2023, a Michigan school-bus driver started feeling dizzy on her afternoon route and radioed to her boss that she needed medical attention. She slowed down to pull over, but it was too late: she lost consciousness. The bus kept moving and was veering into oncoming traffic! As CCTV footage of the incident shows, several kids noticed that something was wrong with the driver and started screaming. For a few agonizing seconds, no one did anything. Then, from the fifth row, seventh grader Dillon Reeves ran up to the unconscious driver and stepped on the break while he calmly steered the school bus to the side of the road. "Someone call 911!" he yelled over the screams. "Call 911! Now!"

None of the kids were injured, and the driver was taken to the hospital. Dillon later received a commendation for his heroism. How did he know how to drive the bus? "I watched the bus driver."

BUSY DAY

Eleven-year-old Davyon Johnson wanted to be an EMT for as long as he could remember, and on a fateful day in December 2021, he got a chance to put his lifesaving instincts into action—twice. The sixth grader's first save took place in his Muskogee, Oklahoma, school. A fellow student, after having accidentally swallowed a water bottle lid, stumbled into Davyon's classroom. Davyon immediately began the Heimlich maneuver (which he'd learned by watching how-to videos) and freed the lid from the kid's throat.

Then, on the drive home from school, Davyon saw a house with flames and smoke pouring out of it! There was a disabled woman with a walker on the porch trying to escape! Davyon knew she wasn't moving fast enough, so he told his mom to turn the car around. She called 911 while Davyon ran up to the burning house and helped get the woman to safety.

A few days later, at a commendation ceremony for the "dual hero," Davyon's principal called him not just a lifesaver but a "kind soul." And an inspiration, as one mother commented on social media: "Way to go!!! My son witnessed [Davyon] doing the Heimlich maneuver and it's all he could talk about for the rest of the week! You, sir, are a true hero!"

While touring Japan, wrestler Andre the Giant allegedly pooped in hotel bathtubs because the toilets were too small for him.

CASHTON MISSED THE CHEW-CHEW TRAIN

It was "chicken nugget day" in the Norman, Oklahoma, school lunchroom in September 2022 when third-grader Cashton York started choking on a nugget. Then he stopped breathing...and started turning blue! The kids called for help from the lone teacher on duty, Jordan Nguyen, but she was on the far side of the cafeteria and might not make it in time.

Sitting across the table from Ashton was eight-year-old Garrett Brown, who knew what to do because his dad had taught him the Heimlich maneuver. Garrett ran over, positioned himself behind the choking boy, and got to work. "By the time I reached Cashton," Nguyen told *Good Morning America*, "the food had already dislodged and he was breathing again."

Garrett was honored with a "Hero Award" from the school, but the best honor came from Cashton's mother, who told Garrett that there are "not enough words to be grateful for saving my son."

HE SEES HER SEIZURE

It was one of Lori Keeney's "worst nightmares" come true. The Oklahoma mom has epilepsy and has daily seizures. Despite this, she likes to take quick swims in her above-ground backyard pool (though she's usually careful to never swim alone). At the end of one such swim in August 2022, Keeney was still in the water after her 10-year-old son Gavin had gotten out and was heading toward the house.

Then it happened.

Keeney lost her motor skills and started convulsing. Gavin didn't notice anything wrong at first, but just before he went inside, he heard splashing. And then, "I heard kind of yelling, but also drowning." He ran back over and quickly climbed the pool ladder, only to see his mother flailing on the far side of the pool. Gavin dove in, swam over, and was able to get Mom's head above the water. Then he carried her back to the ladder, where he held her head above the water while she continued to convulse. A few moments later, after hearing the dogs barking, Keeney's dad, who lives next door, ran over and helped finish the rescue.

Had Gavin gone straight inside, Keeney could have drowned. Thankfully, she took in only a little bit of water and was otherwise fine. The most surreal part for her was watching the security camera footage. "I don't normally get to see him in action and what he gets to do after I'm having a seizure." And this was actually Gavin's second rescue: a year earlier, he'd saved his mom from choking on her food. Keeney said she has "so much pride in him...at the same time, it was heartbreaking to watch." Gavin was made an honorary member of the fire department. And you can bet that from now on, he'll be making sure that Mom gets out of the pool first.

The gospel group Five Blind Boys of Mississippi forced out a member who regained his sight.

A HEROOOIC ACT

Nine-year-old Charli Johnson saved her mother Sharon's life...with a little help from emergency dispatcher Anne Barklimore. In August 2022, the Gold Coast little girl dialed triple-0 (that's Australia's version of 911) and told the dispatcher, "She just kneeled to the ground and she just fainted." Barklimore asked the girl for her suburb and name, to which she calmly answered: "Helensvale. Charli."

The situation was dire; there was no one else home, the ambulance was nearly 20 minutes away, and Sharon Johnson wasn't breathing. "Listen carefully," said Barklimore. "I will tell you how to do resuscitation." After a brief tutorial, Charli got into position and began doing chest compressions. But Mum still wasn't breathing. "Keep doing the compressions." Charli kept it up, counting along with Barklimore, but as the minutes wore on, the little girl was getting tired and more and more distressed about her mother's state. "I need you to keep doing the compressions over and over," said the dispatcher. "Don't give up. I am so proud of you, and your mum is going to be so proud of you!"

Charli didn't give up, and after an exhausting 17 minutes of CPR, the paramedics finally arrived and took over. Johnson, who had a viral infection, made a full recovery. And Charli got a commendation for her bravery. "She held it together. So many older people don't have that composure," said Barklimore. Johnson added that the save "was quite surprising" given that Charli can be "a bit of a ratbag at home."

A CHIP OFF THE OL' BLOCK

Jimmy Karlbon is a former fire chief and current volunteer firefighter in Avenel, New Jersey. But he didn't hear the smoke alarm going off in the middle of a Sunday night in January 2020. Karlbon's wife and two-year-old son also slept through the alarm. Good thing for them that six-year-old Madalyn heard the beeping. She woke up and smelled smoke—it was so thick it started burning her eyes and throat. Madalyn ran down the hallway shouting, "Daddy, the house is on fire, the house is on fire!"

Karlbon got up, and by that point, he couldn't even see through the smoke. He barely had enough time to get his wife and kids out of there. If little Madalyn hadn't acted so fast, the family would have been trapped inside the burning home. "Madalyn," wrote the Avenel Fire Department in a Facebook post, "it goes without saying how bright and smart of a girl you are. This morning proved that!!"

*   *   *

"Why do they call it rush hour when nothing moves?"

—Robin Williams

The unique light pattern flashed by a lighthouse is called its characteristic.

A SPOONFUL OF ASPARTAME

Pronounced "AS-per-tame," this artificial sweetener has been one of the most popular sugar substitutes since its debut in the 1990s. But what exactly is it? And is it safe?

A BRIEF HISTORY OF SUGAR

Humans crave sweets. Yummy, yummy sweets. This craving goes back millions of years to our primate ancestors, who gained necessary bursts of energy from fruits in the trees. The ripest fruits were packed with nutrients such as fiber, potassium, vitamin C, and folate. Those riper fruits also happened to be sweeter. Result: the primates that developed a taste for sweet fruits gained an energy advantage over those that didn't, and—due to natural selection—the "sweet tooth" became so integral to our survival that the tip of the tongue has taste buds specifically designed to detect those yummy, yummy sweets.

SUBBING IN

The earliest evidence of chemically refined sugarcane comes from India circa 500 BC. Archaeologists think it probably first appeared around 8,000 years ago. Yet for most of human history, sugary confections were a rare delicacy. Then came the 20th century, when candy and chocolates began to be mass-produced and everyday life became more sedentary (especially after TV entered the picture). Result: consuming empty calories from sugar—with scant amounts of nutrients that used to naturally accompany it in fruit—resulted in an "obesity epidemic," as the National Institute of Health named it in 2004.

That's why sugar substitutes are a multibillion-dollar industry today. The first artificial sweetener was saccharin (1879), followed by sucralose, acesulfame-K, and xylitol. And so far, none have even come close to overtaking sugar. But we're here to talk specifically about aspartame. Why? Because this non-saccharide sweetener made from a derivative of two amino acids (aspartic acid and phenylalanine) is 200 times sweeter than table sugar, and it can be found in approximately 6,000 foods and beverages. And some studies have linked it to the "big C" (cancer), while others say it's harmless. Before we get to that, let's look at where aspartame came from.

HOW SWEET IT IS

In 1965, a pharmaceutical chemist named James Schlatter was working on an anti-ulcer drug when he went to pick up a piece of paper and licked his finger...and was struck by its sweetness. He traced the taste back to a compound he'd synthesized called aspartame. It soon went into development as a sweetener, but it took nearly two decades for the U.S. Food and Drug Administration to fully approve aspartame, after

More people buy Girl Scout Cookies each year than they do Oreos, Chips Ahoy!, and Milanos.

first approving it in 1974 and then banning it in 1980 when concerns arose that it could cause brain damage. After more testing, aspartame was approved in some foods in 1981 and some beverages in 1983, and then all of them in 1996.

Because aspartame is so much sweeter than sugar, food and beverage manufacturers need to add less to their products, making it much cheaper. But one thing aspartame isn't: good for baking. When it breaks down from heat, it loses its sweetness. That's why there are no cake recipes that call for Equal. But aspartame has had another cloud hanging over it, almost from the beginning, that might finally be sorted out.

THE BIG QUESTION

Does aspartame cause cancer? If so, that's a big problem, considering that it's in *so many* foods. The FDA says we needn't worry: aspartame is "one of the most studied food additives in the human food supply, with more than 200 studies supporting its safety." There have been some studies, however, that shed doubts on those findings. The one that drew the most attention came in 2023 from the International Agency for Research on Cancer (IARC) and called aspartame "possibly carcinogenic"—specifically implicating it in a type of liver cancer called hepatocellular carcinoma.

The response: "The FDA disagrees with IARC's conclusion that these studies support classifying aspartame as a possible carcinogen to humans. FDA scientists reviewed the scientific information included in IARC's review in 2021 when it was first made available and identified significant shortcomings in the studies on which IARC relied."

An IARC spokesperson elaborated on the findings by saying they "shouldn't really be taken as a direct statement that there is a known cancer hazard." According to the World Health Organization, for aspartame to be dangerous, you'd have to consume more than the "daily intake limit of 40 milligrams per kilogram of body weight." That equates to 14.5 Diet Cokes per day for a 155-pound person. Everyday.

So is the science settled? Aspartame is still considered safe...until another study comes to a different conclusion.

A PARTIAL LIST

Here are just a few of the products that contain aspartame—not including all the laxatives, shake mixes, wine coolers, and even pharmaceutical drugs and supplements that have it.

Equal	Sprite Zero	One Cereal
NutraSweet	7 Up Free	Log Cabin Sugar Free Syrup
Canderel	Trident Gum	
Diet Coke	Wrigley's Orbit	Sugar-free Jell-O
Coke Zero	Wrigley's Extra	Skinny Cow Ice Cream
Diet Pepsi	Crystal Light	Schweppes Slimline Tonic
Pepsi Max	General Mills Fiber	Dr Pepper Zero Sugar

There are more trees in Canada (318 billion) than stars in the Milky Way (100 billion).

CELEBRI-JURORS

One of the great things about a jury is that every member is of equal standing. And it gives celebrities a chance to come down to our level...if they even get chosen to serve.

MR. J

In 2009, a 56-year-old man named Laurence Tureaud—whom you might know better as Mr. T—was summoned for jury duty in Chicago. To say the athlete, actor, and motivational speaker was excited to serve is an understatement. Wearing camouflage pants and his trademark mohawk hairstyle, he told reporters, "It's not about *The A-Team*, it's the J-Team—the jury team!" (For our younger readers, *The A-Team* was a 1980s TV show that propelled Mr. T to fame.) But perhaps it was that very fame—and how his larger-than-life persona might have been a distraction—that got Mr. T dismissed from serving. He had at least one disappointed fan in the courtroom: according to the *Chicago Sun-Times*, the defendant's daughter said, "My mom would have picked him" for the jury. Mr. T no doubt pitied the decision. (But he was paid $17.20 for showing up.)

JURORS-IN-CHIEF

- In November 2017, a small motorcade rolled up to a Chicago courthouse. And out of the last car came a man, as described by the AP, "wearing a dark sport coat, dress shirt, but without a tie," who waved to a crowd that had gathered. Ultimately, Barack Obama was dismissed from serving on a jury (maybe he would have been the foreman). But he was paid his $17.20, and he (and his Secret Service agents) got to sit in a little room and watch a juror instruction video. Obama had been called up once before, in 2010, but he got out of it on the grounds that he was president.

- Presidents Bill Clinton and George W. Bush were also called for jury duty after their time in office...and were also dismissed.

- In 2015, Republican presidential candidate Donald Trump got the call. "I have jury duty. Can you believe this?" he said after showing up at the New York State Supreme Court in a stretch limousine. "People are surprised I agreed to do this. I'm not surprised. I think it's the right thing to do," he added. But Trump was among the many jurors dismissed without being called to a case.

Only former U.S. vice president without a gravesite: Walter Mondale.
(He was cremated.)

THE OPRAH FACTOR

One celebrity who did end up serving on a jury was Oprah Winfrey, and it was a murder case. This all took place in 2004, when the "Queen of All Media" was one of the most famous people in the country. The trial took three days, and after a two-hour deliberation, the jury voted to convict. "It's a huge reality check," Winfrey later said. "When your life intersects with others in this way, it is forever changed." (She also made $17.20 per day.)

That would have most likely been the end of it, if not for the Oprah factor. She and the jurors formed a bond, and the jurors went on talk shows, talking about the case, and even reunited on her top-rated daytime talk show. Shortly after the trial, one of the jurors told Greta Van Susteren of Fox News that Oprah was "a joy," and another said that she wasn't a distraction: "Oprah Winfrey is Oprah Winfrey so, of course, you know, you're always aware of the fact that she's present. She's in the room. However, when we were making our decision it was an individual, it was each individual in the room evaluating the evidence in the case and then we worked as a team to come up with a decision and her vote was the same as everyone else's." At the end of that same interview, former San Francisco Assistant D.A. Jim Hammer told Van Susteren that jurors shouldn't deliberate and tell: "You know it's not over until the appeals are over and, if those jurors happen to reveal something that was improper, some evidence that shouldn't have come in, some reference to an outside source, other things that jurors do incorrectly and they do it on national television, there's going to be a new trial. So, I'd be having a Maalox moment or, you know, a Rolaids moment."

WALL OF FAME

When James Marsden played an exaggerated version of himself in the 2023 docu-comedy *Jury Duty*, he told *People* magazine about the time he served on a real jury in the early 2000s, when he was already famous for movies such as *X-Men* and *The Notebook*. "It was a bizarre experience because it was here in L.A., and I walked into the courtroom and there was a wall of headshots of actors who have served jury duty before—in a government building!" That's why he wasn't that surprised when he got chosen to serve (it was "an eviction case or something"), but he *was* surprised when, "In the middle of an opening argument, [the lawyer] turned to me and he goes, 'And I've loved everything you've done.'" No word on whether Marsden's headshot was added to the wall.

The world record for the longest wedding dress train was set in France in 2017. It's more than 5 miles long.

HANKS FOR NOTHING

Tom Hanks got called for jury duty in Los Angeles in 2013, and the 57-year-old Oscar winner ended up on the jury. It was a contentious domestic violence case, so the *Forrest Gump* actor took his job seriously and tried not to be a distraction. But there was nothing Hanks could do when, during a lunch break, he was approached in a stairwell by a staffer who worked for the prosecution. She thanked Hanks for showing up and told him that they were all impressed that someone of his stature didn't try to get out of it. He smiled and said he was just doing his civic duty. Then he continued on.

Hanks later described it as a "very informal, seven-second interchange." But defense lawyers claimed prosecutorial misconduct—as no one from either side is allowed to talk to jurors. The case was scrapped when the defendant—who was facing up to a year in prison if convicted—struck up a plea deal for a lesser charge of disturbing the peace, with a $150 fine.

And that was that. Hanks's time as a juror—and the case—were over. He didn't talk about the trial for a while, but later shared his own verdict in an interview with the *Mail on Sunday*: "Justice was either served or the entire judicial system was discovered to have a fault in it because of where I chose to eat my lunch that day."

"HAPPINESS CHEMICALS" AND ACTIVITIES THAT ACTIVATE THEM

Dopamine (the reward chemical)
- Finishing a task
- Engaging in self-care
- Eating a good meal

Oxytocin (the love hormone)
- Playing with a baby or dog
- Complimenting someone
- Tender physical contact

Endorphin (the painkiller)
- Laughing
- Exercising
- Eating dark chocolate

Serotonin (the mood stabilizer)
- Basking in sunshine
- Walking in nature
- Meditating

In 1952, future president Jimmy Carter averted a meltdown at a Canadian nuclear plant by going inside the reactor and disabling it by hand.

DRYER SHEET HACKS

Dryer sheets are those thin sheets made of what feels like fabric and science, which you throw in with a load of wet clothes in the dryer. When your clothes emerge dry, they also come out softer and static-free, thanks to the dryer sheet. But that's not all these odd little helpers can do, apparently.

Because they reduce static cling, they also make excellent dust cloths, picking up dirt, lint, and pet hair.

Dry, powdery things stick to dryer sheets, which makes them work much better at picking up spills of ingredients like flour, sugar, or baking soda than a dry or wet paper towel.

Hiking, camping, or performing tree maintenance? Bring some dryer sheets, because they can remove sticky tree sap that tends to stick to hands.

A quick brush of a dryer sheet dislodges sand from feet, legs, and other beach-exposed skin.

Many insects hate the smell of dryer sheets, likely due to the presence of the ingredient linalool, a flower-scented chemical. If you're on a hike or hanging outside and don't want to be bugged by bugs, slip a dryer sheet into the back of your shirt or hat, with some of it hanging out.

A dryer sheet can also repel insects in another way. After a car trip, moisten a dryer sheet and use it to cleanly dislodge and wipe away all those dead bugs stuck to the windshield and hood.

Dryer sheets deodorize and absorb unpleasant smells, replacing those odors with their own inoffensive, subtly clean scent. Place one at the bottom of a garbage can before putting in a trash bag, or inside of a vacuum-cleaner bag, in the car, in a duffel bag for workout gear, in suitcases, or in air vents.

Oven racks get grimy, and as an alternative to spray cleaner, dryer sheets' makeup can remove that greasy buildup. Fill up a bathtub with warm water, a little dish soap, and a half dozen dryer sheets. After an overnight soak, and a scrub with those wet dryer sheets, the racks will come out clean and shiny.

Dryer sheets remove tiny bits of gunk from clothes in the dryer, so they can also be used to remove what gunk remains when those garments get ironed. Starchy buildup accumulates on the plate at the bottom of an iron; a dryer sheet takes it away.

The annoying sound of a squeaky shoe is generally caused by a slight space in between the bottom and the liner or insole. Stick a dryer sheet in between those two layers to fill the space and kill the squeak (and make for a better-smelling shoe).

INSECTS A TO Z

Insects (invertebrate arthropods with three body segments and six legs) outnumber humans by about 200 million to one. Here are some unusual facts about some usual and unusual insects.

Ants

Bees sting, and ants bite. Right? Wrong. Ants sting, too—but only the females. For example, the female fire ant will grab your skin with her mandibles (jaws) and then use her stinger to inject you with venom. One genus—the *Formica* ants, which comprise about 30 species—neither bite nor sting; instead, they spray formic acid that dissolves their victims.

Bugs

All bugs are insects, but not all insects are bugs. The main difference? Bugs suck. Literally. They have a straw-like proboscis that pierces the outer layer of skin, then injects saliva to break down the tissue before slurping out a meal. Some bugs, such as mosquitoes and bed bugs, suck animal blood; stink bugs, aphids, cicadas, and leafhoppers suck plant juices. The other difference: bugs hatch as nymphs and then transform into adults, whereas insects undergo complete metamorphosis (egg, larva, pupa, adult). So, even if a fly may be "bugging" you, it's not a bug.

Cockroaches

You can't see a cockroach's head from above. Why not? It's protected by a shield called a *pronotum*, which means they can only look straight ahead. And speaking of cockroach heads, they can live without them for up to two weeks! How? For one, their blood clots in their neck hole, keeping them from bleeding out. Plus they don't breathe through their mouths, instead using *spiracles*, tiny holes on their bodies that air passes through. But cockroaches do use their mouths to eat and drink. They can last for a few months without food, but usually only a week without water.

Death's-head Hawk Moths

This peculiar moth has a distinctive black-and-white pattern on its thorax that looks eerily like a human skull—hence the name. This was the moth used to cover Jodie Foster's mouth on the *Silence of the Lambs* movie poster (except the skull pattern was replaced by a Salvador Dalí photograph of seven nude women arranged to form what looks like a skull). Entomologists are unsure what evolutionary advantage a human skull provides the moth, but it looks pretty cool.

Country with the most languages per capita: the 300,000 people
of Vanuatu speak 138 indigenous languages.

Earwigs

All insects hatch from eggs, if they're lucky. Egg sacs are usually left alone to fend for themselves. Earwig moms, however, don't take any chances. These creepy-looking insects—with oversized pincers on their thorax—remain with the eggs until they hatch, guarding them from predators, and even moving them if need be. They eat mold and other pathogens that can infect the eggs, which will eventually kill the females, but this way, they can lay their eggs where other insects can't even go. And that's why there are always lots of baby earwigs every summer.

Fireflies

Like all beetles, most of the firefly's life is spent in the larval state—up to two years for some of the 2,000 species around the world. And unlike the kid-friendly adult firefly, which is easy to catch and doesn't bite, the larvae of the firefly are known to be ruthless predators that will hunt down slugs, snails, and worms, and then inject them with a paralytic substance before devouring them alive.

Grasshoppers

Even though it sounds likes the buzzes and crackles made by grasshoppers have a pitch, these insects are tone-deaf. They don't even have ears; they hear—or, rather, pick up vibrations—through an organ on their abdomen called a *tympanum*. Grasshoppers communicate via rhythm by rubbing their hind legs against their forewings (in a process called *stridulation*). Each species of grasshopper has a rhythm with a unique signature, allowing members of that species to recognize and respond to one another.

Honeybees

These beneficial insects are heating and air-conditioning pros. Being coldblooded, their hives need to stay between 93° and 95°F. Bees maintain this temperature in winter by huddling together and vibrating their wings, while also filling in any gaps with *propolis* (a resin-like material that bees make from pine tree buds). In summer, "water bees" fly out to find water and bring it back in their abdomens. They regurgitate the water and fan it around, thus cooling the hive as the water evaporates.

Ice Bugs

As their name implies, these small, wingless bugs are *extremophiles*—meaning they thrive in Earth's most extreme environments. For ice bugs, that's at high elevations, sometimes on the edges of frozen glaciers. One reason for their success: they're *omnivorous*—feasting on whatever insects, carrion, or plants are available. What ice bugs can't take are temperatures above 50°F, which result in death for the bugs.

Who introduced the akita, a Japanese dog breed, to the United States? Helen Keller.

Jerusalem Crickets

Not actually crickets (but related), these insects look a little like something out of a horror movie—with their pale body segments, abnormally large heads, and huge mandibles (which can deliver a painful but nonvenomous bite). They aren't named after the city in the Middle East. They don't even live there. Rather, their name comes from an early 20th century American exclamation: "Jerusalem!" (As in, "Jerusalem! Would you look at that cricket?") Because they also kind of resemble potatoes, their other common name is the potato bug. Found throughout the lower western U.S. into Mexico, other names for this odd insect include *niña de la terra*, stone cricket, skull cricket, and devil's baby.

Katydids

Katydids get predators to "leaf" them alone by looking just like a green leaf—right down to the tiny veins. They're also called bush crickets or long-horned grasshoppers, but don't call them cicadas. A lot of people make that mistake. Although katydids and cicadas both live in trees and make a lot of noise, they're quite different: katydids sing at night, and cicadas by day. And cicadas have stout, greenish-brown bodies. They look nothing like a leaf.

Lice

One of the most common reasons for school absenteeism? You guessed it: head lice, which infest an estimated 6 to 12 million U.S. kids each year. In fact, lice can't survive on anything except for human heads—which classifies them as *human obligatory parasites*. Lice can neither fly nor jump; they spread from person to person by crawling really fast when two heads touch. The female lays her eggs and then glues them to hair follicles; the glue is so strong that neither washing nor brushing will get rid of it.

Mosquitoes

This just in: mosquitoes prefer beer drinkers! Why? Entomologists aren't exactly sure, but one study showed that drinking even one beer will get these bugs' attention. It could be because drinking alcohol raises the body temperature and produces sweat, which also attracts mosquitoes. And when you crack open a cold one, a bit of CO_2 fizzles out. Mosquitoes like that, too—and can detect it from up to 100 feet away.

Narcissus Bulb Flies

Ancient Greek mythology told of handsome young Narcissus, who was so enamored by his own reflection that he turned into the narcissus flower—related flowers in the family include daffodils, lilies, and irises. The narcissus bulb fly, which feeds on the

The custom of shaking hands was depicted as early as 900 BC.

daffodil's nectar and pollen, is also quite the looker—you might even mistake one for a bright, fuzzy bumblebee. A closer look reveals that the narcissus bulb fly has just one set of wings...and no stinger. But predators see the markings that mimic a bumblebee and steer clear.

Owl-flies

Named for their big, round eyes and fluffy faces, these two-inch-long predatory flies (with inch-long antennae) look more like dragonflies than owls. That's why owl-flies hang out on branches near dragonflies: so they can blend in with these much stronger predators. Other sneaky owl-fly tactics include pretending to be a twig by sticking out their twig-like abdomen; holding a wing at a weird angle so it looks injured and inedible; and, if all else fails, emitting a malodorous chemical that should finally tell whatever predator is around that this thing ain't worth it.

Perdita Minima Bees

Who's the tiniest bee? *Perdita minima* bee, that's who. These metallic yellow bees nest in the desert soil of the U.S. Southwest. They range in length from 2 mm to 10 mm. For comparison, the average pinky fingernail is 8 mm wide. They're also one of the few bees that can't sting.

Queen Alexandra's Birdwings

The largest butterfly in the world is also one of the most beautiful. And that might lead to its demise. With their nearly 10-inch wingspan, the females' brown-and-yellow patterning has made them a must-have for collectors ever since they were "discovered" in Papua New Guinea in 1906 and named after the queen of Denmark. Due to collection and habitat loss, they're critically endangered and illegal to trade, though a black market thrives.

Rat-tailed Maggots

Rat-tailed maggots (the larvae of the drone fly) could have been called snorkeling maggots. They have a siphon, a long body part at their posterior end that does resemble a rat tail, but allows them to breathe while underwater. Not that they're safe there—because fish love them, rat-tailed maggots are used as ice fishing bait. (They're called "mousies.")

Stick Mantises

Don't confuse the stick mantis with the stick insect. Other than both resembling sticks, these insects couldn't be more different. For one, stick insects can't turn their head—only the mantis can do that (a full 180 degrees!). And stick insects are

If you're average, there are 2,100 photos saved on your smartphone.

herbivores, whereas stick mantises will eat anything they can catch—including stick insects (if they can recognize them).

Trap-jaw Ants

What are the fastest moving parts in the animal kingdom? The mandibles of the trap-jaw ant. They're so fast that scientists have only just recently constructed a camera that can capture them clamping down at a cool 145 mph. The ants use their powerful jaws to strike at prey, or to get away from predators by biting down so fast that they're launched up to 15 inches away. That's the equivalent of a human being able to bite down so hard it would launch him 135 feet away.

Uzi Flies

Uzi flies are parasitoids, or insects that mature within the body of another insect, killing the host in the process. An uzi fly's host of choice is the silkworm: The female lays her eggs between the worm's body segments and then literally glues them there. When those eggs hatch, the uzi larvae feed on the silkworm's innards, build cocoons, and, after about ten days, breaks out of the host. Individual silkworms aren't the only victims of uzi flies: they have been blamed for a 15- to 30-percent drop in silk production in India's silk industry. The good new is that scientists have identified a wasplike insect that acts as a parasitoid for the uzi fly's pupa stage, and they're urging farmers to use the wasps to fight the flies to save the worms.

Viceroy Butterflies

Batesian mimicry (named for English naturalist Henry Walter Bates) occurs when an undangerous species looks like a dangerous one—similar to the aforementioned narcissus bulb fly's bumblebee impression. Viceroy butterflies utilize *Müllerian mimicry* (named for German naturalist Fritz Müller), which occurs when two dangerous species look alike. That's why it's hard to distinguish between a viceroy and the much more famous monarch. Their orange-and-brown wings are quite similar—except the viceroy has an extra black line, and it's a bit smaller. The benefit of Müllerian mimicry: once a predator tries either one of these species—and is met with an unpleasant taste—it will avoid both species for the rest of its life.

Water Boatmen

These bugs appear to "row" on the surface of water like a boat, hence the name. The water boatman has another important feature: a "singing" penis. That's because the insect chirps by rubbing its penis over ridges on its abdomen. At less than half an inch long, water boatmen can generate chirps that reach nearly 100 dB, nearly as loud as a chainsaw. Why so loud? Because they do their calling from underwater in

Heavy metal band name idea: Osmium.
(That's the world's densest metal—twice as dense as lead.)

the middle of rivers. About 99 percent of the sound is lost, and their chirps must be loud enough for prospective mates to hear them from the bank. Water boatmen are not only the loudest of the insects, they're the loudest animal on Earth relative to body size.

Xerces Blue Butterflies

The Xerces blue went extinct in the 1940s, but there aren't a lot of insects that start with x, and we're including them on this list because of their sad and interesting story: it's the first known butterfly species that went extinct in North America due to habitat loss. These gossamer beauties—dark-blue wings with white spots—once fluttered around coastal sand dunes of San Francisco, until the local lotus plant population was wiped out. That was the Xerces blue larva's primary food source. At last report, there was an effort underway to repopulate the dunes with the Palos Verdes blue butterfly, a close relative of the Xerces blue from the Los Angeles area.

Yellow Jackets

Yellow jackets are not bees; they are wasps. Bees lose their stingers when they sting; yellow jackets will keep stinging as long as they perceive you as a danger to their colony. In case you need to get away from one, know that the average human runs 6 to 8 mph, the same speed that yellow jackets fly. An even more dangerous wasp is the hornet, with its larger stinger and 25-mph top flight speed. Drive away, if possible.

Zoraptera

Zoraptera is an order of about 30 species of tiny "angel insects" that live in colonies inside rotting trees and old leaf piles. Measuring just 3 mm long, they feed on fungi and dead arthropod parts. Unlike bees, there's no social organization in Zoraptera colonies. One final insect fact: When Italian entomologist Filippo Silvestri first identified this order in 1913, he combined the Greek *zor* ("pure") and *aptera* ("wingless"). Even though it was later discovered that some species do have wings, the awkward name stuck.

* * *

THE NAME IS OBVIOUS

- A Leatherman brand pocket device seems to have a little gadget for every function, leading one to believe that the tool originated as a leather worker's trusty aide. It didn't. It was invented by a man named Tim Leatherman.
- The Dumpster, the brand name for a large garbage receptacle, was named for its function of receiving "dumped" trash, right? Nope. It's a play on the name of its inventor, George Dempster.

Two most-consumed things on Earth: water and concrete.

UNCLE JOHN'S PAGE OF LISTS

Some random bits from our bottomless files.

6 Pre-Fame Celeb Commercials

1. Sarah Michelle Gellar: Burger King
2. Keanu Reeves: Corn Flakes
3. Brad Pitt: Pringles
4. Leonardo DiCaprio: Bubble Yum
5. Elijah Wood: Cheese

5 Smells Americans Hate the Most (*Popular Science*, 2020)

1. Skunk
2. Mildew
3. Cigarette
4. Gasoline
5. Dog pee on the carpet

10 Worst Fashion Trends of 2022 (HuffPost)

1. Sunglasses at night
2. Y2K aesthetic
3. Floral dresses à la coastal grandmother
4. Low-rise jeans
5. Cargo pants
6. Platform flip-flops
7. Brands that don't take accountability
8. Micro miniskirts
9. Lingerie as evening wear
10. Skinny jeans

Earth in 15 Languages

1. *Aarde* (Dutch)
2. *Bumi* (Indonesian)
3. *Chikyū* (Japanese)
4. *Địa Cầu* (Vietnamese)
5. *Dìqiú* (Chinese)
6. *Ddaear* (Welsh)
7. *Erde* (German)
8. *Jigu* (Korean)
9. *Jorden* (Norwegian)
10. *Maa* (Finnish)
11. *Terre* (French)
12. *Terra* (Italian)
13. *Tierra* (Spanish)
14. *Zemlja* (Russian)
15. *Zemljá* (Ukrainian)

12 Longest Words with Letters in Alphabetical Order

1. Aegilops
2. Beefily
3. Billowy
4. Abhors
5. Accent
6. Access
7. Almost
8. Biopsy
9. Bijoux
10. Billow
11. Chintz
12. Effort

5 Things Invented by Black Women

1. Folding cabinet bed (Sarah Goode, 1885)
2. Modern ironing board (Sarah Boone, 1892)
3. Hairbrush with synthetic bristles (Lyda Newman, 1898)
4. Home security system (Mary Van Brittan Brown, 1966)
5. 3D illusion transmitter (Valerie Thomas, 1980)

Share of Pet Owners by Generation (*Forbes*, 2023)

1. Millennials (33%)
2. Gen X (25%)
3. Baby boomers (24%)
4. Gen Z (16%)
5. Silent generation (2%)

6 Things Found in Osama Bin Laden's Compound

1. Diary
2. Son Hamza's wedding video
3. Video games
4. Disney movies
5. Pornography
6. Conspiracy theory books

Enya is the best-selling Irish singer of all time, and she's never done a solo concert.

GOVERN-MENTAL

From city councils to the highest offices in the land, here are some eye-rolling accounts of oddball political happenings.

ROADWORK AHEAD

In 2013, after Australian contemporary artist Lindy Lee had spent six months sculpting and installing *Cloud Gate* in Sydney's Chinatown district, she was under the impression that it was going to be a permanent display. After all, the city spent $356,000 U.S. dollars on the installation, which consisted of several large bronze "clouds" set into the pavement along two streets.

The installation barely lasted five years, thanks to a light-rail construction project that was slated to go through part of it. Rather than contact Lee, or try to figure out a way around her artwork, the city-contracted workers extracted the bronze clouds with jackhammers, and then resurfaced the street with bitumen (similar to asphalt).

At last report, the broken clouds were stacked up in a storage room. The transport department for New South Wales apologized for the "shoddy removal" of the installation and blamed the construction company. "It's very disappointing," said Lee. "It was an awful lot of effort on my part." She added, "It just feels like the left hand wasn't speaking to the right hand."

PANTS ON FIRE

According to U.S. Rep. George Santos (R-NY), he attended a prestigious private academy in the Bronx, was an actor on the hit Disney Channel show *Hannah Montana*, was the star of his college volleyball team, was a reporter for Brazil's Globo network, was a landlord with 13 properties, worked at Goldman Sachs and Citigroup, produced Broadway's *Spider-Man: Turn Off the Dark*, got mugged in Queens, and survived an assassination attempt. According to fact-checkers, none of that is true. (The House Ethics Committee agreed.)

SO UNTIDY

By the summer of 2020, 80-year-old U.S. Army veteran Dennis Moriarty was getting too old to mow the steep lawn in front of his Kansas City, Missouri, home. His solution: replace the lawn with a 1,500-square-foot wildflower garden. By the next summer, Moriarty's blooming garden was the envy of his neighbors. Then one morning, he saw a man out front of his house taking photos. The man introduced himself as Leon Bowman, Kansas City code inspector, and he informed Moriarty that his "untidy" yard was in violation because "lawns can be no higher than 10 inches." Moriarty had 10 days to remove all the "weeds," or he'd start receiving fines.

"They are certainly not weeds," Moriarty argued. He should know; he'd spent years volunteering in urban community gardens. He explained that this was not a lawn but a "pollinator garden." It uses less water than grass and attracts hummingbirds, butterflies, and bees. Bowman disagreed, called the plants weeds, and issued an official warning.

Moriarty took to Twitter with a post that went viral. "I...planted 10 Native Wildflowers species on my front terrace and now KC CODES has photographed as weeds and I'll be hauled to court."

The city argued that they support "urban gardening," but homeowners often confuse native plants and weeds, and that unmanaged plant growth of any kind is a nuisance. However, much of the public took Moriarty's side, including the *Kansas City Star* in an op-ed: "With all the challenges Kansas City faces—gun violence, homelessness, crumbling abandoned buildings, the lack of affordable housing, trashy vacant lots and so much more—we have one question: Huh?"

Moriarty and the newspaper urged the city to rethink its ordinance. And he did agree to cut down his flowers, but only after the first hard frost in the fall, to encourage greater growth the next year.

SHADY POLITICIAN

In June 2023, Bjørnar Moxnes, leader of Norway's left-wing Red Party, was perusing a gift shop at the Oslo airport when, for some reason, he stole a pair of Hugo Boss sunglasses. Security-camera footage of the act was leaked to the Internet and quickly blew up into a scandal that culminated in Moxnes's resignation.

"A lot of people have asked me how I could do something so stupid," he wrote on Facebook. "I've asked myself that many times in recent weeks. I don't have an adequate explanation."

FOLLOW THE WHITE RABBIT

On Easter Sunday in 2022, the White House was hosting its annual Easter Egg Roll. Because kids are the focus of this event, the banter between the press and the president is expected to be superficial. And it was...until a reporter asked President Biden about a deadly air strike in the Middle East. As Biden was starting to answer, "Pakistan should not, and Afghanistan should be..." a presidential aide briskly walked up and whooshed the president away mid-sentence, before guiding him to a section of the lawn where there were no reporters. The odd part: the aide was dressed up in full costume as the Easter Bunny.

Only time all four Beatles contributed to the same record, post-breakup: Ringo Starr's *Ringo* (1973).

CANADIAN SENSATIONS THAT FLOPPED IN AMERICA

The Canadian entertainment, cultural, and business landscape is loaded with American entities making good in the Great White North. Every so often, something from much-less-populated Canada will expand into the United States. It doesn't always work out for the best. Here are some Canadian icons and household names that couldn't garner much attention in the States.

🍁 CANADIAN HIT: SWISS CHALET

Successful Rise: The first Swiss Chalet opened in 1954 in Toronto as Swiss Chalet Bar-B-Q. The chief attraction on the menu then, as it is now, isn't barbecue at all, but chargrilled rotisserie chicken. Now a sleek sit-down restaurant that serves up plated meals fast—fried chicken, ribs, fries, roast beef, salads, sandwiches, and pies grace the current menu—Swiss Chalet at first embraced an alpine lodge theme, a novelty that quickly helped it spread throughout Canada and into Buffalo, New York, which borders the Canadian province of Ontario.

American Flop: The company moved into the U.S. quickly; a Buffalo outpost was only the fourth ever Swiss Chalet, opening in 1957 following a second Toronto location and a spot in Montreal. While the restaurant would expand across Canada, 80 percent of its 200-plus current locations stand in Ontario. By 2000, only four had opened in the U.S., all of them in Buffalo. Three closed down in 2010, and the fourth in 2020.

🍁 CANADIAN HIT: THE CANADIAN FOOTBALL LEAGUE (CFL)

Successful Rise: As rugby evolved in the early 20th century into what's now known as football in the U.S., it birthed a very similar game in Canada known as Canadian football. With rules and a style of play established and codified by the 1920s, the CFL formed with nine teams in 1958. Canadian football as played in the CFL strongly resembles NFL football, but with some notable differences. For example, the field in Canada spans 110 yards instead of 100, the goalposts stand on the goal lines instead of at the back of the end zones, there's more passing than running, and a team gets three downs on each possession rather than four. While CFL football is very popular in Canada, its reach and financial success has a ceiling—Canada's population is about one-tenth that of the U.S., meaning far fewer TV outlets, and limited revenue. In 1991, the CFL got a big infusion of cash and attention when hockey legend Wayne

Gretzky and movie star John Candy teamed up as minority owners of the Toronto Argonauts, then signed American football player "Rocket" Ismail to a huge contract. Capitalizing on the moment, the CFL looked to the U.S. for a huge, NFL-level TV deal. In 1993, it added its first American team, the Sacramento Gold Miners, and then a year later, six more teams in big cities that didn't have NFL teams at the time: Birmingham, Baltimore, Las Vegas, Memphis, San Antonio, and Shreveport.

American Flop: Not even in football-hungry cities could the CFL attract enough fans to fill stadiums and turn a profit; the style of play was just different enough from that of the NFL to seem foreign and subpar. Nevertheless, the Baltimore Stallions went to the Grey Cup championship game in 1994 and won it in 1995, but poor attendance and the lack of that longed-for American TV contract forced the CFL to abandon its American experiment. After the 1995 Grey Cup, the CFL shut down all its U.S. teams.

🍁 CANADIAN HIT: CORNER GAS

Successful Rise: In the 2000s, most scripted comedies airing in primetime on Canada's major TV networks were imports from the United States. *Corner Gas*—a Canadian-made show about life in the extremely small and rural farming community of Dog River, Saskatchewan—debuted in 2004 on CTV. The action revolved around the operator of the town's only gas station, Brent (played by stand-up comedian and series star Brent Butt), with his friends, two bored police officers and the operator of the adjacent coffee shop. It became the #1 comedy on Canadian TV for all five years of its run, winning every major entertainment award and spawning a hit feature film and animated spin-off.

American Flop: Reruns of *Corner Gas* were sold into syndication in 2007, with cable channel WGN America buying up the exclusive U.S. rights to the smash hit series. It lasted just six months on WGN's daytime schedule before being relegated to a late-night time slot and then disappearing completely.

🍁 CANADIAN HIT: GIANT TIGER

Successful Rise: In the early 20th century, before the rise of "big box" retailers such as K-Mart, Target, and Walmart, the retail market was dominated by so-called "variety" or "discount" chains (including Woolworth, Newberry's, and Ben Franklin) that sold a little bit of everything, from canned goods to housewares to toys to clothes to sporting goods. Canadian traveling salesman Gordon Reid visited some variety stores in the U.S. in the late 1950s and then introduced the concept to Canada, with the first Giant Tiger store opening in Ottawa, Ontario, in 1961. It would take Reid four more years to build up a customer base with his new store idea, with store number two opening in 1965. By the 2000s, a whopping 230 Giant Tiger stores could be found across Canada, primarily in suburban shopping malls and in the downtown shopping districts of

They're just longer: giraffes have the same number of neck bones as humans.

medium and small towns. Giant Tiger customers proved so loyal that when Target tried to enter Canada in the early 2000s, it couldn't gain a foothold; Giant Tiger would expand even more by buying up abandoned and empty Target buildings.

American Flop: Having beat back the threat of Target, an American company, Giant Tiger's Canada-based board of directors felt the time was right to move into the States. In 2004, Giant Tiger opened its first store outside of Canada in Potsdam, New York, home of two colleges: Clarkson University and SUNY Potsdam. Just 30 miles from the Canadian border and thus exposed to Canadian culture, and filled with savings-minded college students, Potsdam remained unfazed by Giant Tiger. The store closed down after five straight years of poor sales.

🍁 CANADIAN HIT: CANADIAN TIRE

Successful Rise: Canadian Tire is a massive business conglomerate in Canada with nearly 1,700 overall locations of all its stores and subsidiaries. The flagship Canadian Tire stores sell tires, auto parts, sporting goods, and housewares. There are also a few hundred Canadian Tire gas stations, a bank, clothing store Mark's, a party supply store, textile companies, and more. Founded in 1922, it's the largest Canadian-based retailer and brings in annual assets of almost $15 billion Canadian dollars.

American Flop: Flush with tens of millions in cash in 1982, Canadian Tire decided to move into the American market by purchasing an existing chain and rebranding it. Instantly, and at a cost of $40 million, 81 outlets of Texas-based auto parts chain White Stores became Canadian Tire. American customers were bewildered by the sudden change of a known entity into a store that proudly proclaimed its Canadian heritage, and had a wide variety of product offerings, that wasn't known in the U.S. (Americans thought the company sold only tires), leading Canadian Tire's U.S. division to sink quickly. Within four years, the endeavor had lost $100 million, forcing Canadian Tire to close half of its American stores and to sell off the other half to Western Auto Supply. Canadian Tire tried to get into the U.S. economy again in the mid-1990s, losing the "Canadian" branding that time. It opened Auto Source, an auto parts superstore, in Indianapolis in 1991, touting in-store stock of 25,000 items, more than double that of the average competitor. By 1994, ten Auto Source mega stores were up and running in Indiana, Ohio, and Kentucky. In 1995, Canadian Tire abruptly shut down the entire chain after discovering that it had lost $60 million on the project.

*   *   *

A MILITARY WORD ORIGIN

In 1915, England's Committee of Imperial Defence called its top-secret armored vehicle program "Tank Supply Committee" to fool German spies into thinking the Brits were only making mobile water carriers. That's how the military tank got its name.

Cold truth: fifteen minutes of shivering burns as many calories as an hour of exercise.

GEODDITIES

These started out as geographical oddities, but we realized there's some odd geology in here as well. Hence, geoddities!

A WATERSHED MOMENT

A watershed is an area of land where all the rainwater and snowmelt empties into the same body of water. The North American continent has two major watersheds, one on either side of the Continental Divide; water on the west side of the divide drains toward the west, while water on the east side drains toward the east. The steep summits of the Rocky Mountains follow this divide from Mexico to Canada. But they're not *all* steep. At Yellowstone National Park in Wyoming is Isa Lake. This lily pad–covered pond is situated in such a way that it drains into the Pacific Watershed *and* the Atlantic Watershed. That means, if two Isa Lake fish buddies get separated, one of them could swim 1,000 miles to the Pacific; the other, 2,000 miles to the Atlantic.

"A FREAK OF NAVIGATION"

Have you ever heard the tale of the passenger steamer SS *Warrimoo* that managed to position itself in two different days, two different months, two different seasons, two different years, and two different centuries...at the same time?

It was New Year's Eve 1899. As the ship was heading west on the Pacific Ocean from Canada to Australia, the navigator told the captain that they were only a few miles from the intersection of the equator and the International Date Line. By positioning the ship diagonally across that point, for that one calm, clear evening, the passengers and crew could stroll back and forth from winter to summer, from the Northern Hemisphere to the Southern Hemisphere, and from the 19th century to the 20th century.

It's a fun story, but did it happen? Snopes calls this one "unproven," and with good reason: navigators back then didn't have the tools to reach such a precise point in the open ocean. In addition, it wasn't reported until a 1942 Canadian news article: "And those aboard were the first people on earth to hail the new century and the last to bid the old century farewell." But according to the fact-checking website, there are no firsthand accounts, or any logbooks, or any evidence at all. Still, as they point out, it *could have happened.*

THE JOINING OF FIJI

Fast forward a century. What might have happened on the steamer from the previous entry almost happened in Fiji, because this archipelago (group of islands) happens to

Chinese equivalent of "old maids": *sheng nu*, or "leftover ladies."

be situated right along the International Date Line. This imaginary line runs north to south, mostly through the Pacific Ocean, going over land only at the poles and zigzagging around the Bering Strait and Samoan Islands.

This line also used to dissect Fiji, but that created major headaches, especially on the three islands through which the line ran. It was neat to be able to walk from today to tomorrow, and then back to yesterday, which is today. However, bookkeeping and planning of anything required compensating for the confusing time change. As the year 2000 was approaching, Fiji's government petitioned to move the line out into the water and off the land. Request approved.

THE REVERSING RAPIDS

The Bay of Fundy, which lies between the Canadian provinces of New Brunswick and Nova Scotia, has the highest tides in the world—28 feet in about 12.5 hours. As the Atlantic Ocean surges, the tides rise in the bay and the water rushes up the Saint John River, effectively reversing the river's flow. That means if you spend a day on an overlook, you'll see raging rapids flowing to the ocean; then a calm, low river during slack tide; and then raging rapids flowing inland. It's awesome to witness but really tough to navigate if you're a ship heading into the city of Saint John. That's why it's navigable only during slack tide.

A STORY OF FIRE AND ICE

Did you know that Iceland, the world's 18th largest island, is closer to North America than it is to Europe? Technically, anyway. It's closer to continental Europe than to the North American mainland, but the closest island to Iceland (146 nautical miles away) is Greenland, which sits on the eastern reaches of the North America tectonic plate. That makes Greenland a part of North America...geographically speaking. Though it's considered a self-governing "autonomous constituent," it belongs to Denmark, making Greenland politically a part of Europe.

Oh, and it's the world's largest island.

As for why Iceland is green and Greenland is white: most of Greenland lies farther north of the Arctic Circle than Iceland does, whereas Iceland (which is 20 times smaller) lies south of it. And get this: almost all of the Mid-Atlantic Ridge, an underwater mountain range, is on the ocean floor...except in Iceland, where the North American and Eurasian plates move past each other on land, creating a volcanically active—and very green—landscape. (Greenland got its name because the Viking Eric the Red, upon returning home from there, made out the icy tundra to be more verdant than it really was.)

A BRIEF HISTORY OF BRIEFS

We at the BRI have a certain affinity for underwear–after all, it's usually the last thing people touch before they pick up a Bathroom Reader. So here's a brief, supportive, and occasionally revealing look at the history of underwear.

3,000 BC | The first garments recognizable as underwear–which go around the midsection and cover private parts and rear-ends–are just regular clothes. It's hot in ancient Egypt, and most men of the lower economic classes don't own much clothing, so a tied linen loincloth or kilt called a *schenti* is pretty much the only thing they wear. (Similar garments were worn by prehistoric man thousands of years before this, and for millennia after, throughout Europe and in the Americas.)

500 BC | The idea of underwear as a way to demonstrate one's sophistication, adhere to beauty standards, and serve some kind of physical function begins in ancient Rome. Upper-class women are expected to wear a *strophium*, a tight wrapping that fits over and just under the bust. It provides support and keeps breasts firmly in place–unsupported or unadorned breasts are unfavorably associated with old women and barbarians, respectively. Under their tunics or togas, Roman men and women wear elaborately folded and tied linen loincloths, or *subligaculum* ("tied on under").

1400s | Men in medieval Europe favor a pants-underwear combo garment called a *braies*, or breeches. Loose-fitting short pants made of linen or wool, the individual legs are tied up at the waist with a drawstring or a separate belt.

1700s | The corset (French for "little body") is the standard item of shape wear for both European men and women. Covering the body from the chest down to the hips, it severely constricts the body, making the torso appear both thin and shapely. That effect is achieved by a structure made from whalebone, wooden splints, or steel. By 1900, it's just for women, but the design has evolved to be less restrictive, aligning with the natural curves of a woman's figure.

Early 1800s | Women begin to wear pantaloons (or drawers), previously worn only by men. On ladies, they are flesh-colored, sometimes cover the bust, and stop at the knees or go all the way down to the ankles, ending in frills and splitting in the middle for when nature calls.

1830s Hoop skirts are highly fashionable. To create a bell shape, an underskirt cage is employed, covered in many layers of thin, frilly skirts called petticoats.

1850s European women start to wear a thin, silken (if not made of silk) sleeveless shirt beneath their corsets, or, occasionally, without a corset. Designed to serve as a protective layer between clothing and bare skin, the camisole (French for "shirt") will eventually become full-length—turning into a slip.

1868 The union suit is patented, and though it's marketed as the next generation in pantaloons for women, it's adopted by men. Providing full coverage of not just the torso but also the arms and legs (with buttoned flaps on the front and rear), it's essentially what's known today as "long johns" or long underwear.

1874 Sporting goods maker C. F. Bennett creates the jockstrap, offering private-parts support to men engaged in the hot new pastime of bicycling. (Riding around on cobblestone streets, present in many American cities of the time, can painfully jostle a man's undercarriage.)

1893 Marie Tucek patents the "breast supporter," or the first-ever bra, designed to lift and keep the bust in place. It features separate cups, shoulder straps, and a hook-and-eye closure, similar to the modern-day garment.

1913 The U.S. Navy adopts the T-shirt as part of its uniform. Short-sleeved, crew-necked, buttonless one-piece garments first made of hot wool and later breathable white cotton, they are designed for wear under a uniform. After the end of World War I in 1918, returning American sailors adopt the undershirt into their civilian wardrobe.

1914 New York socialite Mary Phelps Jacob patents a garment called the "brassiere," the beginning of the end of the corset era. She buys a sheer, backless evening gown for a party, and, realizing that a whalebone corset won't work with the dress, she and her French maid concoct a demure bust-supporting undergarment out of handkerchiefs, ribbon, and cord.

1920s	The dancing, partying female "flappers" of the Jazz Age usher in the era of decorative lingerie. For the first time, underwear is worn on the outside, as a fashion statement, with short flapper dresses originating from tailored slips, and in colors besides white.
1930s	The development of elastics creates a revolution in underwear. Skivvies can now be more comfortable, both formfitting and allowing some give, as opposed to the make-it-fit style of corsets. This decade sees the introduction of the girdle for women and briefs for men, as well as elastic-waisted boxers—like the outerwear worn by fighters, but shorter and made of thinner materials.
1947	Frederick Mellinger, who claims to have invented the push-up bra, opens Frederick's of Hollywood in California, selling all kinds of hard-to-acquire, European-made skivvies—lacy things, bridal lingerie, and novelties. Pinups and cheesecake models such as Bettie Page in the 1950s and beyond will wear such things in their photo shoots, purchased at Frederick's of Hollywood and similar outlets.
Late 1940s	"Bullet bras" come on the scene. Eschewing round cups designed to comfortably fit the bust, these pointed cylinders fuel the "sweater girl" look.
1950s	The "sweater girl" pinups and the popularity of busty movie stars such as Jayne Mansfield lead to a cultural fixation with breasts and a connection between bust size and proper womanhood. Result: underwear companies introduce and aggressively market the "training bra" to preadolescent girls. It provides little support—it's just a way to introduce girls to wearing (and buying) bras.
1950s	French designer Louis Réard popularizes the bikini, a two-piece swimsuit. By the 1960s, the growing feminist movement will influence the widespread adoption of more-comfortable and less-restrictive underwear—and skimpier bikini-style underpants hit stores.
1974	Experimental Austrian American fashion designer Rudi Gernreich (who also invented the topless swimsuit or "monokini") introduces the thong. First a swimsuit—characterized by a thin strip of fabric in the back that, instead of providing coverage, sits inside of the buttocks, showing off the rear-end—it's soon adapted into underwear.
1977	After feeling uncomfortable shopping for lingerie for his wife at a department store—where the selections are far too modest for his

Do you have galeanthropy? It's the belief that you have transformed into a cat.

liking—Roy Raymond opens the first Victoria's Secret store at a mall in Palo Alto, California. Until this time, average stores sell functional and sedate underwear; lacy, racy lingerie is procured at specialty shops or from catalogs. Victoria's Secret takes scandalous skivvies into the mainstream.

1980s   Fashion designer Giorgio Armani unveils boxer briefs. Combining the two major men's underwear styles of the 20th century, they offer support where men need it and provide coverage down to the thighs.

1994   The WonderBra was introduced in the U.S. and Canada in 1955 but doesn't become a phenomenon until the 1990s when manufacturers stop making it a purely functional push-up bra and redesign it as a line of lacy undergarments available in a variety of styles that would look at home in a Victoria's Secret.

2000   Sara Blakely introduces Spanx. Made of stretchy fabrics, the garments are like a more comfortable, more sophisticated girdle. A landmark in shape wear and compression garments, they're worn under clothes to provide a slimmer silhouette.

2010s   The biggest new thing in women's undergarments is an old thing: the bralette. A mix of a training bra and a camisole, it's a lacy, fashion-minded garment designed to wear under shirts but also provide no support in the form of padding or wires. Sociologists think the anti–sexual assault #MeToo movement made many women question beauty standards and avoid unwanted male attention, thus helping drive the sales of bralettes. Their popularity is also helped by the COVID-19 pandemic, when millions of women work from home, and millions of bralettes sell—they're a lot more comfortable than a push-up bra.

*   *   *

HE STARTED A JOKE

"Take my wife, please!" is a very old, very simple one-liner. (The listener thinks the speaker brings up his spouse as an example, only for the speaker to express a desire for her to disappear. Comedy!) It was originated by comic Henny Youngman in the 1940s. Youngman was appearing on a radio program and asked a stagehand to show his wife to her seat. "Take my wife, please," Youngman said. The stagehand thought he was cracking wise; he wasn't. Youngman put the joke in his act right away.

The older the tree, the more carbon it absorbs from the atmosphere.

🗣 MOUTHING OFF 🗣

A CELEBRATION OF OXYGEN

Singers talk singing.

"Singing is a trick to get people to listen to music for longer than they would ordinarily."
—David Byrne

"I love singing. I love it, and it doesn't feel like a chore. It's an expression."
—Rihanna

"When you're singing, you're using extra muscles, and it requires a lot of exercise and breathing. You can't do that if you're a sissy. If I have any fitness advice for people, I'd tell them to sing more. It's good therapy, too."
—Willie Nelson

"There's no half-singing in the shower, you're either a rock star or an opera diva."
—Josh Groban

"Singing is just a feeling set to music."
—Carrie Underwood

"Singing, it's like loving somebody, it's a supreme emotional and physical experience."
—Janis Joplin

"What you must understand is that my voice comes from the energy of the audience. The better they are, the better I get."
—Freddie Mercury

"SINGING IS A WAY OF ESCAPING. IT'S ANOTHER WORLD. I'M NO LONGER ON EARTH."
—Edith Piaf

"If I cannot fly, let me sing."
—Stephen Sondheim

"Singing is like a celebration of oxygen."
—Björk

"I'M MUCH MORE COMFORTABLE SINGING THAN TALKING."
—Kenny Rogers

"WHEN I SING, TROUBLE CAN SIT RIGHT ON MY SHOULDER AND I DON'T EVEN NOTICE."
—Sarah Vaughan

CAMPING WITH DUCT TAPE

It can't just fix every single problem in your house—duct tape can save your life (or just make your next camping trip a little easier)! Here's how.

Fix a Tear: Use duct tape—the good kind, not a cheap dollar-store knock-off—to temporarily seal holes in tents, camp chairs, sleeping bags, air mattresses, coats, rain gear, and other garments. Tape both sides of the tear for extra protection.

Fashion a Rope: If you're stuck at the bottom of a ravine with a roll of duct tape and not much else, be the MacGyver of your group and twist long strips into a rope. It probably won't be strong enough to support your weight and save you, but a duct tape rope is plenty strong to hang your food high enough so the bears can't reach it at night. (It also works as a clothesline.)

Fight Off a Bear: Throw the roll of duct tape at the bear and then run away while it's distracted.

Fight Off Ticks: The last one was a joke. This one is dead serious, as Lyme disease can screw up your life. To protect yourself—especially in tick-filled areas such as tall grass—use bug spray if you have it. And use duct tape around the bottom of your pant legs to block access between your cuffs and boots, where ticks are most likely to get you.

Keep Food Fresh: You don't have sealable baggies or bag clips, so how do you keep your chip bags sealed so the critters can't smell them? Use duct tape.

Make a Splint, Bandage, or Sling: Sprained ankle? Calling Dr. Duct Tape. Use it just like you would an ACE bandage (just don't adhere it to bare skin—use a plastic bag under the tape so the bandage can be easily cut away). If you hurt your arm, you can make a sling out of duct tape the same way you made the rope when you were stuck in that ravine. You can even seal a wound with duct tape (similar to a Band-Aid).

Bye-bye, Blister: If you're on a long hike and you feel your heels or toes starting to blister, get some duct tape between your boots and wherever your foot is starting to hurt. Do it preventively if you have new boots, as a bad blister can botch a backpacking trip.

Repair Your Specs: Anyone with poor eyesight knows how scary it would be to break your glasses in the woods. Before you give up on your busted specs, get out the duct tape and see what you can do to fix them.

Keep Your Pants Up: Start with a strip of duct tape about six inches longer than your waistline. Fold it in half lengthwise so there's no sticky side. Run it through your belt loops, and you can use a shoelace to tie it in place for easy untying later. (Of course, you'll have to spend the rest of the camping trip getting made fun of for your duct-tape belt—but that's better than being made fun of for accidentally mooning everyone.)

Keep Your Shoes On: Duct tape—temporarily extending broken boots' lives since World War II. Use it to repair the sole or replace a shoelace.

Pest Control: If the flies are bugging you, tape two strips back-to-back and hang them near the food (but away from kids) for a chemical-free flytrap. Add a small weight to the bottom to keep the wind from blowing it around.

Spear a Fish: Use plenty of duct tape to firmly attach a knife to the end of a dowel or pole, such as a broom or a strong stick that you've found. Then you can spear a fish.

Fix a Fishing Pole: Or a tent pole that's broken in two. Find a strong, shorter stick to place along the break, then wrap in duct tape until the pole is firm enough to last the rest of the trip.

Break the Wind: If it's rainy and windy and your shelter is lacking, you can make a windbreak with duct-taped plastic bags, as long as you have something to attach it to.

Find Your Way: Stacking rocks (a.k.a. cairns) to mark your place on a trail is frowned upon—so try using a piece of duct tape (a brightly colored one, if you have it) to trace your steps. Attach it only to rocks or fence posts so the duct tape doesn't damage any trees. And try not to leave any behind.

A-Hem: You can use duct tape to hem your pants.

Secure a Picnic Table: Strategically placed duct tape will keep your tablecloth from wreaking havoc when the wind picks up.

Re-Seal a Water Bottle: You've dropped it one too many times, and the thing cracked and now it's leaking. Not any more! Just apply a piece of duct tape.

Keep Your Feet Warm: If your socks or other footwear aren't keeping out the cold, you can use duct tape to insulate the inside of your boots. If you have nothing for your extremities but you do have other clothes or fabric around, you can secure them in place around your feet or hands with duct tape. This could be the step that keeps you from getting frostbite and losing your toes.

See Your Way When You Pee: If you have to do your business in the dark of night, it can be frustrating (and potentially disastrous) fumbling in an attempt to prop up your flashlight or cell phone. Just pull that roll of duct tape off that duct tape utility belt you just made, tape the light to a tree, and have a safe and happy pee with your new hands-free light.

What's the difference between a jalapeño and a chipotle?
They're the same pepper, but a chipotle is dried and smoked.

ALL HAIL THE BITUMINOUS COAL QUEEN!

The Miss America pageant grew out of an early 20th-century practice: industries, companies, small towns, and tourist destinations promoted themselves with beauty contests, crowning a young woman "Miss" or "Queen" of whatever it was they were touting. Was it sexist? Arguably. Was it also a weird slice of Americana? Yes. Bettie Page was the 1951 Miss Food Industry. Here are some others.

Miss Idaho Potato
National Donut Queen
Miss Fabulous Frankfurter
National Pork Queen
Queen of Cuisine
International Posture Queen
Miss Correct Posture
Miss Atomic Bomb
National Catfish Queen
Miss Magic Marker
Miss Lovely Eyes
Miss Food Industry
Blueberry Queen
Miss Diaper Queen
Miss Radio Queen
Miss Gasoline Station
Miss National Laugh Queen
Miss War Worker
Mink Queen
Outdoor Health Queen
Miss Control Tower
Queen of the Pet Festival
May Wine Queen
Queen of the Coal Fields
Pennsylvania Bituminous Coal Queen

Miss Potato Chip
Sweet Corn Queen
Shrimp and Petroleum Queen
Miss Oil Patch
Miss American Vampire (sponsored by *Dark Shadows*)
Miss Polish Job (sponsored by Muller Brothers Automotive in Los Angeles)
Miss Lube Rack (same)
National Uranium Queen
Miss Subways
Miss Prettiest Ankles
Hot Rod Queen
Queen of the Circus
Miss Perfect Back of America
Queen of Anti-Triskaidekaphobia
Miss Klingon Empire
Miss Lemon
Miss Bobbed Hair
Miss Steel Pier
Miss Psywar (psychological warfare)
Miss Drumsticks
Miss Sweater Girl
Most Beautiful Ape in the World (sponsored by *Conquest of the Planet of the Apes*)

KITTY MISCELLANY

Our final article on the domestic house cat is dedicated to Uncle John's feline friends Fizzgig and Mogwai. (No, Fizzgig, get down! It is not lap time! Mogwai, stop clawing the chair. There is still food in your bowl! OK, Fizz...just for two minutes.)

 NINE LIVES TO LIVE

Whether they're getting ganged up on by dogs, or falling from a tree, or even getting caught in an earthquake, domestic house cats seem to have an uncanny ability to not die. That's because they still have their wild instincts; in nature, the slight, slender wildcat is both predator *and* prey. It must be cunning enough to hunt birds, rodents, and reptiles, while always being ready to escape from leopards, wolves, coyotes, raptors, snakes, monitor lizards, and whatever other threats may loom. That renders *Felis catus* both lightning fast and nearly indestructible.

So, it's no surprise that humans would bestow upon the cat nine whole lives, but when exactly that happened has been lost to antiquity. The phrase might have been inspired by—or inspired—the myth of ancient Egyptian sun god Atum-Ra, who could take the form of a cat. His life combined with the life of each of his eight sons meant his kingdom had nine lives. The number nine was also a sacred number in Greece and China. In more modern times, the English proverb first appeared in print in the 1500s: "A cat has nine lives. For three he plays, for three he strays, and for the last three he stays."

Bonus: The number of lives a cat has also depends on where it lives. In Arab countries, cats get six lives. In Spanish-speaking countries, they get seven.

 HEY MAN, PASS THE CATNIP

If you've never seen a cat "get high" on catnip, it's quite the sight to behold. The kitty starts sniffing the catnip like there's no tomorrow, then falls over, writhes around, and makes strange faces while meowing wildly. Then it zones out for a spell, writhes some more, and within about ten minutes is back to normal. (Then the cat is immune to catnip for about two hours.) This state of energetic euphoria comes from a cat *smelling* catnip. When a cat *eats* the stuff, the opposite happens and it gets sluggish. And not all cats are affected by catnip—only about half—and it's hereditary. Kittens and older cats also have less of a reaction.

This leafy green herb from the mint family contains an essential oil called nepetalactone that somehow alters the cat's brain chemistry, but exactly how is yet another cat behavior not fully understood by science.

Bonus: Although catnip doesn't have the same effects on humans, it is said to be as relaxing as chamomile if boiled into tea.

 THE MYSTERY OF THE PENIS SPINE

Another kitty conundrum: the male's penis has hundreds of "spines." Each only a millimeter long, the true purpose of these penis spines is unknown. They might make it more difficult for the female to disengage, or they might make it more stimulating for the female so she will begin ovulation. If the male is spayed early enough, his hormones won't develop the spines.

 PARROTING CATS

Despite the countless videos of cats meowing "hello" on the Internet, cats can't talk. Well, one species, called the margay, can—kind of. This spotted wildcat, a cousin of the domestic house cat, lives in the Amazon, where it preys on small monkeys called pied tamarins. Margays have been observed slinking closer and closer to a troop of pied tamarins...and then—hidden in the underbrush—mimicking their call. When a curious monkey investigates, the margay strikes.

 CAT YEARS EXPLAINED

According to Guinness World Records, the oldest house cat ever—Creme Puff—lived to be 38 years and three days old. In human years, that's 168! The average life span of a cat is 14, which is about 70 for a human. Here's how to calculate your cat's age: Kittens develop quickly—the first year equals 15 human years. The second year is another 9. After that, each cat year equals 4 human years. So, a 10-year-old cat is 56; a 15-year-old cat, 76; and a 21-year-old cat is 100.

 FOR WHOM THE CAT PURRS

Sure, kitty cats purr, but what about the rest of the feline family? Lions, leopards, and jaguars exhibit "purr-like sounds," but it's not true purring. There are wild cats that do purr, including bobcats, cheetahs, pumas, and the Eurasian lynx.

 BIG (SMALL) CATS

House cats are getting bigger, and they have been at least since Viking times. We know this because the Vikings wore cat-fur pelts, so they left behind a lot of cat skeletons. Researchers compared those skeletons to modern ones and found that the house cat has grown 16 percent larger over the past millennium. It hasn't been determined if this is due to genetics or to a change in diet, but most other domesticated species get smaller. Once again, the cat goes against the grain.

HOW DO YOU SPELL THE SOUND A CAT MAKES?

The three most popular variations in English are *mew*, *meow*, and *miaow*. The origin is hard to place because this is an example if onomatopoeia, a word having a spelling inspired by the sound it makes, such as "rumble," "fizz," and "bang" (and "purr"). Dozens of languages have a similar-sounding word, dating back at least to the ancient Egyptians' *mau*—not only their word for "meow" but for "cat" as well.

The word first showed up in Early Modern English as *mew* ("I neuer herd thy catte once mew"). From there, it took on several similar spellings—including both *meow* and *miaow*—until the 1840s, when *miaow* became the preferred British iteration, and *meow* became the preferred American spelling.

Making matters more confusing, *mew* never went away, and it remains an accepted synonym of *meow* and *miaow*. But is there a difference? According to British linguist Neil Turner, "*Mew* is the word for what a cat does when it vocalizes (as a verb) or the name for that sound (as a noun)—the equivalent of *bark* for a dog. *Meow* and *miaow* are onomatopoeic representations of the sound, equivalent to *woof* for dogs." Because all these variations can be used as a noun and a verb, they've become interchangeable.

Bonus: One of YouTube's most-watched videos (it's approaching a quarter of a billion views) is called "Nyan Cat." Uploaded in 2011, it's a crudely animated loop of a cartoon cat with a Pop-Tart body flying through space trailing a rainbow behind it. (The grating yet catchy melody keeps you watching for longer than you really should, until you finally ask yourself, "Why am I still watching this?") *Nyan* is Japanese for "meow."

*   *   *

ALLERGIC TO AWARDS

The American Contact Dermatitis Society, which raises awareness of natural and manmade irritants, annually names a different menace its "Allergen of the Year." Some recent winners:

2000: Blue dyes

2001: Gold

2005: Corticosteroids

2007: Fragrance (all of them)

2008: Nickel

2015: Formaldehyde

2016: Cobalt

2022: Aluminum

2023: Lanolin

About one in 10 people breathe evenly through both nostrils at the same time.

LAST WISHES

These famous people ascribed to the philosophy: when you go out, go out with a bang. Some of them took that literally. Here are some highlights from celebrity funerals with pre-death requests carried out in full.

Celebrity: Hunter S. Thompson
Details: The self-proclaimed "gonzo journalist" wrote about his exploits with firearms and drugs for *Rolling Stone* for decades, most famously in *Fear and Loathing in Las Vegas*, adapted into a movie in 1998. Johnny Depp played Thompson in the film, and the two became such good friends that when the writer died in 2005, the actor made sure his pal's ambitious funeral wishes were carried out. Thompson wanted to be cremated and for his ashes to then be "blasted out of a cannon." Depp footed the $3 million bill to pay for a 153-foot tower in the shape of a fist holding a hallucinogenic peyote button to be built in rural Colorado. A cannon was mounted upon the tower, from which Thompson's ashes were blasted forth.

Celebrity: Alexander the Great
Details: In the 4th century BC, Macedonian-born Alexander the Great conquered most of the Middle East and parts of Asia, amassing in 13 years one of the largest empires of the ancient world, one that stretched from Greece to Egypt to India. His death in 323 BC was a massive event, and his funeral matched the magnitude of the man and the moment. First, his body was placed in a solid gold coffin, which was then placed into another solid gold coffin. Then the whole heavy load was placed into a gold-plated carriage. Pulled by a fleet of 60 horses, the funeral procession took two years, in order for it to reach every major spot in the deceased emperor's land. He was buried twice in Egypt, first in Memphis and then in Alexandria (the exact location of this tomb is now lost to history). The cost of all of that, in 2023 dollars: $600 million.

Celebrity: Aretha Franklin
Details: The "Queen of Soul" died in 2018, and her lavish, carefully staged funeral leaned into the royalty aspect. Franklin had several specific directions laid out in her last will and testament, including a request for three separate public viewings. And at each one, she wanted her body dressed in a different luxurious gown. For her first public viewing, Franklin was adorned in red, a nod to her status as an honorary member of the Delta Sigma Theta Sorority (whose official color is red). At viewing number two, Franklin appeared to well-wishers in a powder-blue dress with shiny shoes. And for the third viewing, Franklin was dressed in a specially made rose-gold

knit gown with pink beaded lace and matching Louboutin heels. For the actual funeral, and burial, Franklin changed clothes again, into a slinky gold dress and sequined shoes. Then she was buried in a gold coffin.

Celebrity: Luke Perry

Details: The 1990s teen idol from *Beverly Hills, 90210* and costar of *Riverdale* died unexpectedly in 2019. A staunch environmentalist, a few months before he died Perry told his daughter that he wanted his burial to be as green, sustainable, and productive as possible. Sophie Perry came through for her father, burying him in an undisclosed location, and without a coffin, instead wrapped in a $1,500 mushroom suit. Made up of biodegradable fabric panels, each section is covered in mushroom spores that speed decomposition of the body, returning it to the earth (as Perry wanted), and encouraging the rapid growth of fungus.

Celebrity: Wolf Johnson

Details: Johnson sang the low, bass-baritone parts for legendary vocal groups the Drifters, the Temptations, and the Platters in the 1980s and 1990s, well beyond their hit-making days but when they were all still major concert draws. Johnson is best known for his solo work, a.k.a. one of the most famous commercial jingles of all time: "I want my baby back, baby back, baby back...Chili's Baby Back Ribs." When he died in 2012, his funeral in Dallas (filmed for a short-lived TLC reality show called *Best Funeral Ever*) adopted Johnson's ad for barbecue as its theme. A choir sang a stirring rendition of the Chili's jingle while guests could gawk at a barbecue sauce fountain, live pigs running around, sculptures of baby back ribs, and a send-off delivered by a minister in a chef's hat.

Celebrity: Michael Jackson

Details: When the King of Pop died of a painkiller overdose in the summer of 2009, it took his family, executors, and event planners two weeks to plan his memorial service. Held at the 20,000-seat Staples Center in Los Angeles, this was the odd funeral with a ticket price: $25 (although scalpers charged as much as $10,000 each). That fee was meant to offset expenses: $11,000 for invitations for VIP guests, $16,000 for flowers, $25,000 for the casket, $35,000 for Jackson's burial clothes, and $1 million for the singer's interment in the Great Mausoleum at Hollywood's Forest Lawn Memorial Park. Jackson's people paid $30,000 for security, but it wasn't enough to keep back the swell on onlookers and well-wishers—the Los Angeles Police Department sent 3,000 officers at an expense of $1.4 million to the city's taxpayers.

Celebrity: Tupac Shakur

Details: The actor and rapper, also known by his stage names 2Pac and Makaveli,

The longest highway in the world, at over 9,000 miles, is Highway 1, which circumnavigates Australia.

made a seemingly offhand request in lyrics of the song "Black Jesuz" about what he wanted to happen to his body after his death. Recorded in August 1996, weeks before he was murdered by gunshot in Las Vegas, Shakur sang: "Cremated, last wishes, *****s smoke my ashes." "Black Jesuz" was recorded with a group Shakur had just formed called the Outlawz, and his fellow rappers in the group saw to it that the request on their song was honored. The Outlawz and Shakur's mother held a small, quiet memorial on a Los Angeles beach where they ate the musician's favorite meal, chicken wings and orange soda. Then they took Shakur's cremains and mixed them with marijuana. Everyone present smoked a little bit of 2Pac.

Celebrity: Fidel Castro

Details: After leading a communist revolution in Cuba, Castro ruled the island nation as a dictator from 1959 until he stepped down in 2008, ceding power to his brother, Raúl. When Fidel died in November 2016, Raúl tried to abide by his brother's wishes but also honor the man in the over-the-top way Raúl felt he deserved. Despite the former leader's wish for not much of a fuss and nothing to be named after him or erected in his honor, Raúl Castro ordered Cuba to be shut down for a nine-day national mourning period. Castro's body was cremated, and his urn went on a three-day tour, visiting most every major city and town in Cuba, the entire event broadcast live on Cuban television and radio. At the end of the journey, Castro's remains arrived in Santiago de Cuba, where they were placed inside a hole carved into a 2.6-ton granite boulder. The opening was then sealed and covered with a large green plaque reading "FIDEL."

A few other bits of famous funeral fun:

- Actress and writer Carrie Fisher was very open and frank about her struggles with mental illness, and owned a giant novelty capsule that looked like a pill of the antidepressant Prozac. When she died in 2016, her brother and daughter agreed that Fisher's cremains should be put inside the pill, because it was her favorite possession.

- *Charlie and the Chocolate Factory* author Roald Dahl was entombed with a few of his favorite things: a snooker cue, a bottle of wine, pencils, a power saw, and chocolate.

- Janis Joplin stipulated in her will that $2,500 be set aside for her friends to have a huge party in her honor. The singer died in 1970, and the allotted-for shindig did take place with all that money, which is the equivalent of about $20,000 in today's dollars.

- The highlight of motorcycle daredevil Evel Knievel's funeral: the red, white, and blue fireworks. (It was held at a stadium in Montana.)

Cows are closer relatives to dolphins than they are to pigs.

THE OLDEST EVER

As the elder statesman of bathroom-forward trivia anthologies, Uncle John appreciates and knows a thing or two about old stuff. Here are some of the oldest, longest-surviving, and most extant things out there.

Oldest dog. A purebred Rafeiro do Alentejo named Bobi was born in Leiria, Portugal, in 1992. In our first draft of this article, Bobi was still wagging and had just celebrated his 31st birthday. Sadly, just a few months later, he passed away—but his age has been proven by Portuguese government records and certified by Guinness World Records, which still makes him the record holder (and a very good boy).

Oldest time capsule. In 2014, city workers in Boston attempting to fix a water leak at the Massachusetts State House uncovered a time capsule that experts dated to 1795. Buried by early American icons Paul Revere and Samuel Adams, the postcard-sized box contained coins, newspaper clippings, and a copper medal bearing the image of George Washington.

Oldest recording of a human voice. In 1857, French inventor Édouard-Léon Scott de Martinville built the first sound-recording device, the phonautograph, using grooved and coated glass and an ear trumpet. Among his recordings, one is that of an anonymous person singing "Au Clair de la Lune," dated to April 1860.

Oldest known film. According to the Internet Movie Database, the most comprehensive record online of all filmed content, the oldest surviving moving image is "Passage de Venus." Six seconds long, it depicts the planet Venus moving in the sky across the sun. It was filmed on December 9, 1874.

Oldest videotape. The first attempt by an American TV network to use videotape to record a program, instead of airing it live, is also the oldest one surviving. On October 13, 1957, CBS aired the Ford-sponsored special *The Edsel Show*, starring Bing Crosby, who personally invested a fortune in the development of video technology.

Oldest hotel. Nishiyama Onsen Keiunkan is a luxurious hotel and hot-spring resort situated near the small village of Minobu in Japan. Fujiwara Mahito opened the business in the year 705, and it's still open—and still run by the founder's descendants—52 generations and more than 1,300 years later.

Oldest recorded story. In 2022, archaeologists exploring an 11,000-year-old site in Sayburç, Turkey, found two carved panels on a bench. One image depicts a man holding up a snake to defend himself against a bull, and the other shows a figure guarding his genitals with his hands as leopards surround him. Dating to the Neolithic era, it's the oldest narrative art ever discovered.

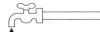

Each year the moon moves about 1.45 inches away from Earth.

TEN-DOLLAR WORDS

If you can ace this anfractuous quiz by matching each word to its meaning, then try not to come across like a palaverous solipsist. Answers are on page 405.

1. Accismus		**a)**	the state of being faithless or disloyal
2. Anfractuous		**b)**	bossy and domineering
3. Clinomania		**c)**	the uncomfortable feeling caused by new underwear
4. Exsanguination		**d)**	a feigned lack of interest in something while actually desiring it
5. Festinate		**e)**	one who is extremely self-absorbed
6. Foofaraw		**f)**	having great volume or bulk; large
7. Imperious		**g)**	labyrinthine; convoluted; unnecessarily complicated
8. Kora		**h)**	the delusion that you are turning into an animal
9. Nimbose		**i)**	the prickly feeling when your limb "falls asleep"
10. Palaverous		**j)**	an excessive desire to stay in bed
11. Paresthesia		**k)**	a great fuss about something insignificant
12. Perfidy		**l)**	confident and cheerful
13. Pot-valiancy		**m)**	to hurry; hasten
14. Sanguine		**n)**	the state of being brave due to drunkenness
15. Shivviness		**o)**	an unpleasant feeling that makes you want to scratch
16. Solipsist		**p)**	cloudy, stormy
17. Testaceous		**q)**	having a hard outer shell
18. Voluminous		**r)**	a musical instrument similar to a harp
19. Yeuk		**s)**	the act of draining a person, animal, or organ of blood
20. Zoanthropy		**t)**	verbose or wordy

The town of California, Pennsylvania, was founded before the state of California.

NICE STORIES

Every now and then we like to lock our inner cynics in a box and share some good news.

FISHY STORY

Call him Ismael. Ismael Lazo, that is. He's a customer service agent at Southwest Airlines in Tampa, Florida. In May 2022, a 19-year-old college student named Kira Rumfola was panicking—her flight home for the summer was about to board, and they weren't letting her bring her beloved pet, Theo, a purple betta fish in a portable carrier. "I'd done it before over the holidays with another airline," she explained. She also said that Theo helped get her through her first time away from home and they'd bonded. "He had a fun little personality," she said. "He liked to do laps around his fishbowl."

Lazo, 35, sympathized with Rumfola but said that Southwest has a strict dogs-and-cats only rule, and there was nothing he could do...to get Theo on the plane. However, "How about if I take your fish home to live with me and my fiancée until you come back for college in the fall?" Although, he added, he didn't know anything about taking care of a fish.

Rumfola thanked him profusely and handed over Theo and all his accessories, and then got on the plane. She texted Lazo when she got home, and he was already on the way to pick up a larger tank.

Four months later, Rumfola returned to Tampa and picked up Theo. He was in perfect health. Lazo told her he likes to swim laps when someone does the dishes. Afterward, Lazo told the *Washington Post*, "To be honest, I was worried about something happening to him on our watch, so I was happy for Kira to have him back."

THE WRITE TIME

Kuttiyamma, a woman from Kottayam, Kerala, India, never got the chance to learn to read; she was born to a low-caste family without educational opportunities, then married at the age of 16. After that, she worked full time as mother and housewife. But after observing her grandchildren studying, Kuttiyamma was motivated to finally hit the books. "I always wanted to learn," she said. "But I could never study because I had to do household chores." Her neighbor, who happens to be a teacher, volunteered to instruct her. In 2020, after studying for months in the mornings and evenings, Kuttiyamma scored an impressive 89 percent on the state literacy exam. She also set a record as the oldest person in India to pass the test for the first time. How old? She was 104. Now she can read books along with her great-great-grandchildren (when she's not outside gardening or feeding her chickens).

The hemiplegic migraine is just a migraine, but it feels like a stroke.

BROKEN RECORD

"Sometimes things like this happen," said Lisa Mahar. "So, if it happened for us, for sure it will happen for others. You can believe that." Three years earlier, in 2019, the Redmond, Washington, woman was on vacation in Ixtapa, Mexico, with her husband, Bernie Wieser. One afternoon, while they were on a fishing boat owned by 75-year-old Nicho Mancia Reyes, Mahar's wedding ring slipped off her finger and into the water! More than a wedding ring, it was a precious family heirloom, with gold from both Lisa and Bernie's families melted into it. Mancia Reyes could see how devastated the woman was, so he vowed to do whatever he could to find her ring.

His daughter, Patricia Mancia, told Seattle's King 5 News, "My father has been going to Ixtapa Island every other couple of weeks. Every time he goes, he would ask waiters, masseuse, snorkeling instructor, everybody around." But every time, the answer was no—no divers or fishermen had found it.

A year passed, then another, then another. By this point, Mancia Reyes's friends were looking for it. Then, one day in 2022, Mancia Reyes came home and said eagerly to his daughter, "Patricia, you won't believe this. We found a ring, and we think It might be theirs!"

It was, and Lisa and Bernie were more than thrilled to get it back. In the interim, Bernie had been diagnosed with cancer. When Lisa's wedding ring finally made it back to them three years later, the cancer was in remission.

STREET SMARTS

Thousands of Americans will experience homelessness at some point in their lives. Two of those were Elmer Alvarez and Roberta Hoskie, strangers who never met until one day in November 2017 when Alvarez, who was living on the streets of New Haven, Connecticut, found a $10,000 check with Hoskie's name on it. Hoskie was currently a real estate broker, but many years earlier, she'd been a single mom without a roof over her head. Rather than cash the check, Alvarez tracked down Hoskie and gave it back to her. "I was just thinking about how that person was feeling by losing an amount of a check like that. I'd be feeling kind of desperate." He'd battled addiction in the past, but he was three years sober and determined to turn his life around.

Blown away by Alvarez's act, Hoskie set him up with an apartment and paid his first seven months' rent while he took real estate classes. At last report, the two former homeless friends were creating a transitional home to set up kids and young adults with aids and services. "He had no idea who the person was behind the check," said Hoskie. "There need to be more people like Elmer Alvarez. He's a golden heart guy."

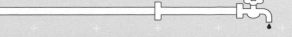

Housecats and tigers share 95.6 percent of their DNA.

THE FAKE BAND CHRONICLES

There's a lot of money to be made in music—so much that some enterprising criminals will pretend to be famous rock and pop stars. It's a surprisingly common phenomenon, and these con artists shockingly get away with it for quite a while... until the jig is eventually up.

NOT REALLY TERRY JACKS

Canadian folk singer Terry Jacks scored exactly one hit single in the United States. In 1974, "Seasons in the Sun" (a translation of a French song by pop poet Rod McKuen) went to #1. Shortly thereafter, Jacks gave up music to become an environmental activist. But then 22 years later, a frequently arrested petty criminal and scam artist named Timothy Wayne McDonald started enriching himself by claiming to be Terry Jacks. After legally changing his name to Terrence Jacques, he surfaced in Colorado Springs in early 1996. McDonald/Jacques appeared on local radio stations, announcing that he was about to release a new album and locally re-record "Seasons in the Sun." The only problem: he was flat broke because he was waiting for a substantial royalty check to come through. With his (fake) reputation, (fake) stardom, and (fake) promises of repayment, Jacques persuaded Colorado Springs residents to house him, feed him, and write him checks.

The media attention—framed as a big potential comeback of a fondly if vaguely remembered 1970s one-hit wonder—spread, and Jacques's past caught up with him. After a few weeks of scamming Colorado residents, he was arrested in a collaborative effort by multiple law enforcement agencies; he'd just been released from an Arizona prison after serving five years on fraud charges. Absconding to Colorado violated his parole. Back in Canada, media outlets tracked down the real Terry Jacks for comment, and the former pop star revealed that Jacques had been impersonating him without authorization since 1978. Jacques would stay at hotels and check into hospitals for medical care under the name "Terry Jacks" and skip town without paying the $1,000-plus bills—which found their way to the actual Terry Jacks. The Jacques scam was such an embarrassment that it contributed to Colorado state representative Jim Riesberg introducing a "Truth in Music Bill," which would require musical acts performing or recording in Colorado to disclose whether they were a tribute act or the genuine article, or face fines of up to $5,000.

During the pandemic, Poland banned flights from Andorra...then abolished the ban upon learning Andorra doesn't have an airport.

PHONY FRANKIE GOES TO HOLLYWOOD

The propulsive, aggressive, explicit dance-pop of Frankie Goes to Hollywood was always more popular in the band's native U.K. than it was stateside. The band released only seven singles in the mid-1980s before infighting, lawsuits, and front man Holly Johnson leaving for a solo career permanently tore the group apart, but all of those songs made the top 40 in England, including the #1 smashes "Two Tribes" and "Relax," the latter of which reached the top 10 in the U.S. and was the band's only American hit. The group built up a small cult following in the U.S. where fans were successfully fooled in 1998, when, more than 10 years after Frankie Goes to Hollywood broke up, a band by the same name started touring North America. At one point booked as the opening act for fellow 1980s band A Flock of Seagulls, lead singer Davey Johnson told reporters that Holly Johnson was dead, but that he was Holly's brother and had played as a session musician (uncredited in the liner notes) on Frankie Goes to Hollywood's debut album, *Welcome to the Pleasuredome.*

That explanation seemed to satiate fans and the music press...until actual Frankie Goes to Hollywood bassist Mark O'Toole noticed that his old group was touring without him and didn't have the authorization to do so. He hired a lawyer and sent warnings to many venues; others involved in the original Frankie music came forward to announce that Davey Johnson was of no relation to Holly Johnson (who was still alive), nor had Davey ever been present for any of the group's recordings. A Flock of Seagulls' front man, Mike Score, promptly dropped the fake band. Nevertheless, the phony Frankie Goes to Hollywood continued to play in small clubs on their own around the U.S. for two more years, until an exposé in *Spin* magazine made them unbookable.

COUNTERFEIT REDBONE

In the early 1970s, Redbone was briefly a major rock 'n' roll sensation. The band is best known for the hits "Maggie," "The Witch Queen of New Orleans," and "Come and Get Your Love," and for being the first major rock band to feature a lineup consisting entirely of Native American musicians. When the board who booked the 2006 Butte-Silver Bow Fair in Montana heard that Redbone wanted to play, they eagerly signed the group to play three shows on three consecutive days for a cut-rate price of just $6,500. But when Redbone showed up for the first show, only two of the promised musicians arrived. Front man Denny Freeman said the rest of Redbone couldn't make it because they'd all contracted the mumps; local musicians filled in on a last-minute basis.

It was a disastrous affair for everyone involved—particularly those affiliated with the actual Redbone. The real band, formed in 1968 by singer and songwriter Pat

Vegas and his brother Lolly, was performing in Wisconsin at the time of the Butte-Silver Bow Fair. The musicians who took the stage in Montana were fraudsters. "I'd like to grab him by the throat and shake him like an old rug," Pat Vegas said of phony Redbone leader Freeman. "I've been in the business for 40 years, and I've never run into anything this blatant," Redbone manager Ron Kurtz told reporters. Freeman had apparently told the fair board that he was a founding member of Redbone; Vegas said he'd never played with his band whatsoever. When caught in his lie, Freeman offered to pay back his $6,500 performance fee.

FAKE FLEETWOOD MAC

There are two distinct periods and sounds in the long history of Fleetwood Mac. There's the late-1970s-and-onward soft rock era, notable for the contributions of guitarist Lindsey Buckingham and singer-songwriter Stevie Nicks, and there's the previous, late 1960s/early 1970s incarnation as a free-flowing jazz-influenced electric blues-rock band. The evolution from one era to the other began when Peter Green and Jeremy Spencer quit in 1970 and 1971, respectively, and then Danny Kirwan was fired in 1972. The rest of the original lineup was left reeling from all the personal and professional tension and wanted to take a break from recording and playing concerts. But band manager Clifford Davis didn't want to lose any momentum and planned an early 1974 tour of the United States, where Fleetwood Mac was gaining in popularity but still wasn't as well-known or recognizable as they were in the U.K.

Undeterred, Davis booked and advertised the shows as Fleetwood Mac concerts, even though the lineup he sent out on the road wasn't Fleetwood Mac at all, but rather a series of largely anonymous session musicians and industry professionals. Among the members of the surreptitiously not-real Fleetwood Mac: Dave Todd, Kirby Gregory, Paul Martinez, Dave Wilkinson, and Craig Collinge.

When the group arrived at a concert hall outside of Pittsburgh for the first show of the tour, promoter Rich Engler immediately realized that these musicians were not Fleetwood Mac—because he knew what its members looked like. Engler told Davis that he would not allow the fraudulent band to take the stage, at which point the manager tried to punch the promoter, who relented and allowed the group to play. For the most part, the audience didn't notice or mind, although a few attendees asked for and received refunds. Engler then called Fleetwood Mac's New York booking agency, warning it of a scam. They didn't believe Engler, and the next show went on as planned in New York. Hearing rumors of the con, *Rolling Stone* sent a reporter to cover the concert. When questioned, Davis claimed that actual Fleetwood Mac drummer Mick Fleetwood had planned to play the show but had to leave abruptly because of a family issue. Fake singer Todd couldn't perform very well due to

laryngitis, so the so-called Fleetwood Mac wound up playing only instrumentals, then engaged in an improvised jam session.

Finally receiving word that their manager was sending out musicians in their stead, Fleetwood Mac sued to put an end to the tour... and fired Davis.

IMPOSTER ZOMBIES

After scaling the pop charts in both the U.S. and the U.K. in 1964 with the moody, atmospheric "She's Not There" and "Tell Her No," the Zombies couldn't maintain their initial success. In 1967, the band released its second album, *Odessey and Oracle*. Now universally regarded as a classic, it flopped everywhere, and the Zombies broke up without any fanfare, the music press not noticing or caring much. But then in 1969, in part to recoup some of the money it spent on the album, the band's U.S. label Date Records released the track "Time of the Season" as a single. The song was a smash, reaching #3 on the pop chart. Suddenly, American concert promoters wanted to hear from the Zombies. But its members were all the way over in the U.K., having formed new bands or left music entirely, unaware of their newfound American popularity.

Rather than reassemble the Zombies, a company called Delta Promotions claimed to have acquired the rights to the Zombies catalog and got a group of young Texas musicians to go out on the road under that name. Seab Meador, guitarist for the 1960s one-hit wonder the Gentlemen ("It's a Cry'n Shame"), met a Delta representative when his band was on tour in Florida, and when he returned home to Dallas, he recruited the rest of the new Zombies: teenage guitarist Mark Ramsey, Ramsey's friend and drummer Frank Beard, and Beard's friend and bassist Dusty Hill. (Beard and Hill used pseudonyms when playing for the "Zombies"; they later went on to comprise two-thirds of ZZ Top.) Delta assured the four musicians that what it was doing was totally legal, and that the real Zombies were actually the fakers, a studio-only act; these new guys were just hired hands to play the songs live.

To prepare the four green musicians for their fraudulent Zombies tour, Delta sent them on a short tour of the South under the name of a different real band: the Rose Garden, a Los Angeles folk rock band and one-hit wonder with the 1967 song "Next Plane to London." This new "Rose Garden" learned only that one song and just played the electric blues they liked for the rest of the set. The gigs went off without a hitch (despite the real Rose Garden having a female lead singer), and the quartet embarked on their tour, as the Zombies, with concerts in Michigan, Wisconsin, and Canada, where they played on television and in a prison. One review of a Michigan show expressed confusion that the re-formed Zombies didn't look or sound like their old selves (they wore cowboy hats and played electric blues, and were conspicuously

First country to launch something man-made into space:
Nazi Germany, with its V2 rocket, in 1944.

missing a keyboard player), and noted that the crowd started to leave early in the set, but no malfeasance was suspected.

Meanwhile, as if to hedge its bets or make more money, Delta Promotions put *another* fake Zombies out on the road. This time, the musicians at least looked like the real Zombies (they dressed in semi-psychedelic clothes) and sounded like them, too. These Zombies were really the Excels, a Marquette, Michigan, band influenced by the Beach Boys who'd scored a few Midwestern radio hits.

In December 1969, *Rolling Stone* ran an article featuring a quote from actual Zombies member Chris White, calling out the imposter groups for "taking money from our fans and dragging down our reputation." The jig was up for both versions of the phony Zombies, but Delta tried the con one more time. They assembled a phony Animals and booked them to play a show in May 1970—where original Animals member Eric Burdon showed up with a baseball bat and a biker gang and threatened violence against the fake band.

* * *

FUNNY (BUT REAL) COURT CASE NAMES

Batman v. Commissioner

Easter Seals Society for Crippled Children v. Playboy Enterprises

United States v. Forty Barrels and Twenty Kegs of Coca-Cola

Demosthenes v. Baal

The California Coalition of Undressed Performers v. Spearmint Rhino

United States v. Forty-three Gallons of Whisky

Death v. Graves

United States v. Ninety-five Barrels (More or Less) Alleged Apple Cider Vinegar

One 1958 Plymouth Sedan v. Pennsylvania

United States v. 12 200-Foot Reels of Super 8MM Film

Schmuck v. United States

South Dakota v. Fifteen Impounded Cats

United States v. 11 ¼ Dozen Packages of Articles Labeled in Part Mrs. Moffat's Shoo-Fly Powders for Drunkenness

Robin Hood v. United States

Association of Irritated Residents v. United States Environmental Protection Agency

Wang v. Poon

Nebraska v. One 1970 2-Door Sedan Rambler (Gremlin)

United States v. Approximately 64,695 Pounds of Shark Fins

United States v. Article Consisting of 50,000 Cardboard Boxes More or Less, Each Containing One Pair of Clacker Balls

Juicy Whip v. Orange Bang

The first chemotherapy drugs were made from mustard gas.

THOSE AMAZING ANIMALS (AND THEIR LEAVINGS)

When it comes to recognizing bathroom achievements, Uncle John doesn't discriminate in favor of humans. Lots of animals out there have waste-elimination habits and procedures that are downright impressive.

BIGGEST POOPER

While studying reptile samples in Cocoa Beach, Florida, some University of Florida herpetologists stopped at a pizza parlor and encountered a Northern curly-tailed lizard with a swollen, overgrown abdomen. Assuming it was pregnant, the scientists gave the lizard a CT scan and discovered it was severely constipated from eating sand covered in pizza grease. The lizard's poop made up nearly 80 percent of its body weight—a record for biggest animal turd in relation to body size.

MOST PROLIFIC POOPER

Guinea pigs are herbivores, so they eat a diet consisting entirely of plants. To get enough nutrition, guinea pigs must eat a lot every day, and since plants are naturally primarily fiber, guinea pigs also poop a lot. A healthy guinea pig will produce between 50 and 100 pellets of poop daily, each one technically its own bowel movement.

MOST VOLUMINOUS POOPER

The blue whale is the largest animal currently inhabiting the Earth, so it stands to reason that it also produces the biggest bowel movements on the planet. According to scientists, in just one session, a blue whale will push out up to 200 liters of waste—that's more than 50 gallons. Those who know say the stuff looks like ping-pong balls, has a consistency comparable to breadcrumbs, and smells just like the average dog doo-doo.

MOST FREQUENT WILD POOPER

Scientists say Canada geese have an inefficient digestive system, their bodies not picking up many life-sustaining nutrients from their diets. So they poop *a lot*. If a Canada goose is normal, it poops at a rate of about once every 12 minutes—mostly while still flying. All that adds up to about two pounds of daily feces.

LEAST FREQUENT POOPER

The demodex mite is like an arachnid but invisible to the human eye. It lives on human skin and in hair follicles, and feeds off other tiny bits that reside on people, but it never lets go of any waste material. The waste simply stays in the mite's body until the mite dies—it has a lifespan of about two weeks. The demodex mite is the only known creature that doesn't excrete waste in some way.

MOST PROLIFIC DOMESTICATED POOPER

If you're going to get a rabbit, prepare to clean up after it. No domesticated animal generates more fecal matter than a deceptively small and cute bunny. In one day, an average healthy rabbit will push out 200 to 300 poop pellets. Accounting for frequency and volume, this is akin to a human having a normal bowel movement every three minutes.

MOST ACTIVE POOPER

Leeches are parasitic toward African hippopotamus species. While hippos swim underwater, leeches sneak into the animal by crawling into the anus and settling near the end of the digestive tract to lay eggs. The hippo fends off those eggs—or the baby leeches that hatch—by sending them out along with their feces. To ensure that the tiny leeches don't immediately swim their way back in and try to make another generation in the rectum, the hippo spins its tail around during defecation to prevent anything from going in.

MOST EFFICIENT WASTE ELIMINATOR

One characteristic of mammals is separate channels for fluid waste and solid waste (pee and poop). Birds are different in that they've got a single, full-service chute called a cloaca, which excretes everything all at once. The reason bird droppings look white with a dark center? The white stuff is urine, and the dark stuff is poo. The ostrich is the only bird that doesn't do all of its business at once: first it disposes of liquid waste through the cloaca, and then it poops.

LEAST COMPLICATED POOPER

Flatworms are an internal parasite that feed off humans and livestock, primarily cows. A flatworm has a digestive system, a simple configuration of a mouth and an intestinal tract, but it doesn't have an anus with which to dispose of body waste. So, it eats food, and that food goes into the body for processing...and then the flatworm sends the waste back out through the mouth.

BEST SMELLING POOPER

Which animal has poop that gives off the most unpleasant odor? It's a multi-way tie between all of them—except the otter. According to those in the know, *spraint*, the leavings of the fuzzy and adorable water-dwelling mammal, smells like fresh fish.

MOST MYSTERIOUS POOPER

Scientists say that the warty comb jellyfish is the only known animal with a disappearing, or retracting, anus. The organ, or the opening, closes up and vanishes into the body of the gelatinous sea creature, emerging only when the animal needs it—to poop. That anus doesn't stay hidden for long, however, because the adult warty comb jellyfish poops about once every hour (the tiniest youngsters go every 10 minutes).

To deter theft, vanilla bean farmers poke a particular pattern of dots on their harvested pods.

RESCUED FROM THE TRASH

Have you ever accidentally thrown away something valuable? It's gut-wrenching. But every so often, these filthy stories have happy endings.

🗑 FIVE IRREPLACEABLE RINGS

Lost: On a Friday morning in Cape Breton, Nova Scotia, in September 2022, Ryan O'Donnell wiped off the kitchen counter and tossed a few items in the trash—including a wadded-up paper towel. Then he took out the garbage, and a little while later, the garbage truck came and took it away. That afternoon, when O'Donnell was out, his wife, Alexandra Stokal, couldn't find her rings. She'd washed them the night before and put them in a paper towel to dry. According to the *National Post*, she lost "her wedding ring, a new engagement ring, an anniversary ring, a ring from her mother to remember her dad after he passed, and a ring from her grandmother."

Stokal called her husband in a panic, and when he told her what he did with the paper towel, "I ran out to my little Fiat, got in. Don't even think I had shoes on, and started chasing garbage trucks." After failing to find the truck, she sped to the waste management facility and told the foreman, J. B. O'Brien, about her predicament. He located the correct truck but warned that her odds were "very slim," and that she'd be dealing with "animal feces, diapers, a lot of food waste, and other stuff in there."

Found: Stokal, O'Brien, and four workers (including the driver) spent hours looking through the mountain of garbage. Once they located an envelope with Stokal's name on it, they knew they were getting close. Then their progress was hampered by garbage bags having been torn apart by the truck's compactor, in an area with thousands of dirty paper towels. Normally, one would avoid un-wadding paper towels from a garbage heap, but this was not a normal situation. Finally, a worker named Chris Ward unfolded a wad...and there were all five rings. Stokal was thrilled and thanked everyone profusely for helping her on this "smelly, long day."

🗑 A FORGOTTEN ARTIST'S LIFE'S WORK

Background: Francis Hines (1920–2016) was an American abstract expressionist best known for creating works in the 1970s and 1980s of various New York City landmarks wrapped in fabric, but he was also an influential painter. After he retired to a Connecticut farmhouse, the artist became mostly forgotten. In 2017, a year after Hines died, a barn where he'd stored most of his art was being sold, and his estate had to comply with a tight deadline to clear everything out. By the time the contractor, George Martin, arrived to haul everything away, there were hundreds of paintings in the dumpster, some more than 50 years old.

Many of the canvases were damaged, but many others were protected by plastic. Not recognizing the signature "F. Hines," Martin had no idea these were the works of a famous artist. He didn't see any reason *not* to take the horde to the landfill.

Rescued: But Martin did notice that lots of the paintings included automotive parts, so he called a mechanic friend, Jared Whipple. At first, Whipple thought about using the paintings to decorate his indoor skate park. But before that, he thought he should see who "F. Hines" was. It didn't take long to find out. With the artist's family's blessing, Whipple has since dedicated his life to "get[ting] Hines into the history books." And those trashed paintings that were going to a skate park? Many are now on display in prestigious galleries and are reportedly worth millions.

🗑 A WINNING LOTTERY TICKET

Background: In March 2023, a 30-year-old woman (who chose to remain anonymous) bought two Sizzling Hot 7's scratch-off tickets at a convenience store in Ovid, Michigan. She scratched the tickets in her car and deduced that neither was a winner, so she stuffed them in a trash bag.

Rescued: The next morning, she had a sudden urge to recheck her work. "I am so glad I decided to look the ticket over again before throwing it away," she said. Why? Because it was a $1 million winner.

🗑 PRECIOUS FAMILY HEIRLOOMS

Background: Frank Lumanovski returned from a summer vacation in January 2023 to his suburban Melbourne, Australia, home only to discover that the door of the freezer was open, and all the food had spoiled. He had to throw it all away.

A few mornings later, Lumanovski realized that he'd forgotten about the box of gold jewelry and 18th-century French bronzed coins that he and his wife had been storing in a box in the freezer. The treasures were worth over $10,000, but even more important was their sentimental value. By the time he'd realized his mistake, the garbage had been taken away.

Rescued: Thus began a frantic search for the truck. He called the trash company as well as a friend who was on the town council. Thankfully, the truck was found before it dumped its load, but 500 bins' worth of garbage had been compacted in the truck, so Lumanovski was told that small box would be like the proverbial "needle in a haystack." Once the truck's 10 tons of garbage were poured out, it took him only five minutes to find his box. The coins were safe, and he let out a big sigh of relief. "I'm still married," he joked afterward, "but I was very close to being divorced."

Only aquatic fungus ever discovered: *Psathyrella aquatica*, found in a river near Crater Lake in Oregon.

PRESIDENTIAL COINAGES, PART III

Our final batch of words and phrases either coined or popularized by presidents will reveal the commander in chief who coined the most coinages. (More coinages on pages 51 and 184.)

OK

Popularized by: Martin Van Buren (1837–41)
Meaning: Affirmative
Origin: This president didn't coin *OK, OK?* But without him it wouldn't have caught on. In 1839, when making fun of illiterate people was all the rage, the *Boston Morning Post* ran a satirical editorial listing obscure (fake) country lingo such as "oll wright" (for "all right") and "oll correct" (for "all correct"). Abbreviations were also in style, so the latter was shortened to "O.K." A year later, when Van Buren was running for reelection, his supporters abbreviated his nickname, Old Kinderhook (the New York town he was from), and adopted the slogan "Vote for O.K." They also formed "O.K. Clubs" and even came up with the hand symbol for OK (connect the tips of the thumb and index finger, and stick the other three fingers up).

Van Buren's critics—such as the editor of the *New York Herald*—mocked his association with his Southern mentor, Andrew Jackson (Van Buren was Jackson's vice president). The newspaper claimed that "O.K." actually stood for "ole kurrek," which is the best that Jackson could manage to spell "all correct," so instead he just signed all his documents "O.K." It was fake news, but it didn't help Van Buren, who lost to William Henry Harrison. *OK* (and its variant, *okay*) has lived on, though, and in a big way. The campaign spread the versatile, easy-to-say word all over the U.S., and as the young nation grew into a superpower and spread its culture beyond its borders, *OK* tagged along. Result: "There are few places left in the world," writes Michael Rosen in *Alphabetical: How Every Letter Tells a Story*, "where an 'OK!' accompanied by a smile and a nod would be misunderstood."

SEPARATION OF CHURCH AND STATE

Coined by: Thomas Jefferson (1801–1809)
Meaning: A philosophical and legal concept concerned with the relationship between religious organizations and government

Origin: The concept of keeping government and religion independent of each other has been around since antiquity, but Jefferson—who certainly had a way with words— came up with the phrase that stuck. It occurred in response to a letter he'd received from the Danbury Baptist Association in 1802, who were concerned that Connecticut's Constitutions lacked specific protections for religious freedom: "What religious privileges we enjoy (as a minor part of the State) we enjoy as favors granted, and not as inalienable rights. And these favors we receive at the expense of such degrading acknowledgments, as are inconsistent with the rights of freemen." Jefferson's response:

> Believing with you that religion is a matter which lies solely between Man & his God, that he owes account to none other for his faith or his worship, that the legitimate powers of government reach actions only, & not opinions, I contemplate with sovereign reverence that act of the whole American people which declared that their legislature should 'make no law respecting an establishment of religion, or prohibiting the free exercise thereof,' thus building a wall of separation between Church & State.

Bonus Words: Jefferson felt it was his obligation to create a distinct lexigraphy for the new nation (so we have him to thank in part for the American English/British English spelling divide). He's been credited with coining at least 110 words—including *belittle, mammoth, authentication, pedicure* (which he borrowed from the French), and *neologize*, which means "to coin new words."

SNOWMAGEDDON

Popularized by: Barack Obama (2009–17)

Meaning: A historic blizzard

Origin: This portmanteau of *snow* and *Armageddon* was borne out of the worst blizzard to hit Washington, D.C., in nearly a century. It was February 2010, and despite most of the city being shut down, President Obama's motorcade was able to make it the few blocks away to the Democratic National Committee's winter meeting, during which he was said to remark, "It's Snowmageddon out there!"

The next day, a local news station posted a story: "'Snowmageddon'—that's what President Barack Obama has dubbed the storm that's shut down Washington and left thousands without power." The word quickly caught on, as evidenced anytime a big blizzard hits. But ten years later, the *Washington Post* countered: "The snowstorm...was a storm for the ages, and our own Capital Weather Gang dubbed it Snowmageddon, a name that stuck and was later used by President Barack Obama and the news media."

Bonus Word: Obama described infrastructure projects that could start right away as *shovel-ready.*

First intern at Pixar: Jonas Rivera. He's now the company's executive vice president.

SQUATTER

Coined by: James Madison (1809–17)

Meaning: One who occupies land or a residence they do not own and refuses to leave

Origin: Just as we are today, in the late 18th century, the United States was facing a homeless crisis. In a 1788 letter to his friend George Washington, Madison described the homeless in Maine: "Many of them and their constituents are only squatters upon other people's land, and they are afraid of being brought to account." Before that, the word *squatter* simply meant "to sit or crouch on one's haunches"—meaning, on your butt, with your legs pressed together (which would make you hard to move).

SUGARCOAT

Coined by: Abraham Lincoln (1861–65)

Meaning: To make something difficult or distasteful appear more pleasant or acceptable

Origin: One of Lincoln's strengths was his ability to talk like a regular person to regular people, while also being a skilled orator. And he did not mince words, as his printer, John D. DeFrees, found out after DeFrees took exception to a passage in the president's letter to Congress, where Lincoln argued that there was nothing in the Constitution that gave Southern states the right to secede: "With rebellion thus sugar-coated they have been drugging the public mind of their section for more than thirty years."

DeFrees complained that Lincoln's misuse of the word *sugar-coated* was "undignified." The verb solely meant "to frost a bitter pill to make it easier to go down." "You ought to remember, Mr. President, that a message to the Congress of the United States is quite a different thing from a speech before a mass meeting in Illinois; that such messages become a part of the history of the country, and should therefore be written with scrupulous care and propriety." Lincoln stood by his metaphorical use of the word, declaring to DeFrees, "The time will never come in this country when the people won't know exactly what *sugar-coated* means."

Bonus Words: Honest Abe is also responsible for *a house divided* and *relocation*. And we'll end with our favorite one. As lexicographer Paul Dickson pointed out in his book, *Words from the White House: Words and Phrases Coined or Popularized by America's Presidents*, "Abraham Lincoln was the first one to use the word *cool*, meaning, 'Hey, that's cool! That's really something.'" Cool!

THE UBER LOST & FOUND INDEX

Wondering where you lost your Danny DeVito Christmas ornament? Maybe it's in the back seat of your last Uber ride. If so, you're not alone. Every April, the rideshare company releases its annual index breaking down the who, what, when, and where of things left behind, based on passenger reports. Here are some findings from 2023's index.

10 MOST COMMONLY FORGOTTEN ITEMS
Clothing, phones, backpacks and purses, wallets, headphones, jewelry, keys, books, laptops, and watches.

10 OF "THE 50 MOST *UNIQUE* LOST ITEMS" REPORTED
Danny DeVito Christmas ornament, an ankle monitor, Statue of Liberty green foam crown, a lightsaber, two painted rat traps, a power of attorney document issued by the Turkish consulate, a bidet, lotion and chicken wings, a slushy machine, and "Tamagotchi, light blue, egg shaped. And nuts."

LOSER TRENDS
- The year 2022 saw a spike in lost Disney and Harry Potter toys, "especially Minnie ears, lightsabers, Disney Magic Bands, and of course, magic wands!"
- There was a "high" increase in lost cannabis and cannabis-related products.
- More gamers left behind a Nintendo Switch than any other gaming device.
- At least 40 passengers left behind fake teeth or dentures.
- Among the pets left behind (and later returned): a toy poodle, two turtles, hamsters, and a rat.

WHERE AND WHEN
- More Uber passengers reported lost items on April 5 and April 9 than any other day of the year; that's also the most forgetful month.
- The most forgetful holiday: New Year's Day.
- Time of day that has the most reports of lost items: 11:00 p.m.
- Passengers are most likely to forget chargers on Mondays, keys on Tuesdays, wallets on Wednesdays, cash on Thursdays, watches and jewelry on Fridays, passports on Saturdays, and groceries on Sundays.

THE 10 MOST "FORGETFUL" CITIES
Jacksonville, FL; San Antonio, TX; Palm Springs, CA; Houston, TX; Salt Lake City, UT; Miami, FL; Atlanta, GA; Indianapolis, IN; Kansas City, KS; St. Louis, MO.

That explains it: "sports jackets" are called that because they were originally made for wearing to the track or ballpark and *watching* sports.

OUR LIVING LANGUAGE

"Fun" used to be no fun at all. Other words have also changed meanings over the centuries.

Word	Modern Meaning	Former Meaning
Villain	a scoundrel or lawbreaker	an uneducated farm laborer
Rocket	a device propelled through the air	a small rock
Pencil	a graphite writing instrument	a very fine paintbrush
Affluent	having an abundance of riches	flowing freely in great quantity
Egregious	conspicuously bad	distinguished or eminent
Travel	to go on a journey	to do arduous work
Warp	to twist or contort	to throw
Nimrod	a buffoon	a skillful hunter
Fool	a naive person	a professional court jester
Leech	a blood-sucking invertebrate	a doctor
Hussy	a disreputable woman	the mistress of a household
Diaper	a garment worn by incontinent people	a white fabric with inlaid diamonds
Silly	lacking in seriousness	pious; blessed
Desire	to want something greatly	to study the stars
Quell	to subdue	to kill
Stripes	decorative parallel lines	lines left on the skin from a lashing
Accent	to add value to or emphasize	to sing
Dinner	the final meal of the day	the first meal of the day
Nuisance	a simple annoyance	heinous injury or harm
Fun	amusement	to cheat or hoax someone
Volatile	increasingly tense	birds, bugs, or other creatures that fly
Addict	one with uncontrollable dependency	to award as a slave
Witch	a person of any gender who practices magic	a man who practices magic
Notorious	infamous	famous
Debacle	a complete failure	to break up ice on a river
Meat	animal flesh prepared for consumption	any solid food
Aftermath	period following an event	second crop of grass after harvesting
Bless	to consecrate by religious rite or word	to consecrate by blood
Wrong	incorrect or not right	twisted or bent
Flux	a state of continuous change	diarrhea

Worst-ever NBA playoff team: the 1952–53 Baltimore Bullets had a 16-54 record.

FABULOUS GAME SHOW FACTS

Everybody gets excited watching TV game shows and fantasizing about winning big themselves. Let's poke some holes in the fantasy with these behind-the-scenes secrets.

- The first ever TV game show in the U.S. was a series called *Cash and Carry*, which aired for one year on the short-lived DuMont Network beginning in 1946. Produced in a supermarket full of only products made by sponsor Libby, contestants had to guess the price of things, what was hidden under a barrel, or what food a mime was silently explaining.

- *Who Wants to Be a Millionaire?* contestants get a "lifeline" to telephone a friend and ask their input in answering a tough question. These potential friends are preselected, and to prevent cheating (including looking up the answer in books or on the Internet), "fully briefed security officers" from the show are sent to watch over them.

- Some of the most successful game show hosts got their emcee gigs after finding fame as contestants on other game shows. In 1980, two years before she'd become cohost on *Wheel of Fortune*, Vanna White appeared on *The Price Is Right*. Future *Studs* host Mark DeCarlo was a contestant on *Tic Tac Dough* and, in 1985, had $115,257 in winnings on *Sale of the Century*. And *Jeopardy!* host Ken Jennings once won 74 straight games of that series.

- Network-produced game shows on daytime TV peaked in 1974, with 29 different ones airing daily. As of 2023, there are just two: *Let's Make a Deal* and *The Price Is Right*, both on CBS.

- When there's a disputed answer and the host audibly asks "judges?" to weigh in? There's not some massive panel of experts. On *Family Feud*, it's two executive producers, and on *Jeopardy!*, it's two writers and a producer, and they're put on the spot.

- Richard Dawson and *Family Feud* producers hated each other so much that when the show was revived in the late 1980s, another host was sought out. Football great Joe Namath auditioned and was a front-runner, but producer Mark Goodson went for likeable stand-up comedian Ray Combs instead.

- Talk show host Merv Griffin is the credited creator of *Jeopardy!* (and author of its theme song), but he acted on a fully formed suggestion from his wife, Julann Wright. Following the 1950s TV quiz show scandal—which briefly ended game shows after producers were found to have fed contestants answers and prearranged outcomes—Wright suggested that the host should just go ahead and

If you never cut or plucked it, your nose hair would grow
to be six feet long over your lifetime.

give contestants the answers, albeit in the form of a question. She thought that contestants could lose money by responding with the incorrect *question*, because it would "put them in jeopardy."

- Who writes the puzzles for *Wheel of Fortune?* Two writers, along with hosts Pat Sajak and Vanna White.

- Nickelodeon's 1980s kids game show *Double Dare* produced its first seasons in Philadelphia. It routinely dumped green slime on contestants, which the show called "gak." That name was taken from Philadelphia street slang for heroin.

- Singer Bert Convy and actor Burt Reynolds cocreated *Win, Lose or Draw*, described as a rip-off of the board game *Pictionary*. The show (1987–90) pitted two celebrity-led teams in a contest of guessing drawn pictures, shot on a set designed to look exactly like Reynolds's living room, where he and Convy conceived the series.

- The "100 people surveyed" whose responses form the basis of questions on *Family Feud* used to be approached in public areas such as shopping malls. Today the surveys are conducted via random phone outreach by an outside company called Applied Research-West; respondents aren't told they're answering as many as 40 questions for *Family Feud*.

- When the Johnson family competed on *Family Feud* in 1981, host Richard Dawson developed a crush on Gretchen Johnson, 23 years his junior. After the Johnsons lost an episode, Dawson asked for Gretchen's phone number, and their first date was at his home, where he made her beef Wellington. They married in 1991 and stayed so until Dawson's death in 2012.

- Until multiple 21st-century *Jeopardy!* contestants set new records, the biggest winner in American game show history was a man named Curtis Warren. He won a total of $1.55 million, comprised primarily of $1.41 million from Fox's *Greed* in 2000, along with jackpots from a 1999 spot on *Win Ben Stein's Money* and a 1986 appearance on *Sale of the Century*.

- A woman appeared on the British version of *Deal or No Deal* in the 2000s and said she wanted to win enough money to afford fertility treatments. She didn't win, but still wound up with the money: pop superstar George Michael saw the episode and secretly gave the contestant enough money to cover her expenses.

- In September 2008, *The Price Is Right* contestant Terry Kneiss won the "Showcase Showdown" when he guessed the exact value of the prize package: $23,743. Kneiss was a regular viewer and he'd memorized the prices of the recurring prizes, giving himself a mental estimate of $23,000. The additional $743 was a guess—which Kneiss derived from his banking PIN—that just happened to be correct.

BE LIKE MIKE?

As one of the most successful boxers of all time, Mike Tyson delivered a lot more blows than he endured. After his fighting days concluded, he continued to deliver hit after hit—in the form of alternately baffling and compelling sound bites.

"I have to dream and reach for the stars, and if I miss a star then I grab a handful of clouds."

"Time is like a book. You have a beginning, a middle, and an end. It's just a cycle."

"You have to feel comfortable being uncomfortable. I'm always comfortable being uncomfortable. And to be comfortable being uncomfortable, I have to hone my discipline, which to me is doing what I have to do, but also doing it like I love it."

"Everyone has a plan 'till they get punched in the mouth."

"I've lived places these other guys can't defecate in."

"I'm a historian, and that freaks me out."

"I'm addicted to perfection. Problem with my life is I was always also addicted to chaos. Perfect chaos."

"At one point, I thought life was about acquiring things. But as I get older, life is totally about losing everything."

"I don't try to intimidate anybody before a fight. That's nonsense. I intimidate people by hitting them."

"It's good to know how to read, but it's dangerous to know how to read and not how to interpret what you're reading."

"I'm a bad guy. But if I was a good guy, nobody would want to pay to see me fight."

"I can talk about humility, but I'm not humble. I mean, if you say, 'I'm humble,' you've just contradicted yourself. But I'm trying to be, man, I'm trying so hard."

"Social media made y'all way too comfortable with disrespecting people and not getting punched in the face for it."

"If they lock me up, at least I'll have a place to stay."

"A man who was friendly with everyone was an enemy to himself."

"My style is impetuous, my defense is impregnable, and I'm ferocious."

"When I fight someone, I want to break his will. I want to take his manhood. I want to rip out his heart and show it to him."

"My biggest weakness is my sensitivity. I am too sensitive a person."

"I guess I'm gonna fade into Bolivian."

First prize given away on *The Price Is Right* (1972): a muskrat fur coat.

NOT EXTINCT AFTER ALL

Not every story about the environment is a sad one.
Take these tales, for example, of animal species thought lost to history,
but who made a surprising and triumphant comeback.

Animal: *Platygonus*

So Dead: Tens of millions of years ago, in the late Cenozoic Era, the plains of what is now North America were dominated by prodigious herds of the *Playtgonus*. Each of these herbivores weighed about 100 pounds and looked like a taller, leaner, less-imposing warthog. By the end of the last Ice Age, about 11,000 years ago, the *Platygonus* had evolved into the *Catagonus*, thought to be the last step on the creature's journey. A *Catagonus* fossil was discovered in Argentina in 1930, a relic of a species thought to have gone extinct thousands of years earlier.

Not Quite: Not only did the *Platygonus* and *Catagonus* genus not die out, but it also continued to evolve. In the 1970s, naturalists discovered a herd of peccaries not far from where the *Catagonus* fossil was discovered. The animal was a modern descendant of *Platygonus*; indigenous people in the Chaco region were aware of the creature, but mainstream scientists had never investigated the area.

Animal: New Guinea highland wild dog

So Dead: This animal is a relative of the dingo, the feral and aggressive dog that roams the wilds of Australia (the closest major landmass to the island nation of Papua New Guinea), and the New Guinea singing dog, a domesticated variant of the highland wild dog. The dogs are so name because they live in packs in remote highlands and mountains; like their domesticated relatives, they also "sing," often in groups and sometimes during mating. Native only to that geographical area, they were the oldest species of dog ever spotted on the planet—until the last one was sighted in the early 1960s, leading to the scientific assessment that the highland dog had died out.

Not Quite: In 2016, two separate expeditions—one led by zoologist James K. McIntyre and the other by researchers from the University of Papua—teamed up to investigate a single muddy paw print believed to belong to a highland dog. It did. Trail cameras the group set up revealed 15 of the animals—adult males and females, and pups—in a wooded area up to 14,000 feet above sea level.

In the 19th century, *twitter* referred to an abscess on a horse's foot.

Animal: Terror skink

So Dead: That name isn't a joke. This lizard grows to a length of 20 inches, and it eats only meat, preferring to kill its prey itself, which it does with its razor-sharp curved teeth. Biologists became aware of the animal's existence only in 1867 via preserved specimens and fossils—it presumably had gone extinct thousands of years earlier, as no live one had been spotted, and one never would...until the late 20th century.

Not Quite: The terror skink is native to New Caledonia, living on two islands with a combined surface area of just 0.35 square miles. It was there in 1993 that the first confirmed spotting of a live terror skink took place. An expedition from a French museum spotted another in 2009, then a few more were seen in 2013 and 2018.

Animal: Coelacanth

So Dead: Tetrapods—four-legged upright vertebrates—evolved from a long line of ancient creatures. Experts believe the first link in that chain may be the coelacanth (pronounced "SEE-luh-cant"), an aquatic creature that lived deep in the ocean 200 million years go. More than 130 million years later, the coelacanth was still present in the planet's oceans while dinosaurs walked the earth. Weighing about 200 pounds and measuring up to six feet long, they're found at ocean depths between 200 and 1600 feet. Fossils of the coelacanth surfaced in the 19th century, and the scientific consensus was that such a large, strange, old creature was a relic from millions of years in the past.

Not Quite: In 1938, a museum curator from South Africa riding on a fishing boat caught a coelacanth in the western Indian Ocean. A monumental find, it was heralded as the most important scientific discovery in decades, and unlocked a lot of clues about how evolution works. Then another species of the creature was discovered in 1998, thousands of miles away, near Indonesia. Biologists think a small but unknown number of coelacanths are still out there in the oceans, but they're at high risk of actual extinction this time, owing to climate change and the manner by which those two examples were found in the 20th century: accidental capture by fishing trawlers.

Animal: *Gracilidris pombero* ants

So Dead: Of the more than 10,000 identified ants on Earth, the *Gracilidris pombero* is one of the oldest—and the newest. The only trace of its existence was a single specimen preserved in amber and tested to date back 15 million years. No record of this particular ant existed before the discovery of the fossil, and none after.

Not Quite: It's likely that the ants evaded human detection for so long by their very nature: they're secretive and stay out of trouble to avoid predators. They're one of a handful of nocturnal ant species, so they leave their burrows only at night. Those burrows also sit so deep underground that only something like construction machinery could ever disturb them. And that's exactly what's happened—starting in

It's illegal to dine out on your birthday in Tajikistan.

2006, *Gracilidris* was identified in the Amazon Basin foothills in Colombia thanks to logging operations.

Animal: Australian night parrot
So Dead: The Australian night parrot was abundant in the state of Queensland up until the 20th century. With yellow, green, brown, and black feathers, the distinctive bird was nocturnal, usually to avoid its natural predators. But some unexpected threats killed off this animal. As settlers from the U.K. arrived in Australia in mass numbers in the late 19th and early 20th centuries, they brought with them cats, for pets, and foxes, for hunting. Within 20 years of their arrival, the fox population became out of control, and the animals were deemed a nuisance and a threat to wildlife. Along with cats, foxes were pegged as the culprit for the elimination of the Australian night parrot. The last live specimen of the bird was noted in 1912.
Not Quite: Probably still hunted by foxes and attempting to go into hiding, the Australian night parrot lived well into the 20th century—a dead one was found in Queensland in 1990. Inspired by that discovery, naturalist John Young spent years trying to find a living Australian night parrot; in 2013, he found and photographed one.

Animal: Bermuda petrel
So Dead: Before humans arrived in the 1500s to colonize what's now called Bermuda, the cahow, or Bermuda petrel, lived in abundance on the island, as demonstrated by fossil records. But with the arrival of humanity came the destruction of the birds' habitat, and invasive species brought by man—cats and pigs—hunted the petrel to extinction. The Europeans on Bermuda didn't mind: the call of the petrel is so loud and terrifying that settlers nicknamed their new home an "island of demons." And while their animals killed off thousands of the birds, the humans plucked eggs out of ground-based nests and ate them. The last recorded instance of a Bermuda petrel on Bermuda dates to 1620.
Not Quite: Two dead birds surfaced in 1935 and 1945. A 1951 expedition found 17 pairs of living cahows (and eight chicks), forced by human encroachment into five small rocky islands in Castle Harbor. Researchers brought the petrel back from extinction, and today there are about 400 examples of the national bird of Bermuda.

*   *   *

"Science is not about building a body of known 'facts.' It is a method for asking awkward questions and subjecting them to a reality check, thus avoiding the human tendency to believe whatever makes us feel good."
—Terry Pratchett

Only palindrome-named song by a palindrome-named artist to be a hit: ABBA's "SOS" (1975).

WEIRD CHEESE

*When we pitched Uncle John this article about the strangest and most
unique cheeses from around the world, he told us about this time he ordered
a burger and they put a piece of cheddar on there instead of American. Not
quite what we meant, because these weird cheeses are really weird.*

Casu Marzu. Made only in Sardinia, Italy, it's soft and spreadable like brie, but
noticeably pungent. It starts out as pecorino; its final taste, texture, and smell are
the result of fermentation, which occurs when the live fly larvae introduced early on
consume the sheep's milk and leave their excrement behind. The cheese is consumed
while the maggots are still alive.

Milbenkäse. This German cheese begins with quark, a soft white spreadable cheese
similar to yogurt. It's flavored with salt and caraway seeds, then placed in a wooden
box for three months. Generous helpings of rye flour and mites jumpstart the aging
process. As the mites eat the cheese and flour, they excrete an enzyme that makes the
cheese age and adopt its bitter, zesty flavor. Milbenkäse fans say it's ready to eat if it
resembles a loaf of bread; true enthusiasts leave the cheese in the mite-filled box for a
year, until the ball turns black.

Chhurpi. A soft version and a hard version of this cheese exist. The hard version can
be eaten and swallowed, but it's so hard after it's dried on a wood fire that it must be
sucked on and then chewed indefinitely. It's as thick, rubbery, and difficult to break
down as bubble gum. It's made from yak milk, dried in the sun or in a low oven, and
is found only in the Himalayan region of Nepal and Tibet. Properly stored (in a yak
skin), hard chhurpi can be consumed for up to 20 years.

Moose cheese. Dairies don't bother with moose cheese because moose produce
milk only five months out of the year, and must be milked in complete silence,
otherwise they get distressed and can stop producing milk permanently. With all
those caveats, only three moose in the world—Juna, Haelga, and Gullan, located on
a farm in Bjursholm, Sweden—produce the milk for moose cheese, resulting in an
annual yield of a little over 600 pounds. All of it is destined for the Algen Hus, a
restaurant operated by the farmers who raise the moose. Moose cheese is similar to
cow milk cheese, only gamier, and available in three styles that cost up to $500 per
pound: hard with rind, feta-like, and blue.

Pule. Crumbly, white, and similar to Greek feta cheese, but thoroughly smoked,
pule is produced on a single farm in Zasavica, a town in Serbia about 50 miles from
Belgrade. Farmers begin by milking by hand a collection of 100 Balkan donkeys, an

endangered animal. It takes about three gallons of milk to make one pound of pule, which packs 60 times more vitamin C than cow milk.

Airag. The milk of virtually any mammal can be used to make cheese—even horses. In Mongolia and eastern Turkey, raw horse milk is fermented until it possesses a heavy cream-like texture and becomes slightly alcoholic. That's called airag, and if it's fermented some more and left to harden, it turns into one of the sourest-tasting cheeses on the planet.

Oscypek. The Vlachs emigrated from the Balkans to the mountainous region of southern Poland about 1,000 years ago. They introduced sheepherding and cheesemaking to the region, and the Vlachs' descendants still perform both tasks in roughly the same ways they did a millennium ago. Made from the milk of sheep that graze freely in the highlands, only about 150 *bacas* (shepherds) know how to properly make oscypek, the signature Vlach cheese. The product is placed into a decorative wooden mold so that the cheese will take on its shape, then soaked in saltwater. (Traditionally formed into the shape of a spindle, novelties like ovals, hearts, and animals are produced on occasion.) Then the cheese in its mold is hung in a wooden hut and smoked with spruce or pine woods. The outside turns golden, the inside gets creamy, and the whole thing tastes like smoke, brine, and chestnuts.

Cougar Gold. Washington State University (home of the Cougars) operates its own creamery, and its primary product is Cougar Gold—unique in that it's distributed in metal cans. A spicier, tangier, nuttier riff on cheddar cheese (but both soft and crumbly), it was invented by WSU dairy husbandry professor N. S. Golding. At the outset of World War II, the U.S. government approached many science professors and invited them to devise new cheese preservation methods, to avoid spoilage in the cheese sent to troops stationed around the globe. Canning food can keep it fresh for years, so Golding struck on the idea of canned cheese. Healthy-to-consume bacteria is what turns milk into cheese (and releases carbon dioxide in the process). Golding's team modified a bacteria culture that would still convert the milk into cheese but cut way down on the carbon dioxide emissions—meaning the cans won't explode. That same culture invented 70 years ago is still in use for making Cougar Gold today.

Lichen cheese. Centuries ago, the indigenous Inuit of Quebec hunted and ate caribou, and would salvage from the animals' stomachs the lichen the caribou had eaten—which, when fermented by stomach acid, turned into a flavorful food that reportedly tastes like cheese. Inspired by that, Montreal-based high-end food distributor Société d'Orignal takes forest-foraged lichen (a moss-like organism that's part fungus and part algae) and roasts, boils, and ferments it. They then impregnate locally raised raw goat milk with the processed lichen, which creates a final product that resembles blue cheese.

Look closely: about one in 10 vegetarian hot dogs contains traces of meat.

THE "MY BLUES NICKNAME IS REALLY GREAT" BLUES

In the early 20th century (and for many decades after), musicians in places such as Chicago and the Mississippi Delta created a distinctly American style called the blues. Powerful, emotional, and deeply evocative, the blues influenced pop, R&B, rock, country...and left us with a legacy of some terrific musician stage names and nicknames as visceral and descriptive as the music.

Homesick James	H-Bomb Ferguson	Peg Leg Sam
Popa Chubby	Little Smokey Smothers	Cow Cow Davenport
Furry Lewis	Mr. Blues	Bo Weavil Jackson
Lazy Lester	Peetie Wheatstraw	Sugar Blue
Barbeque Bob	Guitar Slim	Speckled Red
Smokey Hogg	Harmonica Shah	Snooks Eaglin
Lonesome Sundown	Johnny Drummer	Major Handy
Black Ace	Washboard Sam	Harlem Hamfats
Shakey Jake	Scrapper Blackwell	Louisiana Red
Cousin Joe	Ironing Board Sam	Hollywood Fats
Little Brother Montgomery	Hip Linkchain	Houston Stackhouse
Lil' Ed	Sunnyland Slim	T-Model Ford
Golden "Big" Wheeler	Catfish Keith	Little Hatch
Kid Memphis	Sleepy John Estes	Blind Mississippi Morris
Champion Jack Dupree	Johnny "Big Moose" Walker	Blind Reverend Gary Davis
Drive 'Em Down	Eddie "Cleanhead" Vinson	Paul "Wine" Jones
T.V. Slim	Seasick Steve	Spider John Koerner
Backwards Sam Firk	Baby Tate	Laughing Charley
Bumble Bee Slim	Watermelon Slim	Jazz Gillum

China has more skyscrapers than do the next 13 countries on the list combined.

BEHIND THE LINES: "I SEE DEAD PEOPLE"

Now for a bad joke: what do The Sixth Sense *and* Titanic *have in common?*
Icy dead people. (Get it?) Here's another, courtesy of Robin Williams: "I have
the fifth sense. I smell dead people." These are just two of countless riffs on
a line of dialogue that not only changed the way we watch movies—it altered
the trajectories of the man who wrote it and the boy who spoke it.

RIP for Parody

It's funny that such a deadly serious line from such a dark, moody horror movie
has generated so many laughs over the years. When *The Sixth Sense* was still in
theaters in the autumn of 1999, "I see dead people" was no joke to the millions of
mortified moviegoers who helped spur the modestly budgeted film ($40 million) to an
astonishing $672 million box office haul that outgrossed *Toy Story 2* and *Austin Powers:
The Spy Who Shagged Me* that year. (Only *Star Wars: Episode I–The Phantom Menace*
made more.) Word of mouth was that you had to see *The Sixth Sense* soon before
the big twist at the end got spoiled, and then you had to see it again to see how they
pulled it off. The film was a hit with critics as well, and remains one of only a handful
of horror movies ever to be nominated for Best Picture.

Then came the parodies (like the Robin Williams joke in the intro, which he
told to Jay Leno), and in TV shows and movies—most notably in 2000's surprise-hit
horror spoof, *Scary Movie*. In 2001, a still image of the scene with the text "I see dumb
people" was uploaded to the Internet, which makes it among the first memes.

Spoiler Alert!

It's safe to say that the line wouldn't have had such staying power had it not set up
the most talked-about plot twist of modern cinema, right up there with the twists in
Planet of the Apes and *The Empire Strikes Back*. We won't spoil those two movies here,
but we are going to spoil *The Sixth Sense*...so if you don't know how it ends, you might
want to give it a watch and then come back and read this.

The line comes in a pivotal scene where nine-year-old Cole Sear (Haley Joel
Osment) is lying in a hospital bed with the covers pulled all the way up to his chin.
The air is so cold that his breath can be seen. Cole whispers his big secret—"I see dead
people"—to Dr. Malcolm Crowe (Bruce Willis), a somber child psychologist who wants
to do better for this boy than he did for a crazed former patient who shot him at the
beginning of the movie. Cole explains that the ghosts are "walking around like regular

people. They don't see each other. They only see what they want to see. They don't know they're dead." Right then, the camera cuts to Malcolm's face.

The psychologist doesn't believe the boy at first, but after learning that he's telling the truth, Malcolm tries to help Cole help the dead people make peace. The big twist comes at the end when Malcolm realizes that he himself is one of those dead people—he didn't survive that gunshot. Audiences were like, "Whaaat?" During the previous parts of the movie, it doesn't appear that Malcolm is a ghost, but a series of flashbacks reveal that all the clues were there. It really is a masterstroke of screenwriting.

By the Seat of His Pants

There are two kinds of fiction writers: "plotters" and "pantsers." The former plots the story with a detailed outline before writing; the latter writes "by the seat of their pants." Writer-director M. Night Shyamalan, who was in his late 20s when he wrote *The Sixth Sense*, was an admitted outliner, but was also something of a pantser. How so? He didn't even come up with the idea that Malcolm was a ghost until the end of the fifth draft of the screenplay.

The original idea came to Shyamalan when "[he] saw a wake at a house...and people are walking around in dark clothes, and this child was sitting on the stairs talking to somebody, but nobody's there." He was also inspired by Terry Gilliam's surreal sci-fi drama *12 Monkeys* (1995), starring Bruce Willis as a pensive time traveler who journeys back to the present from an apocalyptic future. At one point he says, "All I see are dead people." It just so happened that *12 Monkey* was set and filmed in Shyamalan's home city of Philadelphia.

The pieces started to come together. Shyamalan's movie would take place in Philadelphia, it would star Bruce Willis, and it would be called *The Sixth Sense* (which Shyamalan thought sounded "cool"). In the first draft, Malcolm was a crime scene photographer whose son sees dead victims of a serial killer. After coming up with the ending's plot twist (and then doing yet another five drafts), Shyamalan flew to Los Angeles, stayed in a hotel room he couldn't afford, and shopped his screenplay around. He started the bidding at $1 million, with the provision that he direct. It was a gutsy move for a young screenwriter whose only credits were two little-known indie films and cowriting the screenplay for *Stuart Little*. Disney ended up securing the rights to *The Sixth Sense* and distributed it through Hollywood Pictures.

Now for the Ironic Twist

The movie line that turned Shyamalan into an instant celebrity nearly doomed his career. In the wake of the film's success, he was being compared to giants like Steven Spielberg and Stanley Kubrick, and the pressure was on. The young auteur's follow-ups—*Unbreakable*, *Signs*, and *The Village*—performed well, but they failed to match the box office or critical reception of *The Sixth Sense*.

Those who know say whale milk has a similar consistency to toothpaste.

How could they, though? Disguised as a typical horror movie, *The Sixth Sense* came out of nowhere and took audiences off guard. No one saw the twist coming because no one was looking for it. Case in point: After viewing a rough cut of the movie, producer Frank Marshall told Shyamalan not to cut to a close-up of Malcolm so quickly after Cole says "I see dead people," because it would give away the twist. But Shyamalan insisted on keeping the close-up, and he was proven right at a test screening for the public, where no one picked up on it.

But when moviegoers walked into *Signs*, *Unbreakable*, and *The Village*, they were expecting a twist. And watching a movie just to guess the twist can take you out of the story. After diminishing box office and harsh reviews for clunkers like *Lady in the Water* and *The Happening*, Shyamalan hit a career low in 2010 with *The Last Airbender*, his live-action adaptation of the hit Nickelodeon cartoon *Avatar: The Last Airbender*. (The movie has a whopping 5 percent on Rotten Tomato's Tomatometer. One sample review, from *The Age*: "This empty, misfired epic from M. Night Shyamalan...is boring and strengthens the claim that he is the worst director working in mainstream cinema today.")

In recent years, it seems that the former wunderkind has gotten his groove back after the thrillers *Split* (2016) and *Knock at the Cabin* (2023) saw a return to form. He's now had a movie open at number one in four different decades.

In 2020, Shyamalan acknowledged that the "I see dead people" twist worked so well because it "didn't have the legacy to deal with. It didn't have my name to deal with. So, it would be interesting if *The Sixth Sense* was the third movie or the fourth movie and how that would've changed the audience's relationship to the film."

The Boy Who Spoke It

The Sixth Sense also made a star out of Haley Joel Osment and will most likely be the movie he's most associated with for the rest of his life. Now approaching middle age, Osment says the "I see dead people" line still follows him, but he isn't haunted by it. Rather, he credits it with launching his career (after he didn't get the part of Anakin Skywalker in *The Phantom Menace*).

But in his *Sixth Sense* audition, he read that pivotal scene and was cast immediately—in large part due to his delivery of that line. (He won it over future *Arrested Development* star Michael Cera.)

But neither Osment nor anyone else on the set that day knew "I see dead people" would become a catchphrase. "It's still amazing to me that nobody, at any point during the production, was like, 'Oh, OK, that's the line. That's going to be the tagline for our movie.'" He also remembers that it was a tough scene for him to film because they were on a refrigerated set so you could see Cole's breath (providing yet another clue—if you were paying attention—that the boy was talking to a ghost).

The U.S. military's B-2 Spirit "Stealth Bomber" cost $65,000 per hour to operate.

NOT INVENTED BY THOMAS EDISON

With more than 1,000 patents to his name, Thomas Edison is regarded as the greatest and most prolific inventor in history. He was indisputably a brilliant man, but by no means did he work alone. He employed a massive team of assistants and scientists and freely borrowed from the work of others in addition to intimidating them. Here's some of what the history books got wrong about the fruitful mind and laboratory of Thomas Edison.

Invention: The electric light bulb

Story: British chemist Joseph Swan figured out how to make the light bulb possible with experiments in the 1850s and 1860s. He determined that a glass-encased complete vacuum with a burning filament would work, but couldn't create a proper vacuum until 1879, whereupon he debuted his invention at a public lecture in Newcastle. It looked like a modern light bulb—but the carbon filament would burn for only a few minutes.

Edison: Edison invented the first *practical* light bulb. He took Swan's design without credit or acknowledgment and replaced the carbon filament with a thinner one made from tungsten. Edison's bulb could burn for as long as 600 hours and helped usher in the age of electric light.

Invention: Wax paper

Story: Photography developed in France in the mid-19th century, and one of the biggest innovators in the field was Jean-Baptiste Gustave Le Gray. Among his developments: he created wax paper in 1851, made by coating paper in paraffin wax, and used it to make photo negatives.

Edison: More than 20 years after wax paper was first widely used in photography, Edison used the absorbent, conductive material when he was working on improving the transmission abilities of the telegraph. He came up with the idea of using paraffin wax paper to prevent the messages from getting wet. Edison probably didn't even steal the concept from Le Gray; wax paper had long been used in the U.S. to wrap candy.

Invention: The electric chair

Story: Edison's biggest and most heated rival in the late 19th century was inventor and industrialist George Westinghouse, who competed against Edison with his

The Statue of Liberty is struck by lightning 600 times each year.

own products built on a form of electricity called alternating current (AC). Edison favored the type of electricity he'd helped develop, direct current (DC), and wanted to discredit Westinghouse's AC electricity; one way he attempted to do so was by publicly executing dogs and horses using AC electricity to demonstrate AC's danger. When a Buffalo dentist named Alfred P. Southwick sought help developing a "more humane" form of capital punishment via electrocution, both Edison and Westinghouse spurned him. However, Edison secretly financed his employee Harold P. Brown's efforts to create the first electric chair—using AC, expressly so that Westinghouse's name would be associated with the newfangled "death machine."

Edison: Thomas Edison supported Brown in secret so he could publicly discredit Westinghouse and drum up public support for DC electricity. Edison funded Brown's research while calling out the brutal inhumanity of capital punishment and the AC electric chair in the press. In 1890, New York became the first state to adopt the electric chair as its form of criminal execution—and despite Edison's best efforts to destroy his competitor, alternating current reigned in the end.

Invention: X-rays

Story: While experimenting with gas-filled tubes and electricity in 1895, German physicist Wilhelm Röntgen discovered electromagnetic radiation inside the invisible light spectrum. He noticed green fluorescent light emanating from a black-paper-wrapped light tube, and after playing around with it, took a photograph of the inside of his wife's hands, producing an image of her bones. Labeled X-ray photography, Röntgen's development made headlines around the world. In Germany, X-rays are still called "Röntgen Rays," and the man who discovered them won the first Nobel Prize in Physics in 1901.

Edison: Reading of Röntgen Rays in scientific journals, Edison sought to re-create and reverse engineer what the German had done. He figured out how to take X-rays and built a machine called a fluoroscope to do it with. Edison patented the first X-ray machine and took all the credit without mentioning his inspiration.

Invention: Motion pictures

Story: In the 1880s, French inventor Louis Le Prince created the first motion picture camera, and he used it to make several short films. In 1890, his work well known in the scientific community by that point, Le Prince was supposed to show his work off at an exhibition in New York. He got on a train in England...and disappeared.

Edison: In the late 1880s, Edison's lab started work on using celluloid film strips to make moving images. Edison put his team on the idea after a visit to his lab from Eadweard Muybridge, who showed off his 1877 device that simulated animation.

Microorganisms outnumber cells in the human body by a 10-to-1 ratio.

In 1891, Edison filed a patent for a moving image camera called the kinetograph and a machine to project them, the kinetoscope, most of it reverse engineered from Le Prince's work, with most of the work conducted by Edison employee William Dickson.

Dickson, angered that Edison failed to give him appropriate credit for his contributions, joined the American Mutoscope Company. In 1898, Edison sued American Mutoscope for trademark infringement, seeking royalties, claiming that he was the sole inventor of cinematography. Louis Le Prince's son, Adolphe, testified for the defense. After 10 years of legal struggles, Edison would eventually lose his lawsuit.

However, Edison had enough patents that, by the 1910s, he had near-total control of the film industry through his Edison Trust. Based in the company town of Fort Lee, New Jersey, Edison sued anyone who tried to make movies without his permission (or without paying royalties for using equipment he claimed to have invented). Three major Fort Lee filmmakers so tired of dealing with Edison that they left New Jersey for Los Angeles, where Edison's litigious ways were harder to enforce. The modern film industry was born when those film bosses, Carl Laemmle, William Fox, and Adolph Zukor, created Universal Studios, Fox Studios, and Paramount Pictures, respectively.

10 TALLEST STATUES IN THE WORLD, IN FEET

1. **The Statue of Unity** (Kevadia, India) – **597**
2. **Spring Temple Buddha** (Zhaocun, China) – **420**
3. **Laykyun Sekkya** (Khatakan Taung, Myanmar) – **380**
4. **Ushiku Great Buddha** (Ibaraki, Japan) – **330**
5. **Sendai Daikannon** (Sendai, Japan) – **330**
6. **Guishan Guanyin of the Thousand Hands and Eyes** (Weishan, China) – **325**
7. **The Big Buddha of Thailand** (Ang Thong Province, Thailand) – **302**
8. **Dai Kannon of Kita no Miyajo park** (Takasaki, Japan) – **289**
9. **The Motherland Calls** (Volgograd, Russia) – **279**
10. **Awaji Kannon** (Awaji Island, Japan) – **260**

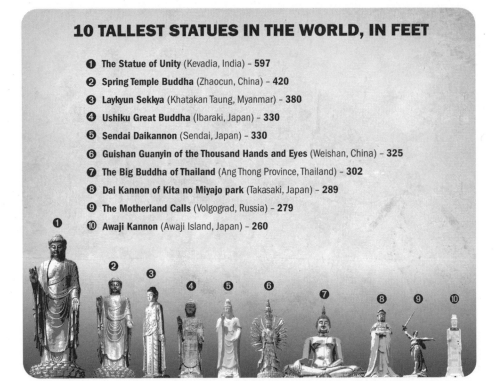

False advertising: cucumbers, radishes, and tomatoes all contain more water than a watermelon.

YOU GOT *WHAT* ON THE BLACK MARKET?

Usually, the "black market" evokes the buying and selling of illegal goods under the authorities' radar. But sometimes, perfectly legal everyday items become so highly in demand that they can be exchanged via sketchy channels, too.

SPAM

Hormel devised SPAM in the 1930s to make a sellable product from a surplus of pork shoulder and ham. During World War II, the inexpensive shelf-stable protein source became extremely popular in Southeast Asia thanks to the cans being supplied to servicemembers stationed there, and it's still an integral part of the Hawaiian cuisine and diet. Since 2017, shoplifting of the still-affordable SPAM—one can cost less than $4 at the time—was such a big problem in Hawaii that store managers around the state had to lock the stuff up as a theft-prevention measure. One Honolulu store was hit by a man who walked inside and stole a case, punching a security guard on his way out. In Oahu, another man grabbed eight cases and got away. Authorities believe that the shoplifted SPAM is an intermediate step in a black-market scheme. Individuals steal huge amounts of SPAM, sell it out of a car trunk or the back of a van (for around the regular retail price), and immediately use the cash to buy drugs.

CIGARETTES

Various state-levied taxes make cigarettes much more expensive in some places. In New York, a pack runs about $14, and in Illinois, the average price is about $9. This creates a black market for cigarettes in the more expensive states—purchased in neighboring jurisdictions where the taxes aren't as high. One study by the University of Illinois found that 75 percent of discarded cigarette packs on Chicago streets came from Indiana; another investigation revealed that 60 percent of all cigarettes purchased in New York were done so illegally, primarily originating in New Jersey.

DOUGHNUTS

The Mexican border city of Juarez is one of the most dangerous places in the world. Cartels enjoy virtual control on all authority, and crime is rampant, particularly murder for those who run afoul of the drug-running enterprise. A nexus point for drugs smuggled from Mexico into the United States, it's also where Sonia Garcia and her sons smuggle goods *out* of the U.S. and into Mexico. Garcia runs the Krispy Kreme doughnut game in Juarez. The city used to have a Krispy Kreme location until

What's the rind on a wheel of brie called? It's a mold named *Penicillium candidum*.

the company shut it down over the volume of crime. So many locals got hooked on the chain's glazed doughnuts that Garcia saw an opportunity. Three or four times each week, one of her sons drives to the Krispy Kreme in El Paso, Texas, and purchases 40 dozen boxes of doughnuts for $5 each. Then, Garcia and her other son set up in Juarez and unload their wares for $8 a box—a markup of 60 percent. Known as the "Krispy Kreme Familia" (a play on the name of local drug cartel, La Familia Michoacana), the Garcias announce their selling spots on Facebook and operate a hotline to handle special doughnut requests.

SALT

The Healthy, Hunger-Free Kids Act was signed into law by President Barack Obama in 2010, setting sweeping new guidelines for school lunch programs nationwide. Developed by a team of nutritionists, one of the biggest new rules was severely limiting the amount of sodium that could be present in cooked school cafeteria meals. The sudden lack of salt proved very noticeable and wildly unpopular with kids, who bemoaned the lack of flavor in their industrial meals. Over the next few years, news reports popped up from around the country regarding high school students who set up black-market salt rings. At Blackford High School in Hartford City, Indiana, for example, one operation brought in bulk table salt from home, loaded up shakers, and sold it to students at a rate of $1 per shake.

PRINTER INK

It's easy (and common) to steal office supplies. Creating a black-market business for office supplies is another thing entirely. Toner, used for printers and photocopy machines, is expensive, but when purchased through illegal channels it's cheap—because it's stolen. In 2013, a man working in the clerical department at Memorial Sloan-Kettering Cancer Center in New York City was discovered to have stolen $1.5 million worth of toner ink, setting up business accounts to order unnecessarily large amounts of toner, then reselling them in the alley behind his workplace. A man who worked in the duplicating department of a big Manhattan law firm falsely ordered $376,000 worth of toner on the company's dime and sold the cartridges (worth between $80 and $259 each) for $10 out of the firm's backdoor.

OTHER ITEMS WITH AN UNLIKELY BUT ROBUST BLACK MARKET:

- Razors
- Hay
- Laundry detergent
- Butter
- eBay accounts
- Maple syrup (in Canada)
- Choco Pies (in North Korea)
- Fruit Roll-Ups (in Israel)

Medieval kings of Europe employed a staffer called the groom of the stool. He helped the king defecate.

SHE FELL FROM THE SKY

It was the deadliest lightning-caused plane crash in history. But from that
tragedy emerged the incredible true story of its only survivor, a 17-year-old girl...
and the rainforest that saved her life. Years later, she would return the favor.

THE CRASH

Just before noon on the muggy Christmas Eve of 1971, a German Peruvian teenager
named Juliane Koepcke and her mother, Maria, boarded LANSA Flight 508 in Lima,
Peru. After a one-hour jaunt over the Amazon rainforest, they would get off at the first
scheduled stopover in Pucallpa. Their final destination: Panguana ecological research
station, in the heart of the jungle. Maria and her husband, Hans-Wilhelm, had
established the station three years prior. The famous German biologists were raising
their daughter there, and the family was eager to spend Christmas together.

A few days earlier, the fair-skinned, blonde, bespectacled teen had graduated from a
German high school in Lima, and she'd persuaded her mother to let her stay an extra few
days to attend a dance and her graduation ceremony. Her father didn't want them flying
LANSA given the airline's poor reputation, but every other flight was sold out. Flight 508
was taking place on LANSA's last remaining working aircraft, a Lockheed L-188A Electra
turboprop (later revealed to be made entirely of spare parts from other planes) that carried
95 passengers and crew. Juliane sat in the window seat of the second-to-last row, her
mother sat in the middle seat, and a Peruvian man on the aisle.

They were about 20 minutes from landing when the blue sky turned dark. The
pilots, feeling the pressure of keeping holiday schedules, made the fateful decision to fly
through a thunderstorm—which that particular plane was not designed to withstand. As
lightning lit up the sky and everything started shaking, overhead compartments popped
open, forcing luggage and Christmas presents to fly about the cabin.

Then Juliane saw a flash strike the right wing! "Now it's all over," said her mother,
as other passengers broke into screams. Nearly two miles up, the aircraft went into a
nosedive...and then it all came apart. The last thing Juliane remembered was being all
by herself in the stormy sky, strapped in to the three-seat bench as it spun like "a falling
maple seed" toward the "broccoli and cauliflower" jungle below. Then she passed out.

THE LANDING

Juliane's bench came to a rest, right side up, on the muddy forest floor. She slipped
off her seatbelt, fell to the ground, and then lay "like an embryo," slipping in and out
of consciousness until Christmas morning. She awoke in a daze, soaked in mud. The

dense canopy of vine-filled trees—which must have cushioned her fall—didn't keep the rain off.

More in shock than in pain, Juliane knew she had a concussion. She was bruised all over. There were deep gashes on her arms and legs. Her collarbone was broken. She'd torn the ACL in her knee. One eye was swollen shut, while the other opened only to a slit. Worse yet, her glasses were gone and she was nearsighted—everything around her was a blur. Despite that, as she recalled years later, "I recognized the sounds of wildlife from Panguana and realized I was in the same jungle." A self-described "jungle child," Juliane had been taught by her parents not only how to survive in the rainforest, but how to not be afraid of all the things that bite and sting.

Juliane tried to stand up, but couldn't. She crawled around for a while, calling for her mother. As Christmas night fell, the concussed 17-year-old stayed near her seat and shivered more than slept. By the next morning, she was still in a fog but becoming more aware. That's when she realized that she might never be rescued. "I was convinced that I would surely die."

After searching unsuccessfully for her mother or any other survivors, Juliane heard something that gave her hope: running water! Her parents had taught her that if she were ever lost in the rainforest, she could follow the course of running water and eventually encounter other people. The high school graduate set her sights on getting back to her family's thatched hut, where their German shepherd, Lobo, and her parakeet, Florian, would surely be waiting for her.

THE JOURNEY

Wearing only a torn sleeveless minidress and one sandal, Juliane started limping down a tiny stream, knowing it would eventually take her to a creek, then to a river, where there would be people—or at least a clearing where search planes could see her.

Her only food: a small bag of candy she'd found among the wreckage. (She'd also found a Christmas cake that was so muddy she didn't take it with her...which she later regretted.) Being the rainy season, the trees weren't bearing any fruit. And she had no knife to cut husks, or any way to start a fire. At night, she tried to sleep under leaves, but the rain washed them away. She later wrote, "Ice-cold drops pelt me, soaking my thin summer dress. The wind makes me shiver to the core. On those bleak nights, as I cower under a tree or in a bush, I feel utterly abandoned." When it wasn't raining, the mosquitoes feasted.

The sounds of the search planes ceased after a few days. As her concussion cleared up, Juliane remembered her survival lessons. With her eyesight compromised, she poked a stick in front of her in shallow water, where biting piranha and venomous stingrays lay in wait. In deeper waters, she knew that the alligator-like caimans make big splashes, but they don't really go after people, so she stuck to deep water when possible.

The Baseball Reliquary has in its collection a fragment of thigh skin from the sport's alleged inventor, Abner Doubleday.

On the fourth day, Juliane followed the sound of vultures and made a gruesome discovery: a bench from the plane, just like the one she'd been strapped to, partially buried upside down in the mud, with three sets of legs (two men and a woman) sticking up. Even though it didn't make sense, Juliane had to make sure the woman wasn't her mother—this woman had polish on her toenails, something her mother never did. "I moved on after a while, but in the first moment after finding them, it was like I was paralyzed."

It took nearly a week, but Juliane finally found a muddy river, albeit an uninhabited section. She waited and waited for a boat. Nothing came, so she slowly made her way downriver, walking along the bank where she could, swimming the rest of the time. After surviving only on rainwater for days, the growing teenager was growing weaker. She knew she had to eat something, so—still in shock—she tried to catch poison dart frogs. Thankfully, she was too slow to get one. Four more days passed.

THE RESCUE

Eleven days after the crash, Juliane woke up on a small sandy riverbank. A few feet away in the water was a small fishing boat that she hadn't noticed earlier. At first, she couldn't believe it was real. No one was around, but there was also a path leading up a small embankment. "I tried to negotiate it, but I had grown so weak, that even by crawling on all fours, I couldn't manage to overcome this little slope. It probably took hours, but I finally made it."

Juliane found an empty hut, with no walls but a roof. She was going to spend the night there, but the floor was too hard, so she made her way back to the riverbank and slept there.

The next morning, Juliane realized that she lacked the strength to keep going downriver. Plus, her arm wound was infested with maggots, and her back was severely sunburned. She'd been attempting to remove the maggots from her arm with a stick, but in the hut was a container of diesel fuel for the boat engine, which she used to flush the wound (as she'd once seen her father do to the family dog when it suffered a similar wound). Then she decided to stay in the hut, where she would wait and hope for rescue.

Just then, she heard somebody coming! Three local fishermen approached on foot. They were shocked to see a filthy, bruised blonde girl with bloodshot eyes (they'd been that way since the crash). As she later recalled, "They thought I was a kind of water goddess—a figure from local legend who is a hybrid of a water dolphin and a blonde, white-skinned woman." But Juliane, who's as fluent in Spanish as she is in German, told them, "I'm a girl who was in the LANSA crash. My name is Juliane." The men fed her and tended to her wounds. The next morning, they took her on an 11-hour river trip to the nearest village with a hospital, where she began her long recovery. An investigation would later conclude that as many as 14 people survived the initial plane crash (which finally put LANSA out of business), most likely thanks to updrafts in the thunderstorm and the cushion of the dense trees. But 17-year-old Juliane Koepcke was the only crash survivor who also survived the jungle.

THE BACKLASH

In the aftermath of the crash, Juliane became a worldwide celebrity. But instead of being applauded for surviving a two-mile freefall and 11 days alone in the Amazon rainforest, she was mocked and even vilified—especially in Europe. The German magazine *Stern* bought exclusive rights to her story, and then implied, according to the *New York Times*, that she was "arrogant and unfeeling." Even worse, the infamous 1972 Italian film, *Miracles Still Happen*, portrayed Juliane as a dolled-up, ditzy blonde who screams at every apparent danger and basically stumbles her way to safety.

Meanwhile, the real Juliane was trying to deal with the grief of losing her mother in a horrific plane crash that she herself had survived. The nightmares alone were almost more than Juliane could handle. "The real mourning set in way later," she told *Vice*, "because after the crash I was constantly being interviewed and interrogated by the air force and police...I couldn't take the sudden fame very well."

She stopped giving interviews for nearly 20 years—and might have stayed silent longer had she not received one of the strangest requests in the history of documentary filmmaking.

THE REDEMPTION

There was one stunning coincidence that had taken place on that fateful Christmas Eve of 1971. Werner Herzog, at the time a 29-year-old German filmmaker who would later rise to fame with such classic documentaries as *Encounters at the End of the World* and *Grizzly Man*, was also originally booked on LANSA Flight 508. His reservation was canceled when he changed his itinerary and booked a later flight to scout locations for a film he was working on.

After the crash, Herzog became obsessed with Juliane's story, but was unable to track her down until 1998, when he asked her to take part in a German TV documentary called *Wings of Hope*. Juliane agreed, and they returned to the crash site in Peru and retraced part of her route out of the jungle. In the film, she matter-of-factly tells her tale as it all comes back to her, occasionally trailing off in thought. Herzog, as he's known to, inserts himself into the story. "The casual way she dealt with the mosquitoes and other vermin," he narrates in his distinctive German accent, "was the first thing that struck us about Juliane."

Figs aren't fruit, botanically speaking. They're inverted flowers.

Thanks to *Wings of Hope*, and to her 2011 memoir, *When I Fell from the Sky*, the world now knows what Juliane Koepcke did. Those two sources provided much of the information for this article, but in recent years, Juliane has given several more interviews—not so much because she wants her own story to be told, but because she knows that by telling it, she can do some real good. "On my lonely 11-day hike back to civilization, I made myself a promise," she told the *New York Times* on the 50th anniversary of the crash. "I vowed that if I stayed alive, I would devote my life to a meaningful cause that served nature and humanity."

LONG LIVE PANGUANA

After losing Maria in the crash, Hans-Wilhelm and Juliane channeled their grief into trying to save that portion of the Amazon from logging. The situation was dire: according to the World Wildlife Fund, "Roughly 1,100 square miles of Peru's forests are cut down every year—around 80 percent of them illegally." While Hans-Wilhelm lobbied the government for official protection in the 1970s—without much success—his daughter continued her field studies in Panguana, first studying butterflies for her graduate thesis, and then bats for her doctorate in mammalogy. In that small patch of jungle alone there are 56 bat species, more than twice in all of Europe.

In 1989, Juliane married entomologist Erich Diller, and has since gone by the name Dr. Juliane Diller. She splits her time between Peru and Germany, where she retired as deputy director at the Bavarian State Collection of Zoology in Munich.

Juliane took over as director of Panguana in 2000 following the death of her father. In 2011, after tirelessly lobbying the public sector, and fundraising in the private sector, her perseverance paid off: the Peruvian government finally designated Panguana as an official conservation area. Now a hot spot for scientists from all over the world, with the help of corporate donors Panguana has grown from its original 445 acres to more than 4,000. And all with the cooperation of the Indigenous Asháninka, who live in a nearby village. The researchers are teaching the locals how unique this particular rainforest is in the world.

In addition to the bats that still have a home thanks to the efforts led by Juliane, also spared from the harvester were 500 species of trees, 160 species of reptiles and amphibians, 380 species of birds, 7 varieties of monkey, and 100 species of fish, along with thousands of species of insects.

And all those years ago, when a battered teen was all alone in that jungle, not a single one of those plants or animals kept her from finding her way home. Juliane will never forget that. "The jungle is as much a part of me as my love for my husband, the music of the people who live along the Amazon and its tributaries, and the scars that remain from the plane crash."

In online games, about 60 percent of female characters are played by male players.

LET'S JUST CALL IT CANADA, EH?

The area was called that as least as far back as the 1500s. But Canada's founders strongly floated the possibility of naming the country something else.

🍁 Oh, Kanata

In 1534, French explorer Jacques Cartier encountered Iroquois near the St. Lawrence River. The Iroquois referred to the region as *Kanata*, which means "village." As European settlers moved into the area, within a decade *Kanata* was appearing on maps, but with the spelling C-A-N-A-D-A. By the 1610s, the entire eastern portion of northern North America was called Canada, and by the 1700s, anything not officially claimed by the United States was known by that name—what's now the state of Louisiana was deemed part of *Canada*. By the 1860s, Upper Canada and Lower Canada had formed into Quebec and united with the province of Ontario, as well as the Maritime provinces of Nova Scotia and New Brunswick, confederated into a new nation. On July 1, 1867, the Dominion of Canada was established.

Before confederation, the chief lawmaking body in the region was the Legislative Assembly of the Province of Canada. It's this chamber that united the separate provinces into the Dominion of Canada (while remaining part of the British commonwealth, with Queen Victoria its figurehead leader) in 1867. This body was also responsible for coming up with the name of the newly formed, hypothetical country. In 1865, its members had submitted ideas for consideration, and heard arguments for more than two dozen potential names.

Acadia. This suggestion was a nod to colonial history. France established the area of New France in the 1600s, which included the colony of Acadia. It eventually became a British territory and was split into the provinces of Quebec, Nova Scotia, Prince Edward Island, and New Brunswick.

Victorialand, Victorialia, Albertland, Albertoria. Hoping to win favor with Queen Victoria while also declaring autonomy, some Canadian leaders proposed naming the country after either Victoria or her husband, Prince Albert.

Albona, New Albion, Albionora. *Albion* derives from a Greek word for "white"; inspired by the White Cliffs of Dover on England's southeastern coast, it's an ancient, classical name for Great Britain or the British Isles. Since Canada was developed in part by the British, lawmakers almost called the country by some variant, including Albona, New Albion, or Albionora, which means "Albion of the North."

King Henry VIII's six wives were all related to him through a common ancestor. (And Anne Boleyn and Catherine Howard were first cousins.)

Britannica, Brittania. Variations on *Britain*.

Borealia. Canada is a very northern place. *Borealia* is Latin for "northern."

Aquilonia. Another Latin-based phrase that means, roughly, "northern."

Norland. It means, roughly, "land in the north."

Vesperia. A Latin phrase lifted from ancient Roman mythology, it translates to "place of the evening star."

Colonia. As in "colony." The country was, after all, a colony of the U.K., even though it was also its own semiautonomous nation under the crown.

Efisga. It's an acronym, in which each letter is taken from the first letter referring to the background of the primary population of Canada at the time: England, France, Ireland, Scotland, Germany, and Aboriginal.

Tupona, Tuponia. Another acronym (and one with an unnecessary extra letter) short for a more formal name: The United Provinces of North America.

Ursalia. Latin for "place of the great bears." There are lots of bears in Canada.

Hochelaga. There are lots of beavers in Canada, so many that the beaver is the nation's official animal. *Hochelaga* means "beaver path" in the Iroquois language, and it was also the name of an indigenous community in what's now Quebec.

Canadensia. *Canada* is an anglicized version of the Iroquois *Kanata*, and *Canadensia* is a false Latin version of "Canada."

Transylvania. Now part of Romania and once a Germanic region, a significant number of people from the area of Transylvania settled in Canada in the 1800s.

Laurentia. European exploration and settlement in Canada started in the area surrounding the St. Lawrence River, named for classical leader and Catholic saint Lawrence of Rome.

Mesopelagia. It means "the land between seas."

Niagarentia. It refers to one of eastern Canada's most majestic natural features: Niagara Falls.

Superior. The representative who suggested *Superior* didn't mean to refer to the border body of water of Lake Superior; he wanted to use it to show the world that this new country was better, or superior, to all others.

Transatlantica. It means "crossing the Atlantic," which is what European settlers had to do to get to the New World.

Canada. The legislature created the Dominion of Canada in 1867. That stayed the official name of the country for 115 years. After several years of effort, the U.K. parliament passed the Canada Act in 1982, which fully severed the country from English rule...and Canada dropped "Dominion of" from the name.

Green beans, pinto beans, and kidney beans are all from the same species of bean.

THE FIRST PLAYER TO...

One way to get into the record books: be the first player to...

WEAR A FACE MASK IN AN NHL GAME

Player: Jacques Plante, goalie for the Montreal Canadiens

Story: On November 1, 1959, at Madison Square Garden, Plante was hit in the face by a puck that came whizzing off the stick of New York Rangers forward Andy Bathgate. Plante wasn't wearing a face mask—and now he had a broken nose and massive cut to show for it. Nearly 30 years earlier, the Montreal Maroons' goalie Clint Benedict wore a leather mask (after a puck broke *his* nose) for a few games, but he didn't like it and it didn't catch on. Prior to that night's game, Plante had made himself a white fiberglass goalie mask with two eye holes, but Canadiens coach Toe Blake would let him wear it only during practice.

After the team doctor stitched Plante up, the goalie told Coach Blake he'd go back on the ice only with his fiberglass mask on. All right, said Blake, but it had to come off as soon as the face healed.

The Canadiens won that game, and then went on a winning streak. The team credited the mask; when Plante's stitches were removed, he played the next game maskless...and they lost. The next night, the mask was back on, and Coach Blake never said another word about it. "When I first put on the mask," recalled Blake, "the boys all told me I would scare the women. They wouldn't come to see the games anymore. I'll tell you something, if I went on the way I was going, pretty soon my face would look worse than the mask." Instead, pretty soon, every NHL goalie was wearing one.

Bonus Fact: Fictional serial killer Jason Voorhees's signature mask, first introduced in 1982's *Friday the 13th Part III*, was a 1970 Jacques Plante Elite FibroSport.

SHATTER AN NBA BACKBOARD

Player: Gus "Honeycomb" Johnson, power forward for the Baltimore Bullets (now the Washington Wizards)

Story: Imagine Charles Barkley traveling back in time to play on a 1960s NBA team, and that's what Hall of Famer Honeycomb Johnson looked like on the court. When the average player was 6'5" (three inches shorter than today) and less than 200 pounds, Johnson—at 6'6" and 235 pounds—wasn't only a little bigger than most other players but faster, too. And he was one of the original "slam dunkers."

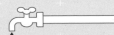

In 1964, while the Bullets were playing against the St. Louis Hawks, 6'6" power forward Bill Bridges was standing in front of the basket, trying to prevent Johnson from dunking. Johnson didn't like that, so he muscled his way in and dunked the ball with such force that the glass backboard shattered. It took half an hour to get a new rim installed, the same length of time it took to get all the glass out of Johnson's hair.

That wouldn't be the last backboard shattered by Johnson, and soon a rule was enacted that all venues had to have backup backboards on hand. They'd need them, thanks to notorious backboard shatterers such as Darryl Dawkins, who shattered two in 1979, and then Michael Jordan, and then the worst of them all: Shaquille O'Neal. After the league "Shaq-proofed" the baskets with stronger steel in 1992—and made it a technical foul to intentionally shatter one—backboards don't break as much any more.

SPIKE A FOOTBALL AFTER AN NFL TOUCHDOWN

Player: Homer Jones, wide receiver for the New York Giants

Story: Though he played in the 1960s, Jones is *still* the NFL's all-time leading receiver with 22.3 yards per catch. He caught 36 touchdowns in 87 games before his career was cut short in 1970. His first touchdown catch came in 1965, and it's the one he's most remembered for. Jones had told himself that the first time he scored a touchdown, "I was gonna throw the ball in the stands, but they changed the rules in the offseason to I think a $500 fine," he later recalled. "And as I crossed the goal line...I thought about that $500 and I threw it on the ground." The crowd roared, and Jones not only invented the spike, but he coined the term for it.

Bonus Fact: In the first ever *Monday Night Football* game in 1970, Jones became the first player in *MNF* history to score a touchdown on a kickoff return.

HIT A HOME RUN

Player: Roscoe Barnes, second baseman for the Chicago White Stockings (now the Cubs)

Story: On May 2, 1876, the National Association of Professional Ball Players, later shortened to the National League, played its first game, marking the birth of the Major Leagues. The game was a lot different back then. The parks (so called because the first baseball fields were in parks) were much larger, so hitting the ball out of one was rare. This was also before the "live ball" era, which made hitting homers easier. And catching the ball on one bounce was an out: that made it poor strategy to hit for distance; instead, batters tried to slap base hits between the infielders.

Average length of time it takes to exhaust a fire extinguisher: 25 seconds.

But not Roscoe Barnes. He'd been called a "seceder" for leaving Boston to play in the new league, and he wanted to make his mark. He stepped up to the plate against Cincinnati Reds ace pitcher Cherokee Fisher. As the *Chicago Tribune* reported, "Barnes, coming to the bat with two men out, made the finest hit of the game, straight down the left field to the carriages, for a clean home run." Notice it said "to the carriages." That's because the long ball was so rare that fans' horse-drawn carriages were parked in the outfield. The ball sailed over them, and then over the fence where hardly anybody was because no one knew how many millions of dollars that ball would be worth some day. (Current whereabouts: unknown.)

THROW A (LEGAL) FORWARD PASS IN COLLEGE FOOTBALL

Player: Bradbury Robinson, quarterback for St. Louis University

Story: Between 1900 and 1905—more than a decade before American football was a professional sport but when college football was wildly popular—there were at least 45 nationwide deaths at the high school and university levels thanks to the violence inherent in the game. In addition to the lack of protective gear for players, there was another critical element of the modern game missing at the time: the forward pass. Up until that point, football play was based on scrums, similar to rugby, and throwing the ball beyond the line of scrimmage was against the rules.

In 1905, amid calls to abolish the game altogether and under pressure from President Theodore Roosevelt to establish safety reforms (Roosevelt's eldest son was on the freshman team at Harvard), representatives from 62 colleges met to institute changes intended to make the game safer. Legalizing the forward pass was just one such change...though there was little enthusiasm for it among the powerhouse schools of the time. There were offensive penalties for incomplete passes and dropped passes; there was also a stigma among football purists, who felt that passing was for "sissies" and didn't count as real football. Just two coaches had interest in the overhand spiral, and today they have credit for introducing it to the game: Howard "Bosey" Reiter of Wesleyan University and Eddie Cochems of St. Louis University.

On September 5, 1906, Cochems's quarterback Bradbury Robinson threw an incomplete pass that resulted in a turnover in a scoreless game against Carroll College. But later in the game, he completed a 20-yard throw to Jack Schneider, and St. Louis University went on to a 22-0 victory. The accomplishment produced little fanfare. However, a month later, Wesleyan quarterback Sam Moore threw a completion to Irwin van Tassel in a game against Yale. That got the press's attention—and inspired other coaches at other schools to incorporate the forward pass into their offenses in the coming years.

Largest ring size on Earth: one man's finger has a 4.78" circumference.

LOST IN TRANSLATION

When signs in foreign countries are written in English, any combination
of words is possible. Here are some real-life examples.

On a store window in Japan: "The toilet is a parking lot."

On a toy plane in Malaysia: "Let the life burning infinite morale!"

On a trash can in China: "Life rubbish."

In a hotel room in Italy: "For a proper service, please turn on the vacuum cleaner when using the shower."

At a dog park in South Korea: "When you defecate your pet, please remove it with defecation envelop."

Outside a forest in Japan: "In case of monkeys are in the forest, you can not find them."

On a trail in China: "Slip carefully"

On a package of steel wool in Asia: "The copper wire sweeps the ball."

On a hotel buffet in Iraq: "Paul is dead."

At an airport in Japan: "Beware of your belongings"

In an airport in India: "Eating carpet strictly prohibited."

On a "wet floor" sign in Singapore: "Execution in progress."

On a menu in South Korea: "Magnetic field, a bowl of rice capped"

On a hammer: "Do not strike any surface other than face."

On a can of compressed air: "Do not abuse or inhale the human body"

On extra-strength glue: "Is a surprise adhesive force. This was a great adhesive. "

On a children's stacking toy: "Don't keep the toy in the mouth to prevent children."

On a toy airplane: "The models made according to the scale of the real thing so that it is lifelike and breathing."

On a meat tenderizer: "The tail with a hanging hole, may receive."

On horse medicine: "Concentrated stomach happy"

In a video for a cooking pan: "Spin the feeling of taste buds."

At a park in Japan: "Do not disturb. Tiny grass is dreaming."

At a zoo in South Korea: "Don't snack on animals."

On a barber shop sign in Vietnam: "Could not connect to translator service"

About a third of all humans possess more than the standard 206 bones.

MUSICAL LISTS

These two pages are brought to you by Franz Liszt.

12 SINGERS WHO GO BY THEIR FIRST NAME

1. Beyoncé (Knowles)
2. Adele (Adkins)
3. Madonna (Ciccone)
4. Beck (Hansen)
5. Prince (Rogers Nelson)
6. Usher (Raymond IV)
7. Kesha (Sebert)
8. Shakira (Mebarak Ripoll)
9. Brandy (Norwood)
10. Jewel (Kilcher)
11. Cher (Sarkisian)
12. Björk (Guðmundsdóttir)

TOP 10 INSTRUMENTS AMERICANS PLAY (*NEWSWEEK*, 2022)

1. Piano/keyboard (27%)
2. Acoustic guitar (20%)
3. Violin (19%)
4. Electric guitar (18%)
5. Drums (18%)
6. Voice/singing (18%)
7. Saxophone (17%)
8. DJ equipment (16%)
9. Trumpet (16%)
10. Bass (16%)

8 TYPES OF MUSICALS

1. Book musicals
2. Jukebox musicals
3. Revue musicals
4. Rock musicals
5. Concept musicals
6. Operettas
7. Pastiche musicals
8. Disney-style musicals

10 BEST-KNOWN CLASSICAL MUSIC PIECES (CLASSIC FM)

1. "Eine kleine Nachtmusik" (Mozart)
2. "Für Elise" (Beethoven)
3. "O mio babbino caro" from *Gianni Schicchi* (Puccini)
4. "Toccata and Fugue in D minor" (Bach)
5. "Symphony No.5 in C minor" (Beethoven)
6. "The Four Seasons" (Vivaldi)
7. "Carmen" (Bizet)
8. "The Blue Danube" (Johann Strauss II)
9. "Boléro" (Ravel)
10. "Flower Duet" from *Lakmé* (Delibes)

5 POPULAR SINGERS WITH THE GREATEST VOCAL RANGE

1. Axl Rose
2. Prince
3. Mariah Carey
4. Steven Tyler
5. Christina Aguilera

TOP-SELLING ALBUMS OF THE 1960s (U.S.)

1960: *The Sound of Music* (Original Broadway Cast)

1961: *Camelot* (Original Broadway Cast)

1962: *West Side Story* (Soundtrack)

1963: *West Side Story* (Soundtrack)

1964: *Hello, Dolly!* (Original Broadway Cast)

1965: *Mary Poppins* (Soundtrack)

1966: *Whipped Cream & Other Delights* (Herb Alpert & the Tijuana Brass)

1967: *More of the Monkees* (The Monkees)

1968: *Are You Experienced?* (The Jimi Hendrix Experience)

1969: *In-A-Gadda-Da-Vida* (Iron Butterfly)

TOP-SELLING ALBUMS OF THE 2000s (U.S.)

2000: *No Strings Attached* (*NSYNC)

2001: *Hybrid Theory* (Linkin Park)

2002: *The Eminem Show* (Eminem)

2003: *Get Rich or Die Tryin'* (50 Cent)

2004: *Confessions* (Usher)

2005: *The Emancipation of Mimi* (Mariah Carey)

2006: *High School Musical* (Various)

2007: *Noël* (Josh Groban)

2008: *Tha Carter III* (Lil Wayne)

2009: *Fearless* (Taylor Swift)

THE SOUNDTRACK FOR YOUR WEEK

1. "Sunday Bloody Sunday" (U2)
2. "Manic Monday" (The Bangles)
3. "Ruby Tuesday" (The Rolling Stones)
4. "Wednesday Morning, 3 A.M." (Simon & Garfunkel)
5. "I Lost Thursday" (They Might Be Giants)
6. "Friday I'm in Love" (The Cure)
7. "One More Saturday Night" (The Grateful Dead)

TOP 10 MUSIC GENRES WORLDWIDE (PRIMESOUND.ORG, 2023)

1. Pop
2. Rock
3. Hip-hop/rap
4. Electronic dance music (EDM)
5. Country
6. Jazz
7. Classical
8. R&B/soul
9. Indie/alternative
10. Latin

IMPACT'S 8 BEST BREAKUP SONGS OF THE 2010s

1. "Marvin's Room" (Drake)
2. "Miss Missing You" (Fall Out Boy)
3. "Somebody That I Used to Know" (Gotye feat. Kimbra)
4. "Nights" (Frank Ocean)
5. "Drunk II" (Mannequin Pussy)
6. "Wrecking Ball" (Miley Cyrus)
7. "The One That Got Away" (Katy Perry)
8. "Don't Hurt Yourself" (Beyoncé feat. Jack White)

5 QUESTIONABLE COUNTRY SONGS

1. "Why'd You Come in Here Lookin' Like That?" (Dolly Parton)
2. "Whose Bed Have Your Boots Been Under?" (Shania Twain)
3. "Who's Cheatin' Who?" (Alan Jackson)
4. "Who's Your Daddy?" (Toby Keith)
5. "Is It Cold in Here (or Is It Just You)?" (Joe Diffie)

BILLBOARD HOT 100 CHART TOPPERS IN 3 SEPARATE DECADES

1. Stevie Wonder
2. Michael Jackson
3. Elton John
4. Janet Jackson
5. Madonna
6. Christina Aguilera
7. Britney Spears
8. Usher

BILLBOARD HOT 100 CHART TOPPER IN 4 SEPARATE DECADES

1. Mariah Carey

Longest rhino horn ever found: just a smidge under five feet.

BATHROOM NEWS

Here's the latest scoop on all the news that involves poop.
(Warning: this page is not for the squeamish.)

Seat of Power

A king is just a man on a throne, after all: to make sure he can always "go" where he wants, the way he wants, it's rumored that newly coronated King Charles III of the United Kingdom always brings a custom-made toilet seat whenever he travels to one of the royal family's country estates or overseas on official state business. Also on his packing list is an ample supply of Velvet, a Kleenex-made high-end toilet paper that costs more and is softer than regular store brands.

No Movement in the Bathroom

In November 2022, firefighters and rescue workers were summoned to the home of Kay Stewart in the English town of Wallsend, North Tyneside. It was on account of a bathroom emergency: her two-year-old potty-training daughter, Harper, was trying to use the commode when she complained that she was "stuck"—she'd somehow removed the toilet seat, stuck it around her neck, and then couldn't get it off. After Stewart and her teenage daughter were unable to remove the seat on their own, they called Tyne and Wear Fire and Rescue Service. A crew used a series of small tools to remove the seat. "Harper gave the firefighter a big hug once he was done," Stewart said.

All Backed Up

One of the claims to fame of the ancient Tofukuji Temple in Kyoto, Japan, is that the sacred Buddhist site is home to the oldest restroom in the country. Or at least it *was*, until October 2022. A 30-year-old man (unnamed in news reports) representing, ironically, the Kyoto Heritage Preservation Association, parked his car in front of the wooden-doored chamber; when he hit the gas to drive away, he didn't realize the vehicle was in reverse. He plowed the car backward through the bathroom door, destroying it as well as the inner walls of the chamber. "We've been told it's going to require a lot of work to restore," a Kyoto Police spokesperson said. Thankfully, the actual pit-style latrines didn't suffer much damage.

Flea Had to Flee

While on tour with his band the Red Hot Chili Peppers in April 2023, bassist Flea walked to a Target store in Minneapolis near his hotel to buy a few things. While taking some photos with employees, he explained in a series of tweets, he was hit

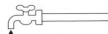

NASA banned beans from in-flight meals because they produce too much flatulence.

with a "major urge to take a s***." Target employees sent him in the direction of the bathrooms, where a line 10 people deep thwarted his efforts. "I'm about to soil my trousers," he said, so he begged to use the employee bathroom. They refused. "I run across the street to some café and ask to use the bathroom," Flea said, only to be denied by the employee on duty, who also threatened to call a security guard for even asking. "I made it by the skin of my teeth to a restaurant a few blocks away."

A Blanket Statement

A TikTok user who goes by the name madwil went viral in early 2023 for sharing her bathroom habits with the world—via an arts-and-crafts interpretation. Parodying and expanding on the TikTok fad of "temperature blankets," in which crocheters add a new line of yarn each day of a year based on the appearance of the sky, madwil made a blanket where each section corresponds to a different day's worth of bowel movement undertaken in 2022. "One row a day in which the color of the yarn was determined by the number of s***s I took the previous day," she says in a video. "The texture of my s*** determined the stitch." By the end of the year, she had a large, 365-row crocheted blanket—primarily brown, green, and other dark shades.

Reeking and Ranking

In January 2023, a second-round match of the Australian Open, part of the "Grand Slam" of professional tennis tournaments, was besieged by a group of seagulls. One wasn't shy about needing to go, and dropped a load from the sky, where it landed right in the middle of the mop of blond hair sported by tennis player Alexander Zverev. He smiled at getting bombed and wiped it off with a towel while the spectators laughed. Zverev ultimately lost the match to opponent Michael Mmoh. It was something of an upset, as Zverev was once ranked...number two.

A Liquid You Shouldn't Flush

A Nashville man (unnamed in news reports) left his rental home in April 2022 following a fight with his partner, the mother of two older teenage boys. During the man's two-month absence, his former partner was arrested and jailed on an unrelated matter, leaving her two sons in the home to fend for themselves. After the boys received an eviction notice, their mother suggested "she would have destroyed the house" before leaving, so the teens did just that: among their destructive acts, they ripped electrical wire out of the walls, nailed a door to the roof, and, most egregious, poured cement into the toilet. They later told their mother they flushed the cement-filled toilet until the handle broke off. The Nashville man returned to an utterly destroyed and empty home upon which the boys had inflicted $200,000 worth of property damage.

Shrews look like they're rodents, but they aren't—they're related to hedgehogs.

A BRIEF HISTORY OF WEATHER MANIPULATION

It's a truism: "You can't control the weather." Well, many humans and organizations through history have wondered, what if we could? Over the last 200 years or so, governments, militaries, and farmers have all had their own reasons for wanting there to be more rain or less rain, and scientists have tried to figure out how to change the weather. Were any of them successful? Kind of...

1841   American meteorologist James Pollard Espy, later a weather consultant to the U.S. government and considered the father of scientific weather forecasting, theorizes in his book The Philosophy of Storms that rainfall could be triggered by fires—but only large, raging wildfires. His logic is related to his convection theory, which holds that air heated by the fire rises into the atmosphere, which attracts other airflows to rush to meet it laterally. That fire creates its own small weather system fueled by convection currents that go on to form cumulus clouds, which produce rain. (Forest fires do occasionally produce rain in this manner, but not much...and not always.)

1871   Scientist Edward Powers publishes *War and Weather.* Powers collects firsthand accounts from soldiers, as well as orally passed-down accounts, of a possible connection between heavy artillery and rainfall. According to numerous witnesses who fought in the Seven Years' War, the Napoleonic Wars, and other conflicts in Europe in the 1700s and 1800s, every major battle was immediately followed by a rainstorm. Powers theorizes that the explosions of cannons and bombs create shock waves so strong that they shake the sky, forcing clouds to then shake off their accumulated precipitation. This legend spread through northern Europe throughout the preceding two centuries, evolving into the notion that cannon fire brings rain but prevents hail. Seeking to avoid crop-destroying, economically devastating hailstorms, farming communities throughout the continent routinely fire cannons as a preventative measure.

1891   Acting on a heavily researched theory that smoke particulates released into the atmosphere act as nuggets of condensation that urge clouds

Oyster mushrooms are carnivores: their excretions paralyze nematode worms so the mushrooms can eat them.

to condense water vapor and create rain (similar to Espy's theory), the U.S. Department of War decides to put the idea to the test. The agency purchases a large volume of gunpowder and explosives ($9,000 worth, or $320,000 in 2023 money) and sets up a test site in Texas that also tests the European cannon theory. After staging hundreds of explosions, the results are inconclusive—it does rain after some of the explosions, but that could easily have just happened naturally.

1930 The birth of sophisticated aviation allows the concept of cloud seeding to be developed—the process by which planes can drop chemicals into clouds to forcibly produce rain. Dutch scientist August W. Veraart uses dry ice (frozen carbon dioxide) and supercooled ice crystals. Results are mild, but promising.

1946 General Electric scientists Dr. Irving Langmuir and Dr. Vincent J. Schaefer are hired by the U.S. Chemical Warfare Board to research how gas masks work, and how to improve them. During cold-weather testing, the pair notice that planes develop ice building from cloud particles. That spurs them to look into how ice accumulates in clouds. In a laboratory setting, they observe that crystals of dry ice applied to supercooled clouds create water ice crystals; those crystals only float within the cloud, not fall. In November 1946, Langmuir and Schaefer send a plane to scatter dry ice pellets into a cloud from above, and the crystals get so enlarged that they fall out of the clouds—in other words, it rains. Langmuir and Schaefer's "cloud-seeding" ideas lead to the discovery that loads of microscopic silver iodide crystals create more rain extraction from clouds than do water-based ice or carbon dioxide–based dry ice.

1947 Military branches come together to work on "Project Cirrus," an emergency, real-world test of cloud seeding. Identifying a hurricane seemingly moving safely out into the Atlantic Ocean near Florida, an air force B-17 bomber drops 175 pounds of dry ice into the storm's cloud cover. Researchers observe that the clouds are altered somewhat, but the dry-ice payload doesn't seem to change the storm's power or precipitation. However, when the hurricane reverses course and makes landfall in Georgia, military higher-ups get scared that Project Cirrus has backfired and made the storm more powerful. (Hurricanes often change direction; Project Cirrus hasn't used nearly enough dry ice to change the storm.)

1954 | William Reich, a psychoanalyst who claims to have grown grass in the desert and cured cancer in a handful of patients, announces that "orgone energy" (a substance he claims to have discovered), abundant in the atmosphere, can be manipulated into producing rain. To execute "cosmic orgone engineering," he develops a cloud-buster, which works like a lightning rod. Made from a series of hollow metal tubes and pipes grounded in orgone-rich material (a natural waterbody), it is aimed at a place in the sky thought to be rich in orgone. (It doesn't work.)

1962 | Between this time and 1983, military personnel secretly run a Project Cirrus successor called Project Stormfury. The goal: weaken hurricanes and tropical storms by flying planes into them and seeding the walls of the eyes, where the power originates, with silver iodide. Results are inconclusive.

1967 | Later revealed in a series of top-secret Congressional hearings, a public disclosure in the mid-1970s, and declassified government documents in the 2010s, the U.S. military wages "Operation Popeye," a five-year battle to make the weather worse in Vietnam. The reason: to ensure a quicker victory for the U.S.-aligned South Vietnamese against the communist Viet Cong during the Vietnam War. High-ranking members of the military theorize that making the troop and supply routes utilized by the Viet Cong impassable, or substantially more difficult to traverse, could secure a win for South Vietnam. Monsoon season in Vietnam is from May to December; a combination of temperatures in the 90°F range, combined with a 90-percent humidity level, high winds, and heavy rains make torrential storms a near daily occurrence. Major cities get as much precipitation in one month during monsoon season as the U.S. state of Arizona receives in one year.

According to research that began in 1966, the Viet Cong's primary access route, the Ho Chi Minh Trail, grows tougher (but not impossible) to navigate during monsoon season, what with the extra rain and mud. Operation Popeye, if effective, would ruin the Ho Chi Minh Trail by stretching out monsoon season and making it more severe. With the Viet Cong trapped, the well-funded, U.S.-led military campaign could know where the enemy fighters congregated and eliminate them through bombing.

Using the cloud-seeding technology developed by General Electric scientists Langmuir and Schaefer in the 1940s, U.S. pilots fly over targeted regions of Vietnam with cargo of silver and lead iodide canisters. Crews ignite and then release the cannisters, sending particle-laden smoke into a storm. If it goes correctly, the newly injected artificial chemicals will cause a chain reaction through the whole weather system, forcefully making it rain longer and harder. They do this consistently, for five years, at an annual cost of $3.6 million ($23 million in 2023 money). Operation Popeye is called off in 1972 after Richard Nixon testified to Congress that the program is a myth, and when results prove inconclusive and impossible to verify.

1969   Troubled by the idea of drought ruining Thailand's agricultural industries, King Bhumibol ordered the formation of the Thailand Royal Rainmaking Project in 1954. More than 80 percent of Thai agriculture depended on direct rainfall, and in 1969, the first rainmaking attempt is conducted at Khao Yai National Park, with dry ice flakes dropped by planes into clouds from above. Some rainfall results, but the Thai crown keeps at it. Later renaming the project the Department of Royal Rainmaking and Agricultural Aviation, the government of Thailand claims that 89 percent of its thousands of annual cloud-seeding projects (which continue to the present day) have resulted in substantial rainfall.

2002   Florida, where hurricanes are a deadly and devastating force of nature each year, is the home of Dyn-O-Mat, a corporation that develops a chemical that founder Peter Cordani claims can reduce the strength of a hurricane. Utilizing and supercharging technology similar to that which makes disposable diapers absorbent, Dyn-O-Gel is a powdered polymer that Dyn-O-Mat says can soak up 1,500 times its weight. If dropped into clouds to remove moisture, the theory goes, the storm uses up all its energy to move out the suddenly heavy water molecules, thereby disarming the hurricane. Then when the rain-gel mixture falls into the ocean, it reportedly dissolves, because saltwater doesn't absorb the same way that fresh water does. Dyn-O-Mat hires a private organization that buys and uses decommissioned military aircraft to drop 9,000 pounds of Dyn-O-Gel into a storm cell brewing off the east coast of Florida. Data released shows that everything goes according to plan. But in 2003, Dyn-O-Gel will be ordered to cease operations. The National Oceanic and Atmospheric Organization claims that while Dyn-O-Gel may have worked on a small storm, it wouldn't be a practical solution for large storm systems, like a tropical cyclone or a hurricane.

We're here for you: according to research, 300 million people around the world are friendless.

OCTOPUS ~~TENTACLES~~ ~~LEGS~~ ARMS

Octopuses are such interesting creatures that we can fill two pages of facts about just their long, squishy, squiggly, sucker-y appendages!

DON'T CALL THEM TENTACLES

- It's not completely wrong to call the arms of the octopus "tentacles"—as long as that word is being used as a generally accepted umbrella term for any elongated, flexible appendage. But, technically, tentacles and arms are different.
- Tentacles are elongated organs—that usually come in pairs—with suckers or hooks at the tips that can both detect and catch prey. (Those four things coming off a slug's head, for instance, are tentacles.) They're also retractable.
- The octopus's arms are shorter than tentacles, thicker at the base, and don't retract. Arms have suckers going up and down their full length. Squids and cuttlefish have eight arms and two even longer feeding tentacles. But octopuses don't need tentacles to feed; their arms are more than capable of doing the job.

THE HEADIEST OF THE HEAD FOOTS

- Octopuses belong to the class of animals known as *Cephalopoda*, which comes from the Greek words for "head foot" because they kind of look like swimming feet with long toes. Other cephalopods include squid, cuttlefish, and nautiluses. But the octopus truly is at the head of the class with the most neurons of all the invertebrates: 500 million. That's about the same as a dog.
- Here's where it gets really weird: more than 60 percent of those neurons are located in the octopus's arms. These interconnected mini brains can not only communicate with one another but perform tasks (such as opening a clam) independently of the brain. As the octopus crawls along the ocean floor, its arms are busy testing the water or reaching into crevices to find prey.

A SUCKER BORN EVERY MINUTE

- Octopuses have 2,240 suckers (that's 280 per arm), each equipped with chemical sensors that allow the animal to feel, taste, and smell its surroundings.
- The suckers are incredibly strong, which makes an octopus a formidable opponent. It can grip a tightly shut clam and—using brains *and* brawn—pry the shell apart.

Fruity fact: limes sink, lemons float.

🐙 TWO LEGS TO STAND ON

- Some species of octopus use their rear two arms like legs. While holding the other six arms up—or in a ball around them—these swift cephalopods literally run across the sea floor faster than if they were crawling on all eight arms (but slower than when jetting themselves backward through the water).
- They don't use the end of the arms like we use our feet; as the end of each arm alternately hits the sea floor, the suckers lift up like rolling tank treads.
- Walking on two feet also allows the octopus to remain camouflaged while moving, which it can't do while crawling on all its arms.

🐙 THE ARMS HAVE EYES

Octopuses can't actually see with their arms, but they have proteins called *opsins* (the same receptors in human eyes) that sense even subtle changes in light. This gives the octopus yet another way to detect movement when reaching into dark places to find food.

🐙 INSTANT TURTLES

Some species of octopus use their arms to carry coconut shells or clam shells around. When a predator approaches, they can quickly hide inside, protecting their soft exterior. Per zoologists, this makes octopuses the only invertebrates that use tools.

🐙 IT'LL GROW BACK

- Lizards can famously grow their tails back, but the replacement tail doesn't get as big or as developed as the original. Not so with the octopus. When it loses an arm, it grows back—exactly as it was before—in about 130 days.
- Because it has a mini brain, a severed arm will stay "alive" for up to five hours. It will wiggle around and even react to pain stimuli. If an octopus's camouflage and ink cloud have failed against a foe, the last resort is to "drop" an arm and then make a quick getaway while the predator goes after the writhing appendage.

🐙 WATCH WHERE YOU STICK THAT THING

The Swiss Army knife that is the octopus has yet another trick up its sleeve: the *hectocotylus*. Or, if you prefer, the sex arm, which is essentially a modified penis. It's found at the tip of a specialized arm on the male with a specialized hook at the end. The details vary from species to species, but it boils down to this: after a bizarre octopus mating ritual, the male inserts the hectocotylus into the female's mantle and deposits the spermatophore (a protein capsule full of sperm). Then (in most species) the male leaves the arm there, and then goes off and dies. The female lays eggs and guards them with her life until she too dies.

A bite from a macaw is about twice as hard as a bite from a German shepherd or tiger shark.

STRANGE LAWSUITS

These days, it seems like people will sue each other over practically anything. Here are some real-life examples of unusual legal battles.

The Plaintiff: Mauro Restrepo

The Defendant: Sophia Adams, owner of Psychic Love Specialist by Sophia in Inglewood, California

The Lawsuit: In September 2021, Restrepo was having marriage troubles, so he went online to find a psychic and selected Adams. At her home parlor, she performed a tarot card reading and, according to the lawsuit, informed Restrepo that he was a victim of *mala suerte*, a curse of "bad luck" placed on him by a "witch hired by his ex-girlfriend." The psychic then told him there's a special crystal that can remove the curse, but it cost $5,100. Restrepo didn't have that kind of money. He claimed that she told him if he didn't buy the crystal, his luck would get worse and his family would be "unhappy and in danger." He gave her a $1,000 deposit. She said she'd order the crystal once she had payment in full.

Two months later, Restrepo sued Adams for "fraud, negligence, emotional distress and civil conspiracy," claiming she had no intention of removing the curse. Furthermore, he said the "PhD" she said she received "for special schooling" was fraudulent. He also named Adams's husband and daughter in the suit, as well as the landlord of the house she ran her business from.

The Psychic Love Specialist herself tells a different story: all she told Restropo after the tarot reading was that he's "unlucky in love." She denied talking about a curse, and said she would have given back the deposit if he didn't want the crystal, if he's just asked.

The Verdict: Case dismissed, on the basis that there wasn't enough evidence to move forward. So Restrepo filed a new complaint; that was dismissed as well. After the third dismissal, the suit was dismissed "without prejudice," which means he can still sue Adams again if he wants.

The Plaintiff: Anjanaffy Njewadda

The Defendant: Showtime, CBS, the New York City Transit Authority, and MTA

The Lawsuit: In 2013, Njewadda was walking down the stairs to the subway at Grand Central station when she tripped, fell, and injured her ankle. She claimed in her lawsuit that she fell because she got scared by a poster advertising the Showtime serial-killer drama *Dexter*. The picture on the poster was of the titular character

First band to use billboards to advertise: The Doors.

(Michael C. Hall) made up to look like a corpse; there's a plastic sheet over his face, and his eyes are wide open. Njewadda said that Showtime intentionally created a hazard for passersby by creating a poster that's "disturbing, provocative, shocking, and fear inducing." And everyone associated with the placement of the ad in the subway station was culpable, too.

The Verdict: In 2019, Judge Shlomo Hagler ruled against Njewadda, conceding, "It is uncontroverted that there was no defect or dangerous condition on the stairs but rather plaintiff's fall was caused by her reaction to the *Dexter* advertisement." But the network has no "duty of care" to ensure their posters don't startle anyone.

The Plaintiff: Phillip White of Los Angeles, California

The Defendant: T. W. Garner Food Co. of Winston-Salem, North Carolina, which makes Texas Pete Original Hot Sauce

The Lawsuit: In 2022, White bought a bottle of Texas Pete's for $3 at a Los Angeles supermarket. But it wasn't until he got home and read the fine print on the bottle that he learned the truth: Texas Pete's is made in...North Carolina! White would have never bought it if he'd known that, so he filed a class action suit against T. W. Garner for false advertising. "By way of its false marketing and labeling," the complaint alleges, Texas Pete's "knowingly and intentionally capitalizes on consumers' desire to partake in the culture and authentic cuisine of one of the most prideful states in America." He's seeking an unspecified amount of damages and for Texas Pete's to change its name and branding.

Garner's legal team countered that it says right there on the label that Texas Pete is made in North Carolina, where it has been manufactured since 1929. In addition, "a reasonable consumer would understand that the trademark symbol next to the 'Texas Pete' name shows that it's a brand." Furthermore, the images on the bottle of the star and cowboy could signify states other than Texas. (The company's website says that hot sauce creator Sam Garner chose "Pete" because it was his son's name and "Texas" because it sounded "American.")

The Verdict: Pending. A judge denied T. W. Garner's motion for dismissal on the grounds that, "though it is true that the imagery of the solo white star and lassoing caricature are not exclusive to the state of Texas," a consumer "could believe—erroneously—that the products originated in Texas." (We'll update this in a future edition, but in the meantime, if you see a bottle of "North Carolina Pete" in the grocery store, you'll know how the case turned out.)

The Plaintiff: Raphael Samuel, a business executive from Mumbai, India

The United States exports more blood plasma each year than it does pickup trucks.

The Defendants: His parents

The Lawsuit: Antinatalism is the philosophical belief that having children is immoral. The thinking goes that very few people end up being truly happy, so it's far too risky to create a person without their consent and subject him or her to a life rife with pain and suffering that will end only in death. But if antinatalism is taken to its logical conclusion, wouldn't that spell the end of our species? That's the point, says Samuel. "If humanity is extinct, Earth and animals would be happier," he told the BBC. "Also no human will then suffer. Human existence is totally pointless." In 2019, when he announced he was suing his parents for having him, he said that when he called to tell them (they're both lawyers), his mother responded, "That's fine, but don't expect me to go easy on you. I will destroy you in court."

The Verdict: At last report, Samuel still hadn't found a lawyer that would represent him, but he said his mother did tell him that she wouldn't have had him if she'd known that's how he would later feel.

Update: In 2023, a TikToker from Hoboken, New Jersey, who goes by "Kass Theaz" drew ire after she claimed to have sued her parents for having her (it's uncertain if she was inspired by Samuel's case). Her fans got upset when they found out she has kids of her own. In a video with more than two million views, Kass Theaz says her kids were adopted, which is different "because it's not my fault that they're here." She also said she didn't *really* sue her parents (her account is listed as "satire"). But as a staunch antinatalist, she advises any expectant mother to hire a psychic to ask her fetus if it really wants to be born.

* * *

THANKS, LIBERACE!

- **He coined a phrase.** In response to a nasty 1954 newspaper review of one of his well-attended concerts, the TV star and pop-classical pianist wrote a sarcastic letter to the critic saying that the write-up prompted him to "laugh all the way to the bank."

- **He broke Barbra Streisand.** In 1963, he invited the 21-year-old future superstar to be his opening act for a monthlong Las Vegas residency. He even played piano while she sang, further ingratiating her to audiences.

- **He was a bathroom innovator.** He hated seeing toilets when he walked into one of the many bathrooms in his Las Vegas mansion, so he designed (and patented) a commode on a spinning pedestal that disappeared into the wall when not in use.

It took the U.K. government until 2015 to pay off its WWI debt—a period of 97 years.

FACTS IN SPAAAACE

"Ground Control to Uncle John. / Ground Control to Uncle John. / Can you hear me, Uncle John? / Can you–" / "Here am I sitting on my porcelain, / fan on in the room, / and I'm reading from the most peculiar book."

- Our universe—which began with a bang about 13.8 billion years ago—is still expanding at 41 to 46 miles per second. At its current size, it would take a beam of light 95 billion light-years to travel across it.

- What color is the universe? Would you believe that it's beige? Or, as astrophysicists call it, "cosmic latte." They've deduced this after adding up all the light from all the galaxies—along with all the visible clouds, gases, and dust—and averaging it out to a color that is close to white but more a shade of cream. Because of the vast size of the universe, the light is diluted so much that space appears almost black.

- A better name for "shooting stars" might be "ionizing chunks." These chunks are usually pebble-sized rocks and/or metals that escaped from comets or the asteroid belt. When they hit Earth's upper atmosphere and collide with air molecules, kinetic energy ionizes the molecules along their path, lighting them up. Meteors' speeds range from 25,000 mph to 160,000 mph. Their trails can be miles long but only a few feet in diameter.

- To give an idea of the scale of the universe, image that the solar system's most distant planet, Neptune, was 33 feet from the Sun. That would mean the closest star, Alpha Centauri, would be a little over 50 *miles* away. The closest galaxy, Canis Major Dwarf Galaxy, would be 331,250 miles away.

- Launched in 1977, the *Voyager 1* probe entered interstellar space in 2012 and is the farthest man-made object from Earth. It takes light from the Sun nearly a day to reach it, and in the time it took you to read this fact, the probe traveled another 1,000 miles.

- Mars used to have a thicker, moister atmosphere that contained rivers, lakes, and seas. Today, most of that water is gone, and scientists say it's the Sun's fault. Mars's atmosphere didn't get quite as thick as Earth's; that allowed the Sun's great energy to strip the lighter hydrogen atoms from the formerly blue planet's upper atmosphere, scattering them into space.

Watch out: the Mediterranean Sea is home to great white sharks, and some of the largest in the world, too.

- You've probably heard of Jupiter's Great Red Spot, a storm larger than the Earth that's been raging for at least 300 years. Saturn's atmosphere has an even weirder feature: a hexagon. This jet stream in the clouds is larger than Jupiter's Great Red Spot, and it's situated over the ringed planet's north pole, on the same plane as the rings. Each of the six equal—and straight—sides is 7,500 miles long. There's nothing else like the hexagon in the solar system, and astronomers won't know what's causing it until they can get a better look beneath the surface of the clouds.

- Something is driving the winds on Neptune to reach ludicrous speeds—much faster than anywhere else in the solar system. That's despite the fact that Neptune is the farthest planet from the Sun; its interior and surface are much colder than those of closer planets. Nevertheless, the fastest jet streams whip around the planet at up to 1,500 mph.

- True or false: astronauts on the International Space Station experience zero gravity. Answer? False. The force of gravity diminishes with distance, and the space station isn't that far away from Earth—so its residents experience 90 percent of the gravity we Earthlings do. So why do the astronauts float? Because they're experiencing what's called *microgravity*. The space station is technically in a "free fall," and so are its inhabitants, all at the same rate. The ISS maintains a stable orbit because the pull of gravity back to Earth is the same as the centrifugal force pulling it away. So the ISS and everything inside it just kind of float around up there...while orbiting at 17,500 mph.

- Nebulae are massive clouds of gases and dust in interstellar space that glow bright in the spiral arms of the Milky Way. Composed mainly of hydrogen and helium, there are a few types of nebulae: supernova remnants are what's left behind after a massive star explodes; planetary nebulae come from stars like our Sun that ended their lives as white dwarves before their solar systems eventually become clouds of dust. The largest are called dark nebulae, and these are where stars are born. One nebula you can see with the naked eye is just below Orion's belt. It will eventually fade out as the growing stars inside it consume the gases as they form new solar systems of their own.

- You've heard the expression "flat as a pancake." How about "flatter than a pizza"? That's how flat the Milky Way is. If our galaxy were the width of a typical 12″ pizza, it would be just an eighth of an inch thick (or 3 mm). This is because galaxies are "planar," meaning they're formed from a giant cloud of gas spinning with angular momentum, resulting in the contents of the galaxy being spread out in a thin plane instead of in a ball.

**Good news: if a black hole doesn't consume enough matter,
it will eventually cease to exist.**

THE KING OF THE LIBRARY

Most of the organization we associate with libraries arose from one man who created
or improved upon already existing concepts. That man: Melvil Dewey, inventor of
the Dewey Decimal System (or Dewey Decimal Classification). And according to
a lot of people, he was a brilliant, quirky...deeply flawed, repugnant man.

HE REQUIRED ORDER, ORGANIZATION, AND EFFICIENCY.

As a child living in upstate New York in the 1850s, Melville Dewey was fascinated
with order and cataloging. He reportedly routinely cataloged the contents of his
family's pantry, and he kept exhaustively detailed accounting records of the money he
earned doing odd jobs as a teenager. Dewey loved school so much that he wept at his
graduation, deciding that his true purpose was to be a teacher. He altered that goal
when, at Amherst College, he worked in the library (a job he continued to do after
he graduated in 1874), which reignited his passion for organization.

Also in 1874: Melville Dewey changed his name. Craving efficiency in even small
things, he eliminated excess letters to shorten his first name to Melvil. In 1879, he
briefly changed his last name, too—to Dui.

HE DEVISED WHAT'S NOW THE MOST PROMINENT LIBRARY CATALOGING SYSTEM WHEN HE WAS 25.

Working in a library all day, Dewey was well aware of the methods libraries used to
organize their collections. The predominant method: alphabetical order, by title,
with no regard for subject matter, author, or language of origin. He was determined
to come up with an improved method, and the idea struck 25-year-old Dewey one
Sunday morning in church in 1876.

Patented and published later that year, the Dewey Decimal System was scalable
for a library of any size or level, and it was as easy to understand as it was complex
in how virtually any topic could receive an assigned, numerical category or
subcategory. The 10 basic categories: Generalities (001–099), Philosophy (100–199),
Religion (200–299), Social Sciences (300–399), Languages (400–499), Natural
Sciences (500–599), Applied Sciences (600–699), Arts and Recreation (700–799),
Literature (800–899), and Geography and History (900–999).

Japanese consumers buy more adult diapers than baby diapers.

HE ESTABLISHED LIBRARY INSTITUTIONS AND WELCOMED WOMEN INTO THE FIELD.

To help spread his Dewey Decimal System, Melvil Dewey founded the American Library Association in 1876. In 1884 at Columbia University, he established the first library secondary school in the United States. But the school refused Dewey the use of a classroom and bristled at his idea to admit women into the program. Nevertheless, he held his first classes, in a storeroom above the campus chapel; there were 17 women and three men in his class. Historians credit Dewey's actions with why library work would eventually become a female-dominated profession.

HE HELPED INVENT THE "SHUSH."

Until the late 19th century, libraries were relatively rowdy places. They became known as a place for quiet study, where librarians would tolerate nothing less than silence and would issue an aggressive "shush!" at anyone not complying. That movement began in part when Dewey printed up and displayed in libraries signs like these: "Readers demand quiet, therefore conversation even in low tones is strictly prohibited. We are required to enforce the rules by personal appeal if necessary, and readers and visitors will spare us this unpleasant duty by strictly observing them."

DEWEY'S CAREER WAS UNDONE BY SCANDAL.

In 1888, Dewey, already the most famous name associated with libraries, took a well-paying position as state librarian of New York. He made so much money that he was able to open the exclusive Lake Placid Club. Because he ran it, he could choose the membership—and explicitly forbade Jewish people, people with a physical disability, and anyone who wasn't White. When the New York State Board of Regents was made aware of this policy in 1904, Dewey was publicly chastised, and he resigned in 1906.

Just after the Lake Placid Club news went public, Dewey was ordered to resign his high-ranking position at the American Library Association. During the group's annual conference, four women alleged that Dewey made unwanted sexual advances. A secretary accused him of similar predatory behavior, and for that he was sued, found liable, and had to pay out hefty compensatory damages.

THE DEWEY DECIMAL SYSTEM CAN AND DOES CHANGE.

Within a few decades of the establishment of the Dewey Decimal System as the premier method of book categorization, ground-level librarians got to work revising it, pointing out and fixing flaws and filling in holes.

In 1939, Dorothy Parker Wesley, librarian at Howard University, a historically Black college, successfully lobbied for a better integration of works by Black authors

First wartime surrender to a robot: during Operation Desert Storm (1991).

throughout the DDS. In Dewey's original classification, "325: International Migration and Colonization" was where anything and everything about Black people or written by Black people went. Imperfect at best (racist at worst), a biography about a Black historical figure would go under the same number as a book about slave ships. Wesley made sure that books by and about Black people were classified according to subject.

The Dewey Decimal System had to change again in the late 20th century to reflect society's growing tolerance and acceptance of gays and lesbians. Previously, books pertaining to the LGBTQ experience were categorized variously in the 100s under "Mental Derangements," in the 360s under "Social Problems–Controversies," and the 600s in "Neurological Disorders." Today, the main heading for LGBTQ books is in the 300s, or "Social Sciences": "306: Culture and Institutions."

DEWEY'S PERSONAL BIASES INFLUENCED THE DEWEY DECIMAL SYSTEM.

Books on religion begin their categorization at 200. A full 90 percent of the 200s are occupied with texts on the history, holy works, and cultural impact of different denominations of Christianity. The Dewey Decimal System doesn't cover other religions until 290, meaning 10 percent of the section is for the world's 4,000 other religions. Islam and Judaism, two widely followed faiths, get one number each.

The language section is another way that Dewey embedded his biases into his system. The entirety of the 400s (from 400 to 499) allows eight whole categories for Germanic languages, including English, to spread out. Meanwhile, Africa, a continent that spawned more than 2,000 languages and dialects, gets just one category, "496: African Languages." A similar arrangement is at play in the 800s, the literature section. English literature, in its various forms, accounts for everything from 800 to 889; the rest of the world's literary traditions are crammed into 890 to 899.

DESPITE FLAWS, THE SYSTEM WORKS.

The original Dewey Decimal System reflected the era in which it was created. The ability to fairly easily revise the classification system means modern library professionals have made it better suited for their users. Several original three-digit Dewey Decimal System codes are no longer used by the library community. Reason: they're woefully outdated, or librarians find that books once shelved in their original places fit better elsewhere.

104 Essays	159 Will
125 Infinity	216 Evil
132 Mental Derangements	376 Education of Women
134 Mesmerism and Clairvoyance	819 Puzzle Activities

LUCKY FINDS

*Ever stumble upon something valuable? It's an incredible feeling. Here's
the latest installment of one of the BRI's regular features.*

Pearls before Dine

The Find: A purple pearl

Where It Was Found: In a bowl of clams at a restaurant

The Story: In August 2022, Scott Overland and his wife were on vacation in
Delaware when they stopped at the Salt Air Restaurant in Rehoboth Beach. They
decided to start with a $14 clam appetizer, but when it arrived, there were peppers
on it; his wife doesn't like them, so they nearly sent the dish back before deciding to
remove the peppers and eat it anyway. "I guess sometimes you get rewarded for not
being a pain at restaurants," said Overland.

That reward came in the form of an uncomfortable bite. At first, the couple
thought the round, purple thing was a piece of candy. But then they noticed a little
indentation in the clamshell...and realized the purple thing had grown there. The
couple was stumped: could this be a purple pearl? Don't pearls grow in oysters?
It turns out that pearls can be many colors, and they can grow in many shelled
mollusks—including the northern quahog clam, which is what the Overlands had
ordered. The pearl was later appraised for $4,071. "Not bad for a bowl of clams!"
exclaimed Overland. The couple decided to keep it and give it their daughter, who
likes purple.

The Lost Weekend

The Find: A class ring

Where It Was Found: Near a creek in New Jersey

The Story: In June 2023, Anthony Dimaria-Sadorski was photographing the sunset
next to a creek in Point Pleasant Borough, New Jersey, a few miles inland from the
ocean, when something shiny caught his eye. The young man dug the object out of
the dirt and saw that it was a class ring...from 1972. He could make out the school
name, so he posted pics of his find on the school's Facebook page.

Not long after, Jim Keelan heard from an old classmate: "Jim, that's got to be you
that they're looking for!" Fifty-one years earlier, when Keelan and his friends were
celebrating their graduation on the Jersey Shore, "We did what young kids do and I
lost my ring that weekend." But having lost it on the beach, he thought he'd never

see it again: "It was toast." Keelan is thrilled to be reunited with his ring, which he's having resized so he can wear it again.

One question remains: how did the ring get so far inland? The leading theory: in November 2012, the ring—along with a whole bunch of other stuff—was swept inland by the historic storm surge wrought by Superstorm Sandy.

Getting a Leg Up

The Find: A prosthetic leg

Where It Was Found: At the bottom of a lake

The Story: Matt Spruitenburg is a scuba diver who volunteers for American River Lost & Found near Sacramento, California. The group looks for stuff people lost in the waterways and then tries to track the owners down. In June 2023, Spruitenburg was swimming in Lake Natoma (a reservoir popular for recreational activities) when he saw the familiar shape of a human leg—bent at the knee—barely visible in the silt. Thankfully, it wasn't a real leg but a prosthetic one, and none too worse for the wear. Spruitenburg posted a selfie with the prosthesis on Lost & Found's Facebook page: "Somebody lose a leg? Yesterday's best find. Now we have to find the owner. These things are expensive."

This leg, specifically, cost $28,000, and it belonged to David Fatta, who lives nearly 2,000 miles away in Jacksonville, Texas. He and a friend went swimming in that lake a year earlier. "I was the first one to pop up out of the water, and I said, 'Holy cow, my leg's gone!'" They couldn't find it in the deep, silty lake, so Fatta had to get along without the leg he'd been using since 2005 after a workplace accident created the need for it. Luckily, his California friend saw the Facebook post and alerted Fatta, who immediately knew it was his leg. The friend flew with the leg to Texas. Fatta added that if he could, he'd give Spruitenburg a big bear hug as thanks.

Keep the Change

The Find: A can full of coins

Where It Was Found: Underneath a kitchen

The Story: "Picture the scene," said auctioneer Gregory Edmund, "you're choosing to re-lay your uneven kitchen floor, you put a pick-axe through the concrete, and just beneath you see a tiny sliver of gold. At the time, you think it must just be a bit of electrical cable, but you find it's a gold round disc and beneath it there are hundreds more." That's how it happened for the unidentified couple from East Yorkshire, England. They retrieved the can full of coins and took it to experts, who informed them that the more than 260 coins in the collection were issued from 1610 to 1727, a tumultuous time in British history.

They were placed under the floorboards in the 18th century by mercantile traders Joseph and Sarah Fernley-Maisters. Like many well-to-do families at the time, the Maisters didn't trust the newly formed Bank of England and its "banknotes" (what we now call cash). Many businesses continued to accept any kind of English coinage in use over the previous century, hence the span of the collection. Why the couple left it there is unknown, but when Sarah died, so too did her family line. It's likely no one knew about her hidden fortune.

The Ellerby hoard (so named for the village where it was found) was expected to pull in about $300,000 at auction, but news of the incredible find sparked a global bidding war for different lots from the coins. They collectively sold for an astonishing £754,000 ($950,000), including one from 1720 that went for £62,400. Edmund called the "absolutely extraordinary" collection "120 years of English history hidden in a pot the same size as a soda can," adding, "I will never see an auction like this again."

* * *

33 NEW YEAR'S RESOLUTIONS LEGENDARY FOLK SINGER WOODY GUTHRIE MADE FOR 1943

1. Work more and better
2. Work by a schedule
3. Wash teeth if any
4. Shave
5. Take bath
6. Eat good—fruit, vegetables, milk
7. Drink very scant if any
8. Write a song a day
9. Wear clean clothes—look good
10. Shine shoes
11. Change socks
12. Change bed clothes often
13. Read lots of good books
14. Listen to radio a lot
15. Learn people better
16. Keep rancho clean
17. Don't get lonesome
18. Stay glad
19. Keep hoping machine running
20. Dream good
21. Bank all extra money
22. Save dough
23. Have company but don't waste time
24. Send Mary and kids money
25. Play and sing good
26. Dance better
27. Help win war—Beat Fascism
28. Love Mama
29. Love Papa
30. Love Pete [his brother]
31. Love everybody
32. Make up your mind
33. Wake up and fight

WHAT'S MY NAME?

Have you ever wanted to look up what something's called, or buy a new one, but you couldn't...because you don't know what it's called? Here are some common things you know of that have names you probably didn't know.

That glass or metal dome that goes over a meal at a fancy restaurant: *cloche*

That big machine you look through at the eye doctor to test your vision: *phoropter*

That wire cage you take off a bottle of champagne to access the cork: *agraffe*

The poles that support a banister and connect it to stairs: *baluster*

The tingly feeling you get when your foot falls asleep: *paresthesia*

Those freestanding stone formations in the American Southwest: *hoodoos*

One of those bicycles with a giant front wheel: *penny-farthing*

That metal thing you stick your foot in at the store to measure your shoe size: *Brannock device*

The white paper box with red lettering that Chinese food comes in: *oyster pail*

The little plastic table they put in a pizza box to prevent the lid from collapsing: *pizza saver*

Those little paper containers they give you in fast food places for ketchup: *souffle cups*

Old men who stand around and watch construction sites: *umarell*

The bottom part of your nose, the little bridge between the nostrils: *columella nasi*

Your smallest toe, like your pinkie but on your foot: *minimus*

That grid of generic photos at the bottom of a website urging you to click: *chumbox*

The little red globes that make up a raspberry: *drupelets*

When you say a word over and over until it sounds weird and nonsensical: *semantic satiation*

A silent letter in a word (like the *k* in *knight*): *aphthong*

That little symbol of three stacked horizontal lines that, when clicked, displays the menu on a website: *hamburger button* (because it looks like a meat patty between two buns)

The pieces of crossing wood in a window frame that separate the individual glass panes: *muntins*

The official name for the day after tomorrow: *overmorrow*

First year nobody at Wimbledon used a wooden racket: 1988.

THE FELINE TIMELINE, PART II

In part I (page 22), you learned how the African wildcat became the domestic house cat and took over the world. Now watch as cats take over pop culture.

1840s | A photographer whose name is lost to history makes a blurry daguerreotype of a small cat drinking from a bowl. It's possibly the first photo of a cat. To say the trend catches on is an understatement; in 2015, there were an estimated 6.5 *billion* cat pics online.

1850s | Around 300,000 cats are employed as mousers in London, and many find their way into homes. Because the Industrial Revolution is in full swing, people aren't growing and storing food as much, keeping the mice numbers down. Result: the cat demands to be fed. It's too expensive to give them people food, so a new profession emerges: cat's meat men. These men (and women) go door to door selling nearly spoiled meat, particularly horse meat, for cheap. The cat-food industry is born.

1861 | In Abraham Lincoln's White House, Tabby and Dixie become the nation's first "First Cats." Lincoln is "fond of dumb animals, especially cats," writes treasury department official Maunsell B. Field. "I have seen him fondle one for an hour." The president even commits the faux pas of feeding Tabby from the table during a formal White House dinner.

1868 | The tradition of "post office cats" launches in England in response to the growing problem of mice and rats eating through mail bags. Every post office is allotted one shilling per week to employ cats, and the pest populations plummet.

1871 | Cats in Victorian England are seen more as exterminators than pets, despite the queen herself owning several. (Her favorite: White Heather, a Persian cat that will be treated like royalty even after the queen dies.) The man who starts changing people's minds is a former cat hater turned fancier named Harrison Weir. To show off the true merits of "possibly the most perfect" animal, Weir organizes the first ever cat show at London's Crystal Palace. It's a rousing success, as 65 cats compete. Several new breeds are introduced, including the first known pair of Siamese cats in England.

Longest parsnip on record: 21 feet, 5.87 inches.

1870s	British photographer Harry Pointer's "Brighton Cats" images would have made him a social-media star were he around today. Specializing in the popular carte de visite photos (the precursor of greeting cards), Pointer photographs cats in humorous settings (such as in a toy pram) and includes whimsical captions (like "Many Happy Returns"). Cats have now claimed a permanent spot in the greeting card and motivational poster markets.
1880s	British artist Louis Wain—who could have schizophrenia or be on the Autism spectrum—starts painting cats, a subject he'll eventually become obsessed with. Some cats are lounging, some are prowling, and some walk on two legs and play golf. Science fiction pioneer H. G. Wells will later write that Wain "made the cat his own. He invented a cat style, a cat society, a whole cat world." Wain's paintings set the stage for 20th-century cartoon cats like Felix, Sylvester, Tom, and Garfield.
1893	Cat (and dog) populations skyrocket, which begins the widespread practice of spaying and neutering. One anonymous U.K. veterinarian does not recommend the "Wellington boot" method—wherein the cat is held facedown inside a boot while the vet uses a knife to…do the deed—opting instead to perform the operation with the patient rolled up in a blanket. He argues against the burgeoning use of anesthetics like chloroform and cocaine, because "even carefully given…they are dangerous." Thankfully for cats, this will change in the next few decades.
1894	It's the first ever cat video! Filmed in Thomas Edison's studio, the short film features two cats in boxing gloves seemingly throwing punches at each other. Fittingly, it's called "Boxing Cats."
1895	Although commonly cited as the first cat show in the United States, this four-day event at New York's Madison Square Garden was predated by two "National Cat Shows" in Boston a few years prior. However, the widely publicized New York event truly begins America's love affair with cat shows and breeding techniques. (The show's winner: a brown tabby Maine coon named Cosey.)
1917	The Association of American Feed Control Officials (AAFCO), formed in 1909, introduces the first legislation designed to set safety regulations for pet food. The organization is still active today.
1918	Cats go to war! They provide World War I soldiers with company while keeping their trenches free of vermin on the Western front. Like ships' cats before them, war cats are highly revered. They can even detect

A century ago, the average American ate 10 pounds of chicken each year. Today, it's 64.

poisonous gas before the soldiers do. An estimated 500,000 cats serve the Allies in World War I. When the war ends, the house cat becomes a bona fide pet in the United States.

1919 — Nearly a decade before Mickey Mouse, the world's first animated movie star is Felix the Cat. Created by Pat Sullivan and Otto Messmer, Felix takes on social issues—such as when he quits his butcher-shop job to fight in the war against rats, or when he organizes a strike in response to a town council ban on cats.

1920s — Thanks in no small part to Felix's popularity, cats are all the rage this decade—as are cat idioms, including *cool cat* and *cat's pajamas* (along with *cat's meow* and *cat's whiskers*, which all mean "cool"). The following decade, Cab Calloway will coin *hep cat*, which later morphs into *hipster*.

1928 — The first "Chief Mouser to the Cabinet Office" is hired to patrol the grounds of 10 Downing Street, where England's prime minister resides. (The most recent chief mouser—and the first to officially be given the title—is Larry, who entered service in 2011 and has outlasted four PMs).

1930s — Spaying and neutering become more commonplace thanks to breakthroughs in anesthesia. Also coming into its own is the pet food industry, which introduces the first canned cat food. Even more importantly, in 1931, the electric can opener is invented.

1935 — A conversation between Albert Einstein and Erwin Schrödinger about the futility of quantum theory leads to the latter's famous thought experiment involving a hypothetical cat. To paraphrase, Schrödinger argues that an element can exist in two states at once only *in theory*. He uses this analogy: if you lock a cat in a box and then come back later, the cat will have a fifty-fifty chance of being alive or dead. In theory, it could be in both states. But once observed (when the box is opened), Schrödinger's cat can be in only one of those states.

1947 — Cats are still mostly outdoor pets because, well, that's where they go to the bathroom. Some owners put sand or ashes in a box, but cats track it all over the house. That's the complaint a Michigan housewife makes to Edward Lowe, who sells sawdust and heavy clay to factories to soak up spills. He recommends absorbent clay for the cat, and it works great. Lowe singlehandedly launches the cat litter industry (and "indoor cats").

1955 — Disneyland opens in California, and Mickey and Minnie are the only mice who are welcome. So park officials put the local stray cats to

The hole in the ozone layer appears in July, gets biggest in October, and disappears in January.

work. Even today, the feral cat population is closely managed. There are feeding stations, and the numbers are kept down by spaying and neutering. Any accidental kittens are adopted out.

1963 Purina Cat Chow hits store shelves. The company's Fancy Feast will follow in 1982. Purina is still the top-selling canned cat food in the United States.

1963 Félicette, a stray petite tuxedo recruited by the French space program, becomes the world's first "astrocat." During her 15-minute trip in a tiny capsule attached to a massive rocket, she endures forces as high as 9.5 g on the way up and, after the rocket detaches, spends a few minutes floating in microgravity 100 miles above the Earth before enduring another 7 g on the way down (that's twice what human astronauts endure). Félicette survives, and to this day, she's the only cat to go to space.

1968 A professional animal handler named Bob Martwick adopts an orange male tabby from a Chicago animal shelter. Given the name Morris, he becomes the official mascot of 9Lives Cat Food until his death a decade later. Every subsequent "Morris" has also been a shelter cat.

1974 Yuko Shimizu, a Japanese illustrator who works for Sanrio founder Shintaro Tsuji, is tasked with creating a cute character to be printed onto clothing products. She draws a white cartoon cat with a red bow and no mouth. Shimizu names her "Kitty." Tsuji adds "Hello," and Hello Kitty debuts on a coin purse a year later. It will soon become the world's second most successful entertainment franchise, after Pokémon (and, fittingly, one place ahead of Mickey Mouse).

1975 Ending a centuries-long tradition, England's Royal Navy bans ships' cats from serving in their fleet. Ironically, it's for the same reason that cats were put there in the first place: hygiene.

1976 Jim Davis, a cartoonist from Indiana, pitches a new comic strip about a dog, only to be told by his editor that "his art was good...but nobody identifies with dogs." So Davis, who grew up on a farm with 25 cats, comes up with a grumpy orange tabby who loves lasagna as much as he hates Mondays. Garfield will go on to become star of the most syndicated comic strip in the world, and America's most famous fictional cat.

1981 Andrew Lloyd Webber finishes adapting T. S. Eliot's 1939 poetry collection, *Old Possum's Book of Practical Cats*, into the musical *Cats*.

The Toyota Camry is named for a *kanmuri*, the Japanese word for "crown."

It premieres in London to rave reviews before becoming a permanent fixture on Broadway.

1984 In response to reports that up to 17 million potential pets are euthanized in America's shelter system each year, the nation's first no-kill animal shelter breaks ground in Kanab, Utah.

1987 Towser dies. Recognized by Guinness World Records as the "most prolific mouser" of all-time, this cat spent all 24 of her years patrolling a U.K. distillery, averaging three mice per day. Kill total: 28,899.

1997 The *Felidae* family tree, which has long been a mystery, finally comes together after geneticists compare DNA from all 37 modern feline species to the bones of their prehistoric progenitors. Now they can determine when each of the eight lineages branched off from their common ancestor. Among the revelations: *Felis catus* belongs to the youngest lineage—the wildcats—which broke off 6.2 million years ago. As sea levels rose and fell, these small, slender wildcats ventured from Eurasia to North America and then back again. After cozying up with humans, they adapted into their modern form and became the most successful of all the felines.

1998 The first cat café opens in Japan and quickly expands into a worldwide fad. At last count, there are 144 cat cafés in North America.

2005 Cats begin their adorable takeover of the Internet when YouTube cofounder Steve Chen uploads the first cat video ("Pajamas and Nick Drake"). This same year, a photo-sharing website called 4Chan launches the "Caturday" tradition of posting cat pics on Saturdays. The following year will see the first viral cat video ("Puppy vs. Cat"), and, a year later, the first LOLcat meme. These aren't just for fun—it's been scientifically proven that viewing funny pics and videos for a few minutes every day "reduces the stress hormone cortisol and increases heart health."

2020– 2023 The COVID-19 pandemic keeps people stuck inside, which leads to a huge increase in both cat and dog adoptions. But as the lockdowns wane and people have to go back to work (while many are still out of work), countless "COVID cats" are abandoned. As these new strays join the feral cats, population centers are overrun. In 2023, New York City officials adopt the controversial "trap, neuter, return" method to reduce the nearly 500,000 cats roaming the Big Apple's streets, which the *New York Times* describes as "extras from a zombie movie."

A proctologist in ancient Egypt was called an *iri*, or "shepherd of the anus."

FABULOUS AND FORGOTTEN FADS

Here's a look at the origins of some of the most popular obsessions from days gone by.

WACKY WALLWALKERS

Japanese American businessman Ken Hakuta lived in Washington, D.C., in the early 1980s. His mother, who had stayed in Japan, liked to send Japanese novelties to her grandchildren. In 1982, she sent over a box of Tako, a sticky, rubbery monster toy. Made from elastic and plastic, Tako resembled octopuses or spiders and had rubbery little legs. When thrown against a wall, the toy would slowly unstick and re-stick itself on the way down, appearing to walk with the aid of its legs. Hakuta became obsessed with the toys meant as a gift for his kids and paid $120,000 for worldwide rights to produce and market them. They totally flopped in the stores where Hakuta had arranged to sell them, until *Washington Post* trends columnist Nina Hyde wrote about the toy, which Hakuta had rebranded the Wacky WallWalker. Suddenly, they exploded locally and, after CBS aired a report about the D.C. fad, Wacky WallWalkers were in high demand across the nation.

By the end of 1983, NBC aired an animated special called *Deck the Halls with Wacky Walls*, in which the toys are imagined as aliens coming to Earth to learn the true meaning of Christmas. Wendy's gave away millions in its kids' meals, and Kellogg's included them as a free toy inside millions of boxes of cereal. The fad died out when people got bored with Wacky WallWalkers; they didn't do much besides slowly descend walls. Nevertheless, Hakuta sold more than 200 million of the globs of goo, and personally netted $20 million off the fad.

HOLLY HOBBIE

In the late 1960s, watercolorist Denise Holly Hobbie painted a series of images recalling a pastoral, idyllic 19th-century New England. Amidst the country scenes was a young girl dressed in a blue patchwork dress and a huge face-obscuring bonnet. The slightly mysterious figure was known only as "blue girl." Hobbie's brother-in-law told the artist that her blue girl paintings would look great on cards, so she sent her work for consideration to greeting card company American Greetings. Art director Rex Connors loved the nostalgic, wholesome imagery, and saw to it that the blue girl appeared on dozens of card designs along with stationery, wrapping paper, and other gift items.

Give it a try: experts say cured pork shoved into a nostril can stop a nosebleed.

American Greetings sold a ton of the designs, and the public clearly wanted more, so it licensed out blue girl as dolls and toys. Knickerbocker Toy Company needed a name, so they named the character after its creator: Holly Hobbie. Dolls of the character in her signature frock and bonnet spurred a revival of rag dolls, not popular since the early 20th century, and Knickerbocker briskly sold a line of toys featuring the character and her newly invented friends: Amy, Heather, Carrie, and Robbie. Kenner also sold a lot of Holly Hobbie ovens, an Easy-Bake Oven–esque toy made to look like a 19th-century woodstove. The concept faded in popularity as the 1970s wore on, and the final nail in the coffin was the failure of a 1980 novel called *The Adventures of Holly Hobbie*, in which the title girl is a ghost who lives in a painting from the early 1800s and helps a living little girl find her missing father.

ROOS

KangaROOS, usually referred to as ROOS, were an early 1980s fad that grew out of the late 1970s fad of jogging. St. Louis–area architect Bob Gamm got really into the running-for-fitness craze but hated to carry his keys with him when he jogged because they weighed him down. So he designed a running shoe outfitted with a tiny cushioned zippered pocket on the side—big enough to hold a house key and a few coins or a folded-up dollar bill or two, but small enough that it wouldn't be cumbersome or interfere with running when filled.

Within a couple of years, more than 700,000 pairs of ROOS were being produced each month. The shoes took off among three distinct sectors of the population—the intended audience of joggers wishing to be unencumbered; kids, who liked the novel secrecy of the pocket; and twentysomethings, who found the ROOS pocket the perfect size to hold a condom or a small packet of cocaine or crack (which also took off in popularity in the early 1980s). ROOS were available in most department and discount stores for the entirety of the 1980s, though sales and popularity declined from their peak in 1982. The shoes were discontinued without fanfare in 1989, then brought back in a nostalgia-fueled rollout after being acquired by Pentland Brands in 1995.

*   *   *

EMERGENCY ROOM HACK

Want to be first in line for treatment at the ER? Here's how they sort patients.

Most Urgent: serious car crash, heart stopped beating, suspected stroke.
Very Urgent: suspected heart attack, severe trouble breathing, large broken bones.
Urgent: fainting, seizure, head injury, asthma attack, temperature over 104 degrees.
Less Urgent: need stitches; broken arm; sore eye, ear, or throat.
Not Urgent: removal of stitches, renewing a prescription, cough or congestion.

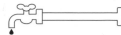

Walmart's workforce is larger than the population of Slovenia.

MAMA ALWAYS SAID...

*Uncle John's mother once told him that life was like a box of chocolates...
no, wait—that's what she told Forrest Gump. Anyway, here's some sage
advice from moms and dads, as recounted by their kids.*

"My father always said, 'Never trust anyone whose TV is bigger than their bookshelf.'"

—Emilia Clarke

"I believe that what we become depends on what our fathers teach us at odd moments, when they aren't trying to teach us. We are formed by little scraps of wisdom."

—Umberto Eco

"My mother said to me, 'If you are a soldier, you will become a general. If you are a monk, you will become the Pope.' Instead, I was a painter, and became Picasso."

—Pablo Picasso

"My father used to say to me, 'It doesn't matter what the profession is, but if they're the best in their field, it will always be fascinating to watch.' And I said, 'Really, Dad? Even like someone who makes pencils?' 'Even someone who makes pencils, it will be fascinating to watch.'"

—Nicolas Cage

"My mama always used to tell me: 'If you can't find somethin' to live for, you best find somethin' to die for.'"

—Tupac Shakur

"When I told my father I was going to be an actor, he said, 'Fine, but study welding just in case.'"

—Robin Williams

"It's like my father always said to me, he said to me, he said, Roseanne Roseannadanna, it's always something. If it isn't one thing—it's another! It's always something."

—Gilda Radner

"AS MY MOM ALWAYS SAID, 'YOU'D RATHER HAVE SMILE LINES THAN FROWN LINES.'"

—Cindy Crawford

"PARENTS CAN ONLY GIVE GOOD ADVICE OR PUT THEM ON THE RIGHT PATHS, BUT THE FINAL FORMING OF A PERSON'S CHARACTER LIES IN THEIR OWN HANDS."

—Anne Frank

THE VERY BEST PETE BESTS

Imagine this: after writing a bunch of songs and playing hundreds of gigs, your band makes it big. What's better is that you did it with some of your best friends. Now imagine that, for whatever reason, you quit that band before the big break, and the band becomes successful—without you in it. It most famously happened to Pete Best, fired as the first drummer of the Beatles. It's happened to lots of other poor saps, too.

Musician: Eric Stefani

Band: No Doubt

Story: In 1986, 19-year-old California Institute of the Arts student Eric Stefani started a ska-punk band called No Doubt. Stefani played keyboards in the band alongside his friend John Spence (who would commit suicide the next year) and his teenage sister, Gwen, as just a way to have fun and blow off steam from his intensive workload studying animation. No Doubt played a lot of gigs almost entirely in and around Orange County, California, until 1990 when an Interscope Records representatives saw one of the band's live shows and signed the group. After the band released two low-selling records, *No Doubt* (1992) and *The Beacon Street Collection* (1995), Interscope hired expensive star producer Matthew Wilder to record No Doubt's next record. That's when Stefani left the group—he didn't want some outside force to control the band's sound, and he wanted to focus on animation. Around the time he starting working full-time for *The Simpsons*, No Doubt—now fronted by his sister, Gwen Stefani, as lead singer—released *Tragic Kingdom*, which would sell 10 million copies on the strength of singles including "Just a Girl" and "Don't Speak."

Musician: Jason Galasso

Band: *NSYNC

Story: In the mid-1990s, private jet company owner Lou Pearlman decided to put together boy bands in the style of New Kids on the Block. He formed the Backstreet Boys and then *NSYNC, recruiting young male singers from the Orlando area. One of those singers was Joey Fatone, who—when realizing that the group needed a fifth performer, and a bass vocalist in particular—recruited an old friend from his high school choir, Jason Galasso. Jason easily passed through the audition process and joined *NSYNC (a name formed by the last letters of the first names of the group's members; the second N comes from "Jason"). But when the band started to prepare for its big launch, Galasso got cold feet—he couldn't master and didn't like the elaborate dance moves required of a boy band, and he didn't care for the kid-oriented pop music he was expected to sing. "I never wanted to be a teen idol," he later told

Dalmatian **comes from an Illyrian word for "sheep."**

VH1. And when it came time to sign a contract that he felt seemed exploitative, Galasso backed out. Lance Bass replaced him, and *NSYNC went on to sell tens of millions of albums—splitting up shortly after suing Pearlman for shady business practices. Galasso went on to build a successful career in real estate.

Musician: Tony Chapman
Band: The Rolling Stones
Story: In the early 1960s, Chapman played drums for a south London garage rock band called the Cliftons. When he heard that another up-and-coming local band called the Rolling Stones needed a drummer, Chapman landed himself an audition, along with one for his Cliftons bandmate bassist Bill Wyman. Both musicians were hired, and played several gigs with the Stones throughout 1962, including a show at Sidcup Art College attended by Keith Richards, who soon joined the band and helped define and refine the band's sound as a mixture of rock 'n' roll with an injection of American blues, played loudly and with as much sleaze as possible. That direction appalled Chapman so much that he quit the band. (The group's schedule also interfered with his job as a traveling salesman.) The Rolling Stones retained Wyman, lured drummer Charlie Watts away from his other band, and Chapman formed a new group called the Preachers, which would serve as the Rolling Stones' opening act in 1965—until the Preachers split up, and former members formed Moon's Train, without Chapman. The drummer ultimately left music, moved to Florida, and became an art dealer.

Musician: Jason Everman
Bands: Nirvana and Soundgarden
Story: When Nirvana guitarist and lead singer Kurt Cobain wanted to add a second guitarist to the trio to enhance its sound in 1989, its then-drummer Chad Channing recommended his childhood friend Jason Everman. Musically, Everman meshed with Nirvana, but personally, he struggled to get along with the other members. During a club tour in 1989, Everman experienced a bout of depression and refused to speak with anybody, alienating his bandmates. Rather than confront Everman, Nirvana canceled the tour midway, drove back to their homebase of Seattle in silence, and just didn't invite Everman to record or play any more gigs. Weeks later, guitarist Hiro Yamamoto quit another Seattle grunge band, Soundgarden, right after the release of its major-label debut, *Louder Than Love*. Everman nailed his audition and played with Soundgarden for more than a year on tour in the U.S. and Europe. After the tour's end, Soundgarden held a band meeting and fired Everman, because he just wasn't a good personality fit. Within a few months, both of Everman's former bands achieved commercial success. The guitarist subsequently quit music and joined the army.

Christmas tree lights can negatively affect Wi-Fi.

IS THIS *YOUR* BOOKMARK?

Books are a great place to leave keepsakes. Of course, if you or a descendant sells those books, or you're leaving things in library books, they're not so secure. Here are some objects that librarians and used-bookstore clerks have reported stumbling on inside their wares.

Tin can lid

A stack of five $20 bills

A pile of hair

Feminine hygiene products

Prophylactics

A winning lottery ticket (for $100)

A photo of Stephen King
(found in *The Shining*)

A five-leaf clover

An elementary school
report card from 1926

Eyeglasses

A dried, flattened, preserved lizard

An airplane ticket from 1970

World War II–era food ration coupons

A peacock feather

A sealed jar of marijuana (in
a hollowed-out book)

A New York State dog license from 1919

Floppy discs

A purchase order for asphalt

A note that reads, "Hi! From a gay guy!"

A video store "Frequent Renter
Card" with no holes punched

A coupon for a free Heineken, valid
only on November 19, 2002

A recipe card for "Fig Sweet Pickles"

A note that says "Go girl" in braille

A fishing hook

A crochet hook

The bottom half of a three-
panel newspaper comic strip

Two identical photos of the same child

A Dora the Explorer journal
(crammed inside another book)

A Book-of-the-Month Club bulk receipt

A letter written in French, on
Christmas, addressed to Enrique

A Page-a-Day calendar entry from 1998

A piece of Big Red chewing gum

A note that says "behave" on one
side with a printed-out recipe
for pot roast on the other

Homemade coupons for "bear hug"

A backstage pass to a Public
Enemy concert

A deceased bookworm

A nine of hearts playing card

Circulation card for a different book

Postcards of Hawaii

Transaction receipt from a defunct
savings and loan association

Coffee sleeve

The most common day to find money on the street in New York City:
the day after Saint Patrick's Day.

A list of books to read (that didn't include the book in which the list was found)

Post-its torn into strips with dollar amounts written on them, to use as play money

A cast of characters to an unwritten play

A cheat sheet for a math test

A note that says "Cheyenne is mean"

An unused Mission of Burma reunion concert ticket

A birthday card written on the back of a postcard issued by a cemetery

A homemade *Mr. Men* book featuring "Mr. Poopy-Loopy Stinky Butt"

A palm-sized homemade book called *My Owl*

A drawing of vegetables with human faces shouting "No!"

A union membership card

A bracelet charm commemorating a 2000 cotillion for "Stacey"

A German beer coaster

Two Post-its, one with a list of Bible verses and the other with half a recipe for cookies

A KitchenAid kettle lid

An invitation to a tea party featuring Iron Man

An empty package from semolina flour

A Korean sleep mask still in the package

A doctor's order for a sigmoidoscopy (to look for a large intestine blockage)

A Garbage Pail Kid card featuring "Roy Bot"

A pawn shop receipt for a

VCR receipt (it cost $50)

A grocery list with only one item written down: "Raisin Bran"

Prepaid long-distance phone card

Security clearance badge for a meeting with Kareem Abdul-Jabbar

Pizza coupons

A stack of school absence excuse forms

A single sheet of toilet paper

Vintage paper doll pieces

Ticket for a county fair from 1910

A $2 bill with "Surprise!" written on it

Vintage advertisement for tooth powder

Key tied on a string

A report from an Australian parole board about an inmate serving time for murder

Ticket for a 1988 Van Halen concert

Red Cross membership card from 1956

A note that says "Favorite pie?" with a drawing of a slice of pie

Vintage Continental Airlines luggage tag

Lion King valentines

Typed recipe for elephant stew calling for one 2,000 lb. elephant cut into small pieces

1964 Topps trading card of John Lennon

A sticker that says "Chicks Hate Me"

Salt and pepper packets

A printout of an electrocardiogram (found in a cookbook titled *Delicious Ways to Control Diabetes*)

Fake dollar bill with a portrait of a dog on it

HOW TO GO TO THE BATHROOM

Pretend you're a microscopic toxin, just hanging out in some poor, unsuspecting human's bloodstream. You won't be there for long, because there's a whole system in place to literally flush you out. Here is exactly how and why the human body makes urine.

A person stays alive, surviving, thriving, and functioning, because of thousands of metabolic processes. Continuously and unrelentingly occurring, these activities happen at every level, down to the cellular, and each produces its own waste. That waste needs to be eliminated from the body as quickly as possible. Most of that waste is transported away as liquid waste and exits as part of urine, which the urinary system collects and sheds through an elaborate and continuous undertaking.

The urinary system consists primarily of two kidneys, two tubes called ureters (one on each kidney), the bladder, and another tube called the urethra. The primary function of the kidneys (or, more accurately, the structures inside them) is the regulation of the chemical composition of the body's fluids, especially the blood. Kidney processes determine the volume, acidity, salinity, and concentration of blood.

Each time the heart pumps, it shoots blood around the body, delivering oxygen and nutrients to where they need to go. Every pump also sends blood into the kidneys, which makes the blood healthy, cleaning and filtering it. The kidneys keep nutrients and oxygen in the blood and send it along, but they also remove what doesn't need to recirculate, including waste products and excess water. And that's what urine is, all ready to go on its grand journey out of the kidneys, through some tubes, into the bladder, then out of the body.

Blood enters the kidneys through the renal arteries. Those branch out into tiny capillaries that directly interact with the renal pyramids. Each kidney is home to about half a dozen renal pyramids, where millions of microscopic workhorses called nephrons filter the blood. Pressure from the blood, and its constant, powerful circulation, helps the nephrons force water and solutions into a capsule, through a membrane. The nephrons flag and remove wastewater and bad stuff; the filtered blood continues to circulate through the body, via the renal veins.

Waste material and excess water collected by the nephrons are then gathered up by the renal pyramids and flow into a holding area in each kidney called the renal

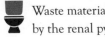

Lost? The state bird of Utah is the California gull.

pelvis. This waste-filled substance is now fully recognizable as urine, made up of about 95 percent water. The remaining five percent of the solution: waste products from around the body, primarily urea, creatinine, ammonia, uric acid, sodium, potassium, hydrogen, and calcium. (Many of those are things the body needs, but the kidneys recognize when we have too much of them and get rid of the excess.) When enough proto-urine is there to move on, the renal pelvises push waste into each kidney's ureter.

Via the narrow tube that is the ureter, the urine moves into the bladder. A hollow, elastic organ, the bladder sits in the middle of the pelvis and exists primarily to store urine until it can be released later at a person's discretion. While that release is voluntary, the processes that fill the bladder happen automatically. Stretch receptors inside the walls of the bladder are activated when the organ has expanded to its limits, or when it's approaching its limits. Those stretch receptors send out an electrical nerve impulse, which travels along the spinal cord all the way up to the brain, sending the message that the bladder is full and needs to be emptied. (The brain, in turn, passes this message on to the conscious mind with feelings of discomfort, urgency, and maybe the sudden need to do the "pee-pee dance.")

The human finds a proper receptacle for their waste—a urinal or a toilet, for example—and that tells the brain that it's time to release the urine. Urine leaves the body via a concerted effort by two sphincters, one involuntarily controlled and the other voluntarily activated. The internal sphincter surrounds the opening (or exit door) of the bladder, allowing urine to pass out. Sensing the flow of wastewater, the external sphincter springs into action. Surrounding the urethra outside the bladder, the external sphincter relaxes.

The area where this activity takes place is just barely inside the body. As urine moves from the bladder, it flows out the urethra, then directly out of the body and into the waiting urinal or toilet.

While you may need to urinate only five or six times a day, the kidneys and the rest of the urinary system are constantly at work, compiling that liquid waste without you knowing about it or doing anything about it. The kidneys filter blood hundreds of times a day, with a total of up to 200 quarts filtered (and refiltered) each 24-hour period.

*   *   *

"When I see a kid throwing a massive tantrum in a grocery store, part of me is like, 'Man, I feel you.'"

—Taylor Swift

Ratio of male to female characters in Shakespeare's plays: 7 to 1.

LIFE IMITATES ART

Countless movies, books, and TV shows are inspired by real-life events. But when real-life events are inspired by fiction, Uncle John takes notice.

ON THE SCREEN: The 2015 James Bond movie, *Spectre*, opens in Mexico City during a Day of the Dead parade—complete with giant floats and marionettes, and marchers dressed in elaborate costumes.

IN REAL LIFE: There is no Day of the Dead parade in Mexico City—or, at least, there wasn't until *Spectre*. Traditionally, *Día de Los Meurtos* is spent at home, or in a cemetery, with friends and family. But the Bond filmmakers had put together such a spectacular parade that people from all over the world started booking trips for the October 2016 event...which didn't exist. So, rather than risk an armada of unhappy tourists, Mexico City's tourism board put on its own Day of the Dead parade...with actual prop floats made for the movie. A quarter of a million people showed up, and it has since become an annual event.

ON THE RADIO: Johnny Cash's 1976 novelty song "One Piece at a Time" (written by Wayne Kemp) is about an auto plant worker who steals one car part every day ("I'd sneak it out of there in a lunchbox in my hand") until he has all the parts to build himself a free car.

IN REAL LIFE: In 2003, a Chinese man identified only as Zhang worked at a motorcycle factory in Chongqing, China, but didn't get paid enough to buy his own bike. So he stole one—you guessed it—"one piece at a time." Unfortunately for Zhang, after spending five years building the stolen bike, he was pulled over by police on his first ride. Unable to provide ownership papers or a driver's license, Zhang was fined and placed on probation, and the bike went back to the factory. (News reports didn't mention if he got fired.)

ON THE SCREEN: The "Prime Directive" has been a part of *Star Trek* since the 1960s original series. This guiding principle of the show's fleet states, in part: "As the right of each sentient species to live in accordance with its normal cultural evolution is considered sacred, no Starfleet personnel may interfere with the normal and healthy development of alien life and culture."

IN REAL LIFE: In 2023, Dr. Pamela Conrad, an astrobiologist at the Carnegie Institution of Science, joined the growing number of voices calling for governmental space agencies—along with their counterparts in the private sector—to adopt a similar directive. Their concern is the "colonial approach" being applied to the next chapter of human spacefaring—to the moon, Mars, and the asteroid belt—to mine them for raw materials. "Oddly enough," Conrad says, "the *Star Trek* series and culture becomes a prime directive for how we could explore space: seeking not to interfere." Canadian scientist Dr. Hilding Neilson, of the native Mi'kmaq people, adds, "I've actually sat and listened to a CEO of a very large company talking about how going to space is the same as when people settled what is now Quebec."

Although NASA still has no Prime Directive when it comes to alien cultures, the space agency's Office of Planetary Protection pledges to "carefully control forward contamination of other worlds by terrestrial organisms and organic materials carried by spacecraft in order to guarantee the integrity of the search and study of extraterrestrial life, if it exists."

ON THE SCREEN: The "Sonic Screwdriver" is a rather ingenious—not to mention budget-saving—device on the BBC's sci-fi serial *Doctor Who*. In one of the device's many functions, the Doctor (a Time Lord from a distant planet) aims the Sonic Screwdriver at a door; it makes a whirring noise, and the door opens.

IN REAL LIFE: In 2010, England's University of Bristol issued a press release announcing that "Ultrasonic engineers...are uncovering how a real life version of the fictional screwdriver—which uses sonic technology to open locks and undo screws—could be created." The harnessing of ultrasonic soundwaves is already being used in the medical field to "separate dead cells from healthy cells." The next step: amplifying these waves to the point where they can actually unscrew a screw just by pointing at it.

ON THE PAGES: In 1944, while the United States was mired in its third year of World War II, DC Comics was preparing to publish the next issue of *Action Comics*. The plot: Superman's archnemesis, Lex Luthor, invents an "atomic bomb" that can completely level a city.

IN REAL LIFE: Shortly before publication, agents from the U.S. Department of Defense ordered DC Comics to shelve the issue, but they wouldn't say why. The reason became clear a year later when American planes dropped two atomic bombs on Japan. The Manhattan Project had been a big secret (to everyone, it seems, but Lex Luthor). DC published the Superman story in 1946.

ON THE SCREEN: Don DeLillo's 1985 novel *White Noise* is a surreal satire about a chemical-freight-train derailment in a midwestern town that causes an "airborne toxic

Dinosaurs didn't roar—they cooed and murmured.

event." Not everyone evacuates in time, and they'll suffer health effects for the rest of their shortened lives. In December 2022, a movie adaptation was released on Netflix.

IN REAL LIFE: Barely two months after the movie came out, a train carrying 20 cars of hazardous materials derailed in East Palestine, Ohio, releasing a toxic cloud that led to an evacuation of the town. *White Noise* had been filmed throughout Ohio the previous year, so you can imagine how odd it must have been to the hundreds of extras who first pretended to evacuate before doing it for real. One extra, an East Palestine resident named Ben Ratner, said that there wasn't a lot to find funny about the accident and its lingering environmental and health effects, but he still did this: "I actually made a meme where I superimposed my face on the [*White Noise*] poster and sent it to my friends."

ON THE SCREEN: *Breaking Bad* (2008–13) featured a middle-aged father named Walter White (Brian Cranston) who gets so good at manufacturing crystal meth that he becomes a distributor himself before being shot by his apprentice, who once looked up to him like a father.

IN REAL LIFE: A middle-aged Alabama man had a similar story: he became known as the best meth cook in the state, so he started making it in large quantities...until he was betrayed by his son, who shot him in the back in 2013 (the same year *Breaking Bad* ended) over an unpaid debt. At last report, the man was serving a 12-year prison sentence. His name? Walter White.

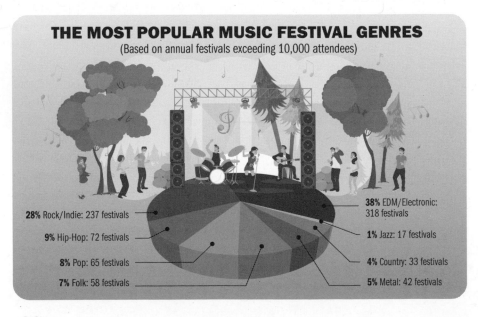

THE MOST POPULAR MUSIC FESTIVAL GENRES
(Based on annual festivals exceeding 10,000 attendees)

28% Rock/Indie: 237 festivals

9% Hip-Hop: 72 festivals

8% Pop: 65 festivals

7% Folk: 58 festivals

38% EDM/Electronic: 318 festivals

1% Jazz: 17 festivals

4% Country: 33 festivals

5% Metal: 42 festivals

Only mammal with a T-shaped tail: the slit-faced bat.

CAKE PHRASES

Who knew the English language had incorporated so many cake-related phrases into the common vernacular?

 Phrase: "Takes the cake"

Meaning: The best

Origin: "Among African Americans in the Old South, one of the highlights of the social season used to be the cakewalking contest. The contestants, couples of all ages, practiced months ahead of time; some even went into training for the event. In these contests a gigantic cake was placed in the exact center of a large circle. The couple who strutted around the cake most gracefully and ingeniously received, from the carefully selected committee of judges, 'the cake.' These contests brought out the newest dance steps, which quickly spread across the country. When the winners gracefully 'cakewalked' past judges, they'd revel in the judges' shouts of, 'That takes the cake!'" (From *Common Phrases: And Where They Come From*, by Myron Korach)

 Phrase: "Cakewalk"

Meaning: Anything easily accomplished or performed with grace and ease

Origin: "Actually, the custom of having a cake as a contest prize goes back much farther than that. In ancient Greece, the cake went to the man who could stick with his drinking the longest. In Ireland, dancing contests used to be held in which the cake was the prize." (From *Dictionary of Word and Phrase Origins, Volume II*, by William and Mary Morris)

 Phrase: "Selling like hotcakes"

Meaning: Selling well and quickly

Origin: "Early public gatherings of all kinds—fairs, carnivals, church socials—crackled with the sizzle and pop of cornmeal batter being fried in hot lard or bear grease. Because the results tasted best when hot, these fritters were called hotcakes. This repast was so popular that those cooking hotcakes could usually sell them as fast as they could cook them. Although pancakes have taken the place of hotcakes, based on our cultural memory we still say fast-moving products sell like hotcakes." (From *I Love It When You Talk Retro*, by Ralph Keyes)

 Phrase: "The icing on the cake"

Meaning: An unexpected bonus that makes a good thing even better

Origin: "The term *icing* is first actually recorded in Elizabeth Raffald's *Experienced*

English Housekeeper (1769): 'Tarts that are iced require a slow oven, or the icing will be brown.' Of roughly equal antiquity with the term icing is *frosting*, which is the preferred word in American English. The metaphorical use of *icing on the cake* for 'desirable extras' first crops up in print in a 1969 issue of *Listener*, but is probably earlier." (From *The Diner's Dictionary*, by John Ayto)

 Phrase: "Cheesecake"

Meaning: A woman photographed in a provocative or titillating way

Origin: "The old story is that in 1912 *New York Journal* photographer James Kane was developing a picture of an actress that included 'more of herself than either he or she expected.' As he looked at it, he searched for the greatest superlative he knew of to express his delight and exclaimed, 'That's real cheesecake!' The word soon became synonymous with photographs of delectable models. In the 1970s, *beefcake* became the male equivalent." (From *The QPB Encyclopedia of Word and Phrase Origins*, by Robert Hendrickson)

 Phrase: "Have your cake and eat it too"

Meaning: To want to consume something but also desiring to preserve it

Origin: "It's an attempt to overcome an either/or situation. It was first written down in 1562 as 'Would you both eat your cake and have your cake?' and somewhere along the line it became, 'Have your cake and eat it too.'" (From *Now You Know Big Book of Answers*, by Doug Lennox)

 Phrase: "Nutty as a fruitcake"

Meaning: Weird, strange, eccentric

Origin: "The origin of this idiom dates back to America in late 1920s. In the expression the adjective 'nutty' was used [as] slang for a foolish person. A slang 'nut' is also used commonly for someone who [is] extremely eccentric in his behavior. The similarity to fruitcakes is clear as fruitcakes contain nuts as well. So the expression 'nutty as a fruitcake' refers to a person who behaves in a strange manner." (From phrases.com)

Phrase: "Shut your cake hole"

Meaning: Stop talking. Immediately.

Origin: "'Shut your pie hole' is common in the U.S. In the U.K. there is a variation: *shut your cake hole*. *Shut your cake hole* came first, and appeared around the mid-1900s. Some speculate it originated in the British Air Force since an early reference of it was printed in Hunt and Pringle's 1943 reference book *Service Slang*." (From *Writing Explained*)

Ancient Roman wedding custom: throwing walnuts at the bride.

BECOME AVERAGE

Artificial intelligence—is there anything the technology can't do? Turns out there's at least one thing: provide inspirational memes that make sense. The new A.I.-powered inspiration generators can be equal parts hilarious, dark, and bizarre. How inspired do you feel by some of our favorites, below?

Above every egg there's a song.

Dare to milk what others see as unmilkable.

Become average.

You have the power to make it so that your dad wakes up in a hospital.

Don't be dull. Be outstandingly dull. Be negative.

Life is a movie where the star is s***.

A spanking might just be the motivation you are looking for.

One day, life will seem pointless. So it's OK to embarrass yourself.

Friendships can fill your life with morons.

Succeed. Make your mom confused.

A vast amount of people become village idiots because they think they're being edgy.

Blood in the urine is actually a message from God, telling you to buy a car.

Don't suffocate enemies. Suffocate some guy named Steve.

Keep on urinating, or you might become harmonious.

A blood sacrifice might just be the solution to all of your problems.

Make sure everyone is aware that you are dumb and famous.

Politicians are flammable.

A wilderness is never just a pair of eyes, but it's not a watermelon.

Most respected be the preacher, for the preacher health the seed, and no individual yet abused his own servant, but wrote a poem about and refuted it, similar to the lion and the gold, for we are employees of his visions, and his servants, until the end of the line.

A chin for a chin, a shrimp for a shrimp.

Together we can make poor people fall down a flight of stairs.

You're hilarious. But so is a fungal infection.

If everyone stopped saying "I just farted" and started saying "kiss me," the world would be a much more confusing place.

Those who know say peeing in space cures a headache.

VIDEO GAME ORIGINS

Ready to hear the stories about how software designers developed the biggest and most popular video games of all time? Just push play! (Or, you know, keep reading.)

ANGRY BIRDS

In 2009, smartphone game publisher Rovio had enough funds to build one game. "Make a game" was the entirety of the direction company bosses gave their only designer, Jaakko Iisalo. He liked to draw animals, so to brainstorm, he sketched birds, drawing them in unrealistic fashions. In one design, he made them round with pointed eyebrows, indicating they were angry. That generated the concept for the game: a flock of birds, so mad about something (it didn't matter what) that they just start breaking things.

Initially, the gameplay featured the smartphone user tapping on a bird, which would make it jump at a structure. Testers didn't quite understand the idea, so Iisalo went back to the drawing board to come up with something to make the bird's launch more dramatic and realistic (and intuitive). He struck on the idea of using a slingshot, and then a catapult. Realizing there wasn't much point to a game without an antagonist, Iisalo turned to something he'd been drawing since he was a kid: a stylized, circular-shaped pig creature.

Angry Birds wasn't much of a hit at first. The game was available on Apple's App Store for three months before the company decided to highlight it and prominently feature it. After that, the app was downloaded 30 million times within the next year. Within five years, it had been played more than three billion times.

THE OREGON TRAIL

In the fall of 1971, three student-teacher friends enrolled at Carleton College in Minnesota were assigned teaching jobs in Minneapolis. Tasked with teaching Jordan Junior High eighth-graders about 19th-century westward expansion, assistant instructor Don Rawitsch designed a board game (hand-drawn on butcher paper) in which players loaded up a covered wagon with supplies and braved the Oregon Trail from Independence, Missouri, to the Willamette River Valley in Oregon. What they faced along the way—wagon trouble, disease, death, bad weather, food thieves, rivers to be forded, the success or failure of hunting and foraging missions—was decided by dice rolls and card draws.

Rawitsch's roommate and fellow student-teacher Bill Heinemann had taken some

Legally, 56 different kinds of fish can be called "snapper" in American restaurants.

primitive computer programming classes and offered to turn the board game into a rudimentary piece of computer software. (A third teacher, Paul Dillenberger, offered to be a debugger.) Rawitsch agreed to the computer game angle, provided his friends could have a working version in time for when he had to teach his lesson—just 10 days away. Working on a computer terminal at Heinemann's school, Bryant Junior High, with the early programming language of BASIC, the trio created *The Oregon Trail*, one of the first pieces of media that could be considered a computer game—but not a video game, because graphics weren't an option on the keyboard-printer-teletype machine setup they used.

Rawitsch's students loved the game, but he put it away after the lesson ended. Three years later, he took a job at a nonprofit software distributor, the Minnesota Educational Computing Consortium. The MECC put Rawitsch's game on its mainframe, accessible by most Minnesota schools, and the game was such a massive hit that MECC spun off a commercial company to sell the game nationally. In the 1980s, they added graphics and sounds for *The Oregon Trail* versions for Apple and Commodore computers. One estimate indicates it's now sold more than 65 million copies.

TOMB RAIDER

Tomb Raider became one of the most popular and top-selling console games of the 1990s and 2000s. Counting its sequels, the *Tomb Raider* franchise has sold about 95 million copies worldwide. Part of the game's success can be tied to its female protagonist. Both in the 1990s and today, titles rarely feature women in a starring role. That attracted girls and young women to the game as well as young men (main character Lara Croft was designed to be noticeably voluptuous and dressed in a revealing outfit). Making the hero a woman was done by U.K. software publisher Core to avoid a potential lawsuit, or accusations that the game cribbed from a familiar movie series. *Tomb Raider* involves archaeologist-adventurer Lara Croft embarking on archaeological expeditions searching for treasure and artifacts. Designer Toby Gard intended to make the title character male, until executives told him to make the raider of tombs a woman so the game wouldn't seemingly rip off the Indiana Jones franchise. So, Gard created a character named Laura Cruz. When told to give the character a name that sounded more English, he flipped through a phone book until he found a name he liked—Laura Cruz became Lara Croft.

* * *

"My belt holds my pants up, but the belt loops hold my belt up. So which one is the real hero?"
—Mitch Hedberg

Country with the most heavy-metal bands: Finland.

IT'S SERENDIPITY: THE TRAVELING WILBURYS

Of all of rock 'n' roll's "supergroups" over the years, arguably none was more super than the Traveling Wilburys, formed in 1988 with George Harrison, Bob Dylan, Roy Orbison, Tom Petty, and Jeff Lynne. We were originally going to share this uncanny origin story in "It's Serendipity" (page 215), but there were far too many happy accidents—and superstars—to fit in one paragraph.

HISTORY LESSON

Way, way back in the 20th century, music artists would release songs, or singles, from their albums on 7″ vinyl records called 45s. The single was the A-side, and the B-side was most often another song from the album that wasn't considered single-worthy. In the 1980s, in an attempt to increase the appeal of 45s, record companies began filling B-sides with unreleased tracks, alternate versions, or other kinds of rarities not available on the album.

That's what Warner Bros. International asked George Harrison for in April 1988: a special B-side track for the European release of "This Is Love," the third single from his *Cloud Nine* album. Did he have anything new, or something he could record in the next few days? Harrison wasn't in England, where his recording studio was. He was in Los Angeles producing a movie. He *could* do a song for the record company, but he'd need to phone a friend.

BOB'S BURGERS

Versions of the band's origin story differ, but it went something like this. All the studios in Los Angeles were booked, and even George Harrison, 45 at the time, who'd risen to fame in the 1960s with the Beatles before embarking on a successful solo career, couldn't get studio space. So he called his friend Bob Dylan, 47, who bridged the gap between folk and rock in the 1960s and is widely regarded as the greatest American songwriter of all time. Dylan happened to have a studio in the garage of his beachfront Malibu home. Harrison also called his friend Jeff Lynne, 41. Though not as well-known as the others, Lynne was a legendary music producer and lead singer of Electric Light Orchestra. He had coproduced *Cloud Nine* with Harrison, and also happened to be in the city, where he was producing an album for their mutual friend Roy Orbison, 52, one of the few remaining giants from rock's early days. Being away from home, Harrison didn't have any of his guitars, but he'd lent one to another mutual friend who lived nearby, Tom Petty, 37, who had risen to fame in the 1970s with his band Tom Petty and the Heartbreakers. Harrison went over to Petty's house to get his guitar; when Petty found out what Harrison needed it for, he replied, "Oh, I was wondering what I was going to do tomorrow."

The original plan was for everyone to hang out while Harrison and Lynne put the new song together. Orbison was there, too, but only because he wanted to "come along and watch." (He and Harrison had been friends since 1963 when Orbison toured England with the Beatles.) As for Dylan, he put on his apron and fired up the barbecue. He'd do the cooking. But when Harrison realized the magnitude of talent that he had assembled in this small studio, he asked for a little help from his friends.

HANDLE WITH CARE

The original plan was for Harrison to write a song on which he would sing and play guitar, and Lynne would add the rest of the instruments. That morning, Harrison had come up with a basic chord progression and a single opening lyric: "Been beat-up and battered around." Then he started writing a bridge in a higher register that he was going to ask Orbison to sing. Petty was eager to help work out the guitar parts. Then Harrison called over to Dylan: "Give us some lyrics, you famous lyricist." Dylan joined them and asked what the song's title was.

Had they been in an actual recording studio, and not in a garage, there wouldn't have been storage boxes stacked up against the wall. But there were, and when Harrison read aloud the words on one of them—"handle with care"—they had their title. The five musicians all sat in a circle with their guitars and worked out the rest of the words and the chorus, which everyone sang on—"Everybody's / got somebody / to leeean on." They recorded the song that afternoon, after which Lynne added the rest of the instruments and mastered it. Harrison had his B-side.

THAT'S NO B-SIDE

"A couple of days later, George came by my office to play the new 'B-side,'" recalled Warner Bros. president Mo Ostin. "Our reaction was immediate. This was a song we knew could *not* be wasted on some B-side. Roy Orbison's vocal was tremendous. I really loved the beautiful guitar figure that George played. The guys had really nailed it. Lenny [Waronker] and I stumbled over each others' words, asking, 'Can't we somehow turn *this* into an album?'"

Harrison was game. (Ostin suspects he was hankering to be part of a band again.) And so were the others, but time was limited as Dylan was prepping for a tour. So they all stuck around and wrote and recorded *Traveling Wilburys Vol. 1* in a couple of weeks (at the home studio of Dave Stewart of the Eurythmics). From the outset,

Harrison wanted everyone—especially the "greatest songwriter of all-time"—to know that this was a band of equals: "We know that you're Bob Dylan and everything, but we're going to just treat you and talk to you like we would anybody else."

"Well, great," answered Dylan. "Believe it or not, I'm in awe of you guys, and it's the same for me."

TONGUE FIRMLY IN CHEEK

What's a Wilbury, you ask? According to Ostin, "George and Jeff had been calling studio equipment (limiters, equalizers) 'wilburys.' So first they named their fivesome the Trembling Wilburys. Jeff suggested 'Traveling' instead. Everyone agreed."

Or, if you prefer the "alternate version" that Monty Python member Michael Palin wrote in the album's liner notes: "Dr. Arthur Noseputty of Cambridge believes they were closely related to the Strangling Dingleberries, which is not a group but a disease." (That's just a snippet. Seek out the entire write-up if you want some fun bathroom reading.)

Yes, this supergroup of Rock & Roll Hall of Famers fully immersed themselves into "Travelers" lore: Dylan's alter ego was Lucky Wilbury, Harrison became Nelson Wilbury, Orbison was Lefty Wilbury, Lynne was Otis Wilbury, and Petty was Charlie T. Wilbury Jr. Harrison said of his spontaneous band: "It's an attitude. Really, anyone can be a Wilbury."

END OF THE LINE

Traveling Wilburys Vol. 1 won the 1990 Grammy Award for Best Rock Performance by a Duo or Group and eventually was certified triple platinum. It also produced two radio hits: "Handle with Care" and "End of the Line," both of which became staples in the waning days of MTV's music video era. *Rolling Stone*'s 4-star review called the album "a low-key masterpiece" from "one of the few rock supergroups actually deserving to be called either super or a group." The album revitalized all five artists' careers and further cemented their status as rock gods.

Plans were underway for a tour and maybe a movie when, tragically, Orbison died of a heart attack in December 1988, less than a month after the album was released. The four remaining Wilburys recorded one more album, *Traveling Wilburys Vol. 3*. (What happened to *Vol. 2*? "That was George's idea," said Lynne. "Let's confuse the buggers!") That third—er, second album did OK, but it didn't quite capture the magic of the first one. But how could it, really? Petty called all of the happy accidents that led to those five men being in that garage that day "cosmic." And, he admitted, "The whole experience was some of the best days of my life, really, and I think it probably was for us all...It really had very little to do with combining a bunch of famous people. It was a bunch of friends that just happened to be really good at making music."

Read this in a well-lit place: *sciophobia* is the fear of shadows.

SIGN NOT IN USE

Life is confusing. These actual signs and warning labels make it even more confusing.

Outside a diner:
**THIS IS THE BACK DOOR
THE FRONT DOOR IS
AROUND BACK**

On a bottle of dog medicine:
MAY CAUSE DROWSINESS
USE CARE WHEN OPERATING A CAR

On a jar of jam:
Tastes Like Grandma
Homemade Jam

At a discount store:
Gift's for Teacher's

*On a fancy bottle of
white wine:*
Brimming with zesty lemon flavor
and freah notes of apple

At the beach:
**PLEASE NO
SMOKING ALCOHOL
ON THE BEACH**

In a parking lot:
**PRIVATE SIGN
DO NOT READ**

On a country road:
SIGN NOT IN USE

On a letter opener:
**Safety Goggles
Recommended**

In a stairwell:
**4
THIRD FLOOR**

On a column at an airport:
**Please Step Around
the Column**

On a workplace safety poster:
**Use brush and dustpan
for glass (not bare
hands)**

*On a carton of "100%
Fruit Juice":*
Contains 27% juice

On a package of meat:
**100% BEEF
~ Made With ~
ALL WHITE MEAT
CHICKEN**

At a public pool:
DO NOT BREATHE
UNDER THE WATER

*On a median covered
with rocks:*
DO NOT MOW

At an appliance store:
Freezer Capacities:
* One person 3–7 cubic ft.
* Small family 8–14 cubic ft.
* Medium to large family
15–25 cubic ft.

An electric highway sign:
WINTER CONDITIONS
DRIVE WITH CAKE

In a parking lot:
DO NOT READ
Under Penalty of Law

On a package of frozen food:
Preheat the Oven to
3500F or 1750C

In an alley near a dumpster:
**GARBAGE ONLY
NO TRASH**

On a jet ski:
NEVER USE A LIT MATCH
TO CHECK FUEL LEVEL

On a city street:
LEFT LANE
MUST
LEFT LANE

On a fishing hook wrapper:
**HARMFUL IF
SWALLOWED**

In a restaurant:
RESTROOM IS FOR
EATING CUSTOMERS
ONLY!!!!

In a public restroom:
CAUTION: DON'T EAT
GUM FROM THE URINAL

On a trailhead restroom:
NO DUMPING

Better use it: *noggin* is a protein found in the skull.

JUST PLANE WEIRD II

Think about it: sitting in a pressurized metal tube zooming 500 mph, 30,000 feet above the ground is weird. These stories make it even weirder.

✈ JUST PLANE FUN

If you've ever flown Southwest Airlines, you've probably witnessed the zany antics the flight crews are known for—such as in 2019, when passengers boarding a Nashville-to-Philadelphia flight were greeted by a flight attendant who was lying on her side in an overhead compartment. The unidentified attendant (as seen on a viral video) is petite, but not quite petite enough for her whole body to fit, so her feet kind of dangle. She remained in the compartment for about ten minutes, bantering with the bemused passengers. When asked to comment on the video, an airline spokesperson said she was "just having a bit of fun." (We recommend you leave this to the professionals and don't try it yourself on your next flight.)

✈ EMOTIONAL SUPPORT [INSERT NAME OF ANIMAL]

It used to be you could bring any furry or feathered friend on a plane, calling the creature your "emotional support animal," and it would get to sit with you. Passengers have gotten away with emotional support ducks, pigs, ponies, turkeys, and even kangaroos. Though it might sound extreme, in many cases these support animals really can help their owners avoid panic attacks. In recent years, however, the airlines have cracked down; now they allow only emotional support cats and dogs in the plane's main cabin.

But one order of animals that has never been allowed on a plane: rodents. In 2018, an elderly woman named Cindy Torok boarded a Frontier Airlines flight from Orlando to Cleveland. Her reservation noted that she was bringing her "emotional support animal" with her. Not a problem...except that, when she got to her seat, the flight crew saw that the support animal was a squirrel. Squirrels are rodents, which are banned from Frontier flights.

Torok was ordered to disembark with her squirrel (named Daisy), so she showed them a note from her psychiatrist explaining she has an anxiety disorder, and said she was staying right there. The flight crew made every other passenger get off the plane so police could remove Torok, all of which caused a two-hour delay. When they wheeled Torok into the gate, she gave a one-finger (the middle) salute to the passengers who were yelling at her, and a thumbs-up to the passengers applauding her for standing her ground. In the end, she had to leave Daisy with her daughter. When asked by

Inside Edition how it was flying without her squirrel, Torok answered, while holding back tears, "It was emotional."

✈ LET'S PLAY "SPOT THE YACHT"!

After being lost for nine days in the South Pacific off the coast of Australia, a Queensland yacht owner named Glenn Ey was out of fuel and his mast had broken in a storm. He had no other choice but to activate his emergency radio beacon. While search-and-rescue teams were preparing to disembark, the Australian Maritime Safety Authority radioed a commercial flight heading into Sydney (after a 14-hour flight from Vancouver) and asked it to join the search. The pilot, Andrew Robertson, alerted the 270 passengers that they were going to drop from 37,000 feet to 4,000 feet:, asking "if everyone could look out their windows." Robertson told anyone with binoculars to use them, as the boat is only 36 feet long. After about 20 minutes, Robertson tilted the plane further toward the water, and, as one of the passengers, a Canadian singer named Jill Barber, recounted, "We're doing this big sweeping right turn and almost immediately they said, 'Oh, we see something!' We were totally ecstatic." Ey's yacht was 270 nautical miles from the coast, so who knows how long it would have taken rescuers to find him without the help of Captain Robertson and his eagle-eyed passengers.

✈ PLAYGROUND ZERO

During an emergency landing, the pilot has to dump the airplane's fuel so it doesn't explode if there's a crash. Standard procedures dictate that the dumping should be done from a high altitude so the fuel will disperse, and never done over populated areas. But there aren't many unpopulated areas in Los Angeles, so the departing Delta plane that was forced to return to LAX for an emergency landing on a January 2020 afternoon dumped all its fuel over not one, not two or three, but *four* elementary schools. That's pretty good aim...and good timing, as this happened while school was in session. According to NPR, the Los Angeles County Fire Department said first responders treated a total of 44 people—both children and adults—for "skin irritation and breathing difficulties" when the fuel fell on the four different schools across the Los Angeles area.

✈ THAT SUCKS!

"There was no warning sign," said Sichuan Airlines pilot Liu Chuanjian. The Chinese plane—heading to the city of Lhasa in May 2018—had just reached 32,000 feet when "suddenly, the windshield just cracked and made a loud bang. The next thing I know, my copilot had been sucked halfway out of the window." Good thing the copilot was

wearing his seatbelt, but it was up to Liu to land the plane on his own—a task made even more difficult by every loose object in the cockpit "floating in the air." Everything was shaking so violently that he couldn't read the gauges or hear the radio. Amazingly, Liu landed safely, and other than some minor injuries to the copilot and a crew member, all 119 passengers were unscathed. Liu was heralded as a hero for his efforts.

✈ DUCT, DUCT, BOOZE

Maxwell Berry's lawyer described his 22-year-old client as a "good man who committed a bad act" and said he's "looking forward to putting this incident behind him." But not until Berry spent 60 days in jail, one year of supervised release, and paid $4,000 in fines and restitution for three counts of assault. But he wasn't the only one who got in trouble during the "indicent." In August 2021, during a Frontier Airlines flight from Philadelphia to Miami, everything was copasetic during Berry's first two drinks, but after he'd ordered his third, the young man in the baseball cap got unruly. First, he "accidentally" brushed an empty glass across one flight attendant's backside. Then he spilled his drink on his own shirt, went to the bathroom, and emerged without the shirt. Then he groped two female flight attendants' breasts and punched a male attendant named Jordan Galarza in the face. Galarza, with the help of some nearby passengers, wrestled Berry back into his seat, where he launched into an expletive-laced tirade, claiming "You guys f***ing suck!" and that his parents are worth more than $2 million. When he tried to get up again, the flight crew duct-taped him to his seat. They even taped his mouth shut. The other passengers cheered and laughed while filming him trying to squirm out of his predicament. When the plane landed, Berry was arrested. Apparently, duct-taping an unruly passenger isn't among the airline's procedures, and the flight crew was suspended. "You can say it looked a bit barbaric," said Galarza, "but it worked perfectly and no one got hurt because of how we did what we did."

* * *

PRO SPORTS NAMING WRONGS

One building with eight names: Since 2018, the NFL's Miami Dolphins play in Hard Rock Stadium. It opened in 1987 as Joe Robbie Stadium, became Pro Player Park in 1996, Pro Player Stadium later in 1996, Dolphins Stadium in 2005, Dolphin Stadium in 2006, Land Shark Stadium in 2009, and Sun Life Stadium in 2010.

Four buildings with one name: Since 1968, the NBA's New York Knicks have played in Madison Square Garden. The arena opened in 1964, and it's the fourth venue to bear that name, following previously closed facilities that opened in 1879, 1890, and 1925.

It's more likely a human will live to the age of 100 than a mouse will live to the age of four.

KITTY CLIPPINGS

*OK, one more cat article. These strange-but-true newspaper stories
prove that whatever century it is, cats will be cats.*

Everything Happened to Everything but the Cat

MILTON, Mass., March 14 (AP)—A cat—a black one—dashed in front of the automobile of Robert C. King of Milton, with this result:

The car went out of control and cut off an electric light pole at the base; gasoline poured from a punctured tank; sparks flew from broken wires, the Boston Edison Company was obliged to cut off electric current in one-third of the town for an hour; firemen had to roll out hose to wash away the gasoline and King went to Milton Hospital, slightly injured.

The cat escaped unscathed.
—*Fort Worth (TX) Star Telegram*, 1942

CATS CAUSE DIVORCE

Kansas City, Mo.— Samuel O'Dell, aged seventy-four, a veteran of the Civil War, obtained a divorce because his wife kept 35 cats.
—*Sausalito (CA) News*, 1912

DRIVER SAVED BY BLACK CAT

Kansas City, July 9 (AP).—A black cat darted across the driveway as Lyle Riley started his car out of the yard during a wind and rainstorm. Riley stopped to avoid hitting the cat. Just then a 100-foot high elm tree crashed down on the car hood, crushing it.

Riley said he believed if he had not stopped, the tree would have fallen across the cab, probably crushing him.
—*New York Daily News*, 1941

Peg-Leg Cat Kills Rat

Fishermen See It, and They Went to the Lake to Fish

Cambridge, NY., May 24—(AP)—W. Artemas Scott and James Bell were back from a Maine fishing trip today—loaded with trout and one very tall tale.

"The story has to do with a cat," said Scott, "a cat, with a wooden leg. Listen..."

"We stayed at a fisherman's cabin and as we dozed in front of the fire we heard staccato taps on the ceiling. The taps seem to cross from one side to another.

"The owner told us the noise was made by his cat.

"'He had a wooden leg,'" Scott said the owner explained. "'Last winter he got caught in a trap and before I found him his right front paw had frozen stiff. I amputated it with a knife and whittled him a good wooden leg.'

"So," said Scott, "the fellow called the animal downstairs and just then a big rat appeared. The cat leaped into action. He dived at the rat and, holding the rat down with its left shoulder, the cat—yes, sir, this is the truth—brought up his wooden leg and just literally pounded the rat to death."
—**Newspaper unknown**, 1937

Wrens can sing at a rate of 36 notes per second.

HOODOO CAT: INDIANA WOMAN BREAKS ARM FLEEING FROM ONE.

Indianapolis, Dec. 31.— Mrs. Elizabeth Flaherty, 60, "hates" cats. As she walked along a street here a few nights ago a large cat approached her in what she took to be a menacing manner.

In her panic to get to the other side of the street, Mrs. Flaherty fell and broke her arm.

—*Dayton (OH) News*, 1933

CAT'S SLY WINK AT MAGISTRATE DECIDES OWNERSHIP CONTEST

An alley cat became the matter of judicial concern in west side court yesterday and the case was disposed of when the cat winked at the magistrate.

John Bonner of 354 West Fifty-second Street and Catherine Borrho of the same address claimed the cat. Magistrate Michael A. Ford told the former to put it through its alleged tricks. Bonner failed. Then the court turned to Miss Borrho with the same invitation.

"Wink at the judge, Pinky," she said.

Pinky slowly closed one eye.

"It's your cat," ruled the magistrate.

—*New York Times*, 1931

CAT WITH WINGS

The most amazing cat in the world, it was revealed yesterday, lives in the Attercliffe district of Sheffield. It has wings.

Apparently just a normal black and white tom cat, about nine months old, when it runs out come the wings, nine or ten inches long, stretched out from each side as a hen stretches its wings when running.

It cannot fly and does not flap them, but it can jump to remarkable heights.

When Mrs. Roebuck, of Candow Street, Sheffield was given the cat as a kitten, it was then normal.

A month or two ago, however, Mrs. Roebuck said she noticed strange lumps appearing just behind its shoulders.

These are its wings. They are covered with fur to match the body.

—*Daily Record* (England), 1939

SMALL PIG IS CONTENTED WITH CAT FOSTER MOTHER

Sussex, New Brunswick, Aug 5.—(U.P.)—You've heard of cats mothering fox pups, squirrels, etc.

Mrs. James Robertson has a cat that is rearing a little pig.

The cat washes her adopted baby in her accustomed way and the little pig follows its feline foster mother about.

—*Indianapolis Star*, 1939

GREATEST PHENOMENON of NATURE.

—An extraordinary TORTOISESHELL TOM CAT, his weight being twelve pounds, length three feet two inches, allowed by judges to be the greatest curiosity ever shown to the public, is at present to be seen at the Ship Tavern, Ivy-lane, Newgate-street, City.

—*Morning Advertiser* (London), 1835

DARK VIEW

—Jasper the cat wears glasses but it's no affectation. The Spokane, Wash., feline's sight is failing and its owner got glasses to cut down any strong glare.

—*Greenwood (MS) Commonwealth*, 1956

There's an asteroid-resistant bunker in Norway filled with Oreos.

🗣 MOUTHING OFF 🗣

I'M SO VAIN

Quotes from folks who could use a slice of humble pie.

"Your father's the biggest movie star in the world, and you're struggling for your little piece of dignity in this extreme shadow."

—Will Smith, on his son Jaden

"I'm offended by that because...and this is going to sound arrogant, but my presence is charity. Just who I am. Just like Obama's is."

—Jay-Z, when asked about his lack of social responsibility

"I started wigs, and now everyone is wearing wigs. I just do whatever I want to do, and people will follow."

—Kylie Jenner

"I am who I am; I can't pretend to be somebody who makes $25,000 a year."

—Gwyneth Paltrow

"I now truly believe it is impossible for me to make a bad movie."

—Jean-Claude Van Damme

"I don't perform. Seals perform."

—Morrissey

"U2 is an original species. There are colors and feelings and emotional terrain that we occupy that is ours and ours alone."

—Bono

"I don't care if you think I'm being bigheaded. This is the only rock 'n' roll band to come out of Los Angeles that's real, and the kids know it."

—Slash

"DON'T SAY I'M NOT TALENTED. IF YOU HAVEN'T NOTICED, I WASN'T MADE —I WAS FOUND."

—Justin Bieber

"I do wish I ruled the world— I think it'd be a better place."

—Courtney Love

"I'M NOT ARROGANT. I'M COCKY. IT'S DIFFERENT. COCKY IS PLAYFUL."

—Adam Levine

"THERE'S A LITTLE PART OF ME THAT THINKS EVERYTHING IS INFLUENCED BY ME, BUT THAT'S JUST MY OWN MEGALOMANIA."

—Quentin Tarantino

YOU CALL THAT ART?

Now for some strange-but-true tales from the world of strange-but-true conceptual art.

BANANA VS. BANANA

"Can a banana taped to a wall be art?" asked Judge Robert N. Scola Jr. in a ruling pertaining to that very thing. In fact, however, there were *two* bananas. The first one came in 2000 from Miami-based conceptual artist Joe Morford, whose work *Banana & Orange* featured a plastic banana duct-taped to a green board, underneath another board with a duct-taped plastic orange. Then, in 2019, the art world was set abuzz by "bad boy" Italian artist Maurizio Cattelan, who's work *Comedian*—a banana duct-taped to a wall at a Miami gallery—went viral, and then was sold to an art collector for $120,000 (just the banana, not the wall). It went on display at the prestigious Perrotin gallery, which wrote that the work "offers insight into how we assign worth and what kind of objects we value."

When Morford found out about Cattelan's banana, he went on his Facebook page and wrote, "I did this in 2000. But some dude steals my junk and pimps it for 120K+ in 2019. Plagiarism...?" The gallery actually sold *three* versions of *Comedian*, ranging from $120,000 to $150,000, to collectors. That's three bananas for close to $390,000 (piece of tape included). And that's how much Morford sought in his copyright infringement lawsuit. Cattelan countered that he'd never even seen Morford's *Banana & Orange* before, and that his work of art is a real banana, not a plastic one.

Cattelan asked for a dismissal, but Judge Scola initially ruled that the case could move forward: "While using silver duct tape to affix a banana to a wall may not espouse the highest degree of creativity, its absurd and farcical nature meets the 'minimal degree of creativity' needed to qualify as original." In the end, he found for Cattelan, citing that there was no proof the defendant had ever seen the original work (which is featured on YouTube), and that it's plausible to believe that two artists could independently come up with the duct-taped banana idea. Quoting philosopher Marshall McLuhan, Judge Scola concluded that art is "anything you can get away with."

DATUNA VS. BANANA

If a questionable artist steals a questionable art piece, is *that* art? Why not? In December 2019, New York–based performance artist David Datuna went to the Miami art gallery to see Maurizio Cattelan's *Comedian*—a banana taped to a wall (see the previous entry) that had already been purchased for $120,000. It was the

The meteor that killed off dinosaurs was the size of Manhattan.

second-to-last day of the show. Datuna's performance art piece, which he filmed on Instagram and called *Hungry Artist*, consisted of him peeling the banana off the wall, then peeling the skin off the banana, then eating it. "I really love this installation," he wrote. "It's very delicious." (And very ripe.) Datuna was escorted out of the gallery by security, but the owner didn't press charges, a gallery spokeswoman calling it "all in good spirits."

Each *Comedian* banana came with a certificate of authenticity and "replacement instructions." Helpful for the couple who bought one of the versions of the work, Billy and Beatrice Cox of Miami. In defense of their purchase, they stated, "We are acutely aware of the blatant absurdity of the fact that *Comedian* is an otherwise inexpensive and perishable piece of produce and a couple inches of duct tape. Ultimately we sense that Cattelan's banana will become an iconic historical object." May it never spoil.

HAANING VS. KUNSTEN

In 2010, Danish artist Jens Haaning made quite a statement with his companion pieces, *An Average Danish Annual Income* and *An Average Austrian Annual Income*. Both frames contained cash—and nothing else. (Denmark had more.) In 2021, Denmark's Kunsten Museum of Modern Art in Aalborg commissioned Haaning to do an update as part of its "Work It Out" show, and, in addition to his fee, they sent him $84,000 worth of banknotes for use in his piece, money required to be returned after the show's completion.

Haaning turned in two works, albeit a bit different from what was agreed upon. He gave the museum two empty frames, with a new title: *Take the Money and Run*. The curators laughed at the joke, and then said (we're paraphrasing), "No, really. Where's our cash?" But Haaning refused to hand over the money, and said the pair of empty frames *was* his piece, take it or leave it. The museum took the empty frames and displayed them anyway. "Jens is known for his conceptual and activistic art with a humoristic touch," said museum director Lasse Andersson. "And he gave us that—but also a bit of a wake-up call as everyone now wonders were did the money go." At last report, Haaning still had it. Humoristic touches aside, the museum does want their money back. "We will of course take the necessary steps to ensure that Jens Haaning complies with his contract."

AI VS. URN

Dropping a Han Dynasty Urn is a performance art piece—captured in three black-and-white photographs in 1995—by Chinese "artist, thinker, activist" Ai Weiwei. That's how the Guggenheim Museum in New York described him when this controversial

piece was on display there in 2018. The first photo shows Ai holding a 2,000-year-old ceremonial urn from the Han Dynasty, valued at $1 million. The second photo shows the urn in the air after he lets go of it. In the third photo, the urn is broken in pieces on the floor.

Ai, who was among China's most famous artists before he moved to New York, reportedly used the money he made selling art to collect a handful of the vases in the 1980s. And he claims that he in fact broke two of them: the photographer didn't click the shutter on time to get the first vase in the air, so Ai had to break a second one for the shot. The vases that he didn't smash, he painted (including one with a Coca-Cola logo).

To say people were upset is an understatement. Some outlets, including the *Guardian*, accused Ai of using fake artifacts because they couldn't imagine anyone just "letting go of an elegant object made with intelligence, imagination, and love more than 2,000 years ago and letting it smash to bits on the ground." (The urns are not fake.) To others, Ai's a hero. "The historical artifact became more exposed in a way the traditional methods of preservation couldn't expose it," wrote the arts magazine *Public Delivery*. When asked why he did it, Ai equates power to value: "It's powerful only because someone thinks it's powerful and invests value in the object." And speaking of value, the photographs of the smashed urn are now worth much more than the intact urn ever was.

MAXIMO VS. VASE

In 2014, the Perez Museum in Miami was setting up for a show of the famous Chinese dissident artist Ai Weiwei's *Colored Vases* (see previous entry about painted Han Dynasty ceramics). Going on display were 16 Han Dynasty vases that Ai painted with various bright colors. On the wall behind them: the three photos that make up *Dropping a Han Dynasty Urn*. In walked Maximo Caminero, a well-known Miami conceptual artist and painter. He walked over to the display table, picked up one of the 2,000-year-old vases, and, just as a curator was saying, "Don't touch," Caminero dropped it.

Caminero claimed his act was in protest against Miami art galleries' lack of focus on local artists (even though plenty of the city's galleries had local art, including Perez). Caminero was arrested and charged with criminal mischief. In his defense, he said the act was a "spontaneous protest" inspired by Ai himself. Caminero didn't know the vase was worth $1 million. He received 18 months' probation and had to pay $10,000 restitution; he also got community service, where he had to teach kids how to paint. How'd Ai react? By stating that the protest itself may be valid but "to damage somebody's work to do that is questionable."

Percentage of American dads who'd never changed a diaper in 1980: 43. In 2023: 3.

THE TOILET PAPER REPORT

And so the news cycle rolls on—with these weird news stories centered around that soft, wonderful, and very necessary luxury that is toilet paper.

HOW TO WIPE OUT TP

It takes a lot of natural resources, including wood and water, to make paper, and in the name of conservation and ecological living, environmental activist Rob Greenfield wants humanity to stop using so much of it. Greenfield especially wants to stop the use, manufacture, and distribution of one specific kind of paper: toilet paper. In 2023, Greenfield toured the United States with his "Grow Your Own Toilet Paper Initiative," constructing a temporary compost toilet in busy downtown areas and offering passersby his sales pitch. Ridding one's life of toilet paper is easy, Greenfield claims—all you have to you is grow some blue spur flower plants and harvest their leaves for use in the bathroom. They're "soft as can be. They're durable. I call them the Charmin of the garden," Greenfield told reporters. "I want to show people that another way is possible. We just buy (toilet paper) at the store and we never think twice about it." Greenfield touts how each leaf is about the size of a sheet of TP, though he reminds adherents that they can't be flushed, but instead tossed in the garbage or buried in a yard.

END OF THE ROLL

Toward the end of the 2022–23 school year, a high school in South Carolina made headlines when an administrator overstepped his powers and tried to deny his students a basic human (or American?) right: to have access to toilet paper when using the facilities. In a May 2023 announcement to students and staff, assistant principal Cornelius Cromer said that Newberry High School would no longer stock its restrooms with toilet paper. Students who anticipated the need would have to stop by the front office to be given a roll before answering the call of nature. Cromer's harsh measure was a response to a schoolwide fad of students flushing entire rolls of TP down school toilets, leading to many clogs and plumbing issues. Hours after issuing the memo, Cromer was overruled, with NHS's human resources officer telling students, staff, and media outlets that the school would not, in fact, ban toilet paper.

GOOD ENOUGH TO EAT

In February 2022, an unnamed woman from Anji, a city in northeast China, ordered a box of boneless fried chicken bites at a Kentucky Fried Chicken outlet, the most popular Western fast-food chain in the country. As she ate the finger-food, she noticed that one was far too chewy and didn't taste like chicken. She pulled it out of her mouth and realized she'd been eating what looked like a wad of toilet paper, soaked in oil, breaded in a coating of flour and KFC's famous 11 herbs and spices, and deep fried along with the chicken. The woman registered an official complaint with the State Administration for Industry and Commerce, which confirmed that it was indeed toilet paper she'd munched and nearly swallowed. The restaurant's management was in the process of negotiating with the woman what would be adequate compensation for her experience.

TOTALLY TUBULAR

In July 2023, firefighters and an official from the Royal Society for the Prevention of Cruelty to Animals descended on a neighborhood in Meanwood, a suburb of the U.K. city of Leeds. The emergency: a resident reported a confused and distressed squirrel lying on the ground with its head hopelessly stuck inside an empty cardboard toilet paper tube. By the time authorities arrived, the squirrel had managed to skitter off and run 30 feet up into a tree. Firefighters rescued the animal by luring it down and freed it while the RSPCA official watched. It's believed that the empty tube was either a piece of litter or had fallen out of a trash can, and the squirrel got it stuck on its head after curiously peering inside.

GAME ON

An independent, solo software publisher named Takahiro Miyazawa created and released in 2023 what's believed to be the first ever video game about toilet paper. Designed for the Nintendo Switch system, *Give Me Toilet Paper!* allows the player to guide a roll of much-needed TP to a man sitting on a toilet with nothing but an empty tube. Players place their Switch controller inside a real empty toilet paper roll and then put it on a flat surface, like a book or piece of cardboard, which guides the onscreen TP as it navigates a series of obstacles (including trap doors, lasers, and spiked "baddie" toilet paper rolls) to successfully reach the pleading man with his pants around his ankles. Cost of the game: a mere $5.

*   *   *

"Vincent van Gogh, you know, people told him,
'You can't be a great painter, you only have one ear.' You know what he said?
'I can't hear you.'"

—Gardner Minshew, NFL quarterback

Scientists have taught an otter with asthma how to use inhalers.

ANSWERS

WHAT AM I? *(Answers for page 110.)*

1. A lawsuit.

2. A field of corn.

3. A feather.

4. Light.

5. A wheelbarrow.

6. The word Chicago.

7. A deck of cards.

8. The word seven.

9. A treadmill.

10. A ruler.

11. The words *eat* and *ate*.

12. Silence.

13. The bird's shadow.

14. Water.

15. A glove.

16. Ice.

17. The word dozens.

18. A skull.

19. The pupil of an eye.

GLADIATORS VS. TRUCKS *(Answers for page 200.)*

1. Gladiator

2. Monster truck

3. Monster truck

4. Gladiator

5. Monster truck

6. Gladiator

7. Monster truck

8. Gladiator

9. Gladiator

10. Monster truck

11. Gladiator

12. Monster truck

13. Monster truck

14. Gladiator

15. Monster truck

16. Gladiator

17. Monster truck

18. Gladiator

19. Monster truck

20. Monster truck

21. Gladiator

22. Monster truck

23. Gladiator

24. Monster truck

25. Gladiator

26. Gladiator

27. Monster truck

28. Monster truck

29. Monster truck

30. Monster truck

31. Gladiator

32. Gladiator

TEN-DOLLAR WORDS *(Answers for page 301.)*

1. d; **2.** g; **3.** j; **4.** s; **5.** m; **6.** k; **7.** b; **8.** r; **9.** p; **10.** t; **11.** i; **12.** a; **13.** n; **14.** l; **15.** c; **16.** e; **17.** q; **18.** f; **19.** o; **20.** h

We are pleased to offer over 150 ebook versions of Portable Press titles—including Bathroom Readers available only in digital format! Visit *www.portablepress.com* to collect them all!

Reader Weird Canada

❑ Uncle John's Bathroom Reader Weird Inventions

❑ Uncle John's Bathroom Reader WISE UP!

❑ Uncle John's Bathroom Reader Wonderful World of Odd

❑ Uncle John's Bathroom Reader Zipper Accidents

❑ Uncle John's Book of Fun

❑ Uncle John's Canoramic Bathroom Reader

❑ Uncle John's Certified Organic Bathroom Reader

❑ Uncle John's Colossal Collection of Quotable Quotes

❑ Uncle John's Creature Feature Bathroom Reader For Kids Only!

❑ Uncle John's Curiously Compelling Bathroom Reader

❑ Uncle John's Did You Know...? Bathroom Reader For Kids Only!

❑ Uncle John's Do-It-Yourself Diary for Infomaniacs Only

❑ Uncle John's Do-It-Yourself Journal for Infomaniacs Only

❑ Uncle John's Electrifying Bathroom Reader For Kids Only!

❑ Uncle John's Electrifying Bathroom Reader For Kids Only! Collectible Edition

❑ Uncle John's Endlessly Engrossing Bathroom Reader

❑ Uncle John's Factastic Bathroom Reader

❑ Uncle John's Facts to Annoy Your Teacher Bathroom Reader For Kids Only!

❑ Uncle John's Fast-Acting Long-Lasting Bathroom Reader

❑ Uncle John's Fully Loaded 25th Anniversary Bathroom Reader

❑ Uncle John's Giant 10th Anniversary Bathroom Reader

❑ Uncle John's Gigantic Bathroom Reader

❑ Uncle John's Great Big Bathroom Reader

❑ Uncle John's Greatest Know on Earth Bathroom Reader

❑ Uncle John's Haunted Outhouse Bathroom Reader For Kids Only!

❑ Uncle John's Heavy Duty Bathroom Reader

❑ Uncle John's Hindsight Is 20/20 Bathroom Reader

❑ Uncle John's How to Toilet Train Your Cat

❑ Uncle John's InfoMania Bathroom Reader For Kids Only!

❑ Uncle John's Legendary Lost Bathroom Reader

❑ Uncle John's Lists That Make You Go Hmmm...

❑ Uncle John's New & Improved Briefs

❑ Uncle John's New & Improved Funniest Ever

❑ Uncle John's Old Faithful 30th Anniversary Bathroom Reader

❑ Uncle John's Perpetually Pleasing Bathroom Reader

❑ Uncle John's Political Briefs

❑ Uncle John's Presents: Book of the Dumb

❑ Uncle John's Presents: Book of the Dumb 2

❑ Uncle John's Presents: Mom's Bathtub Reader

❑ Uncle John's Presents the Ultimate Challenge Trivia Quiz

❑ Uncle John's Robotica

Bathroom Reader

❑ Uncle John's Slightly Irregular Bathroom Reader

❑ Uncle John's Smell-O-Scopic Bathroom Reader For Kids Only!

❑ Uncle John's Supremely Satisfying Bathroom Reader

❑ Uncle John's The Enchanted Toilet Bathroom Reader For Kids Only!

❑ Uncle John's Top Secret Bathroom Reader For Kids Only!

❑ Uncle John's Top Secret Bathroom Reader For Kids Only! Collectible Edition

❑ Uncle John's Totally Quacked Bathroom Reader For Kids Only!

❑ Uncle John's Triumphant 20th Anniversary Bathroom Reader

❑ Uncle John's True Crime

❑ Uncle John's Truth, Trivia, and the Pursuit of Factiness Bathroom Reader

❑ Uncle John's 24-Karat Gold Bathroom Reader

❑ Uncle John's Ultimate Bathroom Reader

❑ Uncle John's Uncanny Bathroom Reader

❑ Uncle John's Unsinkable Bathroom Reader

❑ Uncle John's Unstoppable Bathroom Reader

❑ Uncle John's Weird Weird World

❑ Uncle John's Weird Weird World: Epic

❑ Uncle John's Weird, Wonderful Bathroom Reader

THE LAST PAGE

FELLOW BATHROOM READERS:

The fight for good bathroom reading should never be taken loosely—we must do our duty and sit firmly for what we believe in, even while the rest of the world is taking potshots at us.

We'll be brief. Now that we've proven we're not simply a flush-in-the-pan, we invite you to take the plunge: Sit Down and Be Counted! To find out what the BRI is up to, visit us on the web and take a peek!

GET CONNECTED

Find us online to sign up for our email list, enter exciting giveaways, hear about new releases, and more!

🌐 Website: www.portablepress.com

f Facebook: www.facebook.com/UncleJohnsBathroomReader

📌 Pinterest: www.pinterest.com/portablepress

And visit Uncle John's Blog for fun throughout the year!
www.portablepress.com/blog

Well, we're out of space, and when you've gotta go, you've gotta go. Tanks for all your support. Hope to hear from you soon.

Meanwhile, remember...

Keep on flushin'!